Food, the State, and International Political Economy

F. LaMond Tullis and W. Ladd Hollist, editors

Food, the State, and International Political Economy

Dilemmas of Developing Countries

University of Nebraska Press

Lincoln & London

106772

Library of Congress
Cataloging in Publication Data

Main entry under title:

Food, the state, and international political economy.

Bibliography: p.
1. Food supply – Developing countries.
2. Agriculture and state –
Developing countries.
3. Food industry and trade –
Political aspects –
Developing countries.
I. Tullis, F. LaMond, 1935-
II. Hollist, W. Ladd, 1947-
HD9018.D44F67   1985
338.1'9'1724   85-30893
ISBN 0-8032-4413-4 (alk. paper)

Contents

Introduction

In the 1980s, famine has claimed millions in Ethiopia and other regions of the African Sahel; undernutrition has stalked the highlands of Central and South America and Mexico; food shortages have appeared again in parts of India and Egypt; and numerous countries have reluctantly turned once again to importing vast quantities of cereal grains to feed people against whom weather, rapid population growth, technology, and government policies have conspired to deny sufficient foodstocks. In some areas per capita food production is falling, real prices on much domestically grown traditional food (e.g., beans and maize) are rising, and nutritional standards are dipping. Rural laborers, faced with severe unemployment and underemployment, have increasingly migrated to cities which cannot absorb them. Some have attempted to settle in other countries.[1] In some areas of Africa and Latin America, real incomes among the poor have declined by as much as 40 percent within the past fifteen years. The human suffering is substantial.

The environment is at risk, too. Issues include: soil fertility and its conservation or loss; the long-term use of water resources and the pollution of underground aquifers; crop utilization of unused, underused, and overused lands; atmospheric pollution; population pressures from growth as well as migration; and natural calamities deriving from drought and floods. Each is affected by, and affects, efforts to feed people and to gain the material benefits of agricultural trade.

In addition to the costs to human welfare of hunger and unemployment, and the environmental concerns associated with modern agricultural practices, national security issues related to food and agriculture also confront developing-country governments. They increasingly speak of "food security," or their domestic and international vulnerability to shifts in food and agricultural production and exchange practices. Thus concerned, they tender policies designed to improve food production for their own domestic markets and to limit their international food dependency.

The poignancy of food as a political weapon, and by implication the insecurity that could derive from an international food shortfall or boycott, were driven home when the United States embargoed grain shipments to Russia. Many national governments, especially in industrialized and newly industrializing countries, suddenly found a pressing need to reduce their food and political insecurity by further protecting and subsidizing domestic food production for domestic markets, even when costs exceeded those manifest in international market prices. Some governments found that "cheap food" seemed less desirable than secure food and the political tranquility that such security implied.

We now realize how food and agricultural activities and their humanitarian, environmental, and security consequences are affected by the increasing integration of food and agricultural producers and consumers in *global* markets. While, *globally* speaking, agriculture is a striking production success, many people and even some countries have been rendered worse off in recent years. The reasons for striking success as well as troubling consequences are attributable partly to each country's international policies and to the farmer and business-firm practices they encourage (or discourage). For example, policies encouraging the application of Green Revolution technology in export agriculture have brought notable production success. However, export and product specialization policies advanced and adopted without regard for ancillary impacts have brought troubling consequences to some. Urban-biased policy makers frequently have fostered an increase in exports in order to earn foreign exchange without much regard for impacts on rural employment, nutrition, migration, or domestic food security. Until now, fostering economic growth through export expansion has been the easiest and safest thing to do politically.

The paradox of increased agricultural and food production coupled with deteriorating nutritional and income levels depends significantly upon how a country postures itself vis-à-vis the international political economy.[2] To ameliorate hunger, poverty, and food insecurity, each country will have to consider how it has situated itself in global agricultural markets. Otherwise policies to enhance "rural development" and to create "incentives" for small farmers to produce more food will simply introduce new paradoxes, aggravating all the attendant difficulties so far experienced.[3] Many of these development and trade dilemmas are clarified when viewed from the political-economy perspectives employed in this volume.

With all the attention food and agricultural issues are receiving from governments and international development agencies such as the World Bank, it is not surprising that in the past decade scholars other than agricultural economists and practitioners other than rural development workers have "found" agriculture once again. Food insecurity, astonishing cases of regional famine and hunger, failure of country development plans based on formal economic models that did not make specific provisions for an agricultural sector, and unintended domestic and international political consequences of agricultural trade have all combined to resurrect that interest. This vital sector of each nation's and the world's political economy has now been thrust onto center-stage of the development drama.

This resurgent interest in agriculture is reflected in academe. An interdisciplinary community of scholars has begun serious dialogue over what is increasingly recognized as a linchpin of development. Agricultural economists, political scientists, nutritionists, and sociologists are talking to each other about it. So are more and more mainline economists who have become disillusioned with their first-, second- and even third-generation growth models and who now seek to deal with an agricultural sector they largely ignored as a priority concern for public and private investment.

Many observers of international relations have also turned attention to food and agricultural issues. They now know that both "development" and agricultural issues fundamentally affect developing countries' international relations—specifically how they relate to developed countries. And, there is more at stake than international trade. Add international security and peace. External powers attempt either to exploit or to contain domestic conflicts that arise in part over agriculturally related dilemmas.

The burning issue of development in developing countries, involving matters as diverse as international debt and domestic nutritional adequacy, is an agricultural matter as much as an industrial process, a political-economic transformation as well as a technological one, and they all affect the interrelations of states. Agriculture affects international relations in ways not fully suspected as recently as a decade ago.

Each concern — human welfare, the environment, national security, integrated global markets — is important, has its own body of literature, and involves issues worthy of book-length treatment. We focus on three political economy themes that, to some extent, overlay all these issues: (1) developing countries' food policies (how to produce food, for whom, at what prices); (2) the international political economy of food and agriculture (what trade relations to foster, what foreign food aid to accept or give, what multinational agribusinesses to permit to operate, and what rewards to foster or allow); and, (3) appropriate food-production technologies (what mix of capital-intensive and labor-augmenting technologies to use for domestic and international food markets).

Developing Country Food Policies

Food policies seek to steer production technologies and incentives, food distribution, and domestic and international markets. They therefore help to "determine" who produces and markets food, who gets it, and at what price.

Governments have a bewildering array of potential policy options: Should they intervene in production and distribution? Should they leave the market to work as it will? Conversely, should they act as a private producer who profits from food production? Or should they control production and distribution for political and social reasons? Other, more specific policy decisions include whether or how much the state should emphasize production for export, production for domestic consumption, and production for subsistence living.

Several of this volume's authors (C. McClintock, Sanderson, Homem de Melo) explore these issues. *They show that under certain conditions state policies emphasizing capital-intensive production technologies to serve international markets (and earn needed foreign exchange) may have a largely unfortunate, if unintended, human consequence.*

On the other hand, developing countries desperately need to export almost anything. They must service their debts to international lenders or risk worsened credit standings. They need to buy food they now do not supply domestically. They must import and pay for machinery, spare parts, and perhaps even the raw resources their machines use if they are to maintain present economic activity. The need for foreign exchange is even more acute when the ideology and expectations of a people demand "accelerated development." Pressures increase with success and remain unremitting even in failure.

Presently, foreign exchange earnings and exports go hand in hand. Other foreign currency sources—direct investment, foreign loans, foreign aid, remittances from nationals working abroad, tourism—are inadequate to meet both needs and desires. But every decision to emphasize production for export over domestic consumption, or vice versa, sets the stage for national political action resulting in considerable conflict among the various social classes and economic interests. In a few instances the conflict has erupted in civil war.

Nowhere among developing countries has there been a completely successful reconciliation of agricultural policy makers' export and domestic goals; hardly anywhere have their policies contributed to domestic social and political amity. On the other hand, a very few developing countries have had notable success in harmonizing production increases with more equitable national income distribution (e.g., South Korea and Taiwan), but most show a dismal record here, too (e.g., Brazil, and Mexico). Chapters 4, 5, 7, and 10 provide details.

Governments matter. More than ever before governments are charged with assuring that their people are fed. In the case of developing countries, they must also steer a course for rapid economic growth. In practice (although not necessarily in principle), policies that might assure an adequate food supply and those that might enhance economic growth often prove incompatible. In pursuing rapid economic growth, governments frequently neglect rural development and food security as they almost exclusively emphasize urban-biased, industrial development strategies. In turn, due to agricultural neglect, growth itself is frequently stymied (Tullis, Ch. 8; Hopkins, Ch. 1).

Additional examples further illustrate the far-reaching effects of food policies. Hopkins (Ch. 1), Christensen and Witucki (Ch. 2), and C. McClintock (Ch. 3) demonstrate how price controls intended to assure low-cost food to urban laborers create disincentives to food producers and eventually cause food shortages. Under these conditions, a policy intended to speed industrial economic growth hurts the rural sector and eventually disrupts the overall economic growth that governments earnestly, although narrowly, seek.

Christensen and Witucki (Ch. 2) and C. McClintock (Ch. 3) also show the shortcomings in developing countries' agricultural credit policies. These governments tend to allocate credit to cash-crop, export-oriented, large-scale agricultural producers at the expense of the small farmer. Since the mid-1970s this practice has become particularly pronounced as governments, by promoting agricultural exports, seek to redress balance-of-payments deficits and generate foreign exchange needed to service their foreign debts. Agribusinesses servicing foreign consumers flourish. But small farmers producing for the domestic population remain largely unassisted. A country's ability to meet its food requirements is thus lessened. Frequently it must import food to meet the shortfalls. Under these circumstances the poor suffer most, for food imports frequently cost more, and those export-destined cash crops that nevertheless appear in domestic markets bear a higher "international-economy" price (Sanderson, Ch. 5).

"Showpiece" projects—a policy preference for large, capital-intensive development projects related to food production—is another developing-country predilection that frequently has negative unintended consequences. C. McClintock (Ch. 3) notes the tendency of the Peruvian government to plan and to construct large irrigation and power systems often with lengthy delays and significant cost overruns. Small, conventional food production enterprises are left unassisted. Still, in the face of such projects, the food shortfall in Peru in the mid-1980s was substantial. Incidences of malnutrition were reported among 50 percent of highland children. A series of widely dispersed, smaller irrigation and power systems would have been far more preferable.

Moore (Ch. 4) analyzes the "Saemaul" Movement that South Korea's political leaders introduced in 1970 allegedly to promote rural development, and which they subsequently labeled a great success. The government needed a showpiece to demonstrate commitment to the welfare of its citizens, settling, finally, upon what initially was a grass-roots, village effort. The government captured local initiative and greatly modified and institutionalized it as a state-orchestrated program—the Saemaul Undong (Movement). Moore argues that Saemaul was politically motivated to offset concerns over a rising urban-rural income gap. However, showpiece projects—such as replacing thatch with tile on house roofs along the more traveled roads, and the introduction of "high yield" rice that required high cost inputs (e.g., fertilizer, pesticides) and that proved less profitable to the farmers than their traditional rice crops—introduced more problems than they solved. Moore sees the government seeking to "turn Saemaul into something like a mass political party to support the . . . administration." The result, he argues, was an overall worsening of the quality of life of many rural families.

The International Political Economy of Food

A second principal theme in this volume is that *relations between a nation's food and agricultural activities and the international political economy shape the daily lives of that nation's people.* Many of the relationships that help explain the simultaneous existence of poverty and wealth, or misery amidst plenty, in developing countries relate to this theme and are treated throughout the volume, but especially in chapters by Sanderson (Ch. 5), Mahler (Ch. 6), Bailey (Ch. 7), and Tullis (Ch. 8).

How a society structures its agricultural production relative to international markets is consequential. Sanderson (Ch. 5) demonstrates how the Latin American beef-export industry, in submitting to an international standard of quality, now requires high-cost inputs that drain resources much needed for rural development. Other unfortunate consequences include increased land concentration with negative effects on the rural population, a strain on foodstuff availability as agriculture moves from food grain to feed grain production, and allocation of resources to internationally oriented production that otherwise could have been utilized to reduce rural poverty.

Mahler (Ch. 6) analyzes the dynamics of international sugar, demonstrating how United States and West European sugar import policies—establishing quotas, subsidizing their own beet sugar producers, regulating prices, and otherwise fashioning sugar markets to their liking—have caused ups and downs in that world market. Countries depending on sugar exports for their economic well-being find such market volatility, not to mention the consequences of price setting, to be devastating.

Bailey (Ch. 7) presents the fundamental dilemma confronting

developing countries: should they specialize in cash-crop production
for export or should they pursue food self-sufficiency? Choosing
specialization for export opens developing economies to risks: politically motivated, arbitrary interruptions of trade, insufficient export
earnings, capital-intensive production technologies that displace
rural labor and small farmers, and reliance upon external agents
(transnational corporations). On the other hand, the cost of self-
sufficiency may be the loss of foreign exchange earnings required to
import capital goods for industrialization and to service outstanding
foreign debt. No surer reality confronts developing countries today
than their existing need for foreign exchange. Having based their
economic growth on the import of capital goods and technologies
requiring foreign exchange, breaking with that practice would surely
be disruptive.

Historically, trade relations more than foreign investments have
explained how the international economy affects a developing
nation's food and agricultural activities. Nevertheless, while food-
related transnational corporations are not as important in agriculture as are manufacturing ones in industry,[4] they are now certainly
consequential. For example, transnationals control 80 percent of
international grain marketing,[5] and they increasingly are making
food processing investments in developing countries. Investments in
the Latin American food industry have increased at an annual nominal rate of 11 percent.[6] (In 1978 one fifth of the U.S. direct foreign
investment in the food industry was located in the developing countries, with 80 percent of that in Latin America.[7]) Farmers and agribusinessmen have brought new lands into production and altered
their crop mix to take advantage of global market demand.

Not surprisingly, investors' decisions do not necessarily reflect the
needs of the host country's population. While profitable, processing
of foods, largely for consumer convenience, is costly. One cost of such
high-priced convenience may be a lessened capacity to feed the host
nation's poor.

The international politics of food aid also affect food concerns in
developing countries. Granting the legitimacy of humanitarian intentions associated with food aid, Tullis (Ch. 8) nevertheless shows that
the rationale for considerable aid has been founded on an East-West,
communism-versus-capitalism perspective of international affairs.
Many food-aid donors (principally the U.S.) have thought that by

contributing to a recipient country's economic wellbeing they were enhancing its political stability, thereby lessening the attractiveness of communism. In the case of Latin American countries, what political stability has been obtained rests more on principles of coercion than consensus. If food aid has enhanced stability, it has done so quite often because the recipient government has been made thereby more able to exact compliance. In any event, in such conditions, those who receive the food aid are not necessarily the poor, but those who, if aroused, might challenge the existing political regime. Food aid born of East-West political conflicts has thereby proven unsuited to the enhancement of food security (by diluting pressures for reforms necessary for domestic agricultural improvements) or betterment of the poor.

Beyond these considerations, many times trade relations between a developed and a developing nation turn much less on the needs of the latter and more on the political interests of the developed country.

Technology and Food

For over a decade global food and agricultural production have increased at a rate that would have been unsuspected a quarter century ago. Along with production incentives, improved technology and land-use practices have accounted for much of the increase.

Europe is awash in surpluses that it can sometimes hardly even give away, and America searches frenetically for international markets to receive the mountains of cereals its own people cannot consume. Argentina made the biggest grain export gains in its history after the United States embargoed shipments to Russia following the invasion of Afghanistan. Mexico has developed a horticulture and produce industry that is the envy of every developing country, and its export cattle-feeding operations are world class (Sanderson, Ch. 5). India's Punjab produces notable food and agricultural surpluses. Korea's and Taiwan's success stories are as remarkable as any. Throughout Africa, Asia, and Latin America a capital-intensive Green Revolution technology with its associated quantum leap in food and agricultural production are being applied as never before. On a global scale, per-capita food production has been increasing quite substantially.

Not only has global food and agricultural production increased, many people are also eating "higher up" on the food chain. In some countries cereals once consumed directly are now eaten indirectly via feed-lot animals. Demand is increasing. Farmers and agribusinessmen almost everywhere are affected in what they plant and grow and in the incomes they make.

In the 1970s and 1980s, increased production and dietary shifts enhanced international trade in food and agricultural products — soybeans, frozen chicken, table vegetables, rice, wheat, orange juice concentrate, fruits, beef and meat products. Many traditional export crops from the Third World have also held steady or increased.

Green Revolution technology, food surpluses, dietary shifts from cereal to animal protein, increased international trade, heightened transnational investment in food and agricultural industries — all are doing well. But many of the world's people and perhaps even most of its small developing-country farmers are not, especially in Africa and, to a lesser extent, in Asia[8] and Latin America. We have already seen that humanitarian concerns for them have been rising.

Thus this volume's third principal theme is that *Green Revolution technologies often prove ill-suited to feeding the world's poor.* Instead, those technologies frequently serve to embellish the diets of those who can afford costly foods. While almost all authors in this volume treat, indirectly at least, the impact of technology on food production and food policy, D. McClintock (Ch. 9) and Homem de Melo (Ch. 10) make it their specific focus.

We do not rail against technology as did the Luddites of old, even though some forms of technology do indeed skew income distribution. We do argue that government policies, and therefore people and regimes, make decisions about applying technology that, under some circumstances, have unintended and frequently adverse outcomes. With respect to Green Revolution technology, we show that the problems Keith Griffin (1974) pointed out years ago are still with us and are even manifestly more troublesome in some areas. The fault is not with the technology, necessarily, but rather in failing to identify the social, political, and economic circumstances under which, when applied, technology may not have adverse consequences. It may indeed be true that some countries will require a "revolution" to change such circumstances so that the adversities can subside.

Thus once a decision has been made to modernize agriculture with energy intensive technology, there are ramifications for societies. Because of the way an economy is structured (itself related to social and political power structures), technology may not necessarily contribute to improved income-distribution patterns.

Homem de Melo, a Brazilian agricultural economist, argues (Ch. 10) that his nation's agricultural economy has long been comprised of two subsectors: an export sector and a domestic sector. The latter feeds the population, particularly the rural population and the urban poor. The former generates revenues wanted to finance economic growth and industrial development. When advanced agricultural technologies have been introduced in Brazil, they have been applied mostly to the export sector. That technology is costly, and requires a commitment of society's resources (governments subsidize the financing of the technology). Resources are diverted from the already resource-poor (credit poor) domestic foodstuffs sector, and food security suffers. The subsistence of the poor, specifically the small farmer and the migrant rural laborer, is negatively affected.

D. McClintock (Ch. 9) asks what technologies might prove more suitable. In developing countries agricultural technologies suited to small farmer needs ought to be given priority, he argues. Sensitivity to the socially, politically, and economically disruptive aspects of high-cost agricultural technology ought to be enhanced. Hence, Green Revolution technologies, heavily dependent upon energy resources (oil), ought to be deemphasized. He concludes with specific recommendations of what technologies would be more appropriate for developing countries's agricultural activities.

Conclusion

We have argued, and contributors to this volume show, that domestic and international political economy issues overlay food concerns in almost all their important dimensions: How should societies produce food, for whom, and at what prices? What trade relations ought they to foster? What foreign food aid should they accept or give? What multinational agribusinesses should they allow to operate? What rewards ought they to foster or permit? What mix of capital-intensive and labor-augmenting technologies should societies employ to achieve gains both in domestic and international food markets?

Those developing countries that have concentrated on industrialization, urbanization, physical infrastructure and the required social complements in urban education, housing and health, while paying insufficient attention to agriculture and rural development, have contributed to food shortfalls experienced by many of their people. Capital transfers from the country to the city via cheap food policies and selective subsidies that penalize domestic market agricultural producers and reward agricultural exporters have long exacerbated the problem. Trade practices, foreign aid policies, and the pursuit of foreign exchange at almost any cost, if persistently followed, will surely continue to inhibit domestic income distribution and long-term development objectives.

Among the many needed changes is a substantial restructuring of agriculture's domestic and international political economy relations to better serve both economic growth and human welfare interests in developing countries. In the long run this will better serve the world. Production increases need to be coupled with adequate and reasonably distributed food stocks for the domestic, not just the international market; improved rural employment, not massive worker dislocation; rising nutritional standards among the poor; and reduced political conflict. We can no longer afford to deal with the complex dynamics of food production and distribution through ad hoc policies that, while politically acceptable in the short-term, undermine the whole development effort in the long term. For example, emphasizing cash-crop exports without sufficiently considering associated domestic upheavals in migration, domestic food costs, employment, and nutrition is one practice that requires close scrutiny.

In addition to the many policy recommendations that chapter authors advance, we need to look for additional ways to promote changes that can be achieved at an acceptable political cost. For example, can governments in developing countries tax foreign investment at less than a disincentive rate, establishing a source of credit for small farmers to help get domestic food production in line with agricultural exports? Alternatively, a developing country's government might require highly profitable export groups to fund domestic research and development on basic food production subsystems, including cataloguing incentives that would be required to make them work.

In analyses of how government policies and the international political economy combine to affect food production and consumption, we do not forget that governments are made of people. We allow, indeed hold, that domestic and international social and economic structures impose limits on a government's policies. Even so, governments have options. Will leaders follow a formal development model? If so, which one? What economic sector will they favor? To what social class will they cater? What population will they penalize economically, and for what purpose? What ethical foundations will guide their use of the public treasury?

It probably goes without saying, but it is probably worth saying just the same: If changes needed are ever to come about in the proper magnitude, we need more developing country leaders of conscience, public virtue, and adaptive will than we have experienced in the past. Here, as with specific policies, we have a long way to go. Nevertheless, some rumblings (e.g., in Argentina) in the 1980s leave us thinking that mere mention of the matter is not quite as naive as cynics always point out. It is yet too early to tell if leaders of the quality we need will be forthcoming. In the meantime, the difficulties of our time continue as relentlessly as the ocean tide, awaiting history's moment of truth to arrest them: the right idea and the courage and power to implement it.

Agricultural production and exchange in developing countries, with all their ramifications, are immensely complex. Now, perhaps more than ever before, they should be approached with the best intellect, insight, and political will that the world's nations can muster. A successful approach by such people will have a truly long-term perspective, for leaders will know that business as usual with its short-term expediencies and fire-engine response to crises is part of the problem that faces us.

List of Contributors

JOHN J BAILEY, Associate Professor of Government at Georgetown University, has researched extensively in Latin America and has directed Georgetown's Latin American Studies Program. His publications include "Presidency, Bureaucracy, and Administrative Reform in Mexico: The Secretariat of Programming and Budget" (also translated and published in Spanish), "Agrarian Reform in Mexico," and (with D. H. Roberts) "Mexican Agricultural Policy."

CHERYL CHRISTENSEN is Chief, Africa and Middle East Branch of the International Economics Division of USDA's Economic Research Service. Her frequently cited articles, "World Hunger: A Structural Approach" and (with Lawrence Witucki) "Food Problems and Emerging Policy Responses in Subsaharan Africa," have influenced the thinking of academics and professionals alike. Her intimate acquaintance with extensive African food and agricultural data makes an especially valued contribution to this volume.

W. LADD HOLLIST is an Associate Professor of Political Science and Director of Graduate Studies at the David M. Kennedy Center for International Studies at Brigham Young University. His work has appeared in the *International Studies Quarterly*, *Journal of Politics*, *American Journal of Political Science*, the *Comparative Foreign Policy Yearbook*, and edited volumes. He co-edits the *International Political Economy Yearbook*, sponsored by the International Political Economy section of the International Studies Association.

FERNANDO HOMEM DE MELO, Professor of Economics, Department of

Economics, University of São Paulo, Brazil, is also a senior researcher at São Paulo's Fundação Instituto de Pesquisas Econômicas (FIPE). His research on Brazilian agriculture, technology and rural development is periodically reported by the London-based *Latin American Reports* and regularly by the Brazilian media. His publications include *O Problema Alimentário Brasil: A Importância dos Desequilibrios Tecnológicos* and "Commercial Policy, Technology and Food Prices in Brazil."

RAYMOND F. HOPKINS is Professor of Political Science at Swarthmore College where he also has directed the Center for Social and Policy Studies and the Program for Public Policy. He has been a Fellow at the Woodrow Wilson International Center for Scholars and also held visiting faculty research positions at Harvard's Center for International Affairs and Stanford's Food Research Institute. His numerous publications on food-related matters include *Food, Politics and Agricultural Development, Food Issues in the Global Arena* (with Robert Paarlberg and Mitchel Wallerstein), and *Global Food Interdependence: Challenge to American Policy* (with Donald Puchala).

VINCENT MAHLER is Associate Professor of Political Science at Loyola University of Chicago where he has specialized in North-South Relations. His publications include *Dependency Approaches to International Political Economy: A Cross-National Study*; "Britain, the European Community and the Developing Commonwealth: Dependence, Interdependence and the Political Economy of Sugar"; and, "The Political Economy of North-South Commodity Bargaining: The Case of the International Sugar Agreement."

CYNTHIA MCCLINTOCK is Associate Professor of Political Science, George Washington University. She has researched extensively in Peru, and has published *Peasant Cooperatives and Political Change in Peru* and edited (with Abraham F. Lowenthal) *The Peruvian Experiment Reconsidered*.

DAVID MCCLINTOCK is a Visiting Associate Professor of Political Science at North Carolina State University and concurrently serves as coordinator for science programs for the Center for the Study of Foreign Affairs of the Foreign Service Institute in Washington, D.C. He previously served as food and agriculture adviser to the Department of State's science bureau (OES), and has published *U.S. Food:*

Making the Most of a Global Resource as well as papers and articles relating to international agriculture.

MICK MOORE is a Research Fellow at the Institute of Development Studies (University of Sussex, England). His practical and academic work is in sociological and administrative aspects of rural development in developing countries, especially in South and East Asia. His consultancies include the UN, USAID, the Swedish International Development Authority, and India's National Institute for Rural Development. His publications include *Agriculture and Society in the Low Country* (Sri Lanka) and *Development and the Rural-Urban Divide.*

STEVEN E. SANDERSON is on leave from the University of Florida where he is an Associate Professor of Political Science. He is author of *Agrarian Populism and the Mexican State*; and, *The Transformation of Mexican Agriculture: International Structure and the Politics of Rural Change*; and editor of *The Americas in the New International Division of Labor.* Sanderson spent 1984 as a Council on Foreign Relations Fellow at the Office of the U.S. Trade Representative in Washington, D.C. He is currently Ford Foundation Program Officer for Rural Poverty and Resources, Rio de Janeiro, Brazil.

F. LAMOND TULLIS is Professor of Political Science and Associate Academic Vice President at Brigham Young University. He has authored *Lord and Peasant in Peru*; *Politics and Social Change in Third World Countries*; and, "The Current View on Rural Development: Fad or Breakthrough in Latin America?" Together with W. Ladd Hollist he co-edits the *International Political Economy Yearbook* series. He spent 1983–84 as a Visiting Fellow at the Institute of Development Studies (University of Sussex, England) and the London School of Economics.

LAWRENCE WITUCKI is an agricultural economist with the International Economics Division of USDA's Economic Research Service. He has done research on irrigated agricultural development in the Sudan, and worked for several years in Kenya's Ministry of Agriculture planning projects for external financing. He has written numerous articles on African agricultural development, including several on the African food situation.

PART I

Food Policies
in
Developing Countries

Chapter 1

Food Security, Policy Options and the Evolution of State Responsibility*

RAYMOND F. HOPKINS

Food is important in not only its physical but also its symbolic, cultural, economic, and political roles; it is not surprising, therefore, that shortages produce anxiety and insecurity.

Food insecurity arises at various systems levels—household, national, and international—and does so because of a unit's insufficient "adaptive capacity." Households, the state, or the international system are unable to adjust patterns of food-related activities with a minimum of financial cost or dietary loss.

Ultimately, food insecurity is a national-level problem. It occurs in countries that experience variations in production or inadequate production to meet consumption needs. The countries cannot smooth out production variability through domestic carry-over or have a population whose consumption habits regularly exceed absolute production capacity or lack adequate internal mechanisms for re-allocating domestic food supplies. In such situations, household level actions, at least in the short run, put pressures on national governments which in turn frequently turn to international markets, either for commercial or concessional food imports. In this situation, especially in countries with weak foreign exchange positions, food aid is

*I thank Jenny Broome, my research assistant, for her assistance in preparing this paper. Jenny graduated as a biology major from Swarthmore College in 1984 and plans to pursue advanced studies in the area of food, nutrition, and policy (national and international) in 1985–86.

the most helpful short-term remedy. Ultimately, however, in order to achieve food security, insecure states must establish and carry out national policies to improve their adaptive capacity.

The norms and expectations governing world food system participants must reflect an understanding of the way in which state action to provide food security has shifted substantially over the last several centuries. A changing state role and people's expectations about their state's food-security responsibilities have made food security a practical test of whether a government is a success or a failure.

In order to appreciate this shift to state responsibility for food security, this chapter briefly reviews the importance of food for human life and hence its importance to state security. It then examines elements of food insecurity and also discusses policy options for alleviating that insecurity. A matrix of possible policy steps is presented, with alternative points for improving specific phases of the food system, including ones involving households, national governments, and the international system.

I. Food Security and State Responsibility

Food security stands as a fundamental need, basic to all human needs and the organization of social life.[1] Access to necessary nutrients is fundamental not only to life per se, but also to stable and enduring social order. Since the fifteenth century the major responsibility for food security has shifted from households toward national governments. In the twentieth century some responsibility has also shifted to the international level. However, food security, or lack of it is still thought of as essentially a concern of individuals, families or localities. Increasingly though, this individual food security reflects properties of national and international systems that determine the chances a populace will have to secure adequate nutrition even when adverse conditions arise. Thus the level of food security now depends heavily on policies undertaken at national and international levels.

All human societies have organized their activities to provide for a regular supply of food. The more precarious and minimal the food supply, the more critical food regulation becomes. Historically, securing food was an essential activity for hunting and gathering bands and peasant societies. Virtually all other activities revolved around it. Where people lived, their housing style, their plans for travel, recreation, procreation, and indeed, the very distribution of wealth and status among them were all intimately and directly tied to the exigencies of food procurement and distribution. Enforcing rules that served the aim of food security was a dominant feature of government.[2]

This is hardly surprising. When deprived only of one or two meals people in contemporary no less than earlier primitive societies immediately feel discomfort. An experiment in the United States with volunteers revealed that seemingly average Americans when deprived of food for a few days underwent dramatic changes. They became hostile, lazy and melancholic; furthermore, food became the dominant focus of their attention. They dreamed of food, thought constantly of eating, and their efforts to engage in other activities were continually interrupted by overriding psychological and physiological concerns to secure food (Keys, et al., 1950). Little wonder that in periods of general food insecurity, such as during World War II or 1973–75, governments dramatically increase their attention and action in food matters.[3]

In spite of government efforts, in the 1980s chronic hunger affects an estimated two-thirds of the developing world's population. Most of these people are in Africa and Asia, where 50 to 80 percent fall short of minimal daily caloric requirements. Even when country surpluses exist, many residents can neither grow enough nor purchase enough to meet their daily food needs. Different malnutrition tests yield substantially different estimates of the number of people chronically underfed. The Food and Agriculture Organization (FAO) estimate is about half a billion, while other estimates range from 300 million to 1.3 billion for the mid-1970s (Poleman, 1983). Regardless of uncertainty over the total populace affected, the magnitude of hunger is awesome when one considers the toll it takes on people's quality of life and economic productivity, and their countries' social and political stability. The near chronic famine conditions in Africa in the 1980s serve to underline this point.

Many other important aspects of food, both practical and symbolic, are assumed or overlooked.[4] Food, for example, plays a major role in cultural life, especially in religious and political rituals. Also, food is a key element in a society's economic status. Affluent societies by definition enjoy food abundance. The classic strategy of economic development requires increased food productivity in order to shift labor into industrial and other sectors. Finally, the satisfactory management of a state's food supply is a critical political task; failures are closely related to political upheaval.

Modern transformations, particularly in the nineteenth and twentieth centuries, have dramatically increased the number of individuals and states relying on national and international market exchanges to supply vital food needs. This has increased the vulnerability of many people to production or marketing failures occurring outside their control. The various roles that food plays in human affairs and the growing vulnerability of the world's population to international production and marketing forces testify to the enduring importance of food.

A. The Importance of Food to Individual and State

The important roles food plays in human affairs, both practically and symbolically, are often overlooked in national and international food system examinations. Therefore, before making specific recommendations to improve food security, I will review two broader themes about the global food system: the dimensions of life in which food is important and the various ways food dependency and insecurity arise.

The Physical Role of Food. The existence of chronic malnutrition is hardly new. Throughout history every society's least fortunate have experienced difficulties in securing adequate food. Furthermore, the effects of undernutrition have long been recognized: discomfort, weakness, susceptibility to disease. In poor countries, adequate food and clean water are the most effective means of improving health and preventing disease. This is a view that officials of key UN bodies such as the World Health Organization and UNICEF hold.

Beyond the physiological importance of food and its impact on health, food is important to people's general quality of life. Alan Berg has shown that even the most basic sources of human satisfaction available even to the world's poorest—friendship, the beauty of nature, the joys of exercise and play—are barred to people distracted and weakened by hunger (Berg, 1973).

A final point about the importance of food to human physiology arises from the positive benefits of having more than enough to eat. When food supplies have become ample and readily available, dramatic changes have occurred in the very physical characteristics of a people. The boom in post-World War II Japan, for instance, was characterized not only by rapid economic growth rates but also in rapid average size growth of the Japanese people. Ample food supplies during childhood can account for differences in height and weight of 10 to 30 percent. The physical features of Japanese age cohorts born in the 1950s compared with those of the 1920s and 1930s illustrate the striking difference that nutrition can make.

Two points emerge: First, adequate food can have a pervasive, fundamental and powerfully positive effect on the psychological outlook and the physical size and well-being of people. Second, large numbers of people throughout the world are deprived of these benefits. Insufficient and unreliable food supplies therefore operate as a major constraint on the development of human resources for productive activity and the flourishing of basic human values.

The Symbolic and Cultural Role of Food. Food, unlike most other commodities, also plays an especially important cultural role. Illustrative is the symbolic role food plays in religious rituals or hospitality. Beyond this, communal solidarity and a people's cultural continuity are regularly symbolized religiously through sacred rites that include eating or making offerings of specially prescribed or prepared foods such as unleavened bread, meat and wine. Outside of religious ceremonies, the offering of food is a universal practice simply to acknowledge welcomeness. Consider further the widespread rules that have evolved in various cultures and religious traditions regarding dietary practices. Long after the prohibition against eating pork or killing cattle have lost their rational basis in medical or economic considerations, they continue as distinguishing traits of various peoples.

The role of food in promoting social solidarity and expressing religious values has political ramifications, too. A principal transaction arena for political leaders and followers is a dinner. From fund-raising dinners to feast-day speeches, community leaders use such occasions to affirm their commitment to their followers' interests and to exact from them tributes and contributions for political campaigns. In international affairs the role of food has more egalitarian connotations. The working luncheon and the formal state dinner with its pomp and toasts are institutionalized elements of international diplomacy. By breaking bread together leaders symbolize to each other and to the peoples they represent at least a minimal mutual trust and willingness to collaborate. More than any other commodity, the centrality of food extends beyond its absolute physiological necessity for human life into broad symbolic meanings.

The Economic Role of Food. Food production and consumption are part of every social system's economic activities. The proportion of the labor force involved in various food functions — production, storage, marketing, processing and preparation — reflects a society's capacity to produce above the subsistence level and to enjoy higher standards of living. Likewise, the proportion of income that various groups, particularly poor ones, have to spend for food reflects general economic well-being. A need to study the food system as a special, indispensibly important sector of an economy has been argued by the World Food Council and other international bodies. They propose that food sector studies be undertaken, especially in developing countries. By focusing directly on food, the economics of the entire food system and the bottlenecks to expanding productivity would be highlighted.[5]

A basic case for the importance of food in economic growth and development rests on the role that food surpluses have played in releasing labor from agriculture and in generating savings with which to compensate it for producing nonfood goods and services. The classic economic development strategy has been to use rural-generated surpluses to support urban industrialization. But this traditional model may have to be modified in contemporary developing countries because of distortions in income distribution that it has a tendency to create (Mellor, 1976).

A less often noted economic aspect of food abundance is its integral tie to high standards of living. The capacity to waste food without serious nutritional or economic deficiencies is a characteristic of affluent societies. Surpluses mean redundancy, which in turn signals an adaptive capacity. Countries with surpluses and waste can afford to lose segments of their food systems without repercussions that damage other economic activities. Thus surplus food not only is a generator of economic development but also a characteristic of industrial and developed countries that provides stability and a quality of life that food-waste critics seldom appreciate.

Politics and Food. The management of food prices, markets, and even production has long been a major government concern. Because of food's central importance and the relative unreliability of production and producer income, government intervention in agricultural and food production has been considerable in all countries. Indeed, political economists and historians seeking to explain the basis for competing interests in various historical periods and the outcomes that emerged, such as the creation of colonial systems,[6] have given considerable attention to the politics of controlling markets and establishing special trading relations for food commodities.

When food is in short supply, or when food production or consumption accounts for a large proportion of a group's income, control over prices and marketing is a powerful political instrument. How it is used affects fundamentally the distribution of privilege and a society's prospects for political stability. Where political power limits access to markets except through fixed channels, whether of state buying authorities or favored middlemen, small producer income usually suffers,[7] and the potential for mass discontent is higher. When food supplies are unreliable, stability is also affected. In the wake of food shortages, mid-1970 governments in Bangladesh, Ethiopia, and Niger were overturned. Merely the threat of food price rises fomented violent demonstrations in Egypt in 1977, in Liberia in 1979, and in Tunisia, Morocco and the Dominican Republic in 1984.

Food as a Source of Insecurity. Food scarcity is not new. Throughout history people have experienced hunger. In its acute form hunger becomes famine, that dread condition which has plagued mankind from pre-Biblical times up to the twentieth century. Over a million deaths from food shortages were recorded in China and Russia in the 1920s, and additional hundreds of thousands were noted in Ethiopia in the mid-1980s. Most famine-related deaths are only indirectly the result of food deprivation; they result primarily from maladies associated with widespread hunger — smallpox, cholera, typhus. Sometimes food shortage is not even the real culprit. The 1974 famine in Bangladesh, for example, was really a product of panic high food prices, not absolute food shortages.[8]

Before the African famines of 1983–85 the last *great* food shortage famine occurred in Bengal in 1943. Recurring starvation threats in East Asia and the African Sahel in the early 1970s and 1980s notwithstanding, the overall incidence of and range of people affected by acute hunger has declined, and life expectancy has increased. This is particularly notable in view of the rapid growth in total world population.[9]

Increasingly, famine seems to have resulted not so much from crop failures as from inadequate transport and government policy and mismanagement. With earlier warning and better transport, most of the recent famine-related 1973–74 deaths in Bangladesh and Ethiopia and 1983–85 deaths in several African states could have been avoided (Shepherd, 1975; Alamgir, 1980).

No appeal is more basic or more compelling than a hungry people seeking food. Any successful beggar or experienced foreign aid official can testify to the powerful sympathetic reaction such an appeal engenders. Starvation is an awesome and demoralizing condition for any person or society to face. Nevertheless, the prospects for human suffering resulting from food shortages in the world in the 1980s seem less likely from starvation and famine than those from chronic malnutrition and its attendant debilitating social and economic consequences.

We are not treating the consequences of famine lightly. The point is that institutionalized mechanisms for transporting food over long distances, and the policies for providing food in an emergency gift basis have developed in the last few decades to the point where currently existing emergency mechanisms have been used with success, at least in averting the worst effects of famine. In the 1974 Bangladesh shortages and in similar African ones (1973–74 and 1983–85), while many deaths can be attributed to food shortages (estimates range from thirty thousand to one million Bengali deaths), it must be remembered that much more massive starvation was prevented through the large inflow of food, largely food aid, from other parts of the world.[10]

The long-term concern for the collective interest of the world is chronic hunger. It affects an estimated one quarter to nearly one and a half billion people. Regardless which estimate is most accurate, most hungry people, concentrated in Africa and Asia, fall short of minimal daily caloric requirements in ways that extract a toll on the social, economic and political aspects of their lives and countries.[11]

B. Food Insecurity at Various System Levels

Food security is the assurance of access to adequate nutrition, either through direct effort or exchange at acceptable prices. Its opposite, food insecurity, is best understood as a relative phenomenon. The concept points to a condition of vulnerability in which a system suffering shock cannot maintain its "normal" working parameters. Shocks might take the form of weather-induced production failures or politically induced disruptions brought on by strife or external embargo. A food-insecure system would be forced to cope by extraordinary efforts, making large changes in its normal activity.

At different system levels extreme food insecurity is manifest in different ways. Food insecurity among individuals might be seen in the abnormal body conditions that indicate severe malnutrition (marasmus, kwashiorkor) or in mass migrations from traditional home areas. Whole villages may be found near starvation. Such occasions occur more frequently in poor countries, but are also found in industrialized, wealthy countries.

National food insecurity may be exhibited when states undertake costly new regulatory tasks (such as rationing) and shift trading patterns to import food at the expense of substantial imports of expected capital or consumer goods. The scarcities and high prices in food markets that African states faced in 1983–84 at a time when world prices were at historic lows is a classic example of national food insecurity. African national per capita food supplies were at all-time lows and serious dislocations and drastic changes in state actions have resulted.

International food insecurity may be indicated by global ramifications in which international food prices rise dramatically and lead to substantial and coordinated international resource reallocation. It is a condition most conceivable in wartime. However, in 1973–74, due to a combination of factors, the world did experience a modest insecurity as prices for internationally traded grain doubled and tripled. At this global level, in the absence of worldwide authoritarian organs, international action is difficult. However, the world food conference of 1974, calling for numerous international stockholding and production measures, was the result of a globally felt need to reduce the perceived insecurity at the international level.

It is important to look at each area in some detail.

Individual Household Insecurity. When individuals are unable to grow their own food they must depend upon their income and an institutionalized structure for bringing food into markets where they can purchase it. Most of those suffering chronic malnutrition cannot count on adequate earnings to secure food, nor upon reliable markets in which food will be available. Transportation systems, storage facilities and government policies that encourage production and minimize barriers to food movement are most frequently absent in the very countries where the greatest malnutrition exists. Thus, it is little wonder that peasants are frequently described as being risk averse, hesitant to adopt new agriculture strategies or to mortgage their land to secure agricultural inputs needed to improve dramatically their productivity. As one analyst of peasant behavior suggested, the peasant's situation is much like that of a person standing in the ocean with water up to his neck. The last thing he wants is waves.[12]

The poor in poor countries spend most of their income on food. They eat mostly cereals and starches such as cassava, have low caloric intake and would spend more for food if they could. Table 1.1 reviews data on average per capita and average household expenditures for a selected sample of countries. Of course, the figures for national averages obscure the fact that even in relatively well-off countries, such as Brazil or even the United States, the poorest of the poor live in desperately food-insecure households. Nevertheless, the national indices demonstrate the countries where household insecurity is highest. In these a large number of individuals eat little but cereals and starches and spend a large proportion of the family income to secure their food. It is individuals in such households who are the most insecure and vulnerable. They have little or no ability to adjust to shortfalls in income. Nor can they adjust to shortfalls in their own or national crop yields, if the result requires additional food expenditures. Research into the 1974 famine in Bangladesh indicates that the most substantial factor leading to famine symptoms was not an absolute shortage of stocks in the country but rather the rise in food prices (Johnson and Schuh, 1983; Almagir, 1980). Food security ultimately is

Table 1.1
Average Household Food Insecurity Measures

Country	Cereals as a Percentage of Daily per capita Caloric Intake 1977/80	Percentage of Household Expenditures Spent on Food 1975*		
		Nationwide	Urban	Rural
Bangladesh	84.8	69.0	65.8	72.2
South Korea	76.2	44.0	41.0	47.0
Egypt	64.9	60.7	43.0	78.5
India	64.5	71.3	67.7·	74.9
Kenya	62.5	59.4	43.5	75.2
Tanzania	59.5	59.3	51.2	67.3
USSR	41.7	47.7	43.8	51.7*
Brazil	33.4	50.0	44.0	56.0
Jamaica	31.7	54.5	51.7	57.3
Japan	30.0	35.5	—	—
United Kingdom	20.4	19.6	—	—
West Germany	19.7	21.8	—	—
United States	17.7	21.3	—	—

*Data from 1972, Compendium of Social Statistics.

Sources: World Food Aid Needs and Availabilities (USDA, 1983); Compendium of Social Statistics (UN, 1977); Income Elasticities of Demand for Agricultural Products (Rome: FAO, 1983).

measured by what happens to individuals, and for those with little or no choice in their access to food the condition of insecurity is almost constant.

Microeconomic theory applied in such circumstances helps explain why peasants opt for strategies to stabilize and secure their position rather than optimize income. Thus poor households generally prefer their low-yielding crop varieties that offer greater resistance to weather extremes. That many peasants will rationally choose to plant crops to meet their minimum subsistence needs year in and year out is therefore not surprising. This also accounts for why land-hungry and food-hungry peasants allow others to extract high returns from their labors without great protests as long as the situation minimizes peasant risks. One year of food shortfall can lead to great calamity for a peasant family. One may therefore understand why peasants withdraw from cooperation with national policies that increase their risk.[13]

People at the margin are thus disadvantaged in two ways. First, the quality of their lives and their capacity to produce are undermined by the physiologically debilitating consequences of undernutrition. Second, their capacity to escape from this desperate condition is itself severely constricted by the rational choices they are driven to make: namely, avoiding risks even if the promise is higher *average* profits, and accepting almost any employment or land-access that promises to provide minimal subsistence. Thus chronic food shortages encourage the continuation of exploitative social, economic and political structures and discourage innovation.

National Level Insecurity. Food insecurity is also a national problem. This is both because household-level vulnerabilities require state action for their alleviation and because the very political legitimacy and security of the state are tied to the avoidance of food calamities.

However, the nature of this national food insecurity and its effect are different from those of individuals. Food shortages in social aggregates, whether nation-states or not, increase internal conflict and vulnerability from external forces. A major factor affecting national food security is *import dependency.* The more a country relies upon food imports to meet its needs the greater its potential food insecurity. In general, national food security can be achieved either by adequate domestic production to meet national needs or by imports added to domestic supplies to the level required. Japan, for instance, relies heavily upon imports, but is not a food insecure nation because it has adequate capacity to afford imports — it pays less than 4 percent of its export earnings for cereal imports — and faces a world market in which several suppliers with adequate supplies exist. The national food security of financially strong countries is aptly demonstrated by the ability of the Soviet Union to secure all but a few million tons of grain of the nearly forty million it sought to import in 1980 in spite of a U.S. embargo on seventeen million tons of anticipated supplies (R. Paarlberg, 1980).

In Table 1.2 the potential impact of world food shortages on countries relying on imports is reviewed for selected countries. In general, the larger the proportion of grain imported *and* the larger the proportion of exports needed to pay for such imports, the greater the potential insecurity. In this respect both Egypt and Bangladesh are quite vulnerable, even though both Japan and West Germany import a larger proportion of their cereal needs.

A second major factor affecting the potential insecurity of countries is the *reliability* of their own food production. Large countries with diverse regions, countries with relatively stable weather patterns, and countries which can adapt their agricultural practices to weather variations (e.g., planting early or late, replanting if torrential rain or late-season freezes destroy initial planting) are all advantaged in being able to count on fairly reliable food production. Often government policy discretion is fairly high in shaping this production. The United States and Canada are perhaps the most favored countries in the world in this respect.

Conversely, other countries suffer from the opposite of one or

Table 1.2
Indicators of Potential Food Insecurity

Country	Cereal Imports as a Percentage of Cereal Consumption (by weight) (1980)	Cereal Imports as a Percentage of Export Earnings (in value terms) (1980)
Jamaica	97.0	11.0
Japan	69.9	3.2
Egypt	53.1	39.4
South Korea	49.9	6.1
United Kingdom	24.7*	1.1
West Germany	23.0	0.6
Tanzania	20.9	21.4
Brazil	18.7	7.3
Bangladesh	15.7	47.5
USSR	14.2	7.4
Kenya	12.9	6.1
India	0.3	14.6
United States	0.1*	0.1

*Consumption data used in the calculation is from 1978.

Sources: FAO Trade Yearbook 1983, and US Department of Agriculture World Food Aid Needs and Availabilities, July, 1983; OECD Consumption Statistics, 1964–1978.

more of these conditions. The Soviet Union, for example, has over 90 percent of its grain lands in northern latitudes. As a result, there is a narrow band of time each year during which crops must be planted and harvested. Unfavorable weather during this time, or a contraction of this period owing to a late spring or early fall, leads to dramatic shortfalls. In other countries the failure of a particular weather pattern can have devastating effects as for example in the 1983–84 South African drought or the failure of the monsoons in 1964–65 for the Indian subcontinent. Basically most at-risk states may be found in subsaharan Africa, in South Asia, and in Central America.[14] In 1983–84, well over twenty African states faced emergency food needs as their markets and crops failed for one reason or another and their financial resources were virtually nil. These countries had little choice but to turn to the international community for assistance.

A third factor is *nutritional* and *stock levels*. Variation in production becomes increasingly important the smaller a country's reserves or carry-over stocks and the more its consumption patterns provide little room for adjustment without increased malnutrition. In the United States, people could shift livestock from feed grain to grazing. This would free up large quantities of grain for direct human consumption. People can also usually step up consumption of other types of products—fruits, vegetables, legumes—to compensate for scarce and therefore high-priced grain or meat products. In the poor countries of Africa and Asia, however, no such adjustment is possible. There the bulk of the population is already at a subsistence level. At best such people can shift from a predominantly grain diet to eating root crops such as cassava and searching out uncultivated food supplies such as wild nuts, berries, and tree leaves.

A fourth factor affecting a country's vulnerability to shortages is its *capacity to import* when domestic supplies prove inadequate. Japan imports nearly 70 percent of its total cereal consumption, but because of its strong position as an industrial exporter, it has ample foreign exchange with which to pay for food imports (F. Sanderson, 1978). This is obviously not the case with most countries. In particular, poor developing countries already seeking substantial amounts of foreign assistance to help pay for imports of capital goods and technology to aid in development projects are most vulnerable. In this situation food imports compete directly for scarce foreign exchange and, to the extent commercial food imports become necessary to meet the basic subsistence needs of the country, their cost has a direct, deleterious effect on economic development.

A fifth factor that increases a country's vulnerability to shortages is its internal *capacity to distribute* food supplies. Particularly in Africa internal transportation systems are so inadequate that while some regions may have more than adequate food supplies, particularly of local fruit and vegetable crops or local subsistence crops such as millet, sorghum and cassava, normally none is marketed or exchanged over areas greater than a few miles. Regional shortages elswhere therefore cannot be relieved. The efforts of governmental bodies (e.g., marketing boards or relief agencies) are usually impotent since such groups lack the infrastructure to procure and move commodities from surplus to deficit areas. Moreover, people in deficit areas may have developed little familiarity with foodstuffs from other regions and find such food, even if available, undesirable. While desperate people will eat anything to relieve hunger, food that is less than acceptable often provides fewer benefits than equivalent, high-costing more familiar foodstuffs. Hence a country may frequently turn to food imports even in a time when food surpluses exist in some regions simply because it lacks the institutional mechanisms and national marketing systems to redistribute its own food supplies.

One measure often used to assess adjustment capacity is income elasticity. Where incomes are low, an extra unit of income leads to a fairly high positive expenditure on basic foodstuffs such as grain, while in wealthy countries such elasticities are low. Table 1.3 presents data on price elasticities for selected countries for cereals as a whole. A more detailed analysis of adjustment tendencies in a country would be desirable. This would reveal for a number of distinct food commodities the level of food security achieved in terms of the response a population could make to modest changes in income and/or in price (where price elasticities are calculated). When food security is robust, elasticities would be low and cross-commodity elasticities would be at least moderate. In a low-risk country increased food prices would simply mean less meat in each diet (except for the poorest who ate little meat initially) and in a poor country, e.g., Bangladesh, the substitution might be from rice and wheat to sorghum and cassava. Thus a design for improving food security would not simply note various

Table 1.3
Income Elasticities of Demand for Cereals, 1975

Country	Nationwide	Selected Urban	Rural
Bangladesh	0.70	0.54	0.86
South Korea	0.54*	0.39	
West Germany	0.39		
Egypt	0.34	0.15	0.54
Tanzania	0.32		
India	0.31	0.21	0.42
Jamaica	0.21		
Brazil	0.10		
Japan	0.15		
United Kingdom	0.01		
USSR			
United States	0.07		
Kenya	0.09**		

*Estimated.

The log-inverse determination of elasticities was used for all data except ** where a semi-log determination was used.

Source: Income Elasticities of Demand for Agricultural Products (Rome: FAO 1983), and P. Konandreas, B. Huddleston, and V. Ramangkura, "Food Security: An Insurance Approach," IFPRI Report #4, 1978, p. 67.

elasticities, but also use these to assess the food security status and adjustment capabilities of a country or important groups within a country.

International Level Insecurity. Properties of the international food system and resources available for international factors are the third level for examining food security. The international level impacts a country's food security through the availability of imports at a dependable and equitable price. Once the need to import is established because of national shortfalls, a country's ability to secure food on attractive terms becomes important. Here long-term export marketing guarantees such as those offered by the Australians to some of their poor country customers or the one which the United States negotiated with the Soviet Union to reduce global trade instability may be important vehicles to decrease vulnerability from tight world food markets, especially for those trading in commercial markets. More generally, stock level, market openness and the availability of several sellers can all contribute to an exchange system enhancing the positive effect of the international level to food security, especially for importing countries.[15] In addition, early information allowing a country to anticipate purchase needs so that it can enter the world market at more favorable periods is also a capability that can reduce vulnerability. Finally, the counter-cyclical availability of food aid and donor country and agency recognition of the importance of helping a country achieve food security can mediate against the harmful effects of a national or even a global shortage.

C. Adaptive Capacity

The central concept in assessing food security, at whatever level of social organization, is adaptive capacity. This refers to the ability of a household, a state or the international system to adjust patterns of food-related activities with a minimum of financial cost or dietary loss. Adaptive capacity is central to understanding security properties of many systems, from the back-up systems used to make space vehicles safer to the redundancy built into electric power grids to prevent failure. In a secure world food system households could adapt in a number of ways to particular food crop shortfalls and states and the international community would support such adaptations. In dire cases national and international agencies would stand ready, as is true now only to a limited extent, to provide food directly through emergency relief.

Economists often think in terms of a fungibility (exchangeability) between food and cash. In a food-secure setting this assumption basically holds. But, as insecurity increases, barriers to easy shifting from one food consumption pattern to another are raised and make adjustments costly and fungibility a less accurate assumption. Thus, food security for the poorest households and states requires food not cash. As a measure of security is achieved, various non-food resources including cash become increasingly useful.

Food aid as an instrument to reduce food insecurity in the extreme case must be targeted for direct consumption. As modest degrees of food security are achieved, however, it will be appropriate to use food resources, especially food aid, to reinforce institutions and policies that extend the adaptive capacity of a country and not simply to continue direct relief. Even in dire cases international food aid need not itself be the exact food used to alleviate the nutritional deprivation for which it is targeted.

II. Policy Options for Alleviating Food Insecurity

The state's role in shaping food systems has always been substantial. For centuries states have provided collective goods such as irrigation to aid production. They have regulated markets and imposed standards for food commodities for nearly equal periods. The rise of the nation-state in the last four centuries has also been marked by an increase in government norms and rules regulating and structuring markets.[16] In exceptional periods states have undertaken special measures to provide food to vulnerable populations. The development of the Indian famine code in the last half of the nineteenth century is illustrative of this last type of policy intervention.

To understand how food security must be enhanced we will review some of the many policies recently proposed and analyzed. Policy recommendations aimed at improving food security represent a complex set of actions, not all of which are fully consistent with and most of which compete with one another, at least implicitly, for scarce resources.

A. Matrix of Possible Policy Steps

There are nine useful divisions into which policies can be categorized representing different action levels and food system phases. These are depicted in Figure 1.1. This chart lists a sampling of policies that could enhance adaptive capacity or food security. The distinctions are occasionally blurred since some policies can affect activities in more than one cell in this ninefold matrix. Nevertheless, the classification helps focus attention upon and clarify the expected effects and benefits of particular policies.

Production is the first major phase in food systems for policy attention. Ultimately food is grown on separate land plots by individuals or small groups of people. Increased production, particularly by those currently most food insecure, has been widely accepted by scholars and proclaimed in international meetings as the fundamental solution for the situation of food insecurity.[17]

The distribution of food through markets or other exchange forms is the second phase of food systems. Maintaining a stable exchange framework is critical to food security, which requires not excluding participants either for social/political reasons or because of deteriorating terms of trade, i.e., high or unstable food prices.

The final phase for policy intervention is the vantage point of the consumer. Even with a stable, open market, food security fails if people lose their income or are otherwise denied access to consumption, say through habits that lead to rejection of nutritious food or illness which inhibits digestion. We turn now to exploring how food security can be addressed by actions at the three levels discussed earlier — individual, national, and international.

B. Alternate Points for Improving the Food System

A state's food system's adaptive capacity is improved by sectorial or national policies that increase the supply of or effective demand for food products. Most state policy efforts have addressed supply side factors, attempting to increase production as a solution to food insecurity. With the Keynesian "revolution" in the twentieth century, governments now also regularly aid in the expansion of demand, most commonly through various food subsidies to consumers.

Before the expansion of national and international markets and transport systems, food security depended principally upon separate food production systems. In peasant societies and in the early growth stages of industrial countries this was a region's or country's principal method of achieving food security. It is still *an* important element in food security and in the long run still basic. Nonetheless, presently other government interventions also play an important role; national and international market intervention; food subsidies; and feeding or employment programs that provide the means to purchase food.

The Production Phase. Food produced within one country will either be consumed there or in another region or country. Consumers are ultimately dependent on the producer, whether it be another family member, a surplus agricultural region of one's own country, or a

Figure 1.1
Food Security Policy Steps

Level of Action	Phases for Policy Interventions
	Production
International	1. Remove import barriers to food and agricultural products in industrialized countries
	2. Development funds committed to increasing LDC production, i.e. IFAD
	3. Funding of research into new cropping technologies
	4. Control of negative impacts from private investment in developing countries
National	1. Integrative National Food Policy—targets for degree of self-sufficiency
	2. Appropriate price orientation that enables domestic production to expand and become more reliable
	3. Employment policies to realize adequate demand
Household	1. Use of improved technologies that reduce the vulnerability of rural households to weather fluctuations —irrigation —chemicals —multiple cropping regimes —new crops
	2. Collective buying and use of farm inputs
	3. Multiple crops for hedging

different country. Now, however, it is universally expected that the nation-state will act to insure a secure food supply. A major question for each state, therefore, is to what degree it will pursue policies aimed at producing sufficient food domestically and to what degree it will rely on the international market.

Figure 1.1 *continued*

Phases for Policy Interventions

Market/Distribution

1. International food stock agreements (IWC action)
2. Market-stabilizing bilateral agreements
3. Small country stabilization stocks held by international agencies, e.g., WFP
4. Emergency food support— IEFR and FAO proposals
5. Futures markets

Consumption/Access

1. Emergency food aid reserves
2. IMF fund to cover production shortfalls and price rises
3. Increase the responsibility and predictability of food aid

---

1. Improved use of international markets
2. Nationally held food reserves
3. Reduced market barriers in LDCs
4. Marketing board integration of food aid and imports

1. Food subsidies
2. Feeding programs
3. Nutritional education programs
   — target populations
   — overall national nutrition goals

---

1. Develop skills and understanding of markets
2. Develop marketing strategies for alternative situations
   — use of multiple markets (open and government controlled)
   — alternative middlemen

1. Better sharing and sounder nutritional decisions
2. On-farm reserves
3. Greater flexibility of food tastes

Some popular prescriptions arising after the 1973–75 world food panic argued a "food first" strategy for states, assigning high social and political benefits to national self-sufficiency.[18] Conversely, conventional economic approaches, such as those most World Bank economists pursue, have continued to advocate trade barrier reductions and the reliance on comparative advantage to strengthen both a country's food security and its general economic well-being (D. Johnson, 1983; Bale and Duncan, 1983). In practice, the predominant trend is mixed (e.g., Japan), combining cost inefficient subsidized food production with some reliance on imports, thereby following a partial "comparative advantage" dictum.[19]

The greatest variability in any state's food system tends to come from production phase fluctuations. Production ultimately depends on rather uncontrollable factors. Most notable, there are weather conditions; pest and disease attacks; unforeseen environmental problems; and fluctuating financial constraints, especially in the capital available to poorer farmers and in the price of inputs they must buy.

Most scholars and policy analysts as well as national and international leaders agree that *increased, more reliable*, and *more efficient* food production is the central, most satisfactory answer to a country's food insecurity (Wortman and Cummings, Jr., 1978; W. Brandt, 1980). However, this commitment to enhance production and the goal of self-sufficiency is tempered by various physical and economic limitations facing each country. The social and political advantage to a country of being self-sufficient in food production may be worth sacrificing some degree of economic efficiency as dictated by rules of comparative advantage. However, the degree a country can reasonably accept relative economic losses to achieve domestic self-sufficiency has some limits, especially for poor countries.[20]

Economically competitive increases in production are possible for most countries, either through increasing the intensity of farming and/or from expanding land under production. Achieving greater yields on current agricultural land is especially possible in areas where new seeds, irrigation and fertilizer use have yet to be introduced to any extent. For example, agricultural land currently under rain-fed conditions in Africa has been shown to double its yields with irrigation (World Food Council, 1984). Intercropping legumes and maize show greater yields than when each is grown separately (Hardy, 1977). Such production achievements are frequent and impressive.

However, a cautionary note regarding the value of new technologies must be raised. Their application can lead to regressive income distribution (Griffin, 1974) and can reduce the reliability of production obtainable through greater yield variability (Barker, et al., 1981).

Increases in production are the major goal of agricultural research, but efforts to reduce the variability of production from year to year are also needed, if not by government-supported research then by other government means. Farmers' income, and for many their consumption as well, will be at risk under new farming techniques. Thus policy interventions to enhance production must consider both average yield *and* yield variability, and must move to reduce innovation risks that may accompany efforts to raise yields over time.

State intervention to enhance production has been most widely celebrated in the successes of American agriculture. The county agent system, rural electrification, production price guarantees and research and education support developed between the 1862 Morrill Act and the 1930s depression have paid handsome dividends in high efficiency of production per hour of farm labor and in reducing the rural-urban gap in standards of living.[21]

High producer prices are the classic economic solution for states seeking to stimulate production, and the evidence of their effectiveness at broad levels is impressive. Since the beginning of the Common Agricultural Policy in 1962, with its high guaranteed prices for producers, the European Community has in twenty years shifted from a major net grain importer to a wheat exporter and minor coarse grain importer. The United Kingdom, which joined only in 1972, was by 1983 a surplus wheat producer when it had been a major importer throughout the previous century. European agriculture is both efficient (by and large) and by world standards well rewarded. By developing internal self-sufficiency Europe has reduced its demand for grain imports which would otherwise compete with the increased imports of poorer Third World countries. The protection enjoyed by European farmers may be keenly resented by U.S. and other export interests, but it remains a success story, though a costly one, for priority of domestic production over comparative advantage dictums.

Tropical Africa represents nearly the opposite picture. Here state policies have created production disincentives, owing largely to low effective producer prices. Only Nigeria in the early 1980s was moving to raise local prices above those of the world market to begin to attack the sharp increase in food import dependency that had arisen in the 1970s. A combination of overvalued exchange rates, declining rural-urban terms-of-trade, taxes on agricultural exports and cheap consumer food prices had eroded production incentives to the point where some African countries suffered not only per capita production declines in the 1970s (the only area of the world to do so), but actual total production declines. The state's desire to obtain development capital by capturing rural surpluses and adding them to overseas aid and loans vastly over-estimated its capacity to manage economic development, a misjudgment reinforced by some donors' liberal aid policies, including the World Bank, which has now become quite critical of past practices.[22]

In 1983–1984 food aid to Africa increased to make up for food shortages due to drought and policy failures. One reason the aid has been possible is that world market prices for grain were at near historic lows and both the United States and Europe had surplus stocks. Indeed, for the first time since its original signing in 1967, the European Community provided in 1983 and 1984 more food aid than their minimal pledged amount under the Food Aid Convention.[23]

The state's role in shaping production incentives appears, therefore, not only critical to success in achieving larger and more efficient production, but also in shaping the position a state can take vis-à-vis world market exchanges and the ability to aid other less food secure states.

The Market Phase. While the market phase is mostly under the control of "privately" evolved and dependable institutions, and therefore not as vulnerable to weather fluctuations or non-revolutionary political changes, it can itself cause or at least amplify food insecurity problems. Market operations within a country involve securing and transporting food from a large number of farms into areas of exchange, especially the central urban areas and deficit regions where consumption or export takes place. In a typical marketing system private exchanges allocate how much is consumed and by whom. Markets create prices which can serve as signals to traders and eventually producers. Prices affect, first, the amount of food present in a particular local trading area or, with open international trade, the country as a whole. Secondly, these market signals put forth allocation implications for food production, where favorable price incentives will affect later production.

Table 1.4 gives data from Kenya to illustrate within-country market dependency among different income levels, and suggests that

Table 1.4
Distribution of Household Food Consumption,
By Income Group, in Rural Kenya, 1974–75[a]

Income Group (KShs)	Own Produce as % of Total Food Consumption	Food Purchases as % of Total Food Consumption	Total Value of Food Consumption (KShs)
Under 0	39.03	60.97	2,457
0–999	36.82	63.18	1,244
1,000–1,999	44.00	56.00	1,707
2,000–2,999	45.68	54.32	2,119
3,000–3,999	44.66	55.32	2,671
4,000–5,999	51.78	48.22	2,872
6,000–7,999	54.97	45.03	4,115
8,000 and over	61.45	33.55	4,794
TOTAL	50.00	50.00	2,594

[a]Excludes pastoral and large farm areas.   Source: World Bank, 1982.

poorer elements of the population may be even more dependent on markets than those with higher incomes. This dependence on trade or markets will greatly affect the overall domestic and international economic relations of a particular country, as well as its level of food security.

In recent years there has been an increasing LDC dependence on international market exchanges. For financially strong states such international trade can be a safe route to food security. However, they have a tendency to protect domestic markets and enter and exit the international market just to cover any shortfall, sometimes erratically, as does the USSR. This has increased the instability of grain trade and has affected LDCs negatively. Valdés, for example, has shown that in the 1960s the greatest burden for LDC food importers came from fluctuations in the *quantity* of food they imported, while in the 1970s their financial burden rose to much greater heights due to fluctuations in import *costs* of changing (rising) international prices. In some cases price changes exceed the amount spent on grain imports due to changes in the quantity of imports (Valdés, 1982).

The EECs common agricultural protection policies (CAP) also have a deleterious effect on low-income countries in the commercial market phase. These countries in the 1970s had to bear the cost of fluctuating world food prices while trade barriers designed to help European farmers and to cement the common markets' integration protected European domestic markets from international price rises. The USSR and Japan have in the past suddenly entered the market and created supply shortages which greatly increase grain prices for the countries who already have problems with balance of payments and must sacrifice other development goals so as to import expensive food (R. Paarlberg, 1978).

Variations in grain prices and in the availability of food aid in the 1972–78 period greatly exceeded anything experienced since 1950 (Hopkins and Puchala, eds., 1978). This international grain price unpredictability can be very dangerous to a vulnerable country's food security. Imports needed when international prices are high, as Bangladesh experienced in 1974, take a devastating toll on a country's balance of payments, on government expenditure for development projects, and on political stability.

One state response has been to inaugurate or increase strategic grain reserves. Such stock holding has and will continue to be a method for states to hedge against international price changes and to assure quick food access if a local shortfall occurs. However, most stock-holding schemes of any size in LDCs, especially in Africa, are financially inefficient. Nonetheless, since major exporters no longer hold stock as they did in the 1950s and 1960s, stock reserve schemes of at least modest proportions take on additional political and economic justification.[24] As major trading states now try to hold less stocks, albeit with only partial success, other countries are holding more and developing countries' shares have increased, with China heading the list. This shift in stocks, and the FAO estimates of the size of global stock holding compared to consumption needed to prevent sharp price rises (roughly 18 percent), are depicted in Table 1.5. Of course, stocks in exporting states are especially critical, and these fell much more sharply than world stocks in 1972–74, a period in which stocks in some states, such as Europe, actually rose.

While reliance on international trade to achieve food security will probably increase due to exporting countries' interests and increased LDC food needs, multilateral efforts to assure low-income countries a market participation capacity is desirable. The IMF food facility fund is one potentially helpful example though its use since 1981 has been

Table 1.5
Changes in World Stocks Held
as a Percentage of Food Consumed, 1971–1984

Years	1971	1972	1973	1974	1975	1976	1977	1978	1979	1980	1981	1982	1983	1984
World stocks as a % of Consumption	17	18	14	15	14	14	18	17	19	18	16	18	21	16

Source: *Food Outlook* Statistical Summary (Rome: FAO, 1984 and 1974).

limited. The fund's drawing rights recognize that it is not just production shortfalls that may hurt a country's food security and consequently strain balance of payments because of food imports, but also grain price increases or export crops failures. Long-term food aid guarantees are another potentially helpful mechanism to assure a country's market participation capacity.

Before a country attempts to solve its food insecurity with international solutions, however, it should weigh seriously whether domestic production as a portion of consumption should decline, which may happen either by a country's increasing cash crop or industrial goods production, or by just letting population growth exceed food production. The real terms of trade in food versus other agricultural crops, and the likely changes in import-export levels must be considered. As Table 1.6 indicates, there is some despair for LDCs regardless of what they do in agricultural production as a food security measure. Over the 1970s the international terms of trade for both agricultural raw materials and food have fallen.

Even worse, the role of markets in national food security efforts leaves much to be desired. Many countries with segmented and discriminatory market policies reduce market effectiveness. East Africa has a form of decomposed farm production, with rural markets supplied by the unofficial system and the urban sector supplied mainly by the parastatal. This is due largely to extreme poverty and deteriorat ing physical and governmental structures in East Africa. National policy makers refuse to acknowledge the importance of the indigenous informal sector whose actions are directed more by self-preservation than by policy makers' urban market assumptions.

Even at household levels, peasant farmers must learn to expand their patterns of exchange, not only with each other, but with a variety

Table 1.6
International Terms of Trade Between Manufactured Goods
and Food and Agricultural Commodities: 1973–1981*
(1975–1977 = 100)

Commodity	1973	1974	1975	1976	1977	1978	1979	1980	1981
Food	134	183	125	97	80	76	76	112	93
Agricultural raw materials	130	119	88	109	105	102	109	110	100

*The indices are derived by deflating the indices of nominal prices by the United Nations index of unit values of manufactured goods exported by developed market-economy countries and are generally used to express the terms of trade of primary commodities for manufactured goods.

Sources: UNCTAD, *Monthly Commodity Price Bulletin, 1960–1980 Supplement* (TD/B/C.1/CPB/Add.1) and *January 1982* (TD/B/C.1/CPB/L.10).

of merchants and traders. This means greater use of stock holding on individual farms and an increase in the variety of nutritious comestibles deemed socially acceptable. The role of the state can be large here. Through research and education in effective storage techniques and through nutrition education and market development support for locally grown crops not yet commanding a national market, the state can provide a framework for greater adaptive capacity at the household level. Cultural barriers and market segmentation typical in many countries, especially those in Africa, can thereby be reduced.

At the international level, poor LDCs are most vulnerable and least able to use adjustment alternatives. Valdés and Castillo found that developing countries' abilities "to finance their growing food import requirements" seriously deteriorated in the 1970s. They were squeezed by declining export receipts, a growing oil bill, and an explosion in annual interest payments on foreign debt.[25]

Consumption. The third and for practical purposes the most critical phase for achieving food security is in consumption. People must be able to eat *and* to eat nutritionally adequate amounts and types of food. This *sine qua non* requires that people have the resources (cash or exchange goods) available to obtain food from the market. To achieve this they must have access to resources to produce their own food through their own labor or have other employment to acquire "exchange entitlements" (cash). This view emphasizes that a nation pursue a demand-led food security policy.[26] A state consumption policy aimed at food security therefore cannot focus solely on food production capabilities or markets.

Fundamentally, undernutrition is a result of poverty. This catch-all phrase points toward rural food scarcities, lack of education, and the weakness of vulnerable groups to command state actions. Chronic malnutrition, that is, inadequate amounts of food intake, affects two major groups: the urban poor who lack economic access to food, and the rural landless or near landless. State intervention in some countries, both through employment policies and feeding programs as in China and Sri Lanka, have made significant progress in reducing food insecurity at this consumption phase. Sri Lanka in the 1970s had an average life expectancy much higher than India, but with the same GNP per capita. But its success was not without cost. After 1977 food subsidies were narrowed to a food stamp program to reduce the "burden" on the state (Edirisinghe, 1984).

In many LDCs, 60 to 80 percent of income is spent on food (see Table 1.1). Thus small price rises result in food consumption losses for the poorest members of the population. States in these situations are under a special burden to develop methods for stabilizing supplies and thus prices of food. Supply side measures such as buffer stocks and international reserves, whether physical or financial, in themselves do not guarantee access in the final phase of the food system. Indeed the 1974 Bengali famine was due to price changes and not to a physical shortage of food; the same was true for the 1862–1864 English Lancashire famine. Greater emphasis needs to be placed, therefore, on generating more stable demand through such measures as stable employment opportunities and reliable transport and distribution systems to prevent market profiteering, and on unemployment and ration shop or food stamp systems.

Since the greatest poverty and malnutrition occurs amongst the rural poor, and since they are usually excluded from serious power in many states, attempts to enhance their access to food through market intervention is in order. Egypt may be one of the few exceptions to the urban bias pattern of food subsidies because its cheap bread is widely available in rural as well as urban areas (Von Braun, et al., 1982).

Finally, states must increasingly see food security as an integrated whole. Attempts to eliminate malnutrition merely with price incentives or established exchange patterns will not suffice. To do more will be especially hard for weak states, such as those in Africa. In a semi-subsistence culture some of the strategies for creating adaptive capacity or redundancy in food production that should be considered include storing tubers in the earth, growing drought resistant crops, and storing financial assets such as jewelry. Such methods must be respected and seen as realistic responses to the harsh environment. A state can become more food secure by supplementing these traditional mechanisms through encouraging subsistence farmers to enter a market and grow market-efficient crops. While for a period it is prudent to encourage farmers to continue to grow their risk-averse crops, risk reduction measures for other crops are also in order. Another task must be to ensure that food subsidies for urban food security are affordable and that nutrition policies also reach the rural areas.

III. Conclusion

In 1984 the world food system exhibited three seemingly contradictory problems: high production efficiency and large stocks in leading industrial states, economic recession among farmers rather generally (the worst since the 1930s depression both in northern and southern states), and growing food shortages, particularly in Africa where by the summer of 1984 famine had arisen. How could farm surpluses and growing efficiency exist alongside a failure to resolve hunger? Addressing the answer and the consequence runs straight to the heart of food policy and state food system intervention for reducing insecurity both for producers and consumers.

In the contemporary world, the state's role is critical. For example, in societies where consumption is low the key is to get effective demand and production raised (Mellor and Johnston, 1984). Demand is raised by addressing problems of income distribution and food pricing policies. However, in order for farmers to capture the benefits of cooperation in controlling production to meet a raised effective demand, the state must intervene to prevent "defection." Each farmer must calculate that in facing a common market price which will not be affected by his or her own production, it is in his best interests to produce maximum yields. This holds even though collectively each farmer would be better off planting more modestly.[27] In this example state intervention is needed to provide the collective good of moderate stability (Olson, Jr., 1965; Hopkins, 1965).

We see therefore that improved food production, while essential to food security, must also be accompanied by state efforts at reduction in, or at least a sharing of, risk. In the past, states provided services such as irrigation — a classic collective good — and also established food policies that provided price floors, subsidized inputs or made other guarantees that reduced risks for food producers. One outcome was rapid rural development. Now the state must share in production risks. Under these conditions in the United States the risk-averse tendencies of peasant production have been shown to decline and the more capital-intensive farm and food-production technology emerge; in Japan labor-intensive development preceeded the shift to capital-intensive production, but the lessons are the same (Cochrane, 1979).

The development of the modern industrial state rests upon this revolution in agriculture. The transformation of agricultural production took place through the uniting of new technology and an expanded role for the state in creating an attractive environment for expanded production. With this transformation the state's increased policy role and national industrialization co-occurred throughout Western Europe and North America in the eighteenth through twentieth centuries.

In other parts of the world, especially Latin America, Asia and Africa where late development occurred, this state policy/technology transformation encouraged substantial discontinuities between the state's role and a country's capability for rural transformation. In countries such as Ghana and Tanzania, for example, efforts to transform the rural area toward a socialist model, skipping the capitalist stage of production, have proved disastrous failures. As Goran Hyden points out, peasants facing efforts by states with weak capacity to aggressively transform their economy prefer to exit from the system rather than accept the promised and unrealized collective goods and disciplines of state regulation (Hyden, 1983).

In industrialized states, governments began fairly late — usually not until the twentieth century — to undertake some major risk-reduction roles that require market intervention directly into the buying and selling of grain commodities. In Australia and Canada, Wheat Boards have now been created, while in the United States the Commodity Credit Corporation has bought and sold millions of bushels of grain. The European Community devotes over 70 percent of the

Common Market budget to maintaining its current Common Agricultural Policy (CAP). The CAP is aimed largely at providing farmer subsidies through marketing board purchases so as to maintain high commodity prices stabilized through government agreement. Even in these countries, however, the role of the private sector and of middlemen between producers and consumers has been maintained. Thus in the most advanced industrialized states we find the state's role as a risk reducer for producers (and for consumers) to be a mainstay in smoothing out erratic qualities in the food system and in expanding food production efficiency. An incremental advance in state control has provided a basis for industrial development and has been achieved relatively successfully over several centuries.

In contrast, in Third World countries (most prominently in Africa) the state has attempted to leap into the same role but in ways resulting in serious deformation in the agricultural sector and, in Africa, to a decline in food production. Tragically, efforts to expand the state's role have included the displacement of middlemen from their role in market management. African states unfortunately have shown little competency in their ability to perform such functions through parastatal bodies.

In early industrializing countries, intervention began first in levels of production to reduce risk to producers, secondly in influence over markets, and finally, and only partially, in providing consumer guarantees of access through rights to food as embodied in various targeted food subsidy programs. The developing countries, however, have moved simultaneously into all three areas and have attempted to maintain "cheap" food policies under conditions in which food production per capita and per farm unit of labor were not rising. The result has been a growing dependency on the world trading system for imports—either commercially or on a concessionary or food-aid basis—in order to maintain the implicit guarantees that have arisen between consumers and government.

This excess in late developing states, sometimes grounded in an urban bias, has led to a more rapid development of a dependency on the state for the provision of food security and, in turn, the dependency of many states on the international system as benefactors, especially in Africa but also for some Asian and Central American states. The trends began as early as the twentieth century, but accelerated after World War II, stimulated in part by a system of food aid that was originally established as one mechanism to reduce surpluses in developed countries, particularly the United States. All these developments have contributed to today's food insecurity.

Food insecurity or its absence can operate at three levels: individuals and households, nation-states, and the international system. To alleviate insecurity in today's world we must focus on national policies to enhance food security. We can thereby better understand the kinds of transactions that take place at the international level since many of these (e.g., trade and aid) are necessitated by individual countries' domestic policies. There is considerable evidence, for example, that the Soviet Union's growing dependence on grain imports is clearly a function of its domestic farm policies rather than a foreign policy objective. In the United States, trade policy is shaped more by futures markets, by domestic pressure from domestic producers, and by interests of the United States in exports in general, than by diplomatic or conservation purposes (Soth, 1982). These are clear examples of how the nation-state plays the key role and is inextricably intertwined with national food security and with an international policy framework.[28]

Finally, in looking at the nation-state for food security we must continue to focus on adaptive capacity, especially in lesser-developed countries. Adaptive capacity suggests that food security is higher where people have several options or choices for securing their food. Adaptive capacity offers a simple and potentially operational definition for food security. From this perspective we can see that having advance fallback or adjustment alternatives is the key task for government when seeking to enhance food security and national well-being. For producers this means some form of risk reduction. For consumers it means improved guaranteed access to food. These are the major contributions the state makes to the food system. State policies that enhance or detract from adaptive capacity of individuals and households provide a basic litmus test for the effectiveness of state intervention. Mechanisms for greater adaptive capacity are possible within household units, at the national level through policies such as stock holding, and at the international level through access to international food, especially food-aid guarantees for the most needy.

The framework or basic set of rules, norms, and expectations that govern the participants in the world food system and its various component levels must reflect an understanding of the way in which the expectations for the state to provide food security have shifted substantially over the last several centuries.[29] This has made food security both a government responsibility and a practical test of whether a government is likely to succeed or fail in ensuing years. Riots over food price rises in the Dominican Republic, Tunisia, Morroco, and Egypt in the last decade and coups in Bangladesh, Niger, and Ethiopia all reflected those countries' failures to meet the populace's food security expectations.[30]

Chapter 2

State Policies and Food Scarcity in Subsaharan Africa

CHERYL CHRISTENSEN & LAWRENCE WITUCKI

Subsaharan Africa faces serious food problems, manifested in declining per capita food and agricultural production, chronic malnutrition, rising food aid requirements, and growing reliance on food imports. The problems were dramatized in 1983 by serious food emergencies in twenty-four countries throughout Subsaharan Africa, and during 1984 with continued, or increasingly severe food problems in twenty countries. Subsaharan Africa's food problems have been well cataloged. There are basic weaknesses in the structure and performance of the agricultural sector, the performance of official food marketing systems, infrastructure, and government policies. These weaknesses have been exacerbated by population growth and increased demand; serious natural, economic, and political "shocks"; and more recently, by a severe global recession. Governments are now less able to ignore food problems, and have generally responded by making food self-sufficiency a major national objective, in some cases formulating strategies for increased domestic production. However, few, if any, governments have additional resources available to implement these programs. Hence, hard choices—domestically and internationally—are inevitable.

I. Current Situation

In 1983–84 Subsaharan Africa faced its third major food emergency since the late 1960s (the Sahel drought, 1968–72; East and Southern Africa, 1979–80; West, Southern and East, 1983–84), as twenty-four countries experienced serious food problems. This was followed by another major food emergency in 1984–85, affecting some twenty countries.[1] Six countries—Ethiopia, Sudan, Kenya, Mali, Niger, and

Mozambique — faced the most severe crises. A combination of production shortfalls, refugee flows, civil strife and poverty led to widespread starvation in Ethiopia, with reports of starvation occurring as well in Sudan, Mozambique, Chad, Mali, and Niger.

These emergencies highlight Africa's precarious agricultural situation. Africa's 1983 cereal production was 47.0 million tons, the lowest since 1973, when drought was also pervasive. Production in 1984 was not significantly better. A decade of weak production and rapid population growth leaves Africa in a worse position now than in 1973. Both per capita food and agricultural production have fallen, while most other regions of the world showed increases (Figures 2.1 and 2.2). Hence, while Africa produced 4 percent of the world's cereals in 1972 and had 8.0 percent of the world's population, in 1983 it produced about 2.9 percent of the world's grain and had 8.9 percent of the world's population.

The most recent emergencies differ from previous emergencies in several important ways. First, they affect countries throughout the continent, although some regions (Southern Africa in 1983–84, the

Figure 2.1
Indices of Total Food Production

(% of 1969–71 average)

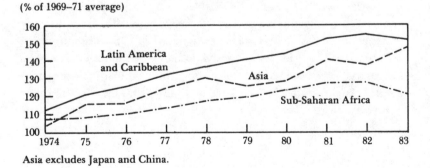

Asia excludes Japan and China.

Source: Economic Research Service, USDA.

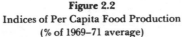

Figure 2.2
Indices of Per Capita Food Production
(% of 1969–71 average)

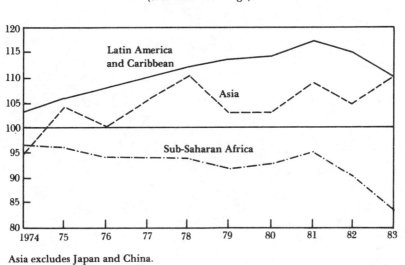

Asia excludes Japan and China.

Source: Economic Research Service, USDA.

Horn and the Sahel in 1984–85) have been more severely affected. Second, trade patterns have been more severely disrupted. South Africa—traditionally an important corn exporter—became a major corn importer in 1983, continued importing in 1984 in the face of a second year of serious drought and faces a third year of drought which makes imports likely in 1985. Since South Africa had previously provided a significant proportion of Subsaharan Africa's corn imports (Figure 2.3), supplies to other countries have been affected. Zimbabwe, also a traditional corn exporter (but on a smaller scale), initially rationed corn in 1984 to avoid imports, but subsequently imported commercially, while receiving substantial food aid. Within the Southern Africa region only Malawi (which largely escaped the drought) has had the capacity to export. Third, worsening financial conditions mean many countries have only a weak capacity to import needed food commercially. Devaluations, often part of "structural adjustment programs," make imports more expensive, while terms of trade, foreign exchange reserves and borrowing capacity have declined.

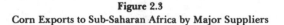

Figure 2.3
Corn Exports to Sub-Saharan Africa by Major Suppliers

Thousand metric tons

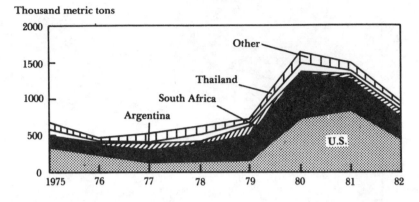

Source: Economic Research Service, USDA.

Because the situation has been so serious and has affected countries in different ways, brief discussions of specific regions are provided.[2]

Southern Africa

The most serious food problem occurred in Southern Africa, where severe drought dramatically reduced production of grain and other crops. South Africa's 1983 corn crop was only 40 percent of normal. Other crops were also reduced and per capita food production dropped below the 1969–71 level. Zimbabwe's grain production was only 1.3 million tons, 55 percent of normal. Both countries had previously been able to export corn. Several smaller Southern African countries (Botswana, Lesotho, Swaziland) also suffered severe production declines. In addition, the southern half of Mozambique experienced total crop failure. Zambia's corn crop was damaged for the second year, and corn imports were about 150,000 tons.

Mozambique experienced large-scale starvation in 1983–84, as the effects of drought exacerbated by civil strife and logistics constraints led to the death of some 100,000 people. The emergency continued into 1984–85, as Mozambique experienced a third year of drought, which exhausted its internal resources for adjusting. Commercial imports of 100,000 tons strained limited foreign exchange reserves, and despite large-scale food aid, starvation was again reported.

West Africa

In West Africa abnormal weather patterns disrupted crop production in many countries throughout 1983. Coastal regions from Ivory Coast to Nigeria suffered from an unusually severe dry season during late 1982 and early 1983. Reduced rainfall and bush fires in several countries (Ivory Coast, Ghana, Togo, Benin and Nigeria) reduced both food crop and export crop production. As a result, export earnings dropped and some countries (especially Ghana) found it difficult to import food to make up for the production shortfalls.

The Sahel faced food emergencies in both 1983–84 and 1984–85, although conditions were far worse in 1984–85. Senegal, Mauritania, Cape Verde, and Gambia all had reduced grain harvests in 1983–84, and Sahelian cereal production fell 10 percent to 4.9 million tons. Drought in northern Senegal was the worst since the devastating Sahelian drought of 1972–73. Cereal production declined one-third to 537,000 tons. Production of peanuts, which normally account for 25 percent of foreign exchange earnings, declined by almost half.

In 1984–85 production fell in all Sahelian countries except Senegal, as severe drought affected Mali, Mauritania, Chad, and Niger. Cereal production in Mali fell to 796 million tons, 25 percent below the last normal crop in 1981–82. In Niger cereal production dropped more than 30 percent, creating large import and food aid needs. Both countries are landlocked, making the delivery of imports difficult and expensive.

East Africa

Ethiopia was the most seriously affected East African country. Drought in the northern highlands in 1981 and 1982 led to crop shortfalls. By 1985, some 7 million people were at risk of starving, and large-scale starvation had occurred in parts of the country, triggering both dramatically increased food aid and migrations of Ethiopian refugees into Sudan, itself affected by a serious drought.

Kenya suffered its worst drought in fifty years, reducing its corn production by 27 percent. Kenya responded to the emergency by importing large quantities of food commercially—about 500,000 tons—while donors allocated more than 500,000 tons. Rapid commercial imports, and relatively smooth handling of food aid, prevented the widespread starvation which characterized several other food emergency countries.

Sudan experienced a second year of drought in 1984–85, which reduced production of its staple crop (sorghum) 30 percent from its already drought-reduced 1983–84 level. Thus Sudan, a sorghum exporter until 1981–82, required imports of more than a million metric tons to cover its own needs. In addition, refugees from Ethiopia, as well as Chad, entered Sudan in large numbers. Combined with large-scale migrations of Sudanese within the country, refugees created additional needs, especially in the rapidly growing camps where starvation occurred.

In addition to food emergencies, Subsaharan Africa has been hit hard by current international economic conditions.[3] Since 1980 African countries have experienced intensified pressure on foreign exchange reserves, coming in part from deteriorating terms of trade, and from macroeconomic changes (higher interest rates, the appreciation of the dollar) which made financing far more costly. The impact of these forces is sobering. Economic growth for African countries peaked in 1974–76 at about 4 percent per year, and declined subsequently, falling to 0.8 percent in 1983 (Table 2.1). Thus real per capita income fell sharply. In addition, inflation rose dramatically, from about 10 percent in 1973 to 28 percent in 1981, before dropping to 17 percent in 1984. Current account deficits rose from $4.5 billion in 1973 to $14.1 billion in 1981, with most of the increase coming between 1978–82. Governments borrowed heavily abroad to finance these deficits, raising indebtedness sixfold, from $11.6 billion in 1973 to $69.3 billion in 1984, and tripling the debt service ratio from 8 percent in 1974 to 24.9 percent in 1984.

It seems clear that, overall, governments were in a far weaker position to cope with the 1983–85 food emergencies than they were in 1973. This situation is reflected in the high food aid requirements witnessed in 1984–85.[4] It is generally recognized, however, that food aid is, at best, a temporary measure, and that the solution of African food problems will ultimately depend on enhanced African food

Table 2.1

Africa:[1] Selected Economic Indicators, 1973-84

	Average[2] 1967–76	1977	1978	1979	1980	1981	1982	1983	1984
	(In percent)								
Economic Growth	4.8	2.3	2.5	2.0	3.0	1.7	1.3	0.8	3.2
Inflation	8.6	24.3	19.3	22.9	22.8	28.0	18.5	26.5	17.0
Terms of trade	0.5	18.1	−8.4	2.7	−2.9	−3.6	−1.7	0.1	3.5
Ratio of external debt to GDP	—	36.0	36.7	37.9	35.7	43.4	49.7	54.6	57.7
Debt service ratio	—	11.9	15.4	15.5	16.5	18.7	22.2	22.6	24.9
	(In billions of U.S. dollars)								
Current account	—	−6.6	−9.3	−9.6	−12.6	−14.1	−13.0	−10.2	−9.4
Overall balance of payments	—	0.7	−0.5	−0.2	−1.4	−2.3	−1.6	−1.5	−0.9
Total outstanding debt	—	31.0	37.1	45.1	50.8	56.3	62.7	66.2	69.3

Sources: IMF, *World Economic Outlook*, September 1984, Occasional Paper No. 32.

[1]African members of the IMF (excluding South Africa).

[2]Compound annual rates of change.   [3]Estimates.

production, greater productivity, and adequate distribution.[5] Without programs to address the fundamental problems underlying the current food problems, there seems little doubt that there will be more life-endangering food emergencies in Subsaharan Africa. Many of the deeper causes of the current situation are explored in the next section of this chapter. Addressing these problems will, in many cases, require policy changes. As the fourth section of the chapter demonstrates, a number of countries have begun policy changes, many designed to meet persistent criticisms and address more basic food problems.

II. Perspectives on African Food Problems and Policy Changes

African food problems have developed, and must be handled, in the context of domestic economic and political patterns and the international economic forces that shape them. Analyses and policies which define food issues narrowly as agricultural sector problems miss much, as many agricultural economists recognize.[6] On the other hand, African food problems are not simply or primarily a reflection of a general African "crisis," as some observers seem to suggest.[7] Food problems will not automatically disappear as a result of general economic or political adjustments: there must be both technological and policy changes within the agricultural sector. The objective of this section of the chapter is to provide a broad perspective on African food problems and the policy adjustment issues being addressed by national governments, international agencies, and scholars alike, which will identify the practical relevance of sectoral, national and international factors without becoming enmeshed in them.

The Agricultural Sector

Much of the analysis of Africa's food problem has focused on the agricultural sector itself, and with good reason. Productivity problems, often reflecting the structure and technological base of food production, abound. In addition, sectoral policies—including producer and consumer pricing policies, as well as those affecting agricultural inputs such as fertilizer and credit—have often acted as serious disincentives to increased production and productivity. Finally, domestic marketing structures often intimately tied to government marketing boards or agencies (parastatals) have frequently been a barrier to increasing marketed food production and making a "cash crop" for African farmers.[8]

Productivity. Aggregate food production has grown very slowly (about 1.8% per year), well below the rates for Asia or Latin America (Christensen and Witucki, 1982). Productivity has been low. Cereal yields are less than half those in Asia, while yields for pulses, roots and tubers are less than two-thirds those in Asia.

Part of the poor production record is explained by the structure of food production and the environment within which African cultivators work. Land tenure patterns vary, but most food production occurs on small farms (under five hectares) by cultivators working with simple hand tools. Complex farming systems have developed to manage delicate environments, maintain soil fertility, and meet the subsistence requirements of rural families.[9] Technological progress in improving staple crop production has been limited. With the exception of hybrid maize, there have been few breakthroughs in breeding improved varieties with higher yields. Several factors constrain such progress.[10] First, production is predominately rainfed, and improved varieties developed predominately for irrigated conditions elsewhere cannot be transferred. Second, location-specific factors (including disease, soil types) have limited the transfer of improved varieties from other regions, while local research efforts have been constrained by lack of experienced personnel, inadequate funding, and poor integration with existing farming practices. Third, production is very labor intensive, and labor is frequently the limiting factor of production. Crop technologies which increase peak labor requirements are often impractical or uneconomical to adopt.

Weak performance in food production has major implications for most African countries, given high population growth rates (2.8 percent per year for Subsaharan Africa) and high urbanization rates. Virtually all analyses of Africa's food prospects indicate that without substantial improvements in production, Subsaharan Africa will become much more dependent on food imports (in some mix of commercial imports and food aid) or will experience even more serious declines in nutritional levels.[11] While many regions of Africa have adequate land to permit area expansion, even under traditional cultivation practices, in other areas population growth is putting pressure on traditional cultivation practices — shortening fallow periods, pushing cultivation into more marginal lands, and sometimes contributing to environmental degradation. The transition to a more "science-based" agriculture is especially critical in such circumtances (Johnson, 1980). Increased food production will not automatically solve nutrition problems, especially those rooted in social and economic inequality; but without increases in production the current situation will become significantly worse.[12]

It is now generally recognized that a strong research base for improved food production technology will require time — at least a decade — to achieve. Short-term increases in production in many cases can be achieved with better availability and use of inputs. However, providing adequate capital and incentives for both immediate and long-term productivity increases in many instances depends on creating a more supportive policy environment than has existed in many African countries.

Policies. Subsaharan governments, like others, have a range of food policy objectives, including welfare protection for consumers, public revenue generation, income creation for farmers, foreign exchange generation, increased food self-sufficiency, price stability, food security, improved nutrition, and regional development and equity (Hanrahan and Christensen, 1981). These objectives frequently conflict, and governments find that their policy instruments are insufficient to achieve them all.[13]

In general, African governments have *de facto* placed highest emphasis on urban consumer welfare, and have tried to maintain low food prices. The political and economic interests behind this ranking of priorities have been analyzed extensively.[14] While most governments set low official retail prices (sometimes but not always subsidizing consumers), they were often unable to meet demand at these prices, and black markets flourished. In large measure as an attempt to limit the cost of retail price policies (and sometimes to try to cover the cost of official marketing agencies), official producer prices for staple food crops were kept low. This contributed to an effective taxation of agriculture and created production and marketing disincentives.

Low procurement prices were accompanied by programs to subsidize inputs in many countries, although inputs were often targeted primarily for export crops. Input delivery was often inefficient, poorly timed, and selectively available. Supplies of subsidized inputs were often inadequate, but could not be expanded given the cost of these subsidies (World Bank, 1981a).

There has been growing recognition of the need to change agricultural pricing policy, by scholars of a wide range of persuasions as well as by African governments, and some progress is being made (as section III shows). However, adjustments in prices alone cannot be an effective "quick fix" for several reasons. First, without productivity-increasing technologies or the use of additional resources, increases in the general level of producer prices may not stimulate additional output (Krishna, 1967). Farmers are more likely to respond to relative prices by shifting resources among crops, as for example between sugar and corn in Kenya or cotton and corn in Tanzania. Second, how significant an incentive a higher producer price constitutes depends on the relative importance of subsistence and market-oriented production, the purchasing power of their cash earnings (affected by the rural-urban terms of trade and availability of desired consumer goods) and their awareness of prices, and the creditability accorded to announcements of official prices (Johnson, 1980). USDA Economic Research Service's (1981) analysis suggests that while farmers are price responsive, traditional cropping patterns and the effect of weather-related yield variability were more significant determinants of output than price changes (USDA/ERS, 1981). Finally, the capacity to respond effectively to recognized incentives is contingent on other factors, including the availability of additional resources (fertilizer, credit, labor), good weather, and an efficient system for input delivery and output marketing. Since the major objective of most governments is to increase *marketed* food production, the structure and operation of the marketing system is particularly important.

Marketing. African governments intervene heavily in the marketing of food commodities, generally as a means of procuring supplies at low official levels and gaining control over food supplies. In some countries, semiautonomous government marketing agencies (parastatals) are the only legal procurement channels (parts of the Sahel, East Africa) while in others, especially in West Africa, they coexist with private traders.

In general, parastatals have been relatively inefficient, and have required heavy subsidies from government revenues. Reasons include poor management and high domestic transportation costs, often coupled with pan-territorial pricing and pressure on margins from low retail prices.[15]

Marketing problems extend beyond those created by institutions, however. Much production comes from small farmers who retain a large portion of the crop for their own consumption. Official marketings fall more than production declines in poor years, and rise dramatically when the harvest is good. Parastatals often have failed to procure bumper crops at official prices, either because they have lacked financing and storage (East Africa) or because they have lacked institutional arrangements to procure from small farmers (Nigeria). Where these problems exist, they create additional disincentives to marketed food production. In addition, basic physical infrastructure is often lacking. Inadequate road networks lead to high domestic transportation cost affecting both the delivery of inputs and the marketing of production. In some regions, primarily Central Africa, marketing is so difficult that farmers are insensitive to price incentives (USDA/ERS, 1981). Higher costs for petroleum and general financial pressure have reduced transportation to rural areas in some countries.

National Context

African food production is also affected by a range of wider national forces, including linkages between sectoral and macroeconomic policies, as well as more purely political factors such as the relative power and organization of domestic groups, the role of the state, and political tensions and instability.

Macroeconomic Policies. In many cases, distorted macroeconomic policies—which typically include rapid inflation, overvalued exchange rates, subsidized credit for preferential customers, high minimum wages for urban workers and depressed rural incentives—can nullify attempts to "get agricultural prices right." As Timmer, Falcon, and Pearson (1983) note, when macroeconomic policies (e.g. budget policies, monetary and fiscal policies, macro-price policies) are badly distorted, the cumulative impact is to put pressure on the economy for major policy reform. As pressures build, food policymakers face a narrowing list of effective policy adjustments because of the linkages between such political and agricultural sectors (Figure 2.4). The constraining macro-environment means that even desirable adjustments in sector policies will not provide the basis for long-run, dynamic growth in rural output and income.

Most African governments have faced serious budgetary problems, which have direct ties both to domestic inflation and to the calls for marketing and public sector reform. A major factor contributing to large budgetary deficits has been the high cost of state marketing operations. Large budget deficits have been covered by borrowing, foreign assistance, and by following expansionary monetary policies. The result has been high domestic inflation rates. In addition, many African countries "imported inflation" as import prices rose significantly and exchange rates were not adjusted.

Exchange rates have been a primary focus, in part because governments have more direct control of them. Many currencies were overvalued, and became increasingly so over the last decade. Overvalued exchange rates generally hurt the agricultural sector by making imports cheaper while making traditional agricultural exports less competitive on world markets. Exchange rates have been one reason

Figure 2.4
Major Connections between Macroeconomic
Policy and Food Policy

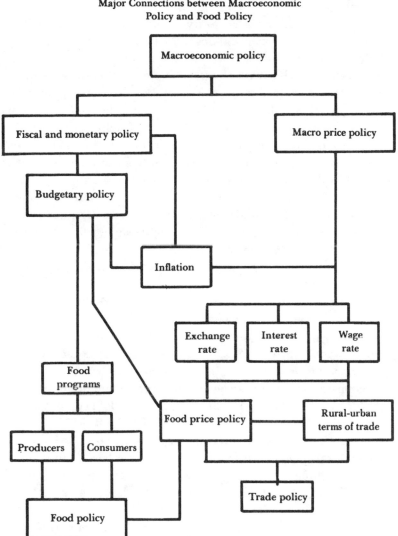

why Africa has lost some of its share of the market in key agricultural commodities, such as coffee (World Bank, 1981; Jansen, 1981). Overvalued exchange rates have been a major reason for deteriorating rural-urban terms of trade, especially when combined with trade regimes that protect relatively inefficient domestic import substituting industries. A number of analysts have thus argued that overvalued exchange rates are an integral part of the "urban bias" found in many countries (Bates, 1981; Lipton, 1977).

Domestic inflation is frequently a major cause of overvalued exchange rates. If a government devalues its currency, but its domestic inflation rates remain significantly higher than those of its major trading partners, its currency will become overvalued again, without any conscious effort to create this effect. Devaluation, without effective steps to lower domestic inflation, will thus be ineffective. This interaction lies at the heart of many structural adjustment program recommendations. The major purpose of a devaluation is to raise the price of internationally traded goods, shifting consumption to nontraded goods. If inflation remains high, however, devaluation will be followed by an increase in the relative price of nontraded goods, which will offset the initial price increases, and thwart the shift from traded to nontraded goods.[16] To be successful in the short run, therefore, devaluation must be accompanied by effective policies to reduce inflation (e.g., lower budget deficits, depress aggregate demand).

Restrictive trade practices also affect Africa's food situation. Tariffs, quotas, import restrictions and licensing procedures are common, and generally necessary to maintaining a fixed exchange rate. Import rationing schemes often adversely affect the flow of both consumer and investment goods to rural areas, while generating revenue used to support government programs and urban-oriented development programs. In addition, as Bates (1981) demonstrates, such regimes frequently provide financial and political benefits to key interest groups, while entailing a general welfare loss. However, the political appeal of such practices often goes beyond those identified, reaching into the political culture of African countries themselves.

Political Factors. The political concerns of many African leaders are generally not simply "economy building," but nation building and regime survival.[17] For many African leaders, ruling countries where religions and ethnic loyalties are strong, and their claims often seen as more legitimate than those of the political regime, the state apparatus—including the state's economic apparatus—is frequently used as a tool for consolidating political power and managing domestic conflict. Hence, state bureaucracies may expand both in size and scope for purely political reasons, in addition to movement in this direction as a result of ideological commitment or political topic.

Within this context, "distorted" economic policies may provide more than an opportunity for competitive rent seeking. They may also be an opportunity for developing alternative systems of power and authority based on the ability to extend authority—using it where it is conferred in order to achieve control in an area where it is not.[18] "Wheeling and dealing," "playing politics," and "power plays" are all imprecise terms pointing to the many ingenious ways in which people in government control others not directly by their authority, but through its extended use. Political machines—or extensive patronage systems—emerge as "unofficial" authority structures built on the extended use of prior authority. Providing economic benefits is, of course, an important method for building these structures, but the rationale for their existence often lies in the political gains derived from expanded authority itself.

The inability to develop a stable political climate can create a legacy of political upheaval which has a major impact on both economic and agricultural performance. Ibingiri (1980) argues that the tendency toward autocratic rule, combined with ethnic and cultural cleavages, leads to a "winner take all" philosophy that significantly shortens the horizons of public officials, focusing primary attention on regime survival and increasing the tendency toward private accumulation.

A second general political factor affecting African food conditions is the role of the state itself. The pattern of extensive state intervention—discussed earlier—is not unique to agriculture. Within most African countries, the state plays a paramount role in economic life, for a variety of historical and ideological reasons. However, the paramount role of the state has not been matched by the capability to act effectively as a state entrepreneur. In part, poor performance can be explained by the shortage of skilled personnel to cover the range of activities undertaken. More generally, however, the root of the problem lies in the inability of the state to perform major entrepreneurial functions, such as risk management. The failure of agricultural institutions must be seen in this wider context.

Finally, as many authors have noted, rural interests are generally not organized to be effective in this political environment.[19] Food producers, often subsistence farmers, have not effectively organized themselves politically. Large farmers, mainly in dualistic systems, are an important counterexample. Second, except for a few cases, political parties at the time of independence were not organized around strong rural interests but more around urban ones. During the post-independence period, African politics has not been dominated by "representational regimes," and political institutions (even when present in local areas) have not served as effective representatives of producers' interests. Indeed, one of the most viable options for peasant producers in this political milieu has been to withdraw from political (and sometimes economic) participation.

International Environment

African countries have faced a series of international shocks, which, coupled with unfavorable weather, have created major economic and agricultural adjustment challenges. The shocks have included higher oil prices, followed by high interest rates and a strong dollar, and more recently, the impact of the global recession before the upturn in 1983 (Balassa, 1983a and 1983b). These shocks reflect Subsaharan Africa's systemic vulnerability—the patterns of costs or constraints imposed by transmission of external shocks and turbulence from the operation of the international system. The extent of the vulnerability is usually contingent on the relative availability and costliness of alternatives that various countries face (Moon, 1984). Balassa (1983a) argues that open market-oriented countries cope better with international shocks (at least through 1978), in part because the economies were more flexible and better able to take advantage of emerging opportunities. However, recent experience has been more mixed, as debt problems have weakened economic performance in many of his test countries. In general, as Moon (1984) notes, shocks and the adjustment costs associated with them are difficult to handle "due to their highly unpredictable and undifferentiated nature." And the costs incurred are high even after the policies are altered. This accounts for much of the dispute over the effectiveness of "structural adjustment" and "stabilization programs" (Moon, 1984).

The interpretation of these international effects (as causes of poor performance or results) and the relative weighting accorded to them lie at the root of many of the differences in strategy between the World Bank's Accelerated Development in Subsaharan Africa and the Lagos

Plan of Action.[20] The Berg report focused heavily on systemic vulnerability and the state's coping ability. Poor performance of the agricultural sector (and especially export agriculture) was identified as a major reason for poor adjustment, and policy reform to speed adjustment was advocated. On the other hand, the Lagos Plan of Action tended to see international disturbances as more potent causes of economic performance problems and focused more extensively on structural distortions arising from their position in the global political economy. Regardless of their perception of the international environment, however, most African countries must now deal with key international actors—such as the IMF and the World Bank—in order to manage their financial problems. Subsaharan countries more than doubled their purchases from the IMF between 1979 (539.72 million SDRs) and 1982 (1.285.3 million SDRs) (IMF, Bureau of Statistics). In addition, as governments reach the limits of their "credit worthiness," they must increasingly enter into stand-by arrangements or arrangements under the extended fund facility with the IMF. Between 1979 and 1982, twenty-seven countries made such agreements, totaling an agreed amount of over 7 billion SDRs (IMF, Treasurers Department). While there is some flexibility in establishing the policy targets associated with IMF conditionality, IMF agreements cover a range of policy areas, such as balance of payments, pricing policy, fiscal and monetary policy, exchange rate policy, and external debt. The dramatic reduction of consumer subsidies, significant adjustments in exchange rates, and constraints on government debt are regular requirements for IMF programs, requirements which governments have much less latitude to ignore in the current environment. In 1983, net financial transfers to the Third World were a negative $11 billion and in 1984 an estimated negative $7 billion.

The combination of domestic food crises, general economic problems, and a changing international economic environment has generated at least a minimal consensus on the need for change. Despite significant disagreements on many points, the Berg Report and the Lagos Plan of Action agree on several key elements. First, both argue that farmers should be given strong cash incentives to produce. Second, both support a focus on small-holder cultivation. While both see the need to improve the agricultural sector to strengthen national economies, the World Bank puts more emphasis on generating additional foreign exchange (via policy reforms that affect export crops) while the Lagos Plan of Action stresses import substitution in food crops and encourages consumption patterns better suited to local production capabilities. Both documents recognize the administrative weaknesses in African countries and the wider implications of them. However, the World Bank stresses cutting back on state functions, so that undertakings are more in line with capabilities, while the African document stresses rapidly increasing the number of skilled managers. As the earlier discussion indicated, while there are pervasive differences in the full scope of Africa's food crises, there is general consensus that much — but not all — of the problem lies in the agricultural sector itself. Making changes that will stimulate appropriate improvements, however, is a more complex problem, and one significantly influenced both by the short-term emergencies countries face, and the medium-term impact of international shocks. In the next section, we explore some of these changes and their possible implications.

III. Policy Patterns and Recent Policy Changes[21]

While many governments responded to weak domestic food production performance, food emergencies, and international uncertainties by announcing programs to increase food self-sufficiency, they were slower to make concrete changes in the key policy instruments at hand: producer price levels, retail prices, marketing structures, and currency exchange rates. Recently, a number of governments have begun to make noticeable changes in prices, with a smaller subset also undertaking changes in marketing practices and currencies. These changes are particularly pronounced in East and Southern Africa, and for this reason relatively more attention will be paid to them in this discussion.

It is important not to exaggerate the significance of recent changes, or to infer from these examples that food policies throughout Subsaharan Africa are rapidly changing. Changes are occurring in a limited number of countries, and their cumulative impact is still unclear.

Nevertheless, it is important to examine recent policy changes for two reasons. First, a variety of prescriptions for policy reform have been made, most based on adjustments in prices, marketing practices and exchange rates.[22] Since many of the changes move in prescribed directions, they need to be examined and assessed. Second, these changes crystallize, for both governments and international agencies, a number of policy issues which need to be addressed in advocating and implementing policy changes.

Producer prices.[23] Many governments reacted to the food crises of the last decade by raising producer prices, although generally not in tandem with international price changes. Domestic prices were low relative to the high world market prices of 1974. Between 1979 and mid-1982, however, a number of countries including Nigeria, Somali, Zimbabwe, Zambia, Kenya, Tanzania, Senegal, Liberia, and Zaire increased official producer prices for some cereals above world market prices (computed at official exchange rates). This pattern continued into 1983, marking a significant departure from historical relationships between official prices and world market prices. In general, price increases in 1981–82 were not enough to raise local prices above delivered import prices with the exception of Zambian wheat and rice. In 1983 and 1984, Zimbabwe and Kenya dropped below world corn prices but Zambia remained above.

With tighter 1983 corn supplies in Southern Africa prices have increased considerably. In April, the South African government approved a 25 percent producer corn price increase to R167.50 per metric ton. Even with the value of the rand at $.90, the new price was equivalent to $150.80 per ton, well above the high U.S. 1983 price of $117.71. Zambia's 1984 harvest corn price of K272.22 per ton, equivalent in December 1983 to $161.00 following depreciation of the kwacha, was near Malawi's late 1983 export offer price of $165, but the cost of importing U.S. corn was about $290. In July 1983, Zambia had increased the corn price for 1984 by 17.5 percent and in November by another 13.9 percent to remain the highest in the region, but drought reduced production slightly.

In August 1983, Zimbabwe, hoping to stimulate large corn plantings by farmers for the 1984 harvest announced a 16.7 percent increase in both corn and sorghum prices to Z$140 a ton, but Zimbabwe's commercial farmers were expecting their costs to increase by 20 percent for the 1984 crops. Smallholders, however, responded, and given the late rains, production increased significantly. Malawi in September increased corn prices by 10 percent, to 122.22 Malawi kwacha per ton, and 1984 production increased slightly.

South African producer corn prices were increased about 30 percent, effective May 1984. With high planting costs and 1983 and 1984's disastrous yields, farmers incurred heavy losses. Debts have escalated and the government has provided financial assistance to commercial farmers. Even so, interest payments have increased by 65 percent and in early 1983 over half the white farmers were in arrears on their loans from cooperatives. Fertilizer purchases were down.

High domestic prices meant that the Maize Board lost money on its exports. The Board has an accumulated deficit of R202 million. Now the corn pricing policy is being reconsidered and quotas may be placed on corn deliveries to the Board for domestic sales, when exports again become necessary. Deliveries for export would not be limited but prices paid farmers would be based on export realization.

These increases translate into much smaller real price increases, given the relative high rate of inflation estimated at 25 percent in Zimbabwe, about 21 percent in Zambia and about 13 percent in South Africa. This is even more true if real prices are examined over a longer time frame (Figures 2.5 to 2.10). Despite significant increases over the past several years, real producer corn prices were below the 1966 level for Kenya and Somalia, and only marginally higher for Zambia, Lesotho, and Zimbabwe. Similarly, despite increases in West Africa, real producer prices were significantly below 1966 levels in Senegal, and relatively constant in Niger. Only in Mali was there a dramatic change in real prices.

Retail Prices. Governments were much more reluctant to increase consumer prices, and in a number of cases left prices unchanged even as producer prices rose. Now, however, a significant number of countries have increased retail prices, and some subsidies are being phased out.

In addition, 1983 retail prices have increased significantly as a result of the drought. Retail corn meal prices have been increasing throughout Southern Africa. In Zambia, the price of this staple food was increased about 30 percent in early 1983 to K0.388, the equivalent of about $0.29 a kilogram. This is 114 percent higher than the price in 1980. In July 1984, prices for meal were increased again by about 10 percent. Besides the increased costs of corn for milling, reduced government subsidies on cornmeal consumption also contributed to increased retail prices. Cornmeal prices in South Africa increased by over 10 percent in 1983 and by another 32 percent in 1984. Unofficial market prices for meal in Namibia (Southwest Africa) were reported in July 1983 to be $0.57 a kilogram.

In Shaba, Zaire, with regional corn supplies very tight, prices of cornmeal doubled from July to November 1983. Wholesale prices in November were Zaires 11.44 per kilogram, or about $0.40.

In early September, Zimbabwe raised its roller meal price by 39.5 percent to Z$0.21 per kilogram or US$0.19 (at the exchange rate of US$0.915), still the cheapest in Southern Africa and about the same as Kenya's.

Marketing

The timing and level of producer and retail prices has important implications for marketing agencies in countries where consumer subsidies often come in the form of parastatal deficits. Hence, for example, Kenyan retail price increases did not match producer price increases, contributing to a substantial rise in the Corn Marketing Board's deficits (Figure 2.11). On the other hand, Zambia's retail price

Figure 2.5

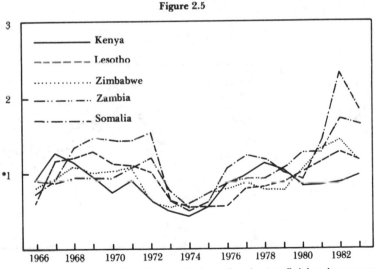

*The point where world market price equals domestic price (at official exchange rates)
Source: Economic Research Service, USDA.

Figure 2.6

Kenya: Price Ratios
Country Price/World Price

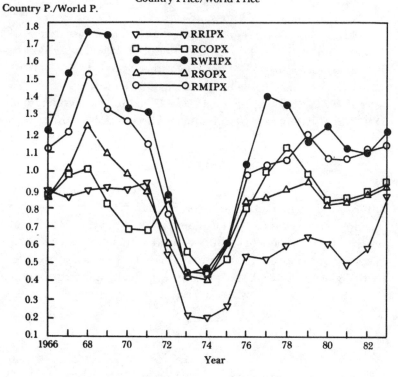

Country P./World P.

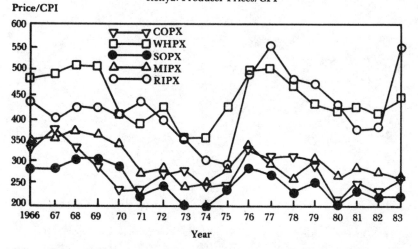

Kenya: Producer Prices/CPI

Price/CPI

Source: Economic Research Service, USDA.

Figure 2.7

Zimbabwe: Price Ratios
Country Price/World Price

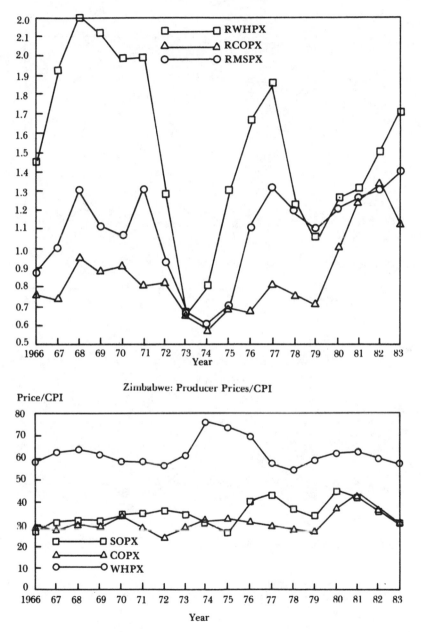

Source: Economic Research Service, USDA.

Figure 2.8

Zambia:Price Ratios
Country Price/World Price

Country P./World P.

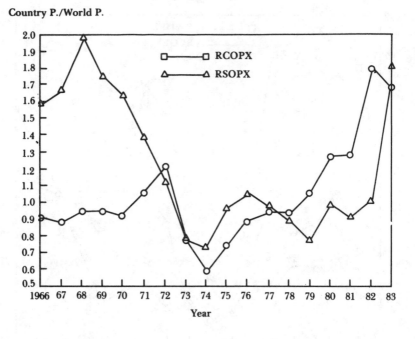

Year

Zambia: Producer Prices/CPI

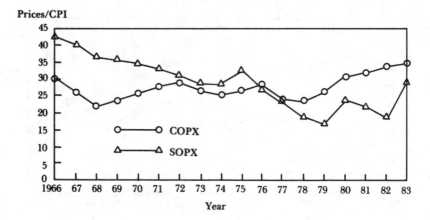

Year

Source: Economic Research Service, USDA.

Figure 2.9

Sudan: Price Ratios
Country Price/World Price

Country P./World P.

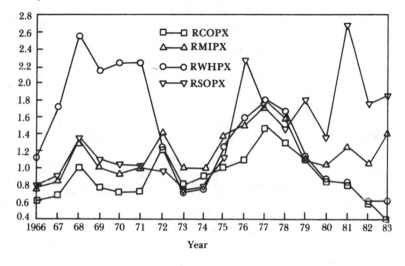

Sudan: Producer Prices/CPI

Price/CPI
(thousands)

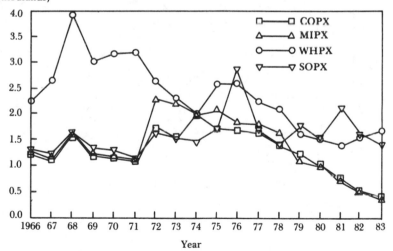

Source: Economic Research Service, USDA.

Figure 2.10

Somalia: Price Ratios
Country Price/World Price

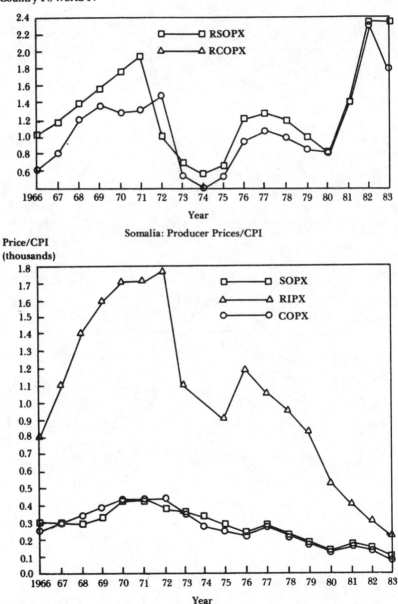

Country P./World P.

Somalia: Producer Prices/CPI

Price/CPI
(thousands)

Year

Source: Economic Research Service, USDA.

increases had more than covered producer price increases in mid-1984 (Table 2.4, p. 69).

Marketing practices have been liberalized over the last two years, although in fewer countries. Some countries changed their marketing policies. Senegal abolished ONCAD (its official cereals marketing board) and has ceased government procurement. Mali's marketing agency is no longer the only purchaser for sorghum and millet, although it continues to control rice procurement. Tanzania has proposed a major restructuring of marketing, returning marketing responsibility to local cooperatives. Zambia has already increased the role of cooperatives, but with mixed results. Kenya is considering marketing reforms to reduce government intervention. However, such steps are difficult, even in a relatively "market-oriented" economy.

Figure 2.11
Kenya: Corn Producer – Retail Price Margins
(1965–1983)

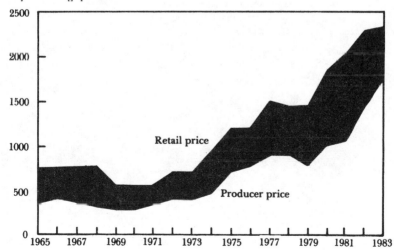

Kenya schillings per ton

Source: Economic Research Service, USDA.

Exchange Rates. Kenya, Zaire, Malawi, Tanzania, Sudan, and Uganda have all devalued their currencies since 1980, the last by sixty times at the end of 1984, with Uganda thus making the most dramatic adjustment.

Yet, despite devaluations, the official rate remained substantially higher than the "black market" rate during this period. In Zimbabwe and Zambia the gap closed somewhat (falling from a black market rate 66 percent higher in 1980 to 58 percent in 1982 in Zimbabwe, and 69 percent to 45 percent in Zambia). In Kenya, however, the gap increased (from a black market rate 10 percent above in 1980 to 30 percent in 1982).[24]

If the unofficial (black market) exchange rate is taken as a guide to overvaluation, currencies required substantial devaluation, with the official rate in 1982 31 percent higher than the black market rate in Kenya, 45 percent in Zambia and 58 percent in Zimbabwe.

Most of these countries have devalued again within the past years and/or their currencies have floated downwards against the dollar. The Zaire was devalued from 6 Zaires to the dollar to 26.9 in 1983. In

Table 2.2
Percent Overvaluation Based on Official
and Black Market Rates

	Lesotho	Zimbawe	Ethiopia	Kenya	Zambia
1970	10.3	34.3	17.1	35.9	35.3
1971	10.4	46.8	17.8	34.5	49.1
1972	16.5	31.2	10.8	32.1	107.1
1973	12.4	26.2	3.8	49.1	93.0
1974	12.9	34.8	16.1	20.0	78.8
1975	14.6	38.5	137.6	19.3	85.22
1976	39.4	167.5	93.2	12.0	161.6
1977	24.6	224.3	97.1	4.2	186.9
1978	4.4	130.0	98.3	8.6	167.6
1979	12.4	109.6	53.2	13.9	81.6
1980	10.0	66.3	35.9	10.3	69.3
1981	9.5	72.7	49.2	20.1	61.3
1982	11.5	58.3	60.4	31.2	45.5
1983	12.6	137.0	70.1	22.0	32.0

Source: USDA, *Pick's Currency Yearbook*.

1982, Uganda instituted the two-tier exchange system. The window one rate was fixed daily by the Bank of Uganda, and was used for essential imports. In October 1983 the rate was Ush 170 to the dollar. The window two rate was set according to offers made by importers. The October 1983 rate was Ush 278 to the dollar. The system was terminated in May 1984. In June 1983 Tanzania devalued by about 25 percent to Tsh 12.2 to the dollar, but the IMF wants a much sharper devaluation. The Kenya shilling in late 1983 was worth about one half of the 1973 value (relative to the dollar) and the Zambian kwacha was worth about half of what it was in 1976.

The recent policy changes in East and Southern Africa (Kenya, Tanzania, Zambia, Zimbabwe) began as politically motivated reactions to food emergencies, coupled in Zimbabwe's case by the political imperatives of the new regime. In part, the changes followed a previously established pattern of raising producer prices in response to a crisis.

All four countries had experienced drought in either 1973 or 1974, although only Tanzania required major imports of corn at that time. Producer prices were increased substantially in Kenya, Tanzania, and Zambia, but remained well below world market levels. Kenya and Zambia concentrated on price increases for maize (the staple crop), while Tanzania raised prices for less preferred "drought-resistant" food crops like millet, sorghum, and cassava. Production in both Kenya and Tanzania rose, reflecting a combination of acreage adjustments and good weather. Neither country could adequately link the production increases to longer term food security, leaving them vulnerable to the next drought. Surpluses in 1978 resulted in storage and procurement problems. Shortly before the 1979 drought became apparent, both countries exported surplus crops at a loss, and Kenya reduced producer prices. Food shortages in 1980 created more severe political and economic problems and a heightened attention to both food issues and the failures of government policies.

Political factors were also important in Zimbabwe. Zimbabwe's 1979 maize harvest was the lowest since the drought of 1973. The new Mugabe government had to import to sustain consumption since decreases in consumption were politically unacceptable. The Mugabe government increased maize prices by 41 percent to stimulate production and ease the concerns of white commercial farmers about the regime's intentions.

The results of the 1979–83 price increases are mixed. Price policy has brought the poorest results in Tanzania. In part this may reflect earlier policy changes, including structural change through villagization and centralization of marketing in the early 1970s. These changes apparently reduced farmers' incentives and disrupted production. Producer corn prices increased fivefold between 1973 and 1980, exceeding domestic inflation. However, aggregate production did not increase much. Food crops expanded at the expense of cash crops. In an attempt to ease this problem, Tanzania recently raised the prices of export crops, and removed export taxes on them. At the same time, it required each village to grow a minimum of 100 hectares of food crops (to limit the shift out of food crops), and plans to reinstitute marketing through local cooperatives (Ellis, 1982).

The price response in Kenya was better, although weather was also better until 1984. Higher prices for corn led to increased production and official marketings in 1981 and 1982. Deliveries reached a record, over 20 percent of the total crop. With a significant small holder sector, Kenya can probably achieve a positive labor supply response, not just increased use of purchased inputs. At the same time, however, it is becoming more difficult to increase corn production in Kenya (Table 2.3).

Arable land and water are severely limited at only 0.14 hectares per person in 1980, and competition among crops is becoming more intense. In recent years, sugar expansion in Western Kenya has displaced corn. While corn area increased substantially in 1981 and 1982, yields remain below 1.7 metric tons per hectare, the level achieved in the mid-1970s. Increased productivity is clearly important.

Corn marketing is also a problem. With small farms now supplying nearly one half the Board's purchases, most from farms under three hectares, logistics are complex. In addition, government constraints on movements of grain across district boundaries inhibit marketing, although it also reflects real government concerns about food security.

Kenya's system of corn pricing and marketing had acceptable results until 1979. Corn production averaged an increase of at least 3 percent a year until the severe setbacks of 1979 and 1980 (see Table 2.3). Kenya's current problems became evident in 1979. The previous years' large corn crops overwhelmed Kenya's marketing facilities. The National Cereals and Produce Board could not handle the large

Table 2.3
Kenya: Selected Prices and Corn Production

	1973	1974	1975	1976	1977	1978	1979	1980	1981	1982	1983
Foreign exchange rates 1 Kenya Shilling =	US$0.142	.14	.135	.119	.121	.13	.136	.133	.110	.092	.075
Kenya's producer corn prices Ksh per M.T.	388.9	464.3	697.9	765.9	888.9	888.9	720	1000	1055	1444	1600
Equivalent in U.S. $ per M.T.	55.22	65.00	94.22	91.14	107.56	115.56	96.32	133	116	132.85	131.70
Kenya's estimated corn production 000 M.T.	1600	1600	1900	2195	2205	1895	1450	1751	2200	2340	2000
U.S. producer corn prices $ per M.T.	75	115	106	98	80	83	93	106	115	93	117.71
U.S. corn prices c.i.f. Rotterdam	110	147	134	123	107	114	134	150	153	126[a]	153[a]
Coffee prices, spot N.Y.C. $ per lb.	0.66	0.69	0.77	1.42	2.41	1.63	1.73	1.56	1.27	1.41	1.33
Petroleum prices, Saudi Arabia $ per bbl.	3.29	11.58	11.53	11.28	12.40	12.70	17.26	28.67	32.50	33.47	29.31
Kenya's consumer price indexes	—	46	55	60.6	69.6	81.4	87.9	100	111.8	134.7	150.2

[a]Estimate   Source: Economic Research Service, USDA.

crops. Export prices for corn were low in 1977 and 1978. Neither the Board nor the government was able or willing to subsidize the exports of corn. As a result, corn spoiled in both farmers' and the Board's hands. Losses were substantial. The government approved a reduced price for the 1979 crop, a price only about 3 percent above that set in 1975. The government, in financial difficulty, dismantled the farm credit programs that year before new credit programs came into effect. Problems were also experienced with input supplies, particularly fertilizer. Corn planting dropped to the lowest level in many years.

The year 1983 brought a partial recurrence of some earlier problems. The large 1982 harvest has strained the resources of the National Cereals and Produce Board. It was again short of storage space. Public finances were severely constrained. Farm credits were restricted and payments to farmers were late. With foreign exchange shortages, imports of fertilizers, chemicals, fuel, and spare parts were restricted. Also, with less favorable weather in 1983 the corn crop was down about 15 percent to about 2 million tons or some 200,000 tons short of estimated consumption needs.

Zambia's case lies in between. In 1981, price increases made Zambian prices the highest in the region, a pattern that continued through 1983 (Table 2.4). Maize acreage increased, and small farmers increased marketings, as did the nucleus of commercial farmers. Unfortunately, Zambia has made little progress in reducing the risks from drought. After an 18.5 percent price increase for 1982, area planted increased again, but drought resulted in a poor crop.

Zambia has been among African countries criticized for public price policies that tended to promulgate prices for agricultural producers that often were lower compared to urban consumer prices, particularly food prices. Since 1978, however, when farm prices were very low relative to consumer prices, a reversal has occurred and corn producer price increases have been more rapid than consumer price increases (see Table 2.4). With a 33.9 percent increase for the 1984 harvest, the corn price is expected to remain above increases in the CPI.

Zambia's 1979 corn harvest was very poor, and marketings dropped about 42 percent to only 336,000 tons. As a result, the cost of cereal imports rose 75 percent, to kwacha 23.1 million (1K = $1.26 in 1979). The 1979 harvest producer corn price was increased by 32.5

Table 2.4
Zambia's Corn Producer Prices Compared to Consumer
Prices, 1970, 1974–1984

Year	Consumer price indexes 1975=100	Farm corn price indexes 1975=100	Farm prices consumer price ratios
1970	72.6	70	97.8
1974	91.8	86	94.7
1975	100	100	100.0
1976	119	126	105.9
1977	142	126	88.7
1978	166	136	81.9
1979	182	180	98.9
1980	203	234	115.3
1981	231	270	116.9
1982	260	320	123.1
1983	314	366	116.6
1984	380	490[a]	128.9

[a]Price increased to K 272.22 per M.T. in November 1983.

Sources: World Bank, Attache reports, IFS.

percent to K100 per ton, or to $3.20 per bushel. In 1980, marketings
were again low, and the producer price was increased another 30
percent. Drought was a factor in these low marketings but incentives
to farmers were also weak. For the 1983 harvest, the corn price was
K203.33 per ton (1K = $0.80) or equivalent to about $4.13 a bushel,
probably the highest official price in Southern Africa. This was so
despite the 25 percent drop in the kwacha's value relative to the
dollar.

Corn plantings in late 1981 and again in 1982 apparently responded favorably to the higher prices but drought damaged the 1982
and 1983 crops. Corn imports have been needed each year since 1979.
Weather in Zambia has only been favorable one year since the higher
corn prices have been in effect. That was for the 1981 harvested crop.
Marketings were good at 693,000 tons. The next year of good weather
will provide a better test of the higher corn prices.

Since the 1970s some reduction has been made in cornmeal consumption subsidies. In 1981, 1982, and 1983 retail cornmeal prices

were 39 percent and 46 percent and 66 percent, respectively, above the producer prices of equal weights of corn. The necessity to import corn, sometimes at high cost, has made the reduction in subsidy costs more difficult. With government financial constraints very severe, there is no readily apparent alternative to taking the IMF conditions for financial assistance and reducing consumer subsidies.

The government has taken a big step in freeing some retail prices from control, including prices of rice, vegetable oil, meats, and beer. Many prices have escalated sharply, and at the same time controls on administered prices have weakened. Labor unions objected to the government-set 5 percent wage increase ceiling for 1983, while the cost of urban living continued to rise sharply. In early 1983 rice prices had about doubled, to $0.56 a pound, fish prices had tripled, dressed chicken was about $1.50 a pound, and regular gasoline prices had been increased about 6 percent, to $3.23 a gallon. After much negotiating the unions agreed to a temporary wage ceiling of 10 percent.

Zimbabwe's increased prices brought a bumper crop, and record marketings, in 1981. However, consumer prices were not raised until 1982. By then the cost of food subsidies had reached $166 million. Given large stocks, and their financial costs, the government did not raise producer corn prices in 1982 or 1983. It had also decided not to announce prices until after planting, limiting their incentives effect. By November of 1983, with corn production reduced by drought, Zimbabwe had taken two major steps to encourage food production. First, it announced minimum guaranteed pre-planting producer prices, and provided price increases. Maize and sorghum were raised from Z120 to Z140 per metric ton and soybeans from Z260 to Z287. Rainfall was poor, however, and the 1984 crop was again abnormally low (1.4 million tons), but smallholders increased production. Consumer subsidies were reduced, and in some cases, totally eliminated. Retail prices for basic food items such as milk, bread, cooking oil and cornmeal rose 14–50 percent. The government has stated its intention to eliminate the remaining subsidies on cornmeal and beef as soon as possible. By late 1983, however, food supplies were very tight, and the Grain Marketing Board began rationing corn. Despite price increases, demand for corn increased dramatically, as two years of drought caused many other subsistence crops to fail, and relief needs both for citizens and for refugees from Mozambique have been high.

Large food imports were necessary to cover current consumption and to build stocks. Severe rationing of foreign exchange was implemented. Imports were cut. This dampened the prospects for an export-led recovery, even though the outlook for exports was better in 1984 than in 1983. Even with normal rainfall in 1985, the recovery from the drought will take time, and development programs will be slowed.

IV. Implications for Policy Analysis

Both the recent history of policy changes and the current situation facing African countries have implications for future studies of food policy in Subsaharan Africa.

First, more attention needs to be paid to the role of food crises in shaping policies. Crises may be important in changing domestic policy and the configuration interests behind them. On the other hand, reactive policies are frequently piecemeal, unstable, and ill suited to development objectives, such as increasing agricultural production, enhancing productivity, or increasing marketed production.

In addition, the current situation suggests a disturbing interaction between standard IMF prescriptions for adjustment and the practical requirements of managing food emergencies. While devaluations may in the long run be beneficial to the food production sector, in the short run they make needed imports more costly. The result is a further weakening of the foreign exchange position of the government or an increase in the appeal for food aid as thinly disguised balance-of-payments support. The other alternative, severely curtailing consumption which is already inadequate, can lead to malnutrition or death for people directly affected by production or economic disasters.

Second, crises may have long-term structural implications which interact with policies. For example, some have argued that repeated drought in Tanzania led peasants to shift away from drought-prone crops (both food and export crops) in favor of more drought-resistant commodities, a tendency reinforced by (but not rooted in) price policy (Swanberg, 1981). In other cases, food crises leave serious problems which policy may need to face. The loss of cattle (and peasant savings) may be such an issue in Southern Africa, especially in predominately subsistence regions where cattle are required for plowing, as well as a common store of wealth.

Third, far more systematic attention needs to be given to the international economic system. The external economic shocks of the last decade have generally weakened both African economies and African states' position in the international system. Without reopening the debate over whether domestic or international factors were more responsible for causing the existing food problems, we can assert that international forces will be important determinants of food policy over the next few years. This is likely for two reasons. The economic performance of many countries in Subsaharan Africa is very dependent on global economic conditions. Balance of payments and debt crises will continue to put pressure on governments which in turn will shape both the priorities of food policy and the resources available for implementing them.

Fourth, and closely related, macroeconomic linkages to agriculture are more important, and need to be systematically incorporated into policy analysis frameworks.

Finally, studies of Subsaharan food policies need to be broadened to include systematic attention to policy implementation. The conventional economic approach to policy often proceeds as though the "government" is a unitary actor, with multiple objectives, which are rationally traded off. While such an approach has merit as a way of examining the costs of alternative policy options, it is weak in explaining the outcome of actual policymaking processes and the full range of risks involved in attempts to actually implement policy reform. An understanding of the multiple actors influencing food policy, their power and interests, is particularly important for policy implementation.

Closer examination of the behavior of key actors and structure of the economy may make it easier to understand the failure of some conventional adjustment prescriptions.

Implementation involves attention to resource availability and structures, as well as politics, however. Many current discussions of policy reform do not sufficiently examine the resource requirements of implementing these changes successfully. This is particularly clear when the long-term effects of policy changes (e.g., enhanced production and productivity, stable marketing patterns) requires the ability to deal with various phases of the cycle of rain-fed agriculture. Without adequate investments, policy reforms are not effectively implemented, for example, leaving farmers with higher announced prices but no payments for the crops they delivered. One important component of any "policy dialogue" must involve the resources necessary to maintain the basic features of the reform.

Perhaps the most difficult part of implementation is assessing the practical implications of weak structures in markets, infrastructure, and industries for the policy adjustment process. While virtually all statements issued highlight the need to take "structural weaknesses" into account in formulating adjustment programs, and this is reflected in the "target levels" established, the key adjustments sought are quite homogeneous. Whether economies—especially those faced with emergencies—adjust (with all the long-term benefits that implies) or simply react in less productive ways presumes "adjustments" which may, in fact, be quite different. Adjustment, rather than reaction, depends in large measure on the wider political stability and the capability of the economy to make sustainable, cumulative changes.

Chapter 3

After Agrarian Reform and Democratic Government: Has Peruvian Agriculture Developed?

CYNTHIA MCCLINTOCK

World hunger is increasing. Third World nations are becoming less and less able to feed themselves and are ever more dependent on food imports from First World nations. These facts are well-known. How can these trends be reversed? Answers to that question are much less clear.

Can some answers be found in Peru? From the promises of its various governments over the last decade, we might have hoped so. In 1968, the government of Juan Velasco Alvarado took power, and proclaimed a "fully participatory social democracy." A sweeping land reform was carried out, second in impact by many criteria only to Cuba within the Latin American region (McClintock, 1981:61; de Janvry, 1981:206). Almost all large haciendas were expropriated, and the enterprises were transformed into cooperatives run by their peasant members. A number of laws were established to encourage the production of foodcrops and to discourage agricultural exports. Yet, as this article will show, Peru did not become more self-sufficient in food, and more Peruvians became hungry.

In 1980, Peru's armed forces, divided among themselves and thoroughly repudiated within the country, returned to the barracks. Open and honest elections were held, and the victor, Fernando Belaúnde Terry, assumed the presidency amid high hopes throughout the country. Peru's new 1979 constitution stipulates in Article 156 that agricultural development is the top national priority. During the presidential campaign, Belaúnde promised immediate actions to guarantee equal terms of trade between the countryside and the city, to provide more technical assistance to the countryside, to facilitate marketing procedures in rural areas, and to emphasize small irrigation systems and land rehabilitation in the national development program (Centro de Investigación de la Universidad del Pacífico, 1980:85). In his inaugural address, Belaúnde emphasized that increased food production must begin at once (*Business Latin America*, August 6, 1980:256). Yet, as this article will demonstrate, several years after Belaúnde's inauguration, the story is the same: food imports are high, per capita agricultural production is falling, and hunger is spreading.

Why, despite strong official commitments to domestic agriculture, is Peru each year less able to feed its people? One important reason is simply that population has increased considerably, at between 2.7 percent and 2.9 percent per year since the 1950s, whereas arable land has not (Martínez and Tealdo, 1982:31). In 1972, crop land per capita was a mere fifth of a hectare — versus about ½ a hectare in 1967 and ¾ of a hectare in 1963 (World Bank, 1981b:5). Peru's .20 ratio of hectare per habitant is below the world average of .33 in 1979, and the lowest of all Latin American countries, except El Salvador (Martínez and Tealdo, 1982:39). The ratio for nearby Bolivia and Ecuador is .61 and .94, respectively (Martínez and Tealdo, 1982:39).

Further, the overall quality of Peru's land is at best fair. Approximately 60 percent of Peru's lands are deficient in nutrients, acids or other organic material (Martínez and Tealdo, 1982:40). Peru's coastal lands, the source of about 60 percent of the country's agricultural product, are river valleys in the midst of desert; if the rivers run dry because of scarce rains in the highlands, or if they flood because of very heavy rains in the highlands, the harvest is ruined. To bring new land under cultivation, expensive new irrigation systems would be necessary in almost all parts of the country (World Bank, 1981b:49).

Yet, Peru's land scarcity does not absolve official agricultural policy for the country's current food difficulties. No recent government has summoned the political will and resources to provide significant new support for food production in Peru. The Velasco government (1968–1975), the first of two military governments, took steps in this direction, but it also took backwards steps and detours. The Velasco government pinned most of its hopes for improved food crop production on the newly established, peasant-managed cooperatives, but yet did little to change the international and national market rules for the cooperatives. Under the second military government of Morales Bermúdez, government support for agriculture declined. And it declined even more dramatically under the formally democratic Belaúnde government.

The Record: Recent Agricultural Performance and Poverty in Peru

Overall, Peruvian agriculture registered only slight production gains in recent years, gains that did not keep pace with the food needs of the growing population (See Table 3.1). Between 1970 and 1981, agricultural production increased only approximately 13 percent, while Peru's population jumped by about 36 percent (Fernández-Baca, 1982:87–88).

Over the last decade, the production of traditional food staples has actually fallen (see Table 3.2). The record for the potato, which is cultivated primarily by peasants in the impoverished Andean highlands and was historically a source of renown for Peru, is especially negative. Average annual per capita potato production fell from 161 kilograms during 1951–55, to 132 kilograms during 1966–70, and down even further to 110 kilograms during 1971–77 (Caballero, 1980:29). The production of wheat and yellow corn, both also grown predominantly in the highlands, dropped also. The record for yellow corn is worse than the figure in Table 3.2 for all types of corn (Alvarez, 1983:45). The decline in highlands food staple production hurts the peasants of this region because they themselves have less to eat and

Table 3.1
Peru's Agricultural Product, 1965–1982

Period	Annual Percentage Increase[a]
1965–1968	−1.3
1970–1977	+2.6
1978–1980	−7.3
1981–1982	+7.0
1983	−16.8

[a]Figures are averages for the period.

Sources: For 1965–1968, Cabieses and Otero (1977:210); for 1970–1978, Matos Mar and Mejía (1980a:90); for 1979, *Agro Noticias*, June 18, 1980, p. 5; for 1980, OAS (1981:13); for 1981, 1982, and 1983, Peru, Presidency of the Republic (1984:238).

Table 3.2

Agricultural Production, 1970–1983: Principal Products

(Thousands of Gross Metric Tons)

	1970	1971	1975	1977	1979	1980	1981	1982	1983
Traditional Exports									
Cotton	248	233	226	173	244	256	286	256	105
Sugar Cane	8,050	8,309	9,418	8,825	7,034	5,600	5,126	6,509	6,380
Coffee	65	71	65	80	105	95	95	90	71
Food Staples									
Potatoes	1,929	1,968	1,640	1,616	1,695	1,713	1,705	1,800	1,200
Wheat	125	122	126	115	102	77	119	101	76
Rice	587	591	537	594	560	430	712	776	798
Other									
Poultry	48	53	130	143	118	143	183	205	206
Beef	85	90	86	87	87	84	90	91	111
Eggs	28	30	50	56	55	60	64	65	68
Corn[a]	615	616	635	734	621	444	587	631	592

[a]Corn variety is unspecified 1970–1980, and "grano seco" for 1981–1983.

Sources: For 1970–1980, Peru, Presidency of the Republic 1982:512); for 1981–1983, Peru, Presidency of the Republic (1984:236 and 659).

because they have less to sell to urban consumers. Among Peru's food staples, production has increased only for rice, which is cultivated primarily on the coast and in lowlands near the jungle.

The decline in food staple production is not a result of an emphasis upon agricultural exports. In contrast to the pattern in various countries discussed in this volume, agricultural exports have not been markedly increasing in Peru (see Table 3.2). Sensitive to the nation's food needs, the military regime issued a number of laws to restrict export crops in favor of food crops. It also placed unusually heavy taxes upon Peru's large sugar estates, and these taxes were one factor in Peru's declining production of sugar, once Peru's most important agricultural export (Alvarez, 1983:165–190). Also, as domestic food demand increased, crops that had once been exported, in particular sugar, were needed for domestic supply; these products, previously "agroindustrial exports," thus became "food crops." Overall, the production of agricultural exports increased at an annual average of only 1.8 percent between 1969 and 1979 (Alvarez, 1983:46). Agricultural exports constituted 14.8 percent of the value of agricultural producion in the 1967–1971 period, but only 7.9 percent in 1976 (Alvarez, 1983:47).

One sector of Peruvian agriculture has registered dramatic gains in recent years: agroindustry oriented towards middle-class consumption. The poultry industry, which has been heavily dominated by transnational enterprises such as Arbor Acres, Hubbard Farm, and Shaver Poultry Breeding, greatly expanded (see Table 3.2). Agroindustrial food processing also increased considerably. Much more bread, pasta, and crackers were produced from the processing of wheatflour; large national and transnational enterprises, particularly Bunge, Nicolini, and Cogorno, have been primary in this industry. The evaporated milk industry, controlled by Carnation and Nestle, also grew dramatically during this period. Overall, between 1970 and 1980, the processed food industry grew 33 percent (Fernández-Baca, 1982:89). To some extent, the expansion of these agroindustries hurt Peru's food-staple production, as will be discussed below.

To supply its new agroindustries and to meet food needs generally, Peru turned increasingly to the First World, especially the United States, for imports (see Table 3.3). Food imports grew from 117 million dollars in 1969 to a staggering 525 million in 1981 (see Table 3.3).

Table 3.3
Food Imports
(Cost in Millions of Dollars of Principal Food Imports)[a]

1960	60[b]
1969	117[b]
1970–1974 (average)	146
1976	261
1979	220
1980	433
1981	525
1982	359
1983	425

[a]Principal imports are wheat, corn, milk products, vegetable oils, and (in some years), beef and rice. Typically, wheat imports are about half the total food import bill.

[b]Figure is for *all* imports, not just principal products.

Sources: For 1969, FitzGerald (1976:65); for 1970–1974, the World Bank (1981b:190–91); for 1976–1981, Peru, Presidency of the Republic (1983:276); for 1982–1983, Peru, Presidency of the Republic (1984:659). The figures for the 1979–1981 period are reported to have been lower in the Presidency's 1984 volume than in its 1983 volume.

During most of the 1970s, food imports were slightly below or above 15 percent of all Peru's imports. Wheat was by far the biggest item in the import bill, usually approximately half the total. In recent years, Peru has paid rather dearly for its dependence upon wheat imports. As Table 3.4 shows, while Peru's imports have increased modestly — approximately 28 percent from the early 1970s to 1981, the cost of the wheat skyrocketed 175 percent during that period (see Table 3.4).

As food supply per capita declined, food prices rose, and Peruvians have not been able to consume daily calorie requirements. During the 1970s, the real average cost per calorie for a low income household in Lima increased about 5 percent (World Bank, 1981b:33). Accordingly, Fernández-Baca (1982:89) reports that between 1972 and 1979, per capita calorie consumption declined from 2,150 daily to 1,595 for middle-class groups, and from 1,934 daily to 1,486 for lower-class groups.

After 1980, the food problem became even more severe. During the eighteen-month period of July 1980–December 1982, the real average cost per calorie for such a household increased much more. During that period, the purchasing power of the minimum wage fell 27

Table 3.4
Wheat Imports

	Volume in Thousands of Tons	Value in Millions of Dollars
1970–1974 (average)	740	73
1976	763	119
1980	830	161
1981	951	201
1982[a]	968[a]	155
1983	N.A.	152

[a]Data from U.S. Department of Agriculture (1983:30, 34). Data do not equate exactly with Peruvian government's data for previous years.

Sources: For 1970–1974, the World Bank (1981b:190–91). Other years from Peru, Presidency of the Republic (1983:276) and Peru, Presidency of the Republic (1984: 659).

percent relative to the cost of a basic food basket for a family of five (*Quehacer*, 21 [February 1983]:11). According to rough estimates for the early 1980s (*Peru Update*, 22 [April/May 1982]:5), the cost of basic foods to the Peruvian worker was excruciatingly high, and higher than in most Latin American countries. A Peruvian, earning the minimum wage, had to work roughly one hour and 43 minutes to buy a kilo of bread and one hour 27 minutes to buy a liter of milk. Average calorie intakes are now significantly below normal requirements in most regions of the country; by some estimates, per capita daily calorie intake is a starvation-level 420 calories in certain highland zones, and at least 40 percent of preschool age children are malnourished.[1]

Malnourished children are increasingly vulnerable to respiratory and gastrointestinal diseases. Infant mortality is rising, and as of 1979 Peru's rate may have been second only to Bolivia in South America (Sivard, 1982:31). Dysentery is the principal cause of death in Peru, and it took the lives of almost five times as many people in 1981 as in 1972, most of them children (Peru, Presidency of the Republic, 1983:540).

The decline in Peruvians' living standards is especially serious because certain regions of the country were already very poor. Table 3.5 shows the socioeconomic disparities between Peru's southern

Table 3.5
Regional Inequalities in Peru

	Life Expectancy (Years at Birth)	Adult Illiteracy (percentage)	Without Potable Water (percentage)	Population Per Physician	Calorie Intake (percentage of FAO requirements)
Southern Highlands[a]	44	53	93	21,650	72[d]
Coast[b]	54	17	67	1,822	N.A.
Fourth World[c]	44	86	91	30,730	86

[a]Averages for the five poorest southern highlands departments, Ayacucho, Huancavelica, Cuzco, Apurimac, and Puno.

[b]Averages for the five main coastal departments, Piura, Lambayeque, La Libertad, Lima, and Ica.

[c]Averages for Mali and Nepal. Figures for other low income Asian and African nations are similar. See World Bank (1983:150–154).

[d]Figure is for northern highlands, probably similar to southern highlands.

Sources: Farm Income per capita from Webb (1977:119–29); figures for 1961. Life Expectancy, Adult Illiteracy, Without Potable Water from Amat y León (1981:Appendices); figures for 1972. Population per Physician from Peru, Presidency of the Republic (1983:543); figures probably for 1972. Calorie Intake from World Bank (1983:35); data for 1980.

highlands and the coast, while Table 3.6 shows that poverty has become worse in the highlands over the last decade. Some of Peru's poorest regions — in particular, Ayacucho, Huancavelica, Apurímac, Cuzco, and Puno — subsist at the poverty levels of such "Fourth World" countries as Niger, Mali, Bangladesh, and Nepal (See Table 3.5). These regions are all located in southern Peru, very high in the Andes. Ayacucho, perhaps the most poverty-stricken of these five regions, is the home of Peru's guerrilla movement, *Sendero Luminoso*.

The Peasant Cooperatives: How did They Affect Peru's Agricultural Development?

Many analysts of Peruvian agriculture blame the nation's food problems on the Velaso government's agrarian reform and on the peasant-run cooperatives established under the reform. In my view, there is no evidence for such a charge against the agrarian reform. In the cooperatives food production did not plummet; nor did it boom, however.

Peru's agrarian reform was a sweeping one.[2] Approximately 8.5 million hectares — somewhat more than 35 percent of all agricultural land — were expropriated. This land was for the most part the best agricultural land in the country; the expropriated lands produce about 60 percent of Peru's agricultural income. By 1980, virtually

Table 3.6
The Increase in Poverty in Peru's Highlands

	Population Density (per square kilometer) (Ayacucho)	Per Capita Income (1972 = 100)[c] (Highlands Farm Families)	Infant Mortality (per 1,000 live births) (Ayacucho)
1940	8.1[a]	N.A.	N.A.
1950	N.A.	106	N.A.
1961	9.3[a]	106	141[a]
1972	10.3[b]	100	197[d]
1980	12.1[b]	82	N.A.

Sources: [a]Larson and Bergman (1969:301, 334); [b]Peru, Presidency of the Republic (1982:463); [c]My calculations, for lower-income among highlands farm families, from Webb (1977:39), Caballero (1981:207–208) and World Bank (1981b:155); [d]Amat y León (1981:Appendix).

no large landowner remained in the countryside. Approximately 375,000 peasants, or 25 percent of all farm families, benefited from the reform in one way or another. Only about one-third of the benefited families made really large gains, becoming permanent members of viable coastal or highlands cooperatives that had previously been profitable haciendas. In contrast, perhaps another third of the "beneficiaries" received very little land. These peasants, however, as well as other peasants who were not formally "beneficiaries" because they received no land at all, were often relieved from feudalistic duties to hacendados who left the region.[3]

Under the reform, about 650 cooperatives were established, which were owned and managed jointly by their members, within a legal framework set by the state. The land of the cooperative could not be sold to individuals, nor put up as collateral for loans. Foreigners were essentially excluded from land ownership. Thus, in Peru, in contrast to many other Latin American and Third World countries, transnational corporations did not control land resources. United States investment in the Peruvian food industry fell during the 1970s, from $46 million in 1970 to $40 million in 1978 in current dollars (Scott, 1980:16). United States investment in the Peruvian food industry also declined as a percentage of U.S. investment in the Latin American food industry, from 10 percent in 1970 to 4 percent in 1978 (Scott, 1980:16).

Within the cooperatives, life certainly improved for their members. Returning almost every year to three cooperatives that I first studied in 1973, I have witnessed firsthand the dramatic changes in members' lives. Men have a new pride, a new self-assurance. When they are asked about the cooperative in comparison to the hacienda, the great majority says that the cooperative is better.[4] When cooperative members are asked why, they usually say that the hacienda owner, the *patrón*, is gone. Said one member of a coastal cooperative in 1975, for example: "Now there are no longer the *patrones* who abused us and punished us." Years later, in 1981, a member of a peasant community belonging to a larger highlands cooperative made a similar comment: "We're better off with the SAIS than with the hacienda; now there is no *patrón*, who was the owner of everything."

The social and material changes in the cooperative were dramatic. New schools, new community centers, new sports stadiums, and new health facilities were constructed. Whereas previously few young people were able to study beyond primary school, by the late 1970s perhaps the majority of families were able to send their teenage sons and daughters to secondary school in the provincial capital. Most members believed, probably for the first time, that their children could lead better lives than they had, and that professional careers would be available to them.

Basic to these improvements were wage increases in the cooperatives. In the three cooperatives I studied, workers' wages approximately doubled in real terms between 1973 and 1980.[5] Data from other enterprises, although less comprehensive and less up-to-date in many cases, also indicate a sharp jump in wages.[6] By the late 1970s, significant percentages of coastal cooperative members had bought their own television sets.

Peruvian cooperative members thus gained from the military government's agrarian reform. However, the cooperative enterprises did not signify a major step forward in Peruvian agricultural development. Government officials apparently hoped that they would do so. Such hopes were, however, unrealistic. The cooperatives performed about as well as could have been expected under the national and international market conditions, which prevailed for them just as they prevailed elsewhere.

Various journalistic articles to the contrary, there is absolutely no evidence of production declines in Peru's cooperatives. Actually, evidence of any kind about production in Peru's cooperatives is limited. The production record of cooperative enterprises is not distinguished from the production record of individual parcels in government statistics. Nor are pre-reform data on production in haciendas available for more than a handful of enterprises, and even these are not always helpful as the products of the enterprise have usually changed somewhat.

However, the cooperative enterprises account for approximately half of Peru's agricultural product, and presumably any major drop in their production would have affected overall production. Peru's agricultural production has, however, increased since the agrarian reform, although, as previously indicated, it has not kept up with population growth. Table 3.1 showed that Peru's agricultural product increased by an average of 2.6 percent per year during 1970–77, the years of implementing and consolidating the reform. Production plummetted in 1978–80 as a result of a devastating drought. The three-year drought was the longest and worst that Peru had suffered in seventy years (*Perú Agrario*, February-March, 1980:10–11). In 1981 and 1982, production recovered. If the cooperative enterprises rather than the drought had been the key factor in the production decline in the late 1970s, production would not have recouped in the early 1980s, as the structure of the cooperatives had not changed. In 1983, natural disasters devastated Peru's agricultural production once again, as aberrations in the El Niño current brought floods to Peru's north coast and drought to the southern highlands.

The data available on Peruvian agricultural production is by crop, not by type of enterprise. As many crops are produced on both cooperative and non-cooperative enterprises, the data tell us little about the impact of the cooperatives on production. As the first section of this chapter showed, the record for some agricultural products has been especially poor, and the record for others good; in neither circumstances are these products from the cooperative enterprises, however. The crops with particularly poor records are the potato, wheat, and yellow corn; 91%, 93%, and 99% of these crops, respectively, are cultivated outside cooperative enterprises (Alvarez, 1983:53). The products with especially good records in recent years are poultry, eggs, and processed wheatflour items, all of which are primarily the output of private agroindustrial concerns. The principal Peruvian products for which at least 25 percent of the total harvest is from cooperative enterprises are sugar, cotton, and rice[7]; as Table 3.2 showed, sugar production has declined, cotton production has been stable or has slightly increased, and rice production has risen considerably.

In the cooperative enterprises for which data are available, production seemed at least as good as before the reform.[8] Horton (1974:108–109), studying a nationwide sample of 23 cooperatives, concluded that production increased in about half the enterprises, stayed the same in roughly 20 percent, and declined in merely 30 percent. Among the three cooperatives I studied, production rose dramatically in one coastal crop enterprise, stayed about the same in a second coastal crop enterprise, and in a large highlands livestock enterprise remained steady until the late 1970s, when a newly constructed large irrigation canal enabled significant production increases.

Why did production not skyrocket in the cooperative enterprises?

First, some type of dislocation is inevitable in any agrarian reform program. In Peru, the new cooperative members needed time to work out relationships with professional agronomists and, at times, to establish stricter on-the-job discipline (McClintock, 1981;221–246 and 305–310). Second, however efficient the new enterprises were, it would have been difficult for them to improve their yields. The yields per hectare of many crops produced in Peru's enterprises are well above world averages. This is the case for sugar, cotton, and rice (Martínez and Tealdo, 1982:44). Productivity is low, on the other hand, for potatoes, wheat, and milk (Martínez and Tealdo, 1982:44).

Perhaps the most important question, however, is why the cooperatives did not turn decisively from producing export crops to producing food crops. Most cooperatives continued to produce what they had as haciendas.[9] In general, this meant food production — primarily sugar, rice, and meat. (Sugar, once a key export, had to be allocated to domestic consumption by the late 1970s.) The only major export crops were cotton, wool, and coffee.

While most cooperatives thus produced food crops, some did not. Indeed, the primary crops in both coastal enterprises that I studied were not basic food crops. The more "successful" of the two enterprises decided, soon after its inauguration as a cooperative, to cultivate substantial amounts of tobacco. Tobacco replaced hybrid seed corn as the most important and most lucrative crop of the enterprise. The second cooperative continued the crop patterns of the hacienda, and asparagus remained its chief product. The asparagus is sold to Germany via a canning factory in the provincial capital. In the Virú valley where these two enterprises are located, my impression is that asparagus and sugar, both originally planted with export prices in mind, now constitute a greater percentage of production than in the 1960s.

Nor did production patterns change greatly in the third cooperative studied, the large highlands livestock enterprise SAIS Cahuide.[10] Meat and wool were the two key products of the enterprise as both a hacienda and a cooperative. The meat — mutton from sheep and beef from cattle — is sold to upper-income families both nearby and in Lima. Most of the wool is exported, primarily to Great Britain. Although the vast lands of this enterprise could produce billions of potatoes, in neither the 1960s nor the 1970s did potatoes constitute more than 1 percent of the enterprise's income.

Thus, during the 1970s, many cooperative enterprises continued to produce goods that were too expensive for most Peruvians to consume. The primary reason was the logic of the market: the cooperatives could earn more by producing these goods. Overall, as I will discuss subsequently, the prices received by the peasants for food crops have been low in Peru, and this is especially the case for the potato (Webb, 1975:117–120). Moreover, for many cooperatives, agricultural innovation would have been expensive and risky. As an illustration, although it would be desirable that enterprises experiment with native Peruvian crops—producing flour from *yuca*, *camote*, or *tarwi*, and mixing it with wheat flour to make a cheaper bread, for example—the government provided no incentives for such undertakings.

Ultimately, the cooperative enterprises cannot be expected to defy the norms of the international food regime without substantial government support and direction. The Velasco government—in contrast to subsequent governments, as we will see in the next section—did provide considerable support to the cooperative enterprises, especially larger, coastal ones. And, the Velasco government did try to encourage food production, but without sufficient vigor. For example, according to the *"pan llevar"* law of the Velasco government, 40 percent of cultivated land was to be devoted to food crops rather than to export or industrial crops, but the law was only minimally enforced. Agrarian Bank interest rates on loans for food production were lower than on other types of loans—but only by a few percentage points. Some enterprises were supposed to sell at least 50 percent of their production of a good on the domestic market, in an effort to make production for export at the higher prices of the international market less attractive.

However, the government should not have been surprised that many enterprises sidestepped these provisions. Whatever the government's regulations, the Agrarian Bank—the only source of working capital for most enterprises—looked first and foremost at the bottom line. The Agrarian Bank, as well as the cooperative members who all shared in the enterprise profits, did not want to see red ink.

Yet, while the cooperatives did not turn toward greater food production, nor did they shift dramatically toward export production;[11] as other articles on this volume indicate, the mere status quo may be no mean achievement in this regard. During the 1970s, many other Latin

American nations were increasing agricultural exports, and indeed, currently international agronomists are advocating such an emphasis for Peru.[12] Luxury fruits and vegetables, such as macadamia nuts, strawberries, avocados, asparagus, and tomatoes are recommended.

Peruvian agriculturalists probably eschewed an export emphasis for various reasons. One factor was presumably the government regulations discussed above. A second factor was members' interest in the production of a slightly larger amount of goods for their own families' consumption. Also, in the cooperatives, members already had their hands full with new responsibilities and challenges, and did not want to embark on production innovations. Members may also have feared that the new products would have provided fewer employment opportunities. Although presumably some export crops are labor-intensive, the primary option that various managers favored — livestock and poultry — were not.[13]

Indeed, while elsewhere in Latin America the absolute number of agricultural jobs declined during the 1970s, in Peru they did not. Agricultural job hours increased in Peru at approximately 3.8 percent per year over the decade.[14] Probably, if Peru's large enterprises had continued under the control of hacendados, fewer jobs would have been created, as neither big labor costs nor big labor pools are in their interest. In contrast, the cooperative members wanted the enterprise to provide jobs, full-time and part-time, for their relatives, wives, sons, and daughters. Yet, not enough jobs were created to meet Peru's employment needs.[15]

Transnational enterprises were not significantly increasing their role in the agricultural export industry during this period, and these corporations rarely affected decisions to produce for domestic consumption versus export. They were, however, increasing their role in food industries that were selling to Peruvian consumers; Bunge, for example, was a pivotal enterprise in wheatflour and animal feed production; Carnation and Nestle were dominant in the evaporated milk industry; and various transnational enterprises controlled the poultry and egg industry. Even when the large firms in the agroindustrial sector were not formally transnationals, they were generally closely tied to them through various mechanisms, and the overall character of Peruvian agroindustry has been characterized as monopolistic (Caballero, 1984:10–11). Various programs and regulations have benefitted certain branches of the agroindustrial sector.

Probably most important, the wheatflour-processing industry was able to buy cheap wheat imports as a result of United States Public Law 480 (Food for Peace). Also, the poultry industry gained from the military government's ban on beef consumption for fifteen days per month during the early 1970s; consumers tended to substitute poultry for beef.

While these agroindustries contributed to the satisfaction of Peruvian food needs, their overall effect on domestic agricultural production is generally believed to have been negative (Fernández-Baca, Parodi-Zevallos, and Tume-Torres, 1983; Fernández-Baca, 1982; Painter, 1983a and 1983b; Caballero, 1984). Most important, these agroindustries have preferred to import their key inputs rather than use domestic supplies or enhance the possibilities for domestic products appropriate to their needs. In the case of the flour-processing industry, as much as 99 percent of the wheat used by industrial mills is imported (Caballero, 1984:11). It is estimated that the import component of the final price for chicken meat is 63 percent, and for a can of evaporated milk, 57 percent (Caballero, 1984:11). The flour-processing industry has not sought out domestic wheat varieties that could be suitable to its needs; the poultry industry has to some extent displaced domestic beef production; and the transnational evaporated milk industries have depressed the development of small-scale fresh-milk dairies (Caballero, 1984:11–13).

Democratic Government: How Has It Affected Peru's Agricultural Development?

Campaigning, Fernando Belaúnde promised that agricultural development would be a top priority, but as president he has not kept that promise. In most respects, the civilian government has done less for agricultural development than its military predecessors.

The terms of trade between the countryside and the city have deteriorated sharply under the civilian government. On-farm prices for agricultural goods have fallen, the cost of key agricultural inputs has risen, and credit has become scarce and dear.

Table 3.7 shows the dramatic change in agricultural price policy for Peru's farmers between the 1970s and 1980s. During the 1970s, under both military governments, on-farm prices for most agricultural products rose at rates above the consumer price index. Indeed,

Table 3.7
On-Farm Prices for Agricultural Products, 1971–1982

	1971–1975	1976–1979	1980	1981–1982
Increase in Consumer Price Index (CPI)	63[b]	199	59	146
Average Increase in On-Farm Prices for Nine Key Agricultural Products[a]	120	236	53	81
Did On-Farm Prices Increase More or Less Than the CPI?	Much more	More	Slightly less	Much less

[a]Products are: potatoes, rice, wheat, beans, cotton, sugar cane, hard corn, sorghum, and soya. Data for sugar cane during 1981–1982 are not available, but figures from U.S. Department of Agriculture (1983:36) for white sugar suggest minimal increase.

[b]See McClintock (1981:357) for sources.

Sources: Statistical Office, Ministry of Agriculture, for product prices. Consumer price index data for 1973–1980 from World Bank (1981b:front matter); for 1982 and 1983 from *Business Latin America*, June 2, 1982 and March 16, 1983.

Table 3.7 shows that the average increase in on-farm prices for nine key agricultural products was almost twice the increase in the consumer price index during the 1971–75 period; in other words, real on-farm prices for agricultural products were increasing sharply. During the 1976–79 period, real on-farm prices were also rising, but only slightly. In 1981 and 1982, however, on-farm prices for agricultural products plummeted in real terms; the consumer price index rose almost twice as much as average on-farm prices. Potato prices fared especially badly; over the biennium, they increased a mere 29 percent, versus 146 percent for the consumer price index.

The current prices are rock-bottom ones. Despite the relatively good price increases for farmers in the 1970s, Peru's producer prices were lower than world market prices even in 1980. Producer prices were about 40 percent below world market prices for rice, 20 percent for sorghum, 12 percent for maize and cotton, and 35 percent for beef as of 1980 (World Bank, 1981b:53).

The key agricultural input in Peru is fertilizer. Until 1978, the military governments encouraged fertilizer sales. The state marketing agency ENCI was established in 1975 with a monopoly on fertilizer sales. Fertilizer prices were subsidized by 30 percent to 45 percent between 1975 and 1977, and costs of fertilizer transport were covered by ENCI to equalize prices throughout Peru and thus benefit remote regions (ENCI, 1977:21). As a result, total fertilizer sales almost doubled between 1975 and 1977 (ENCI, 1977:20).

After 1977, however, fertilizer prices rose markedly.[16] In 1982, the Belaúnde government ended ENCI's monopoly and decontrolled fertilizer prices. Transportation costs are no longer covered in the prices, and prices in the highlands and jungle are currently 20 percent to 45 percent higher than in Lima.[17] In 1982 alone, fertilizer sales plummetted by 34 percent.[18]

As roughly 75 percent of Peru's coastal properties and 10 percent of the country's highland properties are worked with credit,[19] the availability and cost of credit are very important to agriculturalists. Table 3.8 traces credit trends and interest rates in recent years. Agrarian Bank loans became more readily available under the Velasco government. During the second military government, credit became scarcer, but cheaper: interest rates were negative, well below inflation. Under the Belaúnde regime, however, credit became both scarce and expensive. Throughout the period, credit allocations have been biased in favor of "modern" coastal enterprises and against "traditional" highlands peasants.[20]

Yet another trade policy that hurt many Peruvian farmers was the import liberalization program of the Balaúnde government. After 1980, tariffs were reduced on all kinds of food imports, from meat to

Table 3.8
Agricultural Credit

	Annual Trend in Real Credit Available[a] (percentage)	Interest Rate (percentage)
1960–1964	6.5[a]	N.A.
1965–1969	3.9[a]	N.A.
1970–1974	4.3[a]	Between 7 and 12[b]
1975–1979	–7.7[a]	Between 10 and 17[b]
1980	+15.5[b]	33[a]
1981	–7.2[b]	52[a]
1982	–15.0[b]	52[b]

Sources: [a]Martínez and Tealdo (1982:101, 109); [b]Banco Agrario del Perú (1982).

apples. Although 1981 was an excellent year agriculturally, total agricultural imports increased by approximately 18 percent (U.S. Department of Agriculture, 1983:34). In subsequent years, under intense balance-of-payments pressure, the government restored many agricultural tariffs, but generally not to previous levels.

Why have the terms of trade between the countryside and the city deteriorated so markedly under the Belaúnde government? Various factors would seem to be important. First, the Belaúnde government sought the support of the international private and public banks as well as of the International Monetary Fund, and the economic orthodoxy of these organizations quite possibly prompted the government's new "free-market" policies on agricultural interest rates, fertilizer prices, and agricultural import tariffs. At the same time, however, despite likely pressure from international economic agencies, the government maintained state control of on-farm prices for agricultural products and kept these prices low. In policy-making on this score, it would seem that the government was responding to the interest of state marketing agencies and commercial intermediaries generally. As noted previously, despite the low on-farm prices, real food prices to the consumer were rising during this period, and thus the provision of cheaper food to Peru's urban population would not appear to be a primary reason for the government's policies. Another factor may have been ideological. Sharing the prediliction towards private property held by international economic agencies and the United States, the Belaúnde government branded Peru's cooperative system a failure and called for private property in agriculture.[21] The government may thus have designed its particular and unusual agricultural terms-of-trade policies in part to undermine the cooperative enterprises and facilitate a counter agrarian reform.

Whatever the intent of the government's current agricultural policies, the result indeed has been to bankrupt the cooperative enterprises. Land tenure patterns in Peru are currently in flux, and by mid-1983 approximately half the country's coastal cooperatives had subdivided.[22] A few ex-cooperative members will have the capital and expertise to survive the current adverse terms of trade, but most will not. New groups—perhaps drug traffickers, international agro-industrialists, government officials, some ex-hacendados—will probably soon be buying coastal properties, awaiting more favorable terms of trade for agriculture.

The Belaúnde government promised not only better terms of trade for agriculture but also improved levels of public agricultural investment. Overall, it would seem that the government did take some steps to direct agricultural investment toward paths of greater benefit to the nation as a whole—but, very small steps.

Since 1968, Peru's agricultural investment budget has skyrocketed. In real terms, public agricultural investment was about three times higher in 1981 than during one of the 1977 or 1978 biennium years, and it was about six times higher during the 1977–78 biennium than during the 1968–69 biennium.[23] In 1981, approximately 90 billion soles, or 215 million dollars, were spent (Peru, National Planning Institute, 1982:4). As a percentage of total public investment, however, agricultural investment increased more during the 1970s than in the early 1980s. In the 1960s, agricultural investment was only about 8 percent of the total; the percentage climbed to roughly 15 percent by the mid 1970s, and it remained at this level through the early 1980s.[24]

Tragically, however, for the most part these investments seem to have been made neither compassionately nor wisely. With respect to overall public investment programs, equity concerns have been minor. Under the two military governments, Peru's poorest departments in the southern highlands did not receive shares of public investment proportional to their population. Between 1968 and 1980, these five departments (Ayachucho, Huancavelica, Apurímac, Cuzco, and Puno) received only about 8 percent of public investment, but included about 17 percent of Peru's population (QueHacer, 19 [October 1982]:61). The Belaúnde government planned to correct this pattern; in its 1982 public investment program, roughly 21 percent of the budget was allocated to these five departments.[25] However, by 1982 three of these provinces (Ayacucho, Huancavelica, and Apurímac) were wracked by political violence, and it is dubious that the investment plans could have been effectively implemented.

There is a surprising degree of consensus among agronomists that Peru's top priorities for agricultural investment should be the rehabilitation of saline coastal lands and the construction of small-scale irrigation systems in the highlands.[26] Other frequently-cited high priorities are reforestation programs for the highlands in particular, as well as research into the enhancement of the production of native Peruvian crops, especially those that could be processed into flour.[27]

Widely supported among policymakers, these measures became important promises in the 1980 campaign platform of Belaúnde.[28]

These programs are believed to be vital because the quality of much of the land that provides Peru's traditional food staples has been deteriorating. Salinity is a serious problem on Peru's coastal lands, and erosion has been marked in the highlands for decades. Erosion has become an ever more severe problem as the social fabric of peasant-community life has unraveled, and the communities no longer carefully terrace and monitor their plots on the very steep, high Andean mountainsides. Trees are appropriated by peasants for their own purposes, and the land becomes even more vulnerable to erosion. Finally, so that new supplies of highland tubers and highland cereals are fully used to meet Peruvian food needs, new varieties and adaptations of these crops should be developed that are more appealing to urban Peruvians' tastes.

Yet, just like the preceding military regime, the Belaúnde government spent only meager shares of the agricultural investment budget on these kinds of programs. Although the government's documents discuss the need for these programs to some extent, the actual money spent on them has been slight. From the government's reports, it is difficult to identify the funds exclusively for research and for reforestation, as these may often be components of other programs. One or two percent would seem to be a reasonable estimate for 1981, however, and more than three percent is highly unlikely (National Planning Institute, 1982:10-12). The government did launch, for the first time, a program specifically for the improvement of small-scale highlands irrigation, called Meris, and a program specifically for the rehabilitation of saline coastal lands, called Rehatic. As Table 3.9 shows, however, these programs have received scant shares of the agricultural budget. According to data from the Peruvian National Planning Institute (1981:10–12), in 1981 Meris and Rehatic together received about 3.3 billion soles, or roughly 7.8 million dollars – about 4 percent of the overall public agricultural investment budget.

Under all recent governments, by far the lion's share of investment funds have been allocated to high-technology, capital-intensive irrigation projects on Peru's coast. Exact comparisons across the various governments are difficult because of variations in documentary sources; for example, sometimes figures are given for projected investments, and sometimes for actual investments, and these num-

Table 3.9
Irrigation Projects: Costs and Benefits

	Percentage of total public agricultural investment spent on the project in 1981	Cost per hectare[a] (thousands of U.S. $)	Cost per family benefited (thousands of U.S. $)
Majes	41	27.3	163.7
Chira-Piura	22	3.3	16.5
Tinajones	8	2.6	10.1
Rehatic[b]	2.1	1.8	8.6
Meris[c]	1.6	1.2	1.3

[a]Per hectare rehabilitated or brought under cultivation for the first time.

[b]Coastal land rehabilitation, primarily of excessively saline lands.

[c]Small-scale irrigation projects in the highlands.

Source: For cost data, author's calculations from Peru, Presidency of the Republic (1982:298); for percentage of total public agricultural investment, Peru National Planning Institute (1982, vol. 2:10–12).

bers may be very different. By rough calculations, however, since 1970 all governments have spent about 70 percent of Peru's total agricultural investment budget on the nation's three largest high-technology irrigation projects, specifically Majes, Tinajones, and Chira-Piura (Portocarrero, 1982:444; Eguren, 1980:41; Peru, National Planning Institute, 1982:10–12). Table 3.9 shows that under the Belaúnde government the share was approximately 71 percent in 1981; in that year, a fourth mammoth high-technology irrigation project (Jequetepeque-Zaña) was almost another 10 percent of total agricultural investment (Peru, National Planning Institute, 1982: 10–12). On Majes alone, which is the most expensive of the three projects, $600 million has been spent over a decade or so, $391 million during the 1970s and $184 million in 1980 and 1981.[29]

Why has so much money been spent on these massive irrigation projects? Certainly not because of pressure from international development institutions; analysts from the World Bank and similar organizations have been uniformly critical of these projects. Table 3.9 shows one reason for the criticism of these projects: The cost per hectare of land to be cultivated and per family to be benefited is very high. Also, the projects are risky. They are technically very complex, to be executed over decades, and unforeseen engineering problems have indeed arisen. Thus, with respect to Majes, for example, not even the first stage of the project is now complete, despite all the expenditure.

What is the official explanation for these expenditures? The military government emphasized primarily the multipurpose character of Majes. Near Peru's border with Chile, the project would enhance national security. Military officials also point out that Majes did not seem so expensive at inception. Indeed, costs did balloon: for Majes, from $160 million to a staggering $2 billion plus now (*Andean Report*, December 1980:221–223). For their part, Belaúnde government officials maintain that since Majes is underway, it cannot be stopped; contracts have been signed and citizen expectations in the area raised. Recently also, officials have emphasized the potential hydroelectricity gains from the project.

But these explanations are not the full story. Various groups benefit from large, capital-intensive projects and vigorously promote them. In the case of Majes, as of the early 1980s a private international consortium had contributed five times as much capital for the project as the Peruvian government had (Painter, 1983:208). International engineering and construction firms as well as local government officials are usually the biggest winners from these projects. These firms receive handsome sums for their sophisticated technology and expertise. The construction contracts are frequently such plums that the countries who win the contracts may fund a significant part of the project. Of course, international firms rarely promote inexpensive, small-scale irrigation projects as these will not require their skills. Also, grandiose schemes like Majes are attractive to local government officials for their pork-barrel possibilities (*Andean Report*, December 1980:221–223).

Conclusion

The problem of hunger is serious in Peru and has become increasingly serious in the last decade. Highland peasants are no longer able to maintain subsistence living standards as they did in the 1950s and 1960s. As we have seen, by some estimates lower-class groups in highlands zones are on starvation rations, consuming a mere 420 calories per capita daily, and nation-wide are eating way below minimal requirements, only 1,486 calories per capita daily. Hungry peasants have not turned deaf ears to the calls of *Sendero Luminoso*, a Maoist guerrilla group.

Various steps were taken by the Velasco government to develop agriculture. The most important was a sweeping agrarian reform. The reform enhanced the lives of the peasants who became members of new cooperatives. Agricultural production in the cooperatives remained more or less steady. This result was unsatisfactory, as Peru's population was growing and food demand increasing. However, it is very possible that if the enterprises had remained haciendas, they would have shifted more toward export production and away from food production, thereby exacerbating Peru's food problem. The haciendas would probably have been less concerned about food production for resident families and about employment opportunities than the cooperatives were. Hacienda owners would likely also have been more allied to transnational agroindustry.

Agrarian reform was only one measure among many that were probably necessary to the development of Peruvian agriculture so that the country could meet its people's food needs. Numerous measures had gained strong support among agronomists and were widely known to policymakers; indeed, they were highlighted in the 1980 campaign platform of Belaúnde. These steps included the construction of small-scale irrigation projects in the highlands; the rehabilitation of saline lands on the coast; reforestation; the improvement of the terms of trade for agriculture; and research into native Peruvian crops.

Tragically, however, the Belaúnde government apparently forgot its campaign promises. The government did not establish an agricultural policy aimed to benefit the Peruvian peasantry as a whole, or to dramatically increase food production. Rather, different components of the government's agricultural program seemed to reflect the demands and pressures of different groups, international and domestic. The upshot was a terms-of-trade policy that seemed, by most criteria, to be more biased against agriculture than ever before. Both for agricultural cooperatives and individuals, the new terms of trade often brought bankruptcy. This result may not have been displeasing to some Peruvian elites and officials who wanted to reverse the effects of the military government's agrarian reform. Some land is now being purchased by a few groups in Peru with some capital; international agroindustry may soon be playing a more important role in agricultural production and marketing in Peru, with the various effects that have been described elsewhere in this volume.

Although during the last fifteen years the role of international actors in Peruvian agriculture was less pronounced than in many Third World countries, its presence was nevertheless felt. International companies became very active in the wheat, poultry, and dairy industries, and they generally relied heavily on imported inputs, by-passing domestic ones and inhibiting the participation of Peru's peasant producers in these emerging industries. Perhaps the most important role of international actors, however—a role that has tended to be neglected by analysts of the international political economy of agriculture—was in public investment decisions. Private international consortia heavily promoted the military and civilian governments' multi-million dollar white-elephant irrigation projects. Government attention and concern were focused on these extravagant projects rather than on the various small-scale irrigation schemes, research programs, and the like that were more apt to have contributed to Peru's agricultural development.

Since the 1960s, the debate on agricultural policy in Peru seems to have been very narrowly focused. While the military government emphasized agrarian reform and supported cooperative enterprises, the civilian government undermined these enterprises and sought to encourage subdivision of the enterprises among private owners. Over a period of about fifteen years, hacienda workers were asked to become members of cooperatives, working enthusiastically together, and then they were asked to become small farmers, dynamic and entrepreneurial. For these Peruvians, the experience of two dramatic and rapid changes in the rules of the game within such a short period must have been very unsettling.

Focused on the debate over agricultural property structures, Peruvian political leaders seemed to disregard the real food crisis emerging within the country. Agricultural policy was not the primary reason behind this crisis; rather, the dynamics of population growth and land deterioration were probably most crucial. However, it would seem that, to overcome the crisis, a strong political will had to be summoned and policies that were much more supportive of food-staple production had to be implemented. Unfortunately, this has not happened under any recent government.

Chapter 4

Mobilization and Disillusion in Rural South Korea: The Saemaul Movement in Retrospect*

MICK MOORE

The Republic of Korea can claim one of the most impressive economic growth records the world has ever seen.[1] In the three decades since the Korean War it has been transformed from a poor, densely populated and resource-scarce country into a substantial industrial power, and one in which the benefits of economic growth have been widely distributed (Wade, 1983:11). Unlike Taiwan, with which it vies closely and with which it is continually compared, Korea did not begin its post-war development with the advantage of a well-developed agricultural export sector (Ho, 1978:Ch. 4). Since World War Two Korea has remained a substantial net importer of food and agricultural products generally (Kim and Joo, 1982:60–63).

The outside world has naturally looked to Korea for the lessons which may be learned. Equally naturally, it has disagreed about what these lessons might be. A few doctrinaire but influential economists have argued that the lessons lie in adherence to the principle of the freely functioning market-economy: that South Korea has prospered principally because the government has refused to distort seriously the price signals and incentives derived from free internal and inter-

*The author's colleague, Robert Wade, provided invaluable intellectual and practical support for the research upon which this paper is based and helpful comments on an earlier draft. A discussion with Dr. Choe Yang-Boo of the Korean Rural Economics Institute greatly assisted the author in clarifying his understanding of recent developments. The author is however solely responsible for the interpretation presented here. This chapter, in slightly different form, appeared in *Pacific Affairs* 57:4 (Winter 1984/85).

national markets; that it has exploited its comparative advantage and developed initially through mobilizing its least-scarce resource, labor. The evidence suggests that the "market" emphasis in this interpretation is very misleading: the state intervenes heavily and continually, often bypasses the market, and in crucial sectors exerts considerable influence on the major investment decisions of the bigger nominally private economic actors (Wade, 1982:Ch. 8).

Insofar as there is a recognizable South Korea development model its main elements appear to conform equally to the allegedly contradicting doctrines of *dirigiste* central planning and respect for the market mechanism. From the school of competitive capitalism comes an aggressive and state-backed search for export markets, approbation of private profit, and refusal to permit the capital accumulation process to be impeded by either public social welfare expenditures or independent labor organizations which might elevate wages above their low "market-determined" levels. From the *dirigiste* school comes a strategy with strong nationalist and statist elements: the exercise of firm and often extra-legal government controls over "private" investment in the context of an aim to continually upgrade technological capacity; strong government support for private companies pursuing approved projects at home and abroad; attempts to maximize the *national* economic benefit from international economic relations; and unceasing normative pressures on a receptive, relatively homogeneous and socially disciplined population to work unremittingly for the national good and for national survival in the face of the real but continually emphasized military threat from North Korea.

Interpreters of Korea's experience disagree widely about the causes of its economic success. Yet they would probably find themselves in broad agreement that it is in industrial policy that the main clues to this success are to be found. It is true that agriculture has grown fairly fast by international standards.[2] But agriculture has grown far less rapidly than industry and, unlike the industrial sector, evinces relatively few traceable direct connections between, on the one hand, government's intentions and policies and, on the other hand, the direction and rate of agricultural growth. The very respectable rate of growth of agricultural output is most plausibly interpreted as a response to demand pressures from the fast-growing urban sector. Cereal production, which has been the main agricultural policy focus of successive governments faced with high feedgrain and foodgrain import bills, has grown much more slowly than agricultural production as a whole. Between 1950 and 1981 the proportion of cereals in the total value of agricultural production declined from 67 percent to 43 percent. Over the same period horticultural and livestock products increased from 15 percent to 44 percent.[3] This was almost inevitable given Korea's exceptionally high agricultural population density. The possibilities of increasing rice and barley output have been relatively very limited in comparison to the prospects for land-saving, but labor-using, products like vegetables, fruit and livestock for which consumer demand has increased very fast.[4] While in a broad sense the outcome of government economic policy generally, this structural shift in agriculture is contrary to the intentions of agricultural policy in the narrow sense, which has until recently been focused on cereals, a matter we discuss below.

The implication that successful South Korean governments have a great deal to be modest about in relation to their agricultural (and rural development) policies is unlikely to be acceptable to spokesmen for either the Park government of 1961–1979 or the Chun government in power, albeit insecurely, from 1980 to the time of writing. Apart from behaving like all governments in claiming the credit for the considerable agricultural progress, both administrations have trumpeted to the world extravagant claims for what they see as a uniquely successful rural development strategy, the Saemaul Undong (Movement), initiated in 1970. The Saemaul Training School continues to train people from other Third World countries in the anticipation that they can return home and replicate what is allegedly a proven formula for rural development.[5]

The replication of Saemaul is not the subject of this paper. It is not anyway a significant issue, for serious attempts at replication seem rare, and the crudity of South Korean propaganda for Saemaul has ensured that many of the more discerning foreign visitors have quickly seen through it.[6] The issues dealt with here are more important and logically prior. What is Saemaul? What has it achieved? How can one explain its ascent and, now, its decline, within Korea? None of these questions can be answered briefly. And the answers given here are contestable. But the fact that Saemaul is now virtually moribund in the Korean countryside does provide an opportunity to reflect, with the wisdom of hindsight, on its genesis and trajectory and on the wider context into which it fits: the political relationships between the small farm sector and the Korean state.

It is argued here that, despite the exaggerations of official propaganda and the heavy bureaucratic push which lay behind Saemaul, the movement did indeed contain genuine elements of popular mobilization and enthusiasm. But these can be understood only in the context of particular features of the South Korean socio-political tradition and, more importantly, in the context of a series of linked changes in rural policy in Korea in the late 1960s and early 1970s. The enthusiasm for Saemaul is intimately related to a sudden, strong, but temporary upsurge in rural incomes and attention paid to agriculture by government. Neither Saemaul itself nor the policies associated with it could be sustained in the long term. In "capitalist" Korea as in Maoist China, strategies for mobilizing the population under combined political and economic programs have a limited life. The process of politicizing the farm sector, of which Saemaul was a part, now poses threats to the political stability of Korea which cannot easily be managed.

The Background

The essential background to the evolution of Saemaul can be written around three themes: South Korean political culture; the socioeconomic structure of agriculture; and the evolution of the rural-urban divide. It is the latter which provided the immediate stimulus for the creation of the Saemaul Movement by President Park in 1970. The first two, which for present purposes can be treated as relatively invariant, are dealt with first.

South Korean Political Culture

One important feature of Saemaul ideology and practice is a kind of populism which bears more than a passing resemblance to Maoism: an insistence that, under the influence of wise leadership and correct thinking, the people, treated as an undifferentiated mass, can overcome underdevelopment through collective striving. The ultimate key to development lies within the attitudes and behavior of the people themselves. Saemaul Undong is "The New Mind Movement," and is "intended to cure the malaise of idleness and complacency which sprouts in the shade of stability."[7] In this respect Saemaul conforms to and exemplifies some prominent themes in Korean political culture: a strong sense of common national interest and identity; the tendency of the rural population to await and submit to the political initiatives of the central political leadership; and the dearth of direct popular constraints on that leadership, as evinced here by the derogatory terms in which the mentality of the people is characterized.

Ideological and political *étatisme* is a correlate of Korea's long history as a centralized polity (Wright, ed., 1975:3), whether under regal, colonial, bourgeois "democratic," communist or military regimes,[8] and of the Koreans' strong sense of national identity despite (or because of) being hemmed in geographically by China, Japan and the Soviet Union, and having a recorded history of foreign invasions running into three figures. More concretely, in the contemporary era this strong sense of national identity must be related to the absence of major social, cultural or regional differences among South Koreans themselves.[9]

In the past the homogeneity of Korean society meant largely the homogeneity of the rural peasant majority. For the country was characterized by a dearth of powerful intermediaries between the central state in Seoul and the peasantry. A correlate was the strong "villageness" of rural society: a strong sense of solidarity at the level of the individual village (V. Brandt, 1971:12 and *passim*); weak local inter-village and supra-village organizations independent of the state; and a sense of separation and even hostility and competition between adjacent villages. The strength of collective organization and consciousness at the level of the individual village was, and still is, an aspect of the political weakness of rural society as a whole in relation to the centralized state (Wade, 1983; Aqua, 1974).

The tendency of rural Koreans to identify themselves both with village and the national collectivity has a material base in the egalitarian distribution of land and prevalence of genuine family farming. A relatively short term historical perspective would trace this to the events following the collapse of Japanese colonial rule in 1945. A series of land reforms which allowed few exceptions abolished tenancy and imposed a three hectare ownership and cultivation ceiling (Ban, et al., 1980:Ch. 10). And the events of the Korean War eliminated or silenced the more radical elements in the rural population.

Yet in a slightly longer time perspective the land reforms can be seen as having mainly corrected a temporary historical deviation: the high incidence of tenancy was partly the outcome of Japanese colonial rule between 1910 and 1945 (Ban, et al., 1980:284); and the salience of the landlord-tenant issue in the politics of the later 1940s and early 1950s was in large part an aspect of the reaction against colonial rule.

The willingness of Koreans to participate in collective village-level Saemaul projects was in part the product of a strong sense of village identity still in evidence today and, more concretely, of strong common material interests in family-farming, especially in rice production. In 1971, 67 percent of families operating farms cultivated between half a hectare and two hectares, and only 1 percent operated more than three hectares.[10] Eighty-one percent of them obtained more than half their income from agricultural production (see below), and for 72 percent of them rice remained the most important crop in income terms[11], despite the shift to horticultural and livestock production (see above). Seventy-eight percent of farm labor input came from farm family members, 7 percent through exchange labor, and only 15 percent through the hire of wage labor.[12]

The Rural-Urban Divide

In the two decades after land reform, Korea experienced a substantial transfer of labor from agriculture to industry, although the farm population continued to grow in absolute terms until 1976 (Ban, et al., 1980:14). Whether or not agriculture experienced any discernible process of capitalist development and internal class differentiation is not clear. It is certainly not in evidence from the data series on farm income distribution.[13] It is clear that Koreans were much more conscious of the growing gaps between town and country, above all the rapid widening in the 1960s of the gap between average rural and average urban incomes (Choo, 1982:24–25). It is awareness of the political dangers of this disparity which largely explains the launching of Saemaul in 1970.

From the economists' perspective the growing rural-urban income gap may be seen as the natural result of the fast growth of output and labor productivity in the urban manufacturing and export sectors. From the political science perspective it may also be seen as the consequence of the inability of the egalitarian family farm and village-centered Korean peasantry even to frame, let alone enforce, national economic policies to suit its own interests. For a decade and a half after the Korean war the peasantry regularly gave its vote to the groups holding state power despite their pursuit of evidently "urban-biased" economic policies.[14] Throughout the 1950s and 1960s the prices farmers received for their main crops—rice, and to a less extent, barley—were depressed by large-scale American grain imports, largely provided on concessionary terms (Kim and Joo, 1982:32; Ban, et al., 1980:7). In the 1950s the meager agricultural research and extension services were allowed almost to wither away. Some improvement was effected after the ascent to power in 1961 of President Park, whose own rural background is often cited as the reason for his sensitivity to rural issues. A beginning was made in building agriculture research and extension services, notably with the creation of the Office for Rural Development in 1962.[15] Tariff policy was gradually adjusted to give farmers some protection against imports (Kim and Joo, 1982:64–69 and 109–111).

Yet until the end of the 1960s the Park government did nothing to change fundamentally the "urban bias" which was, perhaps in the long-run fortunately, a dominant feature of economic policy. In Korea as in Taiwan (T. H. Lee, 1971), the success of labor-intensive manufactured exports-led growth was predicated upon the "squeezing" of the agricultural sector. Low grain prices kept labor costs down in two ways: Directly, they reduced the reproduction costs and thus wage levels for the industrial labor force; and indirectly, they exerted a continual downward market pressure on urban wage rates by providing a continual supply of ex-rural job seekers eager to escape the even poorer material conditions of farming.

Unlike in Taiwan, in Korea the harshness of the rural-urban sectoral conflict over resources was not mitigated by the spread of industry to rural areas. Capitalizing on the excellent rural infrastructural development undertaken during Japanese colonial rule, Taiwanese manufacturers spread out into the countryside in search of labor and factory sites. Korea by contrast had a very poorly developed rural transport and communications system. Industry and new employment were heavily concentrated around Seoul and Pusan (Ho, 1982). Only in the late 1960s and early 1970s, as part of a general reorientation of policy (see below), was rural road building serious tackled, and even then the emphasis was on inter-provincial national expressways

(Keidel, 1981:130–137). While Taiwanese farm families found compensation for relatively poor agricultural incomes in industrial employment, rural Koreans had few such opportunities. Allowing for the uncertainties of the figures,[16] it seems that in the 1950s the proportion of farm-family income obtained from non-agriculture was similar in the two countries. Yet while that proportion remained at around 20 percent in Korea in the 1960s and early 1970s, in Taiwan it rose steadily to reach 68 percent in 1981. Only in 1977, aided by declining real-producer cereal prices and farm incomes (see below) did the figure begin to rise markedly in Korea. But by 1981 it had only reached 33 percent.[17]

Reorientation of Policy

The absolute accuracy of the official figures on average rural and urban incomes in Korea has been challenged, both by those who believe that they understate and by those who believe that they exaggerate the difference. But a recent thorough reappraisal reveals that, whatever modifying assumptions are made about the data base, the trends over time are very clear, including a major widening of the urban-rural gap in the 1960s (Choo, 1982:24–25). The official figures indicate that average farm household incomes were the same as average urban wage-earners' incomes in 1965, but fell to 67 percent of that level by 1970 (Korea Development Institute, 1982:3). Aware of the political consequences of growing rural discontent, President Park began to take compensatory steps even before the consequences became publicly visible in the shape of the results of the 1971 presidential election. Unlike in previous elections, when rural voters had rather passively supported whichever government happened to be in power, they turned against Park, and the anti-government vote reached a record high of 45 percent of the total (Hahn, 1975:88).

Probably also impelled by the threat of reductions in cheap PL 480 American grain imports, Park had in late 1968 inaugurated what in the next few years amounted to a complete reversal in rural policy. The prices at which the government purchased rice and barley were steadily increased, and within a few years stood well above both international and domestic market prices.[18] Government increased its own involvement in cereal distribution. Having purchased 7 percent of domestic rice production between 1960 and 1969, it purchased

16 percent in the following decade (Korea Development Institute, 1982:8). Since cereals were sold to consumers at a price lower than that paid to farmers, government was subsidizing both cereal producers and consumers. The subsidy on fertilizers also increased very markedly. The subsidies on cereals and fertilizers were mainly financed in an inflationary fashion through central bank credits. This situation could not be tolerated for long (see below). In the meantime, in the first five or so years of the 1970s, farm incomes increased very considerably, the rural-urban income gap narrowed (Choo, 1982:24–25), and farm land prices rocketed (J. H. Lee, 1981:72).

This reversal from urban to rural bias in the sphere of pricing was but one of four major changes in policy affecting farmers which were initiated between 1968 and 1971. The second was the introduction of new high-yielding varieties of rice. These came late to Korea, for its temperate climate did not suit the earlier generations of high-yielding rice diffused in tropical and sub-tropical Asia in the 1960s. The new variety was first introduced in a significant way in Korea in 1971, when it covered only 0.3 percent of the rice area. It has however spread rapidly, covering, according to official figures, 76 percent of the total area in the peak year (1978) (Kim and Joo, 1982:27). Total rice production increased by 50 percent between 1971 and the peak year (1977), equivalent to an annual average increase of 7 percent (Korea, Ministry of Agriculture and Fisheries, Yearbook of Agriculture and Forestry Statistics, annual). This very rapid diffusion of high-yielding rice varieties was largely due to input and output price incentives (see above), the increased use of fertilizer, and the fact that an effective agricultural extension service has been built up in the shape of the Office for Rural Development, and focused heavily on rice.[19]

The mode of agricultural extension was however somewhat unconventional. The Office for Rural Development and the other government agencies involved in extension, notably local government, the irrigation associations and the Saemaul Movement itself, went far beyond what are in other so-called "market economies" conventional extension technique. Massive propaganda campaigns, the physical destruction of seed beds planted with non-high-yielding varieties, highly publicized competitions, adoption quotas for the territories served by public officials, and exchange of government services (credit, subsidized machines, the right to sell paddy to the state at

higher prices than in the open market) were widely used weapons
(Wade, 1982 and 1983). In no sense had the South Korean state suddenly become pro-farmer. It combined price incentives with a battery
of more or less coercive extension methods. Conflicts of interest
between state and rice farmer became especially evident in some areas
around the mid-1970s, when the difference between market prices for
high-yielding price varieties (sold mainly to government) and those
for traditional varieties (preferred by consumers and mainly sold
privately) began to narrow. Since the cost of production for traditional varieties was relatively low, farmers often made more profit
from them, while the state continued to insist that they grow high-
yielding varieties (Kim and Joo, 1982:27; Wade, 1983:23).

The third major policy change to affect farmers from the end of the
1960s was an increase in the proportion of public expenditure devoted to rural areas and agriculture (Ban, et al., 1980:7 and Ch. 6),
especially to road construction (see above). Neither this nor the other
two changes in policy discussed above can be clearly separated from
the Saemaul Movement, the fourth major change in policy, which was
inaugurated in 1970, and to which we now turn.

The Saemaul Movement

Published sources on the Saemaul Movement are abundant. They can
be arranged on an approximate continuum. On one side are the
Korean government publications, which are strongly eulogistic and
normative in tone, but give very little information (and even less
accurate information) on what Saemaul actually is.[20] Studies by
Korean academics[21] contain more concrete information, but are generally silent or reticent on the political aspects of Saemaul, on which
only foreign scholars are free to comment.[22] This author's interpretation of the Saemaul experience is open to dispute, for it emphasizes
the political aspects of Saemaul which official spokesmen would wish
to completely deny. In addition, ideological and programmatic "generalization" of Saemaul (see below) leaves a large area of potential
disagreement over which aspects of government policy should or
should not be viewed as aspects of Saemaul.

There does appear to be general agreement that Saemaul had
modest and almost fortuitous origins, and that it was only after it was
formally launched that an ideology was developed around it and it

became the symbolic focus of the government's development efforts. Saemaul began as a purely rural program in the winter of 1970–71. It initially involved the distribution, to each of almost all of Korea's villages, of 335 bags of cement to be used "for village projects meeting villagers' common needs based upon their general consensus" (Choe, 1978:10). Cynics have suggested that this was merely a convenient way of disposing of a temporary surplus of cement in government hands. Whether or not this was true, the program appears to have been widely welcomed by villagers. It is not surprising that they found good use for cement in, for example, construction of village meeting houses, paved roads and drains. For real incomes had risen substantially in recent years, and villagers had presumably raised their expectations about their physical environment and were willing to contribute cash and labor to do something to improve it. Bear in mind that in Korea there had previously been no rural development program of any kind, that rural areas had been largely neglected by governments, and that administrative responsibility for most aspects of rural society lay, as it does today, with the law-and-order-oriented Ministry of Home Affairs (Aqua, 1974:5). It is understandable that in the circumstances there should have accumulated a potential for village-level community projects.

Apparently encouraged by this early experience, and perhaps also by reports of North Korea's similar Thousand Horses movement, President Park began to take a major interest in Saemaul in 1972 (Choe, 1978:11). The program was expanded and an ideology was built up around it. In these early years there were perhaps five important features of Saemaul.

Firstly, at the local level Saemaul was built entirely around the individual village. The key figure was the village Saemaul leader, who worked alongside the village head. True to the Korean tradition, no attempt was made to organize either projects or local nongovernmental activities at any level other than the individual village (Choe, 1978; Wade, 1983).

Secondly and relatedly, government built upon traditions of village solidarity and inter-village competition by placing villages in competition with one another for resources. In 1972 government assisted only about half of the total number of villages, providing those reckoned to have made the best use of their initial cement allocation with a further allocation of 500 bags of cement and a ton of steel rods (Choe, 1978:11). Thereafter, under the rubric of the so-called "Selective-Sequential Approach," elaborate criteria were developed for classifying villages according to their current stage of Saemaul development ("underdeveloped," "developing," and "developed"). And an equally elaborate points system was put forward to govern promotion of villages from one classification level to the next (Choe, 1978:11–12, 42–44 and *passim*). In practice the application of these formal criteria conflicted with the strong pressures placed on public officials to meet targets. The criteria must have been applied rather loosely. There is no other way in which one can explain the fact that, while in 1973, 53 percent of all villages were classified as "underdeveloped" and only 7 percent as "developed," four years later none were classified as "underdeveloped" and 67 percent as "developed" (Choe, 1978:16 and 44). But the principle of helping only those villages which could help themselves must have had a considerable effect. It is very consistent with the ideological emphasis on locating the causes of development and underdevelopment in the mentality and collective behavior of the people themselves.

The RSU (Rural Saemaul Undong) identifies the major causes of economic stagnation in rural Korea as the farmers' lack of willingness, self-confidence, and determination, including their conservative resistance to change, their wasteful customs of costly ritual and ceremony, and their laziness (Choe, 1978:24).

Thirdly, as is implicit in what is said above, the whole initiative in Saemaul lay with government, especially with the President. As in the sphere of agricultural extension (see above), strong bureaucratic pressures were put on villages to encourage "participation." As a number of critics have pointed out, such pressures extended to the forced donation of land for community projects and the physical removal by officials of conventional ("traditional") thatched roofs in order to "encourage" people to replace them with brightly painted tiles (Choe, 1978:67–68; Aqua, 1974:62–64; and Wade, 1983:19–21).

Fourthly, a major government objective in the early stages of Saemaul was to beautify the countryside, especially that part of it visible to those travelling along major highways between large towns. Replacement of thatch roofs was the main single component. It was claimed that between 1972 and 1977 new roofs were placed in 2.4 million homes, a number equivalent to about a third of all households in the country (Choe, 1978:58). Some villages were completely rebuilt and sometimes relocated, although this may have been confined mainly to "show" villages visible from national highways. Such improvements took place in the context of a relatively successful massive program of re-afforestation. The combined effect is certainly visually delightful, at least from the highways.

Fifthly, Saemaul was a *melange* of activities, including: straightforward political indoctrination, especially in training classes for Saemaul leaders; attempts to encourage villagers to improve their living environment and construct collective facilities; and a range of more conventional agricultural production programs, including the promotion of high-yielding rice varieties and cooperative production teams (Choe, 1978; Wade, 1983).

Having begun as a set of rather diffuse, if intensively promoted, activities focused on the village level, Saemaul was gradually expanded to become even more diffuse, more wide-ranging, and more oriented to levels higher than the village.

In the first place, the "Saemaul" label was attached to an increasing range of government programs, to the extent that it became almost coterminous with all government development activity, especially in rural areas. The proportion of central government development expenditures classified as Saemaul expenditures increased from 4 percent in 1972 to 38 percent in 1978 (Whang, 1981:51).

In the second place, Saemaul was expanded to include, for example, "Factory Saemaul," "Urban Saemaul," "School Saemaul" and the "Nature Preservation Movement" (*Saemaul in New Age*, 1982:90–141). In 1974 Saemaul training was extended to the higher ranks of government, business, finance, education and organized religion (Choe, 1978:35). Factories located in the countryside have been labelled "Saemaul factories," although their substantive connection with Saemaul is obscure. In principle and at the ideological level Saemaul was generalized into something even nearer a national mobilization campaign like China's Cultural Revolution. The crucial difference in practice was that the Korean state remained very firmly in control.

In the third place, Saemaul became institutionalized within the state apparatus. In part this took the form of the development of national and regional headquarters and training schools separate from, if still largely under the control of, the regular administrative structure of the Ministry of Home Affairs. Perhaps more importantly, Saemaul units were created at all levels within public offices. A major purpose, not always accomplished (Wade, 1982:126–128), seems to have been to supplement and improve the mechanisms for monitoring and controlling the work performance of public officials. At this point one has to cease talking of the Korean state as a monolith imposing upon the population. For Saemaul was exploited by the development-oriented central political leadership as an opportunity to bring more pressure to bear on its traditionally otiose public bureaucracy (Aqua, 1974). It is not possible for the outside to say how far this inflation of work-performance targets and monitoring mechanisms actually improved work performance. It certainly led to a great deal of falsification of reports, ritual compliance, and displacement in the form of coercion of villagers by lower-level officials so that their work targets could be formally fulfilled (Wade, 1982:Chs. 5, 7 and 8).

In the fourth place, and relatedly, the creation of Saemaul units within but partially separate from the existing administrative structure appears to have been an aspect of a broader intention to turn Saemaul into something like a mass political party to support the Park administration (Wade, 1983:16). There is certainly political space for such a party in Korea, especially in the rural areas. Since the suppression of the Communists there have always been in Korea competing parties at the national level, although until the legislative elections of February 1985 the main opposition party was widely viewed as a creation of the ruling group itself. Yet even under the Park regime, when inter-party competition was more genuine, the parties themselves were best described as cliques or factions within the business, professional and political elite. None had a mass base, and the "genuine" opposition has been mainly concerned with essentially elite-level issues of civil liberties and the constitution rather than with representing the interests of large population groups (Hahn, 1975:85–88). Insofar as interest groups are organized, they exist almost entirely in urban areas and are in part the creation of the higher bureaucracy. They rarely compete with one another, but exist mainly to provide a channel of communication between the bureaucracy on the one side and business and the mass media on the other (Cho, 1975:80). The major rural economic organizations, the National Agricultural Cooperative Federation and the National Livestock Cooperative Federation, are totally staffed and controlled by the bureaucracy (Ban, et al., 1980:263). In this respect Korea contrasts strongly with Taiwan. Not only do Taiwanese farmers have some (frequently exaggerated) control over the Farmers Associations and Irrigation Associations, but *the* national political party, the KMT, has a mass membership and, although tightly controlled from the top, is an important forum for competition between interests.[23]

In the late 1950s and early 1960s there was little need for a mass party to support Korean governments, for the rural population could be relied upon. But the urban proportion of the population has been increasing, and rural support is no longer assured (see above). So there was a clear rationale for the attempt to use Saemaul to mobilize large sections of the population in support of the regime. As we shall see below, this has not been successful.

The Decline of Saemaul

As Saemaul institutions were being developed at the supra-village level in the mid and late 1970s, its village base was withering away. By 1983 it was almost moribund in the villages. Few new Saemaul projects are undertaken, at least not by villagers themselves. Even in the show villages to which foreign visitors are conducted, the abundant statistics on the village situation and Saemaul achievements have often not been updated for some years. Although the national Saemaul head-quarters maintains an appearance of activism, it appears to be largely divorced from regional and local organization. The fact that the movement is directed by President Chun's younger brother is sometimes taken as an indication of the political importance attributed to control of Saemaul. It is certainly true that Chun has done his best to identify himself with Saemaul in the way that Park did. But rather fragmentary evidence suggests that the President's brother controls the Saemaul headquarters and little else. His position is more symbolic than substantial, and at regional and local levels the Ministry of Home Affairs plays the major controlling role—insofar as there is anything to control.

Since the government would not for a minute admit to the fact that Saemaul is in severe recession, it is very difficult to find evidence to explain the movement's decline. The evidence available to this author suggests the importance of two broad factors. The first is, to paraphrase what the author was told by Korean villagers, "Once we

had rebuilt our houses and widened the road, we ran out of projects."
There is a limit to the range of useful projects which villagers
can undertake on a collective basis and through the use of their
own voluntary labor. The second and perhaps more important factor
is that the motivation to undertake village-level projects or to cooperate with government more generally has been seriously eroded
by changes in the general economic and political environment.

One reason for this is that the program for promoting high-yielding rice varieties — a major feature of both Saemaul and of the general
shift of government attention to rural areas and agriculture around
1970 — has run out of steam. It has already been mentioned above that
by the mid-1970s the rice program was generating increased conflict
between villagers and officials because farmers often found it more
profitable to grow traditional rice varieties. But the acreage under
new varieties was still increasing, and the pressure from above to
continue to promote them gave a wide range of lower-level officials a
target and a sense of purpose, and obliged them to interact extensively with villagers. All this began to change after 1978 when it
became clear that the new varieties had been promoted too heavily.
Their vulnerability to disease and to the early onset of cold weather
before harvest became clear from 1978 onwards, when Korea recorded the first of a series of rather poor harvests. Total rice production peaked in 1977, and has since failed to regain that level. In 1982 it
was only 86 percent of the 1977 level. The area under high yielding
varieties peaked in 1978 at 76 percent of the total rice area. It then fell
rapidly to 27 percent in 1981, recovering somewhat to 33 percent in
the following year.[24]

The Korean bureaucracy did not respond immediately to the
evidence that the high-yielding varieties campaign had been pushed
too far. It was still promoting them heavily at the end of the 1970s
(Wade, 1982). But in very recent years it has come to terms with the fact
that it was losing the battle. Farmers variously report that in the last
"two," "three" or "few" years the pressure on them to cultivate high-
yielding varieties has lifted. They no longer have to agree to cultivate
high-yielding varieties if they are to receive credit or fertilizer from
official sources. The Farmland Development (i.e., Irrigation) Associations, which had been pressed into service as supplementary extension agencies, report that they are no longer expected to fulfill this
function. While cereal self-sufficiency is still an official planning goal,

government attention has shifted away from cereals to other crops, especially to issues of marketing and price stabilization.[25]

The decline in rice production and in the acreage under high-yielding varieties is due not only to technical problems and reduced extension effort. It also reflects a series of reversals since the mid-1970s in the economic relationships between agriculture and the rest of the economy. Agriculture has in various sense become "worse off," absolutely or relatively, and it is the disillusion and resentment which this causes among farmers which in turn explains the declining willingness to cooperate with government or participate in the Saemaul movement.

As discussed above, the shift in the terms of trade in favor of agriculture from the late 1960s was the result of deliberate government policy. It was an attempt to counter market forces which, when allowed to work freely, were resulting in a rising divergence between rural and urban incomes. As Korea became industrialized and labor increasingly scarce, its family farm sector became increasingly unable to compete with foreign suppliers of grains and livestock products, notably the United States, Australia and New Zealand, who could produce cheaply because of high ratios of land and capital to labor in agriculture. But the shift of resources to agriculture, at least on the scale at which it was attempted in the early 1970s, was not sustainable in the longer term, either economically or politically. Because of the strength of the urban interest in cheap food and because of Korea's need to keep manufacturing wages and thus food cheap if its exports were to remain competitive, the burden of supporting agriculture had not been placed directly on food consumers, but assumed by government, and thus taxpayers and the nonagricultural economy as a whole. Both food producers and consumers were subsidized (see above). In both five year periods 1972–1976 and 1977–1981 government deficits on its grain and fertilizer operations, which were, especially in the early period, financed in part in an inflationary fashion by borrowing from the central bank (see above), equalled 15 percent of central government expenditures.[26] From the mid-1970s government began to take steps to reduce these deficits. It proved possible only to contain them rather than cut them substantially, mainly because the fertilizer cost increases occasioned by the 1978 international oil price increases could not for political reasons be passed on to farmers.[27] The burden of cutting agricultural subsidies therefore fell on producer grain prices. Annual increases in the price of grain purchased by government began to fall behind the (high) inflation rate: "The real purchase price of rice began to fall in 1976" (Kim and Joo, 1982:32). The free market price of rice held up rather better than the official purchase price, but it was not high enough to put a halt to a substantial shift in the terms of trade away from agriculture (Table 4.1, column A). From 1976 the government for the first time opened the Korean market to large imports of livestock products (Kim and Joo, 1982:64).

This decline in agricultural protection and subsidy interacted with long-term trends and with the slowing down of the Korean economy at the end of the 1970s to produce a marked deterioration in agricultural incomes in both relative and absolute terms. The rural-urban income gap had already begun to widen again in 1975, and continued to do so (Choo, 1982:24–25; Kim and Joo, 1982:108). Average farm household real disposable income, having increased every year in the decade after 1968, and very substantially in 1969–1973 and again in 1977–1979, fell by 12 percent in 1979–1980. True it recovered again in 1982 (Table 4.1, column A), but the relative fall, compared to both urban incomes and past experience, seems to have affected farmers very deeply.

Disillusion is now rife among Korean farmers. And while declining product prices are cited as one of the main causes of farmers' problems, their disillusion has broader psychological and sociological dimensions. For the other problem cited again and again is the exodus of youth from the village, and the fear that, in sociologists' jargon, the village is no longer reproducing itself as a social unit. As column C in Table 4.1 shows, this fear has a concrete basis. Despite urbanization, population growth has been sufficiently fast that the absolute number of farming households increased every year until 1967 (see above). It then began to fall, but around 1976 the trend rate of decline accelerated noticeably. It averaged 1.1 percent per year between 1968 and 1976, but since 1977 has averaged 2.8 percent per year.

When asked about Saemaul, farmers frequently talk of it not as a movement or a program, but as a period of time – a "golden age" in the early 1970s when their incomes were rapidly improving in both absolute and relative terms, when productive new rice varieties were available for the first time, when fertilizer was cheap, when there was a series of good harvests uninterrupted by drought, flood, plant disease or unseasonal cold weather, and when government was for the first

Table 4.1
Trends in Farm Terms of Trade, Income,
Returns of Labor and Population
1968–1982

Year	Terms of trade= Index of ratio of prices received by farmers for all farm products to all prices paid by farmers (1980=100)	% change over previous year in average real disposable income of farm families*	Index of real returns per hour of farm labor input (1980=100)**	% change over previous year in number of farm families
	A	B	C	D
1968	87	+4%	54	–0.3%
1969	90	+11	62	–1.3
1970	92	+4	63	–2.5
1971	98	+25	74	–0.1
1972	104	+6	85	–1.2
1973	107	+6	90	–0.1
1974	106	+1	109	–2.8
1975	106	+2	110	–0.1
1976	105	+12	119	–1.2
1977	105	+8	120	–1.4
1978	105	+11	133	–3.5
1979	102	–4	117	–2.8
1980	100	–8	100	–0.3
1981	100	+10	109	–5.8
1982	95	N.A.	N.A.	N.A.

*In calculating this figure disposable farm family income (from all sources) has been deflated by the index of prices paid by farm families for consumer goods and services.

**This figure was obtained by dividing average net farm disposable income (gross income minus farm production expenses) and all wages paid by farmers by the average number of human labor hours (from all sources) used in farm production. The figures are deflated in the same way as those in column B.

Sources: Column A: Korea, Economic Planning Board, *Monthly Statistics of Korea*, (June 1983:Table 34); Korea, Economic Planning Board, *Korea Statistical Yearbook* (1981:426–427); and Korea, Ministry of Agriculture and Fisheries, *Yearbook of Agriculture and Forestry Statistics* (1975:Tables 141 and 142).

Column B: Korea, Ministry of Agriculture and Fisheries, *Yearbook of Agriculture and Forestry Statistics*, (1975:Table 14) and (1982:Table 121).

Column C: Ibid (1982:Tables 75 and 77; 1978:Table 79; 1975: Table 85; 1971: Tables 122, 128 and 189).

Column D: Ibid (annual).

time paying attention to the improvement of agriculture and rural life. The outlook of farmers seemed good then — now it is bleak.

The Outlook

There is little likelihood that the government of Korea will be able in the next few years to engineer for the farmers a return to the "golden age" conditions of the early 1970s. The economic pressures to cut grain and fertilizer subsidies, already powerful, will be strengthened by the current jitteriness of the international banking community about Korea's ability to service its massive foreign debt. It becomes increasingly likely that Korea will, formally or informally, become subject to International Monetary Fund "conditionality" if it is to receive further funds to roll over its debt when current loans become due. And "conditionality" spells an assault on public subsidies. In addition, recent changes in the structure of agricultural production pose a threat to the future of family farming which is at present barely recognized in Korea. For the livestock industry, the fastest growing sector within agriculture, is rapidly becoming dominated by large corporations who have moved in from outside agriculture. This is especially in evidence in the dairy sector. Livestock production is becoming very large-scale and capital intensive, and small farmers cannot compete. In recent years the proportion of small farmers raising livestock has declined rapidly (Table 4.2). This decline was reputedly accelerated by the pork and beef price slumps of 1979 occasioned by sudden large increases in imports.[28] Large diversified

Table 4.2
Proportions of Farm Households Rearing
Main Categories of Livestock
1976–1981

Year	Beef/draught cattle*	Hogs	Chickens	Dairy Cattle
1976	51%	39%	53%	neg.
1981	42%	21%	31%	1%

*Almost all are in fact now raised for beef. Beef is, after rice, traditionally the second main product of farming families.

Source: Korea, Ministry of Agriculture and Fisheries, *Yearbook of Agriculture and Forestry Statistics* (1982:Table 9); and National Livestock Cooperative Federation, *Quarterly Review* (Vol. 3, No. 2, June 1983:pp. 82–108).

Table 4.3
Changes in the Ownership Concentration of Livestock Herds
June 1978 to June 1983

| Year | Proportion of total herd owned by the largest 5% of producers: | | | |
	Beef/draught cattle	Hogs	Chickens	Dairy Cattle
June 1978	18%	45%	76%	20%
June 1983	20%	55%	91%	26%

Source: National Livestock Cooperative Federation, *Quarterly Review* (Vol. 3, No. 2, June 1983: pp. 82–108).

corporations are better able to withstand such shocks, and account for an increasing proportion of livestock numbers (Table 4.3). It is reported that Korea is now moving in the same direction as Taiwan, where large corporations handling food-grain imports account for a large and growing proportion of livestock production.[29]

It has been plausibly argued that political stability and the conservatism and quiescence of the family farm-based rural population have made important contributions to the rapid post-war economic growth of Korea, Taiwan and Japan (Hofheinz and Calder, 1982:26). In the medium term the likelihood of continued political quiescence on the part of Korea's farmers must be in doubt. At present the countryside seems far from political ferment, and indeed gave the ruling party its victory in the 1985 legislative elections. But the stimulus for rural dissent is there. Expectations have been raised and then dashed, and the ability of government to meet farmers' economic grievances in the future seems very limited. Farmers have been very heavily integrated into the cash economy and cannot in the future expect to be immune from adverse trends in the national and world economies. Between 1961–1963 and 1979–1981 the proportion of farm production expenditures incurred in cash increased from 38 percent to 72 percent, and the proportion of farmers' agricultural income realized in cash increased from 26 percent to 53 percent.[30] Farm production costs are dominated by industrially produced inputs (fertilizer, agrochemicals and machinery) and by wage costs determined by industrial wages. Most farm income is obtained by selling produce on the market. Recent adverse trends in the farm economy appear to have generated substantial grassroots support for the radical and anti-government Catholic Farmers movement and the smaller Christian (i.e., Protestant) farmers. This author was told by a senior public servant that fear of these organizations is a major reason why government has not, despite continual discussion, taken concrete steps to amend the land laws. Government's desire to encourage farm amalgamation and thus promote a more efficient agriculture requires the legal recognition of land tenancy, which remains formally illegal, although widespread. But it is feared that to raise this issue would permit the Catholic and Christian farmers to make too much political capital out of alleged land speculation in areas close to towns.

Radical observers have in the past often looked for evidence of capitalist differentiation within Korea's small farm sector. Present evidence suggests their concerns were misplaced. The small farm sector remains relatively undifferentiated, but major political contradictions are emerging between, on the one side, the small farm sector as a whole and, on the other, nonagriculture in general and the new corporate livestock producers. Government has for many years been promoting farm amalgamation, but with limited success.[31] The political stability of Korea in the future may depend in large part on how far government can contain these emerging contradictions by speeding up the rate of farm amalgamation (and thus the rate of differentiation within the small farm sector) and, perhaps more importantly, by expanding nonagricultural employment to rural areas.[32] No other nation has ever faced the political problems posed by having industrialized relatively successfully while the farm sector remains so undifferentiated and so cut off from the prospects of supplementing relatively declining farm incomes with part-time industrial employment.

PART II

The International
Political Economy
of Food

The Emergence of the "World Steer": Internationalization and Foreign Domination in Latin American Cattle Production*

STEVEN E. SANDERSON

Despite the many ambiguities surrounding the world market for cattle and meat products, it is generally agreed that the market is, indeed, global.[1] The production, exchange, distribution, and consumption of cattle and meat products have been transformed and "globalized" by improvements in refrigerated shipping, communications, industrial organization, and technology. Since World War II in particular, the Latin American cattle industry has been inserted into that global framework, not only in sales and procurement (i.e., trade), but in technology, stock lines, and methods of processing cattle products.

Given the long history of Latin American primary commodity exports, the internationalization of cattle industries hardly seems surprising. After all, British and U.S. capital in the nineteenth century paved the way for the modernization of beef export production in Mexico and Argentina. Cattle slaughter for trade with foreign powers such as the United Kingdom and the United States dates back at least to the 1849 Gold Rush and subsequent Westward expansion. Likewise, the technology of stock breeding has been dominated by the Western powers, with the universalization of European and North American breeding stock in bovine and hog production, and the more recent appearance of U.S.-based turkey operations in poul-

*An earlier version of this paper was delivered at the 44th International Congress of Americanists at the University of Manchester. It was awarded a 1984 Congress Prize in Economics/Economic History.

try raising. Foreign direct investment now identified with Purina, Bayer, Hoechst, Anderson-Clayton, Ciba-Geigy, and other international giants results from the initiatives of a long chain of predecessors led by such famous barons as William Randolph Hearst and Collis P. Huntington. Their tradition is carried on by modern Ludwigs and their Latin American national analogs.

This study's argument is not that the internationalization of Latin American cattle is a new phenomenon. Rather, it is that (1) the internationalization of cattle production has entered a new phase, qualitatively different from previous modes of external influence; and (2) the political and social consequences of that new mode of internationalization are much more severe and lasting than most advocates of herd modernization or devotees of improving Latin American nutrition through increases in animal protein have appreciated. This argument's essence relies on the contention that the "new wave" of internationalization in cattle is a function of the internationalization of capital at the level of production itself. The international economic integration of the nineteenth century, which relied primarily on commodity circulation, has been supplanted by a holistic integration of the cattle sector *in production*. Before delving into that central *problematica*, however, it is useful to make precise our initial understanding of the emergence of the "world steer."

First of all, the term "world steer" is mainly an artifice to identify cattle production with other global commodities such as cars and consumer luxury goods produced on a global scale according to global strategies. Obviously, in the case of cattle, such a term has special limits. Component parts do not enjoy the easy mobility of other manufacturers (one shudders at the macabre possibility of an international market for steer parts). Likewise, the concept is not intended to convey the idea that a single beast emerges from the internationalization of cattle markets. Local production and climate still govern a variety of cattle breeds and products. Nevertheless, the term involves the international standardization of producer technology and social relations along lines that (1) are transnational in scope (e.g., U.S. feedlot technology, European antibiotics, and Japanese markets for boxed beef), and (2) approach an international standard for consumption and trade (e.g., immunity from major contagious diseases, certain marbling characteristics of the meat, standardized cuts of beef, and so forth).

Table 5.1

Cattle and Buffalo: Numbers in Selected Countries 1960–1982 (in Thousand Head)

	1960	1961	1962	1963	1964	1965	1966	1967	1968	1969	1970	1971
North America	131,606	133,880	137,709	143,230	148,201	151,001	151,790	152,556	153,828	154,917	159,096	163,154
Canada	10,387	10,696	10,933	11,223	11,678	12,128	11,902	11,723	11,677	11,401	11,626	11,985
Costa Rica	901	951	1,006	1,068	1,135	1,211	1,294	1,387	1,355	1,423	1,496	1,574
Dominican Republic	1,132	1,125	1,121	1,115	1,109	1,104	1,099	1,093	1,082	1,090	1,100	1,339
El Salvador	1,110	1,141	1,163	1,194	1,225	1,271	1,322	1,330	1,371	1,410	1,440	1,100
Guatemala	1,062	1,134	1,122	1,263	1,324	1,384	1,328	1,242	1,371	1,376	1,443	1,585
Honduras	1,394	1,411	1,429	1,447	1,465	1,483	1,502	1,380	1,450	1,559	1,578	1,598
Mexico	17,413	17,668	18,453	19,325	20,219	21,078	21,975	22,965	23,294	23,627	24,876	26,053
Nicaragua	1,305	1,291	1,278	1,265	1,252	1,373	1,495	1,616	1,738	1,859	1,980	2,102
Panama	666	763	835	842	891	969	1,011	1,037	1,119	1,157	1,188	1,240
United States	96,236	97,700	100,369	104,488	107,903	109,000	108,862	108,783	109,371	110,015	112,369	114,578
South America	138,686	144,087	148,153	150,621	152,203	156,167	161,697	166,526	170,537	174,107	177,229	180,243
Argentina	45,484	47,494	48,657	48,520	47,213	49,173	51,792	53,120	53,392	53,291	52,260	51,877
Brazil	55,700	57,900	59,800	61,800	63,900	66,100	68,300	70,500	72,900	75,300	78,448	81,131
Chile	2,913	2,990	3,046	3,017	3,062	2,870	2,869	2,884	2,911	2,916	2,931	2,891
Colombia	15,000	15,500	16,000	16,400	16,700	17,000	17,300	17,900	18,700	19,500	20,200	20,508
Ecuador	1,600	1,650	1,700	1,800	1,850	1,900	1,950	2,000	2,100	2,150	2,200	2,250
Peru	3,132	3,242	3,326	3,466	3,625	3,644	3,686	3,700	3,810	4,060	4,127	4,310
Uruguay	8,532	8,792	8,900	8,682	8,698	8,100	8,188	8,570	8,622	8,601	8,564	8,727
Venezuela	6,325	6,519	6,724	6,936	7,155	7,380	7,612	7,852	8,102	8,289	8,499	8,549
Oceania	22,495	23,778	24,631	25,240	25,751	25,617	25,154	26,017	27,465	29,216	30,939	33,192
Australia	16,503	17,332	18,033	18,549	19,055	18,816	17,936	18,270	19,218	20,61	22,162	24,373
New Zealand	5,992	6,446	6,598	6,691	6,696	6,801	7,218	7,747	8,247	8,605	8,777	8,819

Source: 1960–1982 *Foreign Agriculture Circulars, Livestock and Meat* FLM 10–78 and FLM 7–81.

Such standardization was obviously inadequate in the unsuccessful efforts of Argentine producers to penetrate European markets with jerked beef in the nineteenth century. Likewise, to some extent, a lack of internationally acceptable hygiene standards still hampers Latin American live cattle exports (although these standards often suspiciously resemble non-tariff trade barriers protecting U.S. and EEC cattle producers). The near-universalization of internationally acceptable hygiene standards appears as a byproduct of the greater international integration of the late-twentieth century.

Although we will be unable to treat the entire question in this chapter, when we discuss the internationalization of cattle production we are not simply addressing cattle as a commodity category but as a key element in the "foodgrain-feedgrain-livestock complex." That is, we will note throughout that the exigencies of modern cattle raising for the international—and increasingly Latin American national markets—involve changes in cropping patterns in basic foodstuff production, reductions in land available for traditional crops, and a transformation of cattle raising itself toward a more industrialized model.

Also important, "foreign domination" and "internationalization" in the Latin American cattle industry are not synonymous. In fact, the foreign domination of the "modern" sector of Latin American cattle raising—most recently by transnational corporations and merchants—has resulted in a deeper process of internationalization. When we speak of internationalization here, we include not only the effects of trade and investment activities on the external sector, but also the "internalization" of international norms in the industry. Such internalization of the global patterns of cattle production include the substitution of internationally preferred cuts of meat for national cuts, the elimination of traditional lean beef technology in favor of confinement feeding, and increases in per capita beef consumption in certain socio-economic strata. It also signifies that the internationalization of Latin American cattle production does not in the first instance depend on the presence of the transnational corporation. While such corporations are obviously central to the accumulation of capital on a world scale, the nationality of beef cattle enterprises is mainly interesting for its correlation with technological and managerial internationalization. Currently, national firms in Brazil, Mexico, and Argentina all subscribe to the essential principles of international trade promotion and product homogenization; they are as effective as transnationals in the propagation of a "world steer," despite the lesser participation of foreign capital in their firms.

The source of this process of international integration of the livestock complex is the internationalization of capital, through trade, direct foreign investment, and the transnationalization of productive processes themselves. Yet, while transnational corporations are the integrative thread for national capital, they are not the motor force of the internationalization of capital itself. The transnational corporation is an integrator of national structures in the global logic of capital. That internationalization does not depend on the multinational or national character of individual capitals, but on the process of accumulation on a world scale (Barkin and Suárez, 1982:26; Palloix, 1977; Clairmonte, 1980). Obviously, such internationalization takes place partly through trade in the private sector and export promotion programs of national governments. However, the homogenization of tastes for certain products (and the productive processes they imply) shows that there is little difference in the creation of a luxury commodity for foreign consumers and its creation for domestic elites at the expense of the rural poor. In fact, in the case of cattle and other rural products, it makes no difference at all that prime international cuts of meat are consumed domestically or abroad; the point is that they are produced according to an international standard with great costs in basic foodstuffs and rural resources. In the absence of fundamental changes in technology and social relations of production, simply cutting off international trade in cattle and livestock products, as a number of observers have advocated, may therefore have no rural development dividend.

The Political Character of Cattle Industry Development

Although not necessarily apparent at first glance, in Latin America the raising and slaughter of cattle is a profoundly political process. For one thing, livestock-producing countries struggling in the mid-1980s to meet external payments obligations (viz., Argentina, Brazil, Mexico) will seek to stimulate exports of cattle, meat and byproducts. Argentina's economic recovery is clearly linked to primary commodity exports, led by beef and wheat. And Mexico's frontier cattle industry offers one of few non-petroleum outlets for trade in a period of economic stabilization.

Even beyond the immediacy of the economic crisis, however, politics intrude on cattle raising, for the present course pits small-scale and large-scale producers against each other. It also strikes at the heart of current efforts to reduce poverty in rural areas. Indeed, in many areas it makes the situation more desperate. This is its most damaging political and social feature. Such a judgment does not square with the mainstream of thought emanating from many international development assistance institutions. Developmentalists have focused on the technical requirements for increasing the yield and dynamism of Latin American cattle herds: improving stock lines, controlling slaughter, increasing carcass weights, and improving reproduction rates. Given the structural difficulties limiting Latin American cattle raising, these concerns have not been without merit. Likewise, there has been substantial enthusiasm for the export potential of Latin American beef cattle (and, not incidentally, their growing potential as consumers of transnational inputs, feedgrains, and medicaments).

This is not to say that cattle raising and herd modernization are inherently bad for an integrated rural development strategy. In fact, such a determination depends on the character of the entire feedgrain-foodgrain-livestock complex, and not simply cattle raising per se. One could certainly conceive of models of rural development in which cattle raising could play an important part, not only in farm labor, but in the economic well-being of the unit. Unfortunately, however, in Latin American societies the most frequent structural conflict is between traditionally based modes of cattle raising and the international industrialization of livestock enterprises in general. Traditional livestock raising is giving way to internationalized modes of poultry, feedgrain, and cattle raising with grave implications for "peasant" or small farmer traditions of animal husbandry. In this transitional climate, the trend favors the modernization of cattle raising in a direction jeopardizing the future of backyard and small-scale enterprises.

This chapter is much too short to evaluate the merits — and certainly not the intentions — of the "modernization" approach to cattle herd development. Suffice it to say that the perspectives of those who have advocated such strategies have not included a complete analysis of the consequences for general rural development. From a purely distributive perspective, the development of larger and more scientifically managed cattle herds and products has had little to do with the nutritional exigencies of the rural poor. As Table 5.2 shows, per capita consumption of beef and veal in Latin America is quite low compared with other countries of the hemisphere, with the notable exceptions of Argentina and Uruguay. Interestingly, per capita consumption does not rise in the countries making the most spectacular advances in beef and veal production (viz., Brazil, Costa Rica, and Honduras for some of the most extreme cases). Even in those cases (Mexico, in particular) where per capita consumption has risen, the benefit to the lower strata of consumers is not evident.

Data from national household consumption surveys in Brazil and Mexico show that lower income groups enjoy little or no animal protein. In Mexico, one-third of rural families never eat meat or eggs, and 59 percent never drink milk.[2] Although aggregate data (Table 5.1) show increases in the Mexican cattle herd over the past two

Table 5.2
Per Capita Beef and Veal Consumption,
Latin America (kgs)

COUNTRY	1961	1970	1980
Argentina	83.2	82.4	88.8
Brazil	18.4	18.6	16.9
Colombia	19.2	19.5	22.7
Costa Rica	11.4	12.1	16.7
Dominican Republic	7.0	6.5	7.0
El Salvador	8.0	5.9	7.3
Guatemala	8.3	7.6	11.1
Honduras	7.2	4.9	5.9
Mexico	9.1	10.6	14.6
Nicaragua	12.9	15.4	11.8
Panama	19.3	22.4	26.0
Uruguay	79.0	77.8	75.2

Source: U.S. Department of Agriculture, *Livestock and Meat Situation*, various issues.

decades, there is little evidence to suggest that such increases result in better protein for the poor and nutritionally deprived. Likewise, in Brazil from 1965 to 1975 the share of worker's income required to purchase a kilo of meat increased by more than 100 percent, during a time when worker's real income declined precipitously (Wood, 1982:225), and per capita beef and veal consumption actually declined (Table 5.2). While indirect, these data, combined with the demographic explosion of the poor in Brazil and Mexico, hardly suggest that cattle herd increases relate to better nutrition for the poor. While inferences for other countries require more case studies than are possible here, there is no reason to expect a different experience among the poor in those countries.

In addition to the obvious inequality in distribution of animal protein within Latin America, it is important to realize that much of the herd increase found in Latin American countries represents export promotion efforts. While increased cattle product consumption is sometimes a byproduct of increased cattle herds, a closer association is between cattle herd increases and export expansion.[3] This is especially true, of course, in periods of economic stabilization characterized by currency devaluation and export promotion when real incomes among the poor decline and the relative prices of Latin American livestock improve on the international market.

The political aspects of cattle raising in Latin America also include the technology of production itself. First, traditional range-fed cattle are land-extensive animals, requiring little labor and low levels of capital investment. In countries with an open frontier (modern Brazil, Argentina in the 19th century, the U.S. during Westward expansion), cattle function as productive occupants of the land, which are typically followed by proprietary claims issued by their owners (Foweraker, 1981). In countries or regions without frontiers (and those countries with closing frontiers) cattle tend to push land out of agricultural use and to dispossess peasant farmers to a great extent. This has been particularly evident in twentieth-century Mexican cattle legislation, which provides generous *coeficientes de agostadero* under the agrarian reform law,[4] and *certificados de inafectabilidad* immunizing cattle raisers from the land limits prevailing under the agrarian reform code. More recently, 1981 reforms to the Mexican agrarian code permit cattlemen to obtain certificates of immunity even though they engage in the planting and sale of forage crops. Such "reforms" of the agrarian code remove one of the most important avenues for agrarian reform claims: claims against cattlemen whose land was proved to be susceptible to agricultural use.

In addition to the generous provisions for large cattle landholdings in Mexico, the internationalization of the industry threatens traditional agriculture and artisan modes of rural survival in several ways. Most obviously, the export orientation of the Mexican frontier cattle industry combined with the increased urban market for beef requires that land previously dedicated to agricultural purposes be usurped by cattle enterprises. One of the most painful examples of such appropriation of public purpose can be found in the execution of the *Plan Chontalpa*, described in great relief by David Barkin (1978). Other examples abound, including the current deforestation of Chiapas and Tabasco (Fernández and Fernández) for the sake of provisioning the domestic beef market (U.N., CEPAL, 1975). Aside from the awesome ecological devastation left in the wake of the *ganaderización* of many previously agricultural zones and rainforests in southern Mexico and the Brazilian Amazon, there is a real threat to traditional wood-gathering and charcoal production carried on by peasants as important market activities.

In slightly more subtle fashion, certain modes of cattle herd modernization threaten some artisan crafts and the *traspatio* (backyard) mode of cattle rearing. In Mexico, the export of increasing numbers of live cattle during the past two decades has been accompanied by a dramatic increase in imports of cattle hides and byproducts, as shown in Table 5.3. The fact that Mexico's export cattle are processed in the United States (after feeding) differentiates the industry across national boundaries. Consumers of hides, horns and lard—principally artisans and poor consumers—require that their primary inputs be reimported at a price above domestic market prices for hides or under supply constraints harming the industry.

Regarding the *traspatio* industry, it is well known that the beef cattle industry suffers periodic price crises resulting in contractions, high slaughter rates, and poor beef-to-feed price ratios. As overgrazing, drought, and poor land-use management force the petty producer onto the forage and feedgrain market, prices of such commodities often determine the viability of small producers. High cost imports or uneven domestic supplies of such key feedgrains as sorghum and oilseed cake/meal have tended to wash out small producers from the

Table 5.3
Certain U.S. Exports to Mexico, 1971 and 1979[a]

Commodity	1971 Volume (lb)	1971 Value (US$)	1979 Volume (lb)	1979 Value (US$)
Non-fat Dry Milk	30,357,698	4,526,723[b]	33,059,671	2,900,790
Wheat	7,337,474	11,267,181	43,289,593	86,515,803
Rice	1,322,552	115,671	31,927,870	82,340,650
Barley	205,870	235,348	2,310,358	3,900,790
Corn	629,941	1,101,579	34,502,513	50,076,383
Grain Sorghum	479,357	653,458	52,910,016	67,610,623
Oranges	384,603	23,268	–	–
Limes	349,850	16,364	–	–
Grapefruit	338,000	17,900	–	–
Grapes	456,902	40,122	1,101,952	133,011
Raisins	3,754,544	442,426	434,776	243,383
Beans	18,795,352	1,588,495	47,249,917	3,858,648
Animal Feed	2,392	106,641	38,355	3,665,496
Cattle Hides	(#)2,194,779	15,714,815	10,698,177	41,823,529
Soybeans	2,031,198	5,807,932	14,977,437	51,921,422
Animal Fats, Oils	4,052,220	340,752	4,523,89	891,572
Soya Oil	363,240	41,128	1,177,755	178,665

[a]Source: U.S. Department of Commerce, Commodity Trade Schedule B.
[b]1967 dollars.

industry. So has the encroachment of cattle on the land tenure system.

Another production consequence of the internationalization of cattle production comes from the regional centralization (i.e., industry rationalization) of slaughter. According to the Meat Import Act of 1964, the United States will only import beef from slaughterhouses determined to comply with U.S. standards of hygiene. The consequent "Latin Americanization" of those standards by countries attempting to increase beef and cattle exports to the United States has removed the small producer from the focus of slaughter. This phenomenon has, among other effects, the tendency to create new intermediaries who traffic in live cattle bought from small producers in the hinterland and delivered to regional slaughterhouses at great profit. Such commercial brokerage undercuts local slaughter facilities that consist of little more than hammer, hoist, and saw and serve local markets with native cuts of meat. Likewise, higher prices for feed-grains and their distribution through the marketplace disadvantage money-short local producers and cause them to exit the industry in hard times. A clear case of local concentration in livestock raising came in the 1979 hog production crisis in Mexico, during which a combination of high feed prices and low livestock prices forced many small producers to slaughter their herds. What industry specialists would call a simple "liquidation phase" of the livestock cycle meant that many small animal raisers would never reenter the market at all.

A final, and most important facet of the politics of the cattle indus-try in Latin America involves the strain on foodstuff production. Such pressures from the rise of modern cattle raising extend well beyond the already cited deforestation and land tenure distortions. Also to be considered is the remarkable diversion of prime agricul-tural land in many Latin American countries away from agricultural crops for human consumption in favor of feedgrains for prime cattle, hogs, and poultry. As Table 5.4 shows, Argentina, Brazil and Mexico have, since 1960, skyrocketed in their production of soya—only a small fraction of which is suitable for human consumption as oil.[5] Argentina and Mexico both show a stunning increase in grain sor-ghum production during the same time period. Focusing the infer-ence more clearly, we find that Mexican crop data indicate that increases in oleaginous crops—especially soya—have come, as cor-

Table 5.4

Soya Production in Argentina, Brazil, and Mexico, 1950–1980[a]

(1000 Tons)

Country	1950	1955	1960	1965	1970	1975	1980[b]
Argentina	1	—	1	17	27	485	3,800
Brazil	61	119	271	523	1,509	9,892	15,040
Mexico	—	—	5	58	215	599	280[c]

[a]Source: Secretaría de Agricultura y Recursos Hidráulicos, Dirección General de Economía Agrícola (Mexico), IV:3, *Principales Indicadores de la Producción Mundial para Cultivos Básicos* (Mexico: March 1980).

[b]1980 data are from U.S. Department of Agriculture, *Agricultural Situation: Western Hemisphere. Review of 1980 and Outlook for 1981* (Washington D.C.: USGPO, 1981).

[c]1980 Mexican production fell 400,000 tons from the previous year, and, as such, may not reflect general increases as clearly as a moving average might.

roborated by Homem de Melo in this volume (Chapter 8), at the expense of domestic production of such crops as corn, wheat, and beans (see Table 5.4).

The unstated concomitant to the change in cropping patterns away from corn, wheat and beans to feedgrains has been the incorporation of traditional providers of basic foods into the cattle complex, at the expense of their traditional communities and, often, their livelihood. Therein lies the most significant political aspect of the internationalization of cattle production: the existential threat to the peasantry in countries with a large, poor rural population dependent upon agriculture for survival.

The Mechanics of Internationalization

The Trade Imperative

Trade in Latin American cattle and meat has roots as profound and unshakeable as the colonial tradition that spawned it. While world trade in livestock totals only 7 percent of world meat production, it is an increasingly important aspect of the Latin American cattle complex. Latin American beef exports represented from 1974–1976 12.3 percent of world beef exports, 1.0 percent of country merchandise exports, and three-fourths of total Third World beef exports.[6] The largest providers of chilled beef for the world market include Argentina, Mexico, and Brazil, with the first two achieving international standing beside France and Australia.

Of course, the great cattle trading economies of Argentina, Southern Brazil, Uruguay, and North Mexico have not developed under the same circumstances. Nor are these "old cattle" systems modal representatives of the newer entrants in international cattle and meat trade, such as the Dominican Republic and selected Central American countries. Likewise, some nations of Latin America have a highly diversified trade (Argentina, Mexico, Brazil) with the United States, Europe and Japan; some are strictly tied to Europe (Uruguay); and some are totally dependent for trade on the United States (the Dominican Republic and Panama). As graphically displayed in a recent report from Winrock International (1981; Figures 11 and 12), Latin America's participation in global cattle and meat trade is split between those countries who essentially serve the European countries and those who serve the United States, with both sets attempting to reach the lucrative Japanese markets as well. Naturally, such distinct trading systems create differences in the characteristics of individual national cattle production systems. Those differences reveal some of the modes of internationalization experienced in the sector over the post-war decades.

One of the most interesting variations in international cattle trade appears in the north of Mexico.[7] In the Mexican livestock and meat sector, trade and the standardization of production have been the motivating forces behind a split in the Mexican cattle system and a subsequent shift in the control of the cattle production system from producer to processor and feed mill. In the 1940s and 1950s the United States and Mexico formed a binational commission for the eradication of *aftosa* (foot and mouth disease) among Mexican cattle. The result of that binational collaboration was a system of export controls over live cattle and the internationalization of slaughter facilities along U.S. lines. Specifically, the northern zone of Mexico has been declared to be quarantine-free. Cattle from those states certified by the Mexican government for trade can be sold abroad. There is an embargo, however, on interstate trade between the "international zone" and the

Table 5.5
Production by Crop Type, Federal Irrigation Districts, Mexico, 1970–1978[a]

Crop Type	%			Change in Area, (ha) 1970–78
	1969–70	1974–75	1977–78	
Grains	59.50	57.79	53.73	– 205,416
Other Foods	3.25	3.23	3.77	+ 36,375
Forage	4.63	6.72	7.78	+127,084
Oleaginous	12.96	18.67	16.50	+190,898
Textiles	13.39	6.01	9.09	– 50,126
Industrial	3.50	4.20	4.61	+ 56,542
Fruits	1.99	2.36	3.80	+ 68,916
Flowers	0.08	0.02	0.02	– 1,329
Seeds	0.02	0.02	0.04	+ 677
Others	0.68	0.98	0.66	+ 3,531

[a]Source: Secretaría de Agricultura y Recursos Hidráulicos, Dirección General de Economía Agrícola, *Estadística agrícola*, 1969–78.

Table 5.6

U.S. Imports of Cattle from Mexico, 1940–1980, Excluding Breeding Animals and Cows for Dairy Purposes and Imports from Mexico as a Percentage of U.S. Imports

(Number of Head)

Year	Under 200 pounds			200 to 699 pounds			700 pounds and over			Total		
	U.S. Imports	from Mexico	% from Mexico	U.S. Imports	from Mexico	% from Mexico	U.S. Imports	from Mexico	% from Mexico	U.S. Imports	from Mexico	% from Mexico
1940	104,602	29,921	28.6	346,289	336,207	97.1	169,720	44,715	26.3	620,611	410,843	66.2
1941	102,195	39,776	38.9	412,312	402,120	97.5	205,488	54,253	26.4	719,995	496,149	68.9
1942	66,518	13,503	20.3	386,495	377,407	97.6	180,054	64,575	35.9	633,067	455,485	71.9
1943	14,269	8,283	58.0	502,909	501,592	99.7	77,520	77,309	99.7	594,698	587,184	98.7
1944	5,861	310	5.3	276,297	275,259	99.6	25,696	25,531	99.4	307,854	301,100	97.8
1945	7,742	1,315	13.5	393,672	392,132	99.6	41,995	41,917	99.8	445,409	435,361	97.7
1946a	10,053	708	7.0	413,665	410,552	99.2	25,915	25,714	99.2	449,633	436,874	97.2
1947b	7,642	0	–	2,010	638	31.7	888	792	89.2	10,540	1,430	13.6
1948	23,571	–	–	96,335	–	–	214,645	–	–	334,551	–	–
1949	41,535	–	–	126,614	–	–	194,916	–	–	363,065	–	–
1950	38,985	–	–	179,709	–	–	173,000	–	–	391,694	–	–
1951	15,609	–	–	51,107	–	–	117,479	–	–	184,195	–	–
1952c	810	96	11.8	82,280	81,185	98.6	47,491	43,617	91.8	131,031	124,898	95.3
1953d	4,000	485	12.1	102,831	101,901	99.1	48,320	25,364	52.5	155,151	127,750	82.3
1954	2,872	–	–	3,377	–	–	46,798	–	–	53,277	–	–
1955e	3,795	539	14.2	191,849	189,631	98.8	73,696	56,153	76.2	269,340	246,323	91.4
1956	4,419	848	19.1	97,984	96,594	98.5	14,038	11,124	79.2	116,441	108,566	93.2
1957	18,400	7,914	43.0	434,901	283,842	65.3	230,272	44,236	19.2	683,573	335,992	49.1
1958	16,811	3,231	19.2	776,837	403,166	51.9	311,724	80,589	25.8	1,105,732	486,986	44.0
1959	31,775	1,037	3.2	503,725	317,095	62.9	135,956	45,697	33.6	671,456	363,829	54.2

Year											
1960	33,852	1,773	5.2	509,584	369,113	72.4	80,496	19,631	24.4	623,932	390,517	66.6
1961	37,620	3,655	23.2	835,451	497,999	59.6	125,070	36,410	29.1	997,781	543,064	54.4
1962	66,240	24,925	37.6	1,041,564	690,228	66.3	108,937	36,732	33.7	1,216,741	751,885	61.8
1963	63,739	27,120	42.5	688,938	540,099	78.4	69,163	18,123	26.2	821,840	585,342	71.2
1964	63,876	13,162	20.6	403,375	315,962	78.3	47,657	1,777	3.7	514,903	330,901	64.3
1965	80,991	15,921	20.9	863,771	504,285	58.4	150,603	14,077	9.3	1,095,365	535,260	48.8
1966	126,494	22,293	17.6	828,128	547,287	66.1	105,380	14,505	13.7	1,060,002	584,085	55.1
1967	97,738	13,553	10.8	607,842	485,929	79.9	21,920	3,936	17.9	727,500	500,418	68.8
1968	147,396	13,052	8.8	802,547	687,912	85.7	58,509	1,344	2.3	1,008,452	702,308	69.6
1969	159,143	32,459	20.4	792,356	773,829	97.6	46,679	4,099	8.8	998,178	810,387	81.2
1970	168,933	45,475	26.9	906,992	889,809	98.1	31,824	1,299	4.1	1,107,749	936,583	84.5
1971	158,689	32,467	20.4	748,873	718,642	95.9	25,583	1,100	4.3	933,145	752,209	80.6
1972	173,336	42,502	24.5	939,163	869,527	92.3	31,363	3,738	11.9	1,143,867	915,767	80.0
1973	143,851	15,213	10.6	783,851	634,697	80.9	77,417	22,744	29.4	1,005,119	672,654	66.9
1974	77,602	3,464	4.4	413,777	395,505	95.7	55,239	35,323	63.9	546,618	434,092	79.4
1975	9,966	592	5.9	220,851	190,062	86.0	149,459	5,385	3.6	380,276	196,039	51.5
1976	119,765	4,748	3.9	562,707	492,319	87.5	266,167	10,294	3.8	948,639	507,361	53.4
1977	132,317	3,305	2.4	718,047	571,198	79.5	250,371	4,867	1.9	1,100,735	579,370	52.6
1978	154,692	12,297	7.9	873,542	794,451	90.9	209,401	8,073	3.8	1,237,735	814,821	65.8
1979	146,034	1,963	1.3	430,726	376,491	87.4	137,320	1,045	0.7	714,080	379,499	53.1
1980	135,515	4,135	3.0	382,325	327,695	85.7	148,540	—	—	666,480	331,830	49.7

[a] Imports prohibited beginning December 27, 1946, due to outbreak of foot-and-mouth disease.

[b] Cattle imports shown in 1947 actually entered the United States in December 1946 after the customs office closed their books.

[c] Imports resumed September 1, 1952.

[d] Imports prohibited beginning May 23, 1953.

[e] Embargo removed January 1, 1955.

Source: United States Department of Agriculture, *Livestock and Meat Situation*, Economic Research Service, various issues.

southern states not certified as disease-free. Simultaneously, a system of slaughterhouses was established to conform with the requirements of the U.S. Meat Inspection Act that all foreign meat processors trading with the United States had to demonstrate conformity with U.S. sanitation requirements. The *empacadoras* T.I.F. (*tipo inspección federal*) (federally licensed meat packers) — almost all of which are in the north of the country — grew up in the service of the U.S. consumer market, not the domestic Mexican market.[8]

In addition to the segmentation of the Mexican beef production system, a feeder cattle system arose in response to the rationalization of the U.S. cattle complex itself. As point-of-production feedlots and slaughterhouses displaced the old regional centers for cattle processing after World War II,[9] the cattle complex of the greater Southwest U.S. came to integrate the North of Mexico as well. Large cattle enterprises specializing in purebred feeder calves sold on contract to U.S. feedlots for finishing became the "engine of growth" for the export cattle and beef trade. From the 1940s Mexico has provided the vast bulk of U.S. imports of feeder calves (200–699 pound-classification; see Table 5.6). U.S. cattle analysts readily acknowledge the attractiveness of Mexican frontier feeder steers because of their large frames, low weights, and rapid feedlot weight gain characteristics.

Part of the rapid growth in border cattle trade between the United States and Mexico has been a function of the rationalization of the U.S. industry, partly due to production contracting from the United States, demand pull from U.S. feedlots and intermediaries, and conscious policy initiatives of the U.S. government. In addition to the bilateral cooperation in disease eradication, and the growth of *empacadoras* T.I.F., in the 1970s *maquila* beef operations (processed meats) boomed along the Mexican-U.S. frontier. Maquila plants, processing live cattle imports from the United States in the free zones of the north of Mexico and shipping the boned meat and offal to Japan or back to the United States, have become important centers of economic activity. The consumer market for these products in Japan seems secure, and the maquila operations not only provide an outlet for exports from the United States, but an opportunity for expansion by the Mexican meatpacking industry. Maquila beef totalled 2.7 million pounds in its best year (1979) (U.S. Department of Agriculture, 1980a), though operations have been derailed to some extent recently by the collapse in Mexico of the financial and industrial consortium Grupo Alfa. In recent interviews, Texas State Department of Agriculture officials remarked on the great traffic in Mexican cattle being shipped to the United States for fattening and then returned to Mexico for slaughter and sale in the tourist and institutional food market. That, too, has presumably been halted by the foreign exchange crisis in the Mexican economy in the mid-1980s. The Mexican trade in cattle has also responded to structural changes in the international cattle market, as will be shown momentarily.

Still in the area of trade, it is important to note that the increases in production of cattle in Latin American countries (Table 5.7) seem to be directly associated with a greater world deficit in feedgrains and foodgrains. The U.S. Department of Agriculture (1978b) recently concluded that Latin American countries will suffer deficits in feed and provide a burgeoning market for U.S. feedgrains during the 1980s, largely due to increases in cattle production. Recent research has indicated at the global level that the total grain deficit for developing regions will increase by 1985 to 93 million tons, as grain feeding of livestock increases from 50 to 79 million tons in the same period (Winrock International, 1981:8). So, although world trade in livestock totals only 7 percent of total world meat production, that percentage forces Third World countries — and Latin American economies in particular — to exploit their comparative advantage in producing large-frame, low weight, rapid feeding live cattle for export, and to suffer growing grain deficits related to domes-

Table 5.7
Latin American Cattle Production and
Feedgrain Imports

Year	Cattle Numbers	Value of Feed Imports (Millions of $U.S.)
1976	247,079	88.2
1977	250,099	169.0
1978	248,086	159.9
1979	248,294	222.5
1980	249,620	300.6

Sources: U.S. Department of Agriculture, *Foreign Agriculture Circular, Livestock and Meat*, FLM 10–78, FLM 7–81; *Agricultural Situation: Western Hemisphere: Review of 1980 and Outlook for 1981*.

tic feeding, all to provide beef to a market dedicated to a great extent to developed-world consumers and their own wealthy urban consumers.

The Emergence of a World Cattle Cycle

One of the most interesting points of evidence demonstrating the internationalization of the Latin American cattle complex is the emergence of a world cattle cycle. Cattle cycles involve a dynamic disjuncture in the marketplace involving price, supply and demand. A cattle cycle is defined as the period from one low point in cattle numbers to the next low point.[10] Such cycles are conventionally described by a lagged response in cattle numbers to market prices. Low prices cause producers to increase slaughter rates and reduce inventories or leave the business. Initially, then, increases in slaughter lower prices, which are already falling. After this initial "liquidation" phase of the cycle, supply begins to shorten and prices begin to increase. With better prices, cattlemen begin to rebuild herds by holding back breeding stock, which further stimulates prices. This "building" phase of the cycle continues until the price response induces the next liquidation. Cattle cycles, like other primary goods market cycles, are imperfect and variable in duration. They are also susceptible to monopoly intervention and state policy changes.

The United States, as the hemisphere's leading cattle producer, has experienced eight cattle cycles in the past century (Simpson, 1979b). At the international level, it is more difficult to associate all productive systems with a single cycle, because of national differences in economic growth rates, policy priorities toward the cattle industry, and herd sizes among the various countries. Nevertheless, some convincing evidence is available to show that the U.S. cycle is a leading factor in world fluctuations in production, especially in the export sector. This certainly is the case with the leading exporters of beef and cattle to the United States, including Mexico, Panama, the Dominican Republic, and many other Latin American countries. Even in such cases, however, the relationship is complex and subtle.

As Table 5.1 shows, cattle numbers in various regions do not fluctuate directly with U.S. cattle numbers; in fact, as might be expected, the larger the region the less sensitive the numbers are to the anticipated fluctuations of the cattle cycle. Even in cases intimately associated with the U.S. beef cattle production system — e.g., Mexico and Australia—the relationship between the U.S. cycle and their production is not obvious. Mexico and Brazil, in particular, have continued to build herd numbers very slowly over the past two decades, without great sensitivity to the U.S. cycle apparent in aggregate herd statistics.[11] Nevertheless, the U.S. cattle cycle by its very nature affects the major providers of live cattle and beef imports to the United States, among whom must be counted Mexico and Canada, as well as Oceania. It is reasonable to assume that the lagged producer response which is the essence of the cattle cycle at the national level is also a factor at the international level, intervening in the association between, say, the United States and Mexico, and making the relationship appear less obvious. Likewise, we can hypothesize that the aggregation of the "modern," internationalized element of the national cattle herd in Latin American countries with traditional domestic providers desensitizes the herd to purely international fluctuations.

Despite the complexity of the association, however, Figures 5.1 and 5.2 show the great consonance among various national cattle cycles.[12] Developed-country cattle producers seem to be more sensitive to the world cattle cycle than underdeveloped-country producers, as might be expected from the greater market flexibility of their systems. Thus, Canada and Australia tend to reproduce the U.S. cycle more closely than do Mexico and Brazil. We can hypothesize that if the aggregate cattle numbers were broken down according to their destination— domestic or international—the association in the cases of Brazil and Mexico would match that of Canada and Australia more closely. The trade imperative and agribusiness investment assures some congruity between Latin American cattle cycles and that of the United States. While the "dual" nature of Latin American cattle raising may confuse the statistical representation of the regional cattle cycle, trade in cattle and meat is inordinately important to Latin America.

Shifts in Control of the Cattle Complex

Another important point to be derived from the close association between the U.S. cattle cycle and the rest of the hemisphere is that national states are not in full command of their livestock complexes. That rather obvious assertion has grave consequences for attempts to derive a conscientious strategy for delivering more animal protein to the mass of the nation's population. With the trade imperative and

Figure 5.1.
The Cattle Cycle Movement for Canada, Mexico,
and the United States, 1960–1982[a]

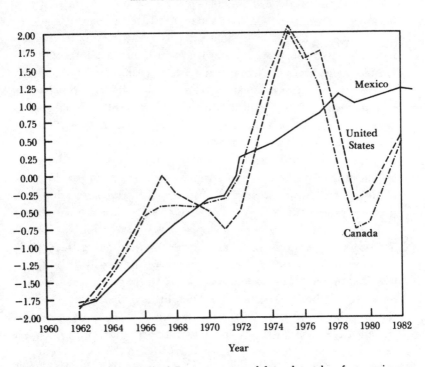

[a]Plots are based on standardized Z-scores computed from data taken from various issues of the U.S. Department of Agriculture, *Livestock and Meat Situation*.

Figure 5.2
Z Scores for Cattle Cycle in Selected Countries

Plot of Canada by year   Symbol used is A
Plot of Mexico by year   Symbol used is B
Plot of USA by year   Symbol used is C
Plot of Argentina by year   Symbol used is D
Plot of Brazil by year   Symbol used is E
Plot of Australia by year   Symbol used is F

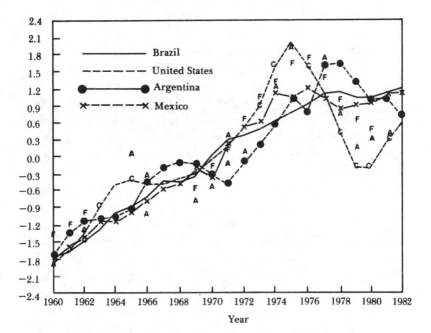

the emergence of a world cattle cycle comes a shift in the control of production in the cattle complex. The traditional Latin American model assumes that the producer/rancher controls herd size, reproduction rates, and slaughter according to a calculus of land resources, weather conditions, and prices available in the market (to the extent that he participates in a market). Due to the internationalization of cattle production in the late twentieth century, however, that producer control has gradually eroded. It is most obvious in advanced capitalist agricultural systems such as that found in the United States, where feed mills lease sows for farrow in order to create future markets for their feed and additives. Similar situations are found in contract providers of feeder cattle for feedlots. The traditional cow-calf operator of the High Plains of Texas, for example, has become more integrated into a feedlot-centered beef system, and raises more feeders for "order buyers" who may provide only finance capital to "custom feed" calves for future sale. The rancher has, in some circumstances, joined the poultry farmer as a wage laborer for the feedlot and its intermediary customers.

In Latin America, because of the relatively recent appearance of such phenomena, such situations do not exist in such great number. But there are signs to indicate that the integration of the cattle complex increasingly emanates from the slaughterhouse and the feedmill, or in some cases from the stock breeding company and the feedlot. A central impetus for this relationship—in addition to the roles of feedmill, feedlot, and slaughterhouse as providers of capital and technology—is the producer contract, which has increasingly come to dominate market relationships in cattle as in other commodities, such as tobacco, tomatoes, and canning goods.

It is well known that U.S. feedlots and order buyers contract for Mexican feeder cattle production in order to achieve a greater vertical coordination among phases of the industry and to avoid the painful possibilities of ownership in the more volatile aspects of cattle production: stock raising. Finances, breeding stock, resources for artificial insemination, antibiotics—even whole feedlot facilities—are readily available from international companies specializing in such services. One need only visit a state cattle fair in Mexico to meet representatives of U.S., European, and Canadian firms selling their technologically advanced wares to the enterprising Mexican cattleman.

But, of course, producer contracts have their difficulties from a developmental standpoint: They specify the quality, breed and delivery—among other conditions—to be adhered to by the producer. Industry advocates contend that such insistence on U.S. quality enhances the modernization process, as do the confinement feeding and other technological "packages" which are the necessary concomitants to a successful international beef or feeder calf operation.

Part of the shift in control in the livestock complex also comes from the organization of transnational corporations. Transnational beef corporations have affiliates in at least a dozen Latin American countries, and several in each of the largest markets (Argentina, Brazil, Mexico, and Venezuela).[13] In addition to the famous Ludwig venture in Brazil, Volkswagen, Gulf and Western, and the King Ranch all hold beef production and processing enterprises in Latin America. It is interesting to note that over the century, direct foreign investment in the industry has tended to diminish as local holders supplant the former giants (such as Swift and Wilson in Mexico and Argentina). That in itself does not affect the nature of internationalization in the industry. Whether the agent is Swift and Wilson in the Argentine industry of the late nineteenth century or Bremer and Grupo Alfa in pork processing in the 1970s, the dynamic of internationalization remains a function of the standardization of production, the reproduction of the labor process, and the valorization of capital.

In addition to those growing enterprises specializing in export-processing of fresh meat (e.g., the maquila beef mentioned earlier), and the direct foreign investment still found in meatpacking and processing, the feedmills have had an important impact in the generation of new cattle activities as well as the change in cropping patterns accompanying livestock development in Latin America. From Purina to Quaker Oats, livestock feed in Latin America has provided an indirect impetus to the cattle industry. Systematic evidence abounds showing the diversion of foodstuff production toward feedgrains to support transnational and local feedmills, which in turn stimulates local producers of dairy and beef cattle.

Conclusion

The international standardization of cattle production, exchange, distribution and consumption—the emergence of the "world steer"

—has had its own technical and economic logic not unlike the modern development of other internationally traded commodities. But its very nature has led it away from one of its putative goals in Latin America, national rural development. The emergence of the world steer has shifted power away from the primary producer; it has "disarticulated" consumption from the national economy (and certainly from the rural economy); and, it has created negative effects in foodstuff production and land tenure. The combined effect has been to help make the poor poorer, the malnourished more malnourished, and the heralded era of "rural development" a bureaucratic nightmare.

The political significance of these changes in the Latin American cattle industry is great. First, the international cattle complex does not correspond to the necessary development of agricultural growth patterns and institutions genuinely responsive to domestic needs, whether those needs be conceived as more popular consumption of cheap animal protein, a broader base of cattle raising enterprises, nutrition for the rural poor, or satisfying the basic consumer needs of the urban population (with the exception of upper strata of that population). Beef production tends to serve a small proportion of the Latin American population in most countries. It reduces the amount of land dedicated to food production in countries without expanding frontiers. It dispossesses marginal peasants or changes their livelihood from one based on food production to one dependent on feedgrain production. And it does not generate ecologically sound technologies amenable to small-scale production. Although these are tendencies and not laws of cattle production in the present epoch, when we speak of changes in any of these elements, we are, in effect, speaking of profound changes in the character of agricultural internationalization and agribusiness accumulation.

Second, regarding the generation of employment in agriculture or non-urban occupations, modern cattle raising tends to be profoundly capital intensive and labor saving. While traditional cattle enterprises have never been particularly labor intensive, the modern cattle enterprise reduces that contribution further, via the ascendance of boxed beef (which removes the bulk of skilled meat cutting from farm to retail outlet), regional concentration of slaughter in urban centers (cutting out previously important local *rastros*), and confinement feeding (eliminating the range hands, who were previously the only claim to labor generation available to cattle raising).

Finally, in ways too similar to other internationalized commodities—citrus, winter vegetables, grains, and others—the state in Latin America has less "policy space" to maneuver against the vicissitudes of the international market in cattle and feedgrains when the system of production extends beyond the realm of its control. For reasons of foreign exchange needed by the national economy, political power enjoyed by cattlemen, and cultural suasion issued by the urban elites, the political possibilities of controlling or limiting cattle herd modernization are reduced as the international dimensions of its development are extended. But, in the case of the collapse of external markets or their prices, the availability of boxed beef and t-bone steaks is not likely to assuage the hunger of the population marginalized by the modern beef cattle industry.

Some would dismiss these consequences as being transitory. Suppose this were an arguable position and that the evidence sustained it. The political and economic implications of the world steer would still be serious, even with progressive institutions dedicated to genuinely development-oriented cattle raising—a condition not found in most Latin American countries today. We can now see that a more important implication for the future of Latin American cattle herd development is that the character of modern production at the global level has differentiated the process so as to threaten the viability of "national" production systems. This is the true meaning of the "world steer," as it is with the "world car" and other globalized commodities. We now face an epoch in which the meat on consumers' tables will have been developed in Europe and North America, bred in Latin America, fed with export grains from the key producing countries (which itself is processed by multinational corporations), slaughtered under international standards, and consumed in the communities most removed from their point of origin. And, as in the case of other global commodities, such a mode of productive organization leaves little room for the state to exercise policies designed to reapprehend national control of its rural development.

International traders and transnational managers will hardly see the difficulties in such a model of cattle modernization. But national politicians and rural development advocates have another mandate.

Even if we concede the virtue of increasing animal protein as a part of the agricultural and cattle product of Latin American countries, national control over such a development process is eroding from an already attenuated base established in the era of the export enclave. If Latin American countries must pursue the elusive goal of developing a cattle system in Latin America more consonant with national development and nutrition, current dynamics described in this study show the emergence of the world steer to be less a promise than a threat.

Chapter 6

Controlling International Commodity Prices and Supplies: The Evolution of United States Sugar Policy*

VINCENT A. MAHLER

The internationalization of agriculture is often thought of as a recent phenomenon. For many commodities it is (see, for example, the analyses of the beef and soya industries by Sanderson and Homem de Melo in this volume). But for at least one major commodity, sugar, this is manifestly not the case. Nearly all of the characteristics associated with the postwar globalization of agriculture—vertically integrated markets, extensive foreign investment, a problematic impact on development and distribution in peripheral areas—have been part of the world sugar trade not for decades but for centuries.

This chapter reviews one of the most revealing components of this long and rich history, the evolution of the sugar trade between the United States and the Third World. The sugar trade has figured prominently in North-South relations since the dawn of the modern era, and was an important mechanism of the early expansion of "metropole" influence into peripheral areas. Moreover, sugar continues to be a major American import from the Third World; the policies that regulate it remain a matter of considerable concern both to Third World producers and to policymakers in the United States.

Has the character of the sugar trade changed over time? What have been the political, economic and social interests at stake? What lessons does this experience offer for current trade in other agricultural

*The research for this chapter was supported in part by a Grant for Research into European Integration from the Commission of the European Community.

commodities? Close attention to these questions in the context of a single narrow area of North-South agricultural trade will complement more general analyses of global agriculture and offer a good sense of the complex interplay between domestic and international forces that has shaped American policy toward the Third World over the last three centuries.[1]

The Origins of the American Sugar Trade
with the Third World

In light of today's debate over the intrusion of global forces into peripheral countries, it is ironic that one of the earliest examples of opposition to a dominant metropole's systematic economic constraints was the anti-imperialist movement leading to the American Revolution. By the 1770s Britain's North American subjects were arguing against the mother country's interference in terms not very different from those that contemporary critics of global political-economic structures employ. By the eve of the Revolution, a large body of colonial opinion had come to believe that the colonies' own economic well-being was, to use dos Santos' (1971:226) familiar description of global asymmetry, "conditioned by the development and expansion of another economy to which [they were] subjected," and in relation to which their own interests were of distinctly secondary importance.

Of the factors leading to the American independence movement, British efforts to regulate the colonial trade in cane sugar were among the most important.[2] It is often forgotten how central a role Caribbean sugar played in the world political-economic system of the seventeenth and eighteenth centuries.[3] Indeed, in comparison to the West Indian sugar-producing islands, the colonies of mainland North America were themselves of marginal economic significance in the eyes of the colonial powers. As put by Morison et al. (1969:48), "the extension of sugar culture around 1650 made even the smallest [Caribbean island] immensely valuable. . . . Far more money and men were spent on defending and capturing these islands in the colonial era than on the continental colonies that became the United States because they were much more profitable to their owners."

Throughout the seventeenth and eighteenth centuries the sugar trade grew ever more important. In Britain, for example, sugar consumption increased rapidly during this period; sugar was Britain's single leading import for every year from 1701 to 1814 (Thomas, 1979:376). The close proximity of so profitable a trade proved irresistible to the settlers of the less well-endowed British colonies of North America. The New England and Middle Atlantic colonies in particular had been settled more for religious than for economic reasons and, unlike the Southern colonies, they grew few of the agricultural staples (such as tobacco or rice) that were of interest to the English home market. Most of the goods produced in the Northern colonies were, indeed, consciously excluded from the English market: the British prohibited imports of colonial wheat, salted meats and other products in an effort to protect the rural aristocracy, who still dominated British politics, from low-cost colonial competition.

Largely excluded from the English market, the Northern colonies turned to the booming West Indies in an effort to sell their products and earn the foreign exchange they needed to purchase essential manufactured goods from Britain. The British West Indies came to be provisioned largely from Continental America: planters subsisted on colonial salted pork, onions, potatoes and flour; slaves ate low-quality codfish from New England; plantation buildings were constructed from wood cut in colonial forests; horses came from Rhode Island breeders; and even the boxes and barrels used to ship sugar and molasses were of North American oak and pine.

In return for these provisions, the Northern colonies received the only products the West Indies had to offer – sugar and molasses. Several associated industries soon emerged. For example, a major distillery industry was rapidly established in New England port cities: by 1750 some 60 firms in Boston and 30 in Newport were engaged in distilling sugar into rum. For colonial merchants rum had many uses, most of them of dubious morality but unquestionably good economics. Some was used for local consumption; rum quickly became the favorite alcoholic beverage of the lower classes. Some was used in the Indian trade, which was at this time still fairly substantial. Most importantly, the Northern colonies became closely involved in the slave trade: ships from Boston, Newport and New York acquired slaves in West Africa, transported them to the West Indies for use in the sugar plantations, returned to the colonies laden with sugar for the distilleries, sailed back to the West Indies with provisions, returned to the colonies for rum, and then sailed to England for manufactured goods or to West Africa for more slaves. By 1771 the more complex American variant of the notorious, but extremely profitable, "triangular" trade in sugar and slaves was fully a quarter as large as that of the English one (Rothbard, 1976:213).

During the seventeenth century the American sugar trade was conducted exclusively with the British West Indies. By the early eighteenth century, however, British West Indian sugar was becoming less and less attractive as soil exhaustion took a toll and plantation owners who had made their fortunes returned to England to spend them in style, turning their plantations over to poorly paid overseers. American merchants began to trade more and more extensively with French growers in Guadeloupe, Martinique and St. Domingue (now Haiti) where the soil was more fertile and management more efficient, and where prices ranged from a quarter to a half below those of the colonists' fellow imperial subjects in the British West Indies.[4] The French government encouraged this trade; it desired revenues from rum produced in its colonial possessions, but was reluctant to introduce rum into the French domestic market for fear of offending politically influential brandy interests.

Planters in the British West Indies argued vigorously that foreign competition would unacceptably undercut their prices and, after years of lobbying, in 1733 were able to prevail upon the British Parliament to pass a Molasses Act levying a prohibitive duty on foreign sugar imported into the English colonies. However, fortunately for the American colonists, British administrators on the scene were sympathetic to the colonists' arguments against the serious enforcement of legislation that would enable "a few pamper'd Creolians . . . [to] roll in their guilded equipages through the streets of London at the expense of two million American subjects" (cited in Carman, 1930:200). In practice, as put by one commentator, "there was one saving grace: no British regulation was more cheerfully evaded and less adequately enforced" (Rothbard, 1976:213).

For over 30 years the Molasses Act was regularly renewed at five-year intervals and just as regularly ignored.[5] Only with the onset of the Seven Years' War in Europe and its North American counterpart, the French and Indian War, did pressure again mount to control the colonists' trade with the French West Indies. With the British declaration of war against France, the colonial trade with Guadeloupe, Martinique and St. Domingue was transformed from a technically illegal but tolerated trade with a foreign country to a case of trafficking with an enemy in time of war—a circumstance which nevertheless did little to dampen it. Moreover, the British became increasingly annoyed at the substantial financial outlays necessary to maintain a military force in North America; the cost of protecting the ungrateful continental colonies seemed to far exceed any benefits derived, and there was serious pressure to force the colonists to contribute more to their own defense. Finally, and more generally, mercantilism as an economic theory was becoming fully established at this time; the mercantilists' notion that supply should be confined within the colonial fold seemed thoroughly justified in theory as well as in practice.

In 1764, a year after the end of the French and Indian War, Parliament passed an American Revenue Act (Sugar Act) which attempted to put some teeth into the enforcement of restrictions on the extra-imperial sugar trade. The wholly unrealistic duty on foreign sugar imports of the Molasses Act (which averaged 100 percent) was halved, but measures were taken to strictly enforce what remained a very stringent tariff. Under newly established "general writs of assistance" customs agents were permitted to break into and enter private warehouses, stores and even homes, to search for smuggled goods without the previous requirement that they obtain a specific writ (search warrant) indicating the premises to be searched and the basis for the search. Moreover, customs agents were absolved of the Common Law provision that they were personally liable for damages from unsuccessful searches; all that was required was a determination of "probable cause" on the part of the authorities.

The colonists' reaction to the Sugar Act was swift and hostile. On this issue the traditionally fractious Northern colonies were united. An incident in Newport was typical:

When . . . John Robinson seized the ship *Polly* in April, 1765 for smuggling molasses he should not have been surprised to receive the full treatment from populace and [local] judiciary alike. . . . The vessel was seized in Dighton, on the Massachusetts side of Narragansett Bay. The first step for Robinson and his aids was to have the crew bring the *Polly* to Newport to be condemned in court. But they could find no one to serve on such an obnoxious voyage. That night a large group of citizens carried away the whole cargo; . . . Robinson [later] found that his prize capture . . . had been run aground, stripped of sailing rigging and other equipment, and her bottom drilled full of holes. No sooner had Robinson arrived in Dighton than he was arrested and sued for three thousand pounds in damages by Job Smith for seizing his vessel. . . . The suit would eventually be suspended . . . [but meanwhile] Robinson was forced to spend the night in jail . . . (Rothbard, 1976:65).

Opposition to the Sugar Act rapidly advanced from the contention that the levy was too high to the broader contention that any levy imposed by a mother country on its colonial subjects without their consent was in itself illegal — was, in the words of James Otis, contrary to "the laws of nature and of Nations, the Voice of Universal Reason and of God." Sam Adams speculated on the precedent established by the Sugar Act: "For if our trade may be taxed, why not our land? Why not the produce of our land and everything we possess or make use of? This we apprehend annihilates our charter rights to govern ourselves." The New York Assembly summarized the principle it saw as being at issue: "Exemption from burthen of ungranted, involuntary taxes must be the grand principle of every free state," without which "there can be no liberty, no happiness, no security." The narrow issue of economic self-determination had been transformed into a broader ideal of national self-determination that was sufficient to see the colonists through a long and bitter struggle that eventually led to full political independence.[6]

The Sugar Trade in the Nineteenth Century: Decline and Recovery

In 1781 the British surrendered at Yorktown; the American colonists had, against all odds, achieved independence from one of the world's greatest powers. For a time New England merchants were able to conduct their version of the triangular trade more or less freely, subject only to interference from British and French privateers — and, before long, the new American government: one of the first acts of the new Federal Congress was a sugar tariff, enacted for the purpose of raising revenue.

But not long after the colonists had achieved their hard-won right of free commerce, several factors served to undermine the sugar trade that had for so long been essential to the economic prosperity of the Northern colonies. For one thing, New England and the Middle Atlantic colonies rapidly began to develop manufacturing industries of their own, reducing the pressing demand for foreign exchange to pay for essential imports from Britain; industrial development had been spurred by the need to develop alternate sources of supply during the early years of independence and by the imposition of high protective tariffs on manufactured imports. In addition, the Louisiana Purchase of 1803 incorporated into the United States a small, but rapidly growing, sugar industry near New Orleans that helped meet domestic needs, particularly in the territory beyond the Appalachians. Finally, and most important, there was the abolition of the slave trade by both Britain and the United States in 1808.[7] Without the international slave trade, American commerce with the West Indies lost much of its rationale — only a small proportion of New England's sugar refining and distilling capacity had ever been directed to domestic consumption.[8]

With the decline in the world trade in sugar and slaves in the early nineteenth century, the sugar industry in the United States went into a steep decline. American tastes in alcohol turned from rum to cheaper domestically produced whiskey, and sugar for direct consumption remained very much a luxury.

Only in the 1850s did the price of sugar drop (largely because of improvements in refining techniques) to a point at which it could attract a domestic mass market in the United States. American sugar consumption increased very rapidly in the 1850s — from a per capita annual consumption of 18 pounds in 1850 to 31½ pounds in 1858. Part of the new demand was met by expansion of Louisiana cane production, but an increasing quantity of raw sugar began to be imported from the Caribbean, especially Cuba.

Thus began a relationship that would persist for more than a century: in time Cuba became as thoroughly tied to the United States economy as any underdeveloped country before or since. It is noteworthy from the perspective of contemporary critiques of North-South agricultural trade that American tariffs on imported sugar were from the beginning steeply graduated by level of processing, with the tariff on raw sugar less than half that on fully refined sugar. As a result, Cuban sugar was generally exported in a nearly raw state, discouraging local processing and allowing the expansion of the refining industry in the United States.[9] A classic example of raw-materials-for-processed-goods complementarity was established:

Cuba's principal industry was almost entirely dependent not on local stimuli but on the vicissitudes of the American market to the North on which Cuba in turn relied for most manufactured essentials.

The burgeoning American refining industry stalled temporarily during the Civil War when the government levied stiff taxes on sugar — still deemed a luxury — to help finance the war effort. After the war, however, demand soon resumed. But the Louisiana cane sugar producing area, previously a major source of supply, went into a decline in the Reconstruction period: Louisiana plantations had suffered damage and neglect during the war and were, moreover, now forced to employ free rather than slave labor.[10] This left the United States without a significant domestic source of sugar, and the already close relationship with Cuba intensified.

While the Cubans were becoming more closely drawn into the American orbit, they were at the same time gradually being excluded from alternate markets on the European Continent. In 1747 a Prussian, Andreas Marggraf, had discovered that sugar indistinguishable from that derived from cane could be produced from beetroot, a crop that had previously been cultivated only for fodder. A strong impetus for the expansion of beet sugar production came when the British blockade during the Napoleonic Wars cut off much of Western Europe from Caribbean cane sugar supplies. Even after the blockade ended there was strong sentiment throughout the Continent to achieve self-sufficiency in food rather than rely on trade over British-dominated shipping lanes. European beet sugar production rose rapidly throughout the nineteenth century, encouraged by heavy government subsidies and extensive tariff protection.[11] By the late nineteenth century the Continent had become largely self-sufficient in sugar, putting severe pressure on Cuba and other major exporters in the Caribbean. Cuba was thus faced with both a pull and a push effect in its relationship with the United States: at the same time that it was being drawn into the United States market it was being excluded from alternative markets in Europe.

In time Cuban producers became subject to competition from beet sugar even in the American market. Beet sugar production became established much more slowly in the United States than in Europe, in part because of technical backwardness and in part because of the inexpensive and secure source of supply afforded by Cuba. But by the

1890s both of these obstacles were being overcome: Claus Spreckels, Henry T. Oxnard and other American entrepreneurs in the West, least accessible to the Caribbean, began applying efficient beet refining methods developed in Germany, while the United States Congress, encouraged by Western and Louisiana interest, began to follow the Continental European method of subsidizing domestic sugar production and protecting it from foreign competition.[12] The culmination of protective efforts in this period was the Dingley Tariff of 1897, which increased the duty on sugar imports sufficiently to stimulate significant domestic production.[13] From the late 1890s beet sugar production rose rapidly and beet sugar growing and refining became an important industry in such states as Colorado, Michigan, Utah, Idaho and California.

Cuban and other Caribbean producers were thus confronted with pressure on their prices from several directions. Paradoxically, as Cuban growers faced increased competition in American import markets they became ever more reliant on American financial resources: Cuban growers, perpetually short of cash, were forced increasingly to rely on American investment to maintain operations.

The dependence of Cuba on the United States was formalized after the 1898 war with Spain. Politically, Cuba became tied to the United States by the Platt Amendment to its constitution, which formally allowed American military intervention to ensure "the preservation of Cuban independence [and] the maintenance of a government adequate for the protection of life, property and individual liberty. . . ."[14] Economically, Cuba was linked to the United States with the enactment in 1903 of a reciprocal tariff reduction of about 20 percent which granted Cuban and American exporters preference in each others' markets over other suppliers. By the mid-1920s not only was the United States the largest source by far of Cuban imports and outlet for Cuban exports, but almost two-thirds of the total Cuban sugar production was controlled by American firms (Thomas, 1971:56). When sugar prices climbed, as they did in the 1920s as a result of the disruption of European beet sugar production in World War I, national euphoria set in: this was the period of Cuba's "Dance of the Millions." When sugar prices fell, as they did in the depression of the 1930s, the Cuban economy was thoroughly and utterly devastated.

Sugar from 1934 to 1974:
Forty Years of a Thoroughly Managed Market

The impact of the depression of the 1930s on Cuba is perhaps best illustrated by a few representative statistics. In 1929, Cuba produced 5.8 million tons of sugar, 4.2 million for the American market; by 1932 Cuban production had fallen to only 2.6 million tons, of which 1.8 million were exported to the United States. By 1933 world sugar prices had fallen from their postwar sugar boom high of 13 cents per pound to 0.71 cents per pound, the lowest price ever recorded (D. G. Johnson, 1974:23; Thomas, 1971:562). By 1933 thirty of the 163 Cuban sugar mills operating in 1929 had closed permanently and nearly all of the rest had instituted massive layoffs and struggled on only with extensive government subsidies.

The worldwide depression affected American sugar producers almost as seriously as Cuban. The first official response to catastrophically low world prices was the traditional remedy of raising tariffs to protect domestic producers from foreign competition—the high Smoot-Hawley tariff was passed in 1930. But it was soon clear that the situation had become too serious for this standard remedy; protection actually led to overproduction, and thus to even lower prices. The effect of higher tariffs on Cuba was to plunge it even deeper into economic and political dislocation (Cuba suffered a period of extensive political violence at this time), damaging not only the Cuban economy, but also the American business interests that controlled two-thirds of Cuban sugar production and American exporters of manufactured goods who relied on their preferred position in the Cuban market.

In response to this crisis, President Roosevelt offered a dramatic new remedy. The Jones-Costigan Act, proposed by Roosevelt and passed by Congress in 1934, abandoned the system of tariffs that had long governed the sugar market in favor of a comprehensive system of quotas that allocated total estimated American sugar consumption among domestic producers and foreign suppliers—a direct curtailment of supply to meet demand. The quota provisions of Jones-Costigan were incorporated into a series of successive Sugar Acts that would govern the American sugar market for 40 years.[15]

Sugar quota legislation began as an ad hoc program intended to protect American sugar producers from the historically low sugar

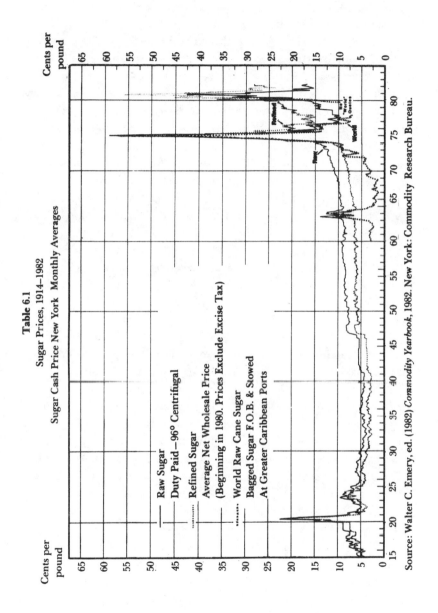

Table 6.1

Sugar Prices, 1914–1982

Sugar Cash Price New York Monthly Averages

Raw Sugar
Duty Paid – 96° Centrifugal

Refined Sugar
Average Net Wholesale Price
(Beginning in 1980, Prices Exclude Excise Tax)

World Raw Cane Sugar
Bagged Sugar F.O.B. & Stowed
At Greater Caribbean Ports

Source: Walter C. Emery, ed. (1982) *Commodity Yearbook*, 1982. New York: Commodity Research Bureau.

prices that prevailed worldwide in the 1930s without unduly disrupting Cuban production. As the Sugar Program continued in operation, however, it established a momentum of its own. As was becoming typical of American agricultural programs, the Sugar Program thoroughly sheltered the price of sugar on the American market from the world market: an administered price objective was achieved by means of acreage restrictions, direct payments to farmers and, if necessary, direct government purchases. Unlike most agricultural programs, however, the Sugar Program offered quotas on the American market at protected prices to *foreign* as well as domestic suppliers, at first mainly to Cuba but eventually to over 30 foreign sugar producers.

The immediate effect of the Jones-Costigan Act on Cuba was to raise the prices Cuban producers received for their sugar and to protect their share of the American market. Over the long run, however, American quota administrators tended to favor American producers in allocating increases in domestic consumption, and the Cuban share of the total American market gradually declined from some 50 percent in the 1920s to about 35 percent in the 1950s. In addition, Cuba was forced to make substantial reciprocal concessions to American exporters for a wide range of industrial products; American manufacturers of the 1930s were beginning to experience serious competition in export markets from the Japanese that preference in the Cuban market helped to alleviate (Thomas, 1971:693).

During the Second World War, a period of disruption in sugar production worldwide and of high world market prices, the Sugar Act was suspended. Cuba continued, however, to supply the American market under bulk purchasing arrangements at below world market prices.[16] In the 1948 reinstatement of the Sugar Act, the criteria governing the size of sugar quotas and the countries to receive them, never entirely clearcut, became even more vague than previously, opening the possibility that quotas would be used to advance American public or private objectives. Moreover, the United States Secretary of Agriculture was permitted to withhold or increase Sugar Act quotas at his discretion if he determined that a country had infringed in any way "fair and equitable treatment to the nationals of the United States, its commerce, navigation or industry" (cited in Gerber, 1977:117). The immediate intention of this provision seems to have been to offer leverage for the collection of Cuban private debts to American institutions, but the long-range effect was to increase the arbitrariness of the granting of quotas to foreign suppliers in a way that allowed considerable room for abuse. From the point of view of Cubans (and, from the late 1940s, of the Filipinos and several Latin American producers who were granted increased shares of the American market) the relaxation of straightforward methods of quota allocation to foreign suppliers made for great uncertainty. As put by O'Connor (1972:62),

The single most important decision of the Cuban economy, the size of the American quota, was determined by . . . authorities with whom Cuba had no official standing. . . . The affront to national sovereignty inherent in this satellitic relationship should be obvious.

The Boycott of Cuba

Fidel Castro came to power in Cuba in 1959. After an initial period of uncertainty, it became increasingly clear that his relationship with the United States would be one of hostility: a bitter war of words was soon accompanied by Cuban expropriation of American property and flirtation with the Soviet Union. In June 1960 matters came to a head when Castro demanded that American-owned oil companies in Cuba process Russian crude or face expropriation. The companies, with U.S. State Department encouragement, refused. Hostilities escalated rapidly, and Castro proceeded to carry out his threat. The U.S. Congress soon retaliated, using the most powerful weapon at its disposal: on July 6, 1960, it passed a bill extending the Sugar Act of 1956 but granting the President discretion to alter Cuba's sugar quota "in such amount or amounts as he shall find . . . to be in the national interest" (Gerber, 1976:112). Acting under the authority of this bill, President Eisenhower promptly reduced the Cuban quota to zero, in one stroke depriving Cuba of the single market that accounted for the bulk of its exports. "This action," Eisenhower commented, "amounts to economic sanctions against Cuba. Now we must look ahead to other moves—economic, diplomatic, strategic" (cited in Thomas, 1971:1289).

Castro immediately turned for help to Cuba's new ally, the Soviet Union. The Soviets and the Eastern European countries quickly purchased most of the remaining Cuban sugar for 1960, and in December the Soviet Union signed a formal agreement to buy 2.7 million tons of Cuban sugar at a very favorable price.

Ironically, the Soviet rescue of Cuba actually reduced the price that other Third World sugar producers received for their sugar. The Soviet Union and Eastern European countries had long been largely self-sufficient in beet sugar and before long the Soviets began to dispose of unneeded Cuban sugar on the world market, depressing the prices on which many Third World sugar producers relied.[17]

The Demise of the Sugar Program

Immediately after the exclusion of Cuban sugar from the American market the Secretary of Agriculture was authorized to obtain temporary replacement sugar for 1961. Fortunately for the United States, the early 1960s were a time of surplus sugar production worldwide and low world prices, and obtaining sugar to compensate for that formerly received from Cuba did not prove difficult.

In 1962 the American government sought formally to alter the sugar quota system to reflect the loss of the single largest quota recipient, Cuba. The prospect of reallocating the Cuban quota brought foreign lobbyists to Washington in force, to the point that they became a focus of considerable Congressional and public concern. Congressmen of both parties voiced their suspicion that foreign lobbyists were using more than persuasion in their efforts to achieve quotas for their countries; criticism centered on Congressman Harold Cooley, House Agriculture Committee Chairman, whose imperious dealings with foreign sugar lobbyists and close relations with the domestic industry led to his nickname "Sugar King."[18]

Public and Congressional concern of the early 1960s was noted by the Kennedy Administration, which was skeptical of the country-quota system and preferred an overall import quota that would be fulfilled by foreign suppliers on a competitive basis, with the difference between the U.S. domestic price and the prevailing world price recouped by an import fee on sugar imports into the United States. But the administration was unable to pierce the sugar "subgovernment" and eventually withdrew most of its proposals when it became clear that they would not be enacted. The sugar bill that emerged from a House-Senate conference committee in 1962 represented a major expansion of the country-quota system to accommodate a reallocation of the Cuban quotas to over two dozen countries. The sugar lobby had weathered the storm and emerged with its power enhanced.

During the 1960s and the first half of the 1970s the sugar sub-government seemed invincible, and occasional calls for reform — from both liberal critics of interest group self-regulation and free-market conservatives — met with little success. In the words of one of its critics, the sugar lobby represented a classic example of "a complex problem . . . dealt with [by] the coalescing of power among those who have the interest or the yen to deal with it" (Cater, 1964:20; see also Lowi, 1969).

Sugar growers and refiners responded to this criticism by arguing that American domestic sugar production simply could not survive without government protection. In many respects, the structure of the world sugar market of this time bore out their claim, at least in part. Sugar lobbyists pointed out that of total world sugar production in the early 1970s, some three-quarters was produced for domestic consumption and never entered world trade at all; the Soviet Union and most Western European countries, for example, were both major producers and major consumers of sugar and in each case producers' prices were subsidized by the government and sheltered from the world market. Of the quarter of world sugar production that did enter the world market, about half was tied up in long-term purchasing agreements at fixed subsidized prices, arrangements similar in many respects to the U.S. Sugar Act; Britain, for example, purchased sugar at subsidized prices from the Commonwealth countries under the Commonwealth Sugar Agreement, while the Soviet Union, of course, maintained its long-term purchasing agreement with Cuba.

This left only about an eighth of total world sugar production to enter the "free" market. Since shortages among domestic suppliers under the long-term arrangements were overcome by tapping the small residual world market, a bad harvest in a single major producer could send world prices through the roof. But since production from an exceptionally good harvest in any major producer would usually be disposed of on the world market, free market prices could as easily fall very low, sometimes below the cost of production. As put by one commentator,

Trade takes place on the unstable and normally unremunerative residual world market because exporters have other markets at stable and remunerative prices. No major sugar industry could continue in production on its sales to the residual world market alone (Smith, 1975:46).

In the view of sugar producers and their supporters, the Sugar Act represented a mechanism that did no more for them than was done for producers in most other developed countries, shielding them from "dump prices, distressed merchandise prices for sugar that has no home" (Representative Mark Andrews of North Dakota, quoted in 1978 *Congressional Quarterly Almanac*, p. 465).

It was in this context that the Sugar Act of 1948 was regularly renewed with only minor adjustments, most of them concerned with increasing the domestic share of U.S. sugar consumption (about 60% of total U.S. consumption in the early 1970s, which represented a gradual increase from about 50% in the 1950s) or shuffling the shares of foreign suppliers, whose number by the early 1970s had grown to more than 30.[19] Although the Sugar Program had many articulate critics, it also had a very firm base of support in Congress from cane sugar states such as Louisiana and Hawaii, beet sugar states such as California, Idaho, Utah, Colorado and Michigan, and several urban, industrial states that were home to cane sugar refineries. The Sugar Program neared its 40th anniversary in a form at least as protective of the domestic and foreign suppliers of the American market as the original Jones-Costigan Act that was hastily devised in 1934 in the depths of the depression, and its continuance seemed assured for the indefinite future.

Suddenly, though, the low world market prices from which the American market was so thoroughly sheltered shifted dramatically. In late 1973 sugar prices, stagnant since the 1950s, began to climb as they had never done before. Part of the reason was that sugar stocks were depleted by poor harvests in Cuba and the Soviet Union in the early 1970s and a poor Western European harvest in 1973–1974. In addition, prospects for demand seemed better than usual due to American concern over the health risks of artificial sweeteners. Finally, demand for sugar was increasing rapidly in a number of countries of the Third World, particularly the "newly industrializing countries" of Asia and Latin America; historically, sugar has been one of the first commodities to increase in consumption with a rise in income.[20]

All of these factors redounded on the small world market and, spurred by pressure from commodity market speculators, served to

Table 6.2
World Sugar Prices, 1973–1982

Sugar "11" (World) New York   Weekly High, Low & Close of Nearest Futures

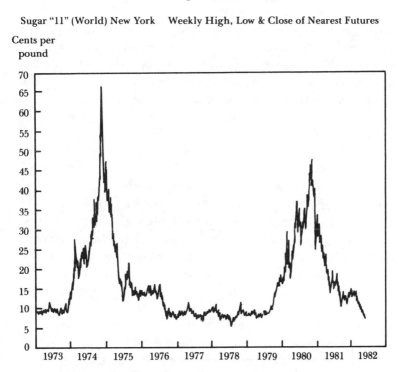

Source: Walter C. Emery, ed. (1982) *Commodity Yearbook*, 1982. New York: Commodity Research Bureau.

increase sugar prices dramatically: world market prices for raw sugar rose from under 10 cents per pound in 1972 to a peak in late 1974 of almost 60 cents per pound.

Suddenly the very rationale of the Sugar Program was turned on its head, as world prices rose to levels several times the price objective of the proposed five-year renewal of the Sugar Act, scheduled to expire on December 31, 1974. An increasing number of Congressmen found it difficult to vote for another renewal of the Sugar Act at a time when sugar prices were at historic highs, particularly since certain provisions allowed for direct payment to producers (according to volume) irrespective of market prices.[21] Matters were not helped by the fact that a large proportion of direct payments to "farmers" actually went to large-scale corporate producers, or by the embarrassingly large profits sugar refiners began to report in 1974.

One of the key characteristics of self-regulating "subgovernments" is that they operate unobtrusively, and when they are opened up to intense public scrutiny they often are subject to broader political forces from which they are able in ordinary times to shelter themselves. In this case, radically higher prices brought together a large and very diverse coalition in opposition to continuation of the Sugar Program (Ripley and Franklin, 1980:117–119). The core of the coalition was an unusual alliance of consumer-minded liberal Congressmen who objected to the sugar "profiteering" they had long criticized, and conservative Republicans, particularly from suburban areas, who were influenced not only by resistance to high prices by their constituents but also by an ideological predisposition against government interference in the economy. To this core were added a number of Congressmen with narrower interests: many members of the Congressional Black Caucus, for example, resented the fact that South Africa received a sugar quota under the act, while several Congressmen objected to the quota granted Venezuela in light of the 1973 increase in the price of Venezuelan oil.

Perhaps as important as the coalescence of opposition to the extension of the Sugar Program were strains in the sugar lobby itself. One of the major areas of strained relations was between growers and refiners. The central argument of sugar growers was that sugar prices were indicative of a genuine global shortage, and that Congress should thus significantly increase price supports within the framework of a long-term extension of the Sugar Program in order to encourage domestic self-sufficiency. Refiners, on the other hand, were convinced that the very high sugar prices of 1974 would be temporary and preferred not to be locked into a long-term commitment to substantially higher prices; this was particularly true of cane refiners who relied on imported cane.

By the time it reached committee stage the extension of the Sugar Act was attracting a great deal of adverse publicity, and its backers thought it necessary to make a number of concessions in order to bolster their support. Among other modifications to the earlier versions of the Sugar Act were provisions imposing an annual ceiling on sugar subsidy payments to any one producer, thus eliminating the embarrassingly large payments to owners of very large acreage, and several provisions to insure that increases in support prices would be passed on to farmers and not retained at the refining and marketing stages. Each of these proposals may have attracted some outside support for the bill, but each also served to dampen the enthusiasm of important earlier supporters: large producers, especially those in Hawaii, were opposed to limitations on maximum payments, while refiners were unenthusiastic about pass-on provisions.

In addition, provisions were added to the bill imposing a minimum wage that domestic growers were required to pay to sugar workers in an effort to attract support from organized labor. These proposals did result in some labor support, but they also contributed to a decline in enthusiasm for the bill on the part of some of its staunchest supporters; as put by House Agriculture Committee chairman, W. R. Poage, "I do not know why they do not bring the legislation they want and try to pass it on its own merits rather than try to pass it as the tail of a sugar program. . . . We have got to confine this to a sugar program and not make a social welfare program out of it" (*Congressional Quarterly Almanac*, 1974, p. 228).

In the end, in a vote that surprised even the critics of the Sugar Program, the bill in the House of Representatives to extend the program for five years was defeated on June 5, 1974, by a vote of 209 to 175. Despite several last-ditch attempts in the final weeks of the 93rd Congress to construct a stopgap extension of the Sugar Program, the program finally expired on December 31, 1974, ending 40 years of a thoroughly managed market for sugar.

Sugar's Seven Years in the Wilderness

For the first time since the depression, the American sugar market operated largely without government protection.[22] For a time, high prices allowed domestic sugar producers to take the loss of sugar subsidies and price protection in stride, and former holders of foreign quotas were compensated for their loss of guaranteed access to the American market by high world prices. Before long, however, the world price of sugar began to decline sharply from its 1974 high, and by late 1976 wholesale sugar prices had plunged to about 8 cents per pound, below the break-even price of most American producers. Growers and refiners alike pleaded for government protection, complaining that they were being forced to compete with foreign producers' residual sugar at a time when most foreign sugar producers enjoyed substantial government support of one sort or another.[23]

By 1977 pressure was building for the government to offer some measure of support to the domestic sugar industry. After temporary action by President Carter to support sugar at what was considered a break-even price of 13.5 cents per pound, Congress in mid-1977 passed a temporary measure of its own (the de la Garza Amendment) to support sugar at about 14 cents per pound through the 1978 crop year.

In 1977 the international community as a whole was also attempting to come to grips with disastrously low world prices. In September 1977, representatives of more than 70 countries convened in Geneva in an effort to negotiate a multilateral agreement to stabilize the price of sugar. After several weeks of complex and at times acrimonious negotiations, agreement was finally reached on October 7, 1977 on a mechanism to assign production quotas to major sugar producers and to establish a buffer stock to support the world price of sugar within the relatively wide range of 11 and 21 cents per pound.[24]

In an atmosphere of generally poor prospects for North-South economic management, the International Sugar Agreement (ISA) seemed to stand out as a modest but genuine success: producing and consuming countries bargained in good faith in pursuit of a goal — price stability — that was in the interest of both. Although neither side was entirely satisfied with the price objectives and quotas agreed upon, each had been willing to make concessions in the interest of escaping the extreme instability of sugar prices of the recent past.

The Carter Administration considered the completion of the ISA negotiations a prime example of successful North-South interaction, a case of the "management" of international economic "interdependence" to which many of its leading spokesmen attached great importance. Senate ratification of the ISA was thus one of the administration's important foreign policy objectives.

Sugar lobbies in the United States also favored ISA ratification, but they added emphatically that it alone was insufficient to protect their interests and that backup quotas and payments were needed if the industry were to remain solvent: the ISA's lower price objective (11 cents per pound) was, in their view, simply too low for American producers to cover their costs. (Ironically, lobbyists for manufacturers of high fructose corn syrup [HFCS], the main competitor of beet and cane sugar in the United States, also argued for high sugar price supports; they felt they could make inroads into the sweeteners market only if sugar prices were high.)

Senate ratification of the International Sugar Agreement thus became for the sugar lobby a vehicle to force the Carter Administration to support an acceptable *domestic* sugar program to supplement the ISA mechanisms. The administration found itself caught between conflicting desires. On the one hand it strongly favored Senate ratification of the ISA, particularly as other countries ratified the treaty and the United States began to look like a holdout in delaying ratification of a treaty it had originally strongly supported. On the other hand, though, the administration was firm in its conviction that large supplementary domestic sugar price supports would be inflationary and were directly contrary to the administration's stated goals of easing inflation and of deregulation in the interest of enhanced competition. Throughout 1978 sugar policy was the object of a truly byzantine series of maneuvers within Congress and by the administration. Central to the maneuvering was the stubborn refusal of generally liberal and internationalist Senator Frank Church of Idaho (a major beet sugar state) to move the ISA through the Senate Foreign Relations Committee, of which he was chairman, unless acceptable supplementary sugar price supports were forthcoming. Finally, after a full year of complex wrangling during 1978, a House-Senate conference committee hammered out a delicately balanced bill which the full Senate approved — only to see the House vote it down 194 to 177.

In 1979 the whole process began again. After another long year of proposals and counterproposals the House again killed a sugar price support bill, this time by a margin of over 90 votes. Once again sugar producers were frustrated in their efforts to achieve price protection, and the administration was just as frustrated in its efforts to achieve ratification of the ISA.

But, as is often the case in Congress, seemingly decisive action was in the end far from decisive. After consecutive defeats on the House floor, the administration and key members of Congress with an interest in sugar took matters into their own hands. Within weeks the administration came to an agreement with Frank Church in which Church allowed the ISA to reach the Senate floor in exchange for action by Agriculture Secretary Bob Bergland to use existing law to maintain a temporary sugar "market objective" of 15.8 cents per pound, lower than the 17 cents per pound Church had long demanded, but higher than the administration preferred or the ISA provided for. Within weeks of this informal agreement, the International Sugar Agreement was voted out of the Senate Foreign Relations Committee, where it had been stalled for over two years. It passed the Senate by a vote of 80 to 11.

Recent Sugar Legislation:
Moving Away from the Market in the Reagan Administration

By late 1979 the world market again began to intrude on the American domestic market: bad weather and crop diseases depleted harvests in Cuba and the Soviet Union, while a portion of Brazil's crop was used in its ambitious gasohol project. Ironically, just as American sugar production again became subject to reasonably generous price supports, the problem of low-cost competition that was behind the demand for such supports receded and they again became unnecessary. By fall 1980, sugar prices had risen as high as 45 cents per pound on futures markets, far above current domestic support prices.

But by mid-1981 the high sugar prices of 1980 had proven as ephemeral as those of 1974, and by late 1981, sugar futures had fallen to about 13 cents per pound. Serious pressure was again exerted to resuscitate comprehensive price supports as part of the 1981 farm bill. Although the budget-cutting Reagan Administration at first opposed sugar price supports as too costly and contrary to free market principles, the program was heavily lobbied and the administration eventually shifted its position in an all-out effort to attract necessary Southern Democratic support for its budget program. As put by John B. Breaux, Louisiana Democrat and sugar-state "boll weevil," when asked whether his vote on Gramm-Latta could be bought, "no, but it can be rented" (*Congressional Quarterly Weekly Report*, July 4, 1981, p. 1169).

Later in the year, the administration's backing of sugar price supports came under increasing criticism, especially in the House, the traditional hotbed of opposition to the sugar program. But in the end, just before Congress's adjournment on December 19, 1981, the House approved by two votes a broad four-year farm bill that included a commitment to support sugar at 17 cents per pound in the 1982 crop year, 17.5 cents in 1983, 17.75 cents in 1984 and 18 cents in 1985. After almost seven years of makeshift sugar support policies, the government was again committed to a formal program of comprehensive sugar price supports over an extended period.

The first component of the current program is a nonrecourse loan program under which sugar producers may use sugar as collateral for loans from the government at the established support rate. At any time up to the loan's maturation date, a processer may choose to forego the sugar and keep the loan if this proves to be more profitable than selling the sugar on the market. In order to avoid budget expenses, all loans are offered and mature in the same year.

The second, and decisive, component of the program relies on the control of imports in order to support domestic prices. When the bill was first passed in 1981 this was accomplished through a combination of custom duties and import fees, which were extended to the degree necessary to bring sugar to a desired "market stabilization price," the domestic support price plus an allowance for transportation, insurance, handling and other costs of marketing sugar. The first line of protection was a customs duty that could range up to 2.8125 cents per pound.[25] A second line of defense was the ability of the President to impose at his discretion import fees on agricultural products of up to 50 percent ad valorem, a blanket power established under the Agricultural Adjustment Act of 1933.[26]

Immediately after the Farm Bill came into effect, President Reagan took the action necessary to impose import fees sufficient to achieve the desired market stabilization price for sugar. Before long, however, world prices fell so low that it became impossible to defend the market

Table 6.3
United States Sugar Import Quotas
(short tons, raw value)

	Percentage share	1984 quota year
Argentina	4.3	131,150
Australia	8.3	253,150
Barbados	0.7	21,350
Belize	1.1	33,550
Bolivia	0.8	24,400
Brazil	14.5	442,250
Canada	1.1	33,550
Colombia	2.4	73,200
Costa Rica	2.1	64,050
Dominican Republic	17.6	536,800
Ecuador	1.1	33,550
El Salvador	3.0	91,500
Fiji	0.7	21,350
Guatemala	4.8	146,400
Guyana	1.2	36,600
Haiti	0.3	16,500[a]
Honduras	2.1	64,050
India	0.8	24,400
Ivory Coast	0.3	16,500[a]
Jamaica	1.1	33,550
Malagasy	0.3	16,500[a]
Malawi	0.7	21,350
Mauritius	1.1	33,550
Mexico	0.3	16,500[a]
Mozambique	1.3	39,650
Nicaragua	2.1	6,000[b]
Panama	2.9	88,450
Paraguay	0.3	16,500[a]
Peru	4.1	125,050
Philippines	13.5	411,750
St. Kitts	0.3	16,500[a]
South Africa	2.3	70,150
Swaziland	1.6	48,800
Taiwan	1.2	36,600
Thailand	1.4	42,700
Trinidad	0.7	21,350
Zimbabwe	1.2	36,600

[a]These countries are entitled to deliver either their percentage market share or the flat rate minimum of 16,500 short tons, whichever is the greater.

[b]Reduced to 6,000 tons in May, 1983.

Source: Computed from Womach (1983); U.S. Department of Agriculture (1984).

stabilization price even with the imposition of the maximum 50 percent ad valorem import fee. It became evident that without some action a substantial amount of sugar, up to 1 million tons, might have to be acquired by the government under the nonrecourse loan program.

On May 5, 1982, President Reagan took action to fundamentally alter existing U.S. programs by returning to a policy similar to the pre-1974 policy of formal import quotas for foreign suppliers of the American market at a price related to that of the domestic price guarantee. The quota allocations were determined by averaging a country's sugar exports to the United States for the seven years between 1975 and 1981 (after having discarded the highest and lowest years) and using this as the basis for dividing up the total United States import quota. (See Table 6.3.)

The effect on sugar exports was contradictory. On the one hand, the import quotas were (as was their intention) quite restricted: In contrast to the approximately 5 million tons of sugar that had entered the U.S. market during the 1970s the quotas since 1982 have totaled only about three million tons, which has unquestionably had a depressing effect on the world market price. On the other hand, countries awarded quotas in the U.S. market received a premium price for the sugar they did export to the United States, a price tied to the domestic U. S. support price which was more than twice what they could receive on the world market. Thus, while the quotas did prompt a negative reaction by many Third World sugar exporters, their opposition was muted by the fact that most quota recipients undoubtedly benefited financially from subsidized access to the United States market (even for less sugar) at prices much higher than the depressed world price.

One of the most controversial aspects of the new United States sugar policy has been its politicization. In May, 1983, the Reagan administration revised the quotas it had established for Nicaragua — which, as has been indicated, had been based on the average of recent sugar exports the United States — slashing its quota from 58,800 tons to only 6,000 tons and reallocating the balance of the Nicaraguan quota to countries viewed as friendlier to the United States.[27] Nicaragua immediately filed a complaint with the General Agreement on Tariffs and Trade charging that the United States had unfairly discriminated against it for political reasons.

More generally, there have been the inevitable difficulties of administering almost any quota program, even when the quotas have been determined by the objective standard of recent export performance. Some countries, such as Mexico, Peru, and Canada, whose exports to the United States had recently declined, received relatively high quotas because of large exports in the 1970s, while others, whose sugar exports to the United States had risen sharply in recent years (sometimes with the assistance of U.S. aid programs), received quotas far lower than their current exports.

At present the United States is in the fourth year of the 1981 Farm Bill, which is scheduled to expire at the end of 1985. Although the provisions of the bill affecting sugar could technically be amended at any time, it is almost certain that the sugar provisions will continue until the expiration of the Act as a whole. In 1985, however, there is some prospect that the sugar program will be seriously curtailed or even eliminated. Once again, the program faces articulate criticism on both the consumer-oriented left and the free-market right. Although President Reagan supported the sugar bill in 1981 and imposed quotas in 1982, he did so reluctantly. Should the government continue to be faced with unprecedented budget deficits, it is possible that he will attempt to atone for his previous actions by supporting the complete or partial deregulation of American sugar production.

On the other hand, the sugar industry retains most of its earlier supporters (less, of course, many cane sugar refiners, whose business has been seriously damaged by import quotas) and has in addition attracted new support from what may seem on the surface an unlikely quarter. As has been mentioned, the current sugar program has attracted backing from lobbyists for the corn/maize sweetener industry, the primary *competitor* of sugar in the United States. Only with a generous sugar support bill, corn sweetener interests reason, will their product be competitive; producers of corn sweeteners are no more able to compete with world sugar at six cents per pound than are domestic sugar producers, but they compete quite effectively with sugar at the domestic support price. As a result, their share of the American caloric sweeteners market has increased dramatically over the last decade to the point that they now represent over 40 percent of all United States caloric sweetener consumption (see Table 6.4). From the perspective of the United States domestic sugar industry this tacit alliance with the powerful corn industry is something of a deal with the devil. On the one hand, sugar producers welcome any support in maintaining a program they view as absolutely essential to their survival. On the other hand, however, their own price protection has allowed their main competitor to dramatically expand its share of the market. As a result, while the long-term prospects of the domestic *sweetener* industry in the United States are excellent, largely because of protection from foreign production, the prospects of the sugar industry itself are not as good, even if the sugar program is renewed in 1985.[28]

Conclusion

In viewing this case study in retrospect, it is difficult not to be impressed by the pervasively hierarchical character of the American-Third World sugar trade at every stage of its long history. The sugar trade was an invention of the West, created and maintained solely to satisfy the desires of the West, that nevertheless has had a profoundly disruptive impact on the people and societies it has touched. In surveying North-South sugar relations, there is no doubt whatever which countries and groups are of the "core" and which are of the "periphery"; the asymmetry of the sugar trade has been painfully evident for more than three centuries.

But in the case of the sugar trade the precise nature of this asymmetry has varied considerably over time, and its present character is quite different from the traditional notion of exploitation, whereby dominant countries (or transnational classes) use their advantaged position to intrude into Third World economies in search of essential labor or material resources for which they offer little in return.[29] In contrast to this traditional model, the prevailing theme of the North-South sugar trade since the mid-nineteenth century has been the eagerness of developed countries to promote the *domestic* production of sugar through subsidies and protective mechanisms, creating subsidized competition that Third World exporters have found very difficult to overcome. Thus, the extraordinarily intense exploitation in the eighteenth century Caribbean of land—almost complete cash crop cultivation with virtually all necessities imported—and labor— the revitalization of slavery after a thousand years of disuse—was replaced in the nineteenth century by the introduction of higher cost, but subsidized and protected, beet sugar in the European and American "core." Similarly, United States sugar policy shifted in 1974 from

Table 6.4
Caloric and Non-Caloric Sweeteners: Per Capita Consumption in U.S. Pounds, 1970-83, U.S.A.

Calendar	Caloric — Refined cane and beet sugar — U.S. grown sugar Beet	Cane	Total	Cane Sugar Imported	Total	Total	Corn sweeteners[1] Corn syrup HFCS	Glucose	Dextrose	Total	Minor caloric[1] Honey	Edible syrups	Total	Total	Noncaloric[2] Saccharin	Aspartame	Total
	(Pounds)																
1970	31.3	25.0	56.3	45.4	70.4	101.7	.7	14.0	4.6	19.3	1.0	.5	1.5	122.5	5.8	—	5.8
1971	30.6	22.9	53.5	48.6	71.5	102.1	.9	14.9	5.0	20.8	.9	.5	1.4	124.3	5.1	—	5.1
1972	30.3	25.3	55.6	46.7	72.0	102.3	1.3	15.4	4.4	21.1	1.0	.5	1.5	124.9	5.1	—	5.1
1973	30.2	24.7	54.9	45.9	70.6	100.8	2.1	16.5	4.8	23.4	.9	.5	1.4	125.6	5.1	—	5.1
1974	25.8	20.8	46.6	49.0	69.8	95.6	3.0	17.2	4.9	25.1	.7	.4	1.1	121.8	5.9	—	5.9
1975	30.1	24.6	54.7	34.4	59.0	89.1	5.0	17.5	5.0	27.5	1.0	.4	1.4	118.0	6.2	—	6.2
1976	32.0	22.4	54.4	39.0	61.4	93.4	7.2	17.5	5.0	29.7	.9	.4	1.3	124.4	6.1	—	6.1
1977	29.8	22.9	52.7	41.5	64.4	94.2	9.5	17.6	4.1	31.2	1.0	.4	1.4	126.8	6.6	—	6.6
1978	27.4	22.9	50.3	41.2	64.1	91.5	12.1	17.8	3.8	33.7	1.1	.4	1.5	126.7	6.9	—	6.9
1979	26.5	21.1	47.6	41.7	62.8	89.3	14.9	17.9	3.6	36.4	1.0	.4	1.4	127.1	7.0	—	7.0
1980	26.9	24.3	51.2	32.5	56.8	83.7	19.2	17.6	3.5	40.3	.8	.4	1.2	125.2	7.1	—	7.1
1981	25.6	21.5	47.1	32.4	53.8	79.5	23.3	17.8	3.5	44.6	.8	.4	1.2	125.3	7.2	—	7.2
1982	25.4	23.5	49.8	24.9	48.4	73.8	26.7	18.0	3.5	48.2	.9	.4	1.3	123.3	7.3	1.0	7.3
1983[3]	23.1	24.0	47.1	23.9	47.9	71.0	29.8	17.9	3.4	51.1	1.2	.4	1.6	123.7	7.2	2.0	7.2

[1]Dry basis. [2]Sugar sweetness equivalent—assumes saccharin is 300 times as sweet as sugar, and aspartame is 200 times as sweet as sugar. [3]Estimate.

Source: U.S. Department of Agriculture/ERS (1984d).

the 1934–1974 policy of fixed sugar quotas at subsidized prices to a policy of protecting American producers *from* lower priced Third World competition; since 1975 most Third World suppliers of the American market have been more "independent" than previously, but their independence is a decidedly mixed blessing in that it entails less protection from the vicissitudes of the world market than was afforded by the earlier Sugar Program. Indeed, as Third World sugar producers enter the mid-1980s they are at least as likely to be troubled by the possibility of being shouldered out of traditional markets because of a rise of protectionism in the West and an increase in the use of corn sweeteners produced in developed countries as by the closeness of their integration into markets in developed countries.

More generally, contemporary North-South relations seem to an ever increasing extent to be characterized by an eagerness of developed countries to promote domestic production of primary products that compete with products produced — usually more cheaply — in the Third World. It is, in fact, arguable whether for Third World countries the more common plight is exploitation or neglect: for every case of headlong, inequitable, foreign-oriented growth there would appear to be several cases of countries so marginal that they do not even attract exploitation. It is in these cases that unregulated capitalism, in the sense of seeking the highest short-term rate of profit attainable regardless of other considerations, is perhaps most pernicious: capital simply shuns unprofitable areas, confining them to the backwaters of the world economy. One is reminded of Joan Robinson's (1962:45) trenchant observation that "the misery of being exploited by the capitalists is nothing compared to the misery of not being exploited at all."

In examining relationships of this sort, there are at least two broad areas that can be singled out as being in need of special attention. First, there is a need for further analysis of the interplay between domestic and international factors that helps shape international economic policies. Third World critics of existing global structures have performed a very valuable service in directing attention to such linkages, particularly through their insistence on the tenuousness of autonomous policies in Third World countries, that are forced to operate within a conditioning international environment dominated by the developed countries. They have, though, been less attentive to the consequences for the Third World of essentially domestic policies of advanced industrial countries, which have often been at least as significant in determining the impact of the West on the Third World as have explicit foreign policies. Nineteenth century efforts to promote beet sugar were, for example, the result of policies designed to achieve domestic self-sufficiency in food and satisfy rural constituencies; the impact on Third World sugar producers has, nevertheless, been profound.[30] Similarly, the byzantine maneuvers over sugar policy in the U.S. Congress have been the product of competing domestic interests, but they too have had an important, if unanticipated, impact on Third World sugar producers. A key element of the asymmetry inherent in North-South relations is the way in which the offhand (at least in the broad scheme of things) actions of Western countries can nonetheless have profound consequences for underdeveloped areas.

A second area that deserves close attention is the interplay between political and economic factors in determining North-South relations. Third World critics of existing international trade structures emphasize the importance of economic disparities that skew international economic relations to the benefit of rich countries, and it is in this that another of their important contributions lies: it is difficult to see how traditional notions of free enterprise, supply and demand, and comparative advantage apply to an international market as hierarchical as the sugar market. But (and this is a point that critics do not as often stress) there are times when political concerns of developed countries override their apparent economic self-interest. The abolition of the slave trade by Britain and the United States in 1808 and of slavery itself in the British Empire in 1834 were, for example, products of a political movement that opposed some very powerful economic interests. Similarly, the American break with Cuba in 1960 was largely a triumph of political hostility at the cost of some economic loss. The irony of the Cuban break with the United States is that within months of Cuba's unwanted grant of economic "independence" from the United States it was forced to enter into at least as close a relationship with the Soviet Union, suggesting, perhaps, that another element of North-South asymmetry is that economic necessity is more inclined to overcome political will for small and poor countries than for large and rich countries. The Soviet Union, after all, was already self-sufficient in sugar when it agreed to purchase most of the Cuban harvest.

Both of these are areas that have been neglected but in which the recent revival of an earlier tradition of political economy has helped to reawaken interest. The intention of this case study has been to contribute to the development of this tradition by filling in the broad strokes painted by more general theorists of North-South relations with contextually sensitive historical detail.

Chapter 7

Politics and Agricultural Policies in the Western Hemisphere: A Survey of Trends and Implications in the 1980s*

JOHN J BAILEY

This chapter describes trends in agricultural policies in Canada, the United States, and Latin America since the latter 1970s and identifies significant political issues relating to national domestic affairs and interstate conflict and cooperation. It is convenient to use the 1970s as a starting point because the tight food market of 1973–74 alerted a broader audience to important emerging trends in global agriculture.

The Western Hemisphere, while closely integrated with the rest of the world, is interesting to consider because market and social interactions are intense and extensive, and a broad array of national and international private and public bodies are organized to think and act in regional terms. Further, the region is the home base of a turf-conscious superpower whose attempts to reconcile military-strategic interests with development concerns have pointed toward regional initiatives in which agriculture has figured prominently.

Our approach treats agriculture rather broadly and eclectically. Given the scope of the topic and the brevity of space, the result is more a satellite photograph than a detailed atlas. Even so, several countries

*The staff of the Economic Research Service of the USDA, especially Donna Roberts, Lisa Shapiro, and Paul Trapido, provided helpful advice. Adhip Chaudhuri, Mary Ott and Mitchell Seligson made suggestions for revisions, as did the project coordinators. The usual disclaimers apply.

(e.g., Panama, Paraguay, Barbados) fall outside the categories we propose and must be excluded. Nevertheless, a satellite view allows us to examine the broad sweep of trends that have enormous consequences in this hemisphere. Our goal is to synthesize recent studies in the context of rather widely accepted arguments in the conviction that ". . . the contradictions inherent in the region's pattern of growth must be analysed, sharpened and brought home to all social groups within the region and within the rich developed countries" (Barraclough, 1977:477).

The overriding goal of agricultural policy in Western Hemispheric countries (as elsewhere) is rapid, sustained economic growth. Agriculture contributes to this goal in two ways: providing commodities for the domestic market both for industrial use and food consumption, and for the international market to generate foreign exchange to finance imports. The argument in brief is that in settings of ample resources, relatively equal income distribution, advanced technology, and relatively limited reliance on imports for sustained growth, this twofold agricultural purpose may create tensions, but these can be managed through normal political processes. Such is the case of the United States and Canada. By contrast, in settings of relatively limited resources, grossly unequal income distribution, simple technology, and great reliance on imports to sustain growth, the domestic and external goals of agriculture come into such serious conflict that the resulting tensions frequently cannot be managed by normal political processes. Moreover, under acute conditions, the conflicts also produce a genuine economic dilemma where emphasis on one goal causes damage to the prospects of the other being realized.

The dilemma for a developing country, starkly put, is whether to emphasize production specialization and exports, or whether to strive for domestic agricultural self-sufficiency. Emphasizing exports means increasing the potential to earn more foreign exchange. Selecting agriculture for that function implies emphasizing an area in which a country has a comparative advantage in exporting the product. The extra foreign exchange earnings will, it is thought, enhance the country's import and debt repayment capabilities and also finance food imports to satisfy any resulting domestic food deficits.

However, such a specialization and trade strategy puts a country at a fivefold potential risk. (1) It may become vulnerable to the international market if export earnings are insufficient (due, for example, to the tendency of primary products to fluctuate in earnings to a greater extent than manufactured goods); (2) in exceptional circumstances, a country can become vulnerable to arbitrary interruptions in the market, as through politically motivated embargoes; (3) the additional investment in export-oriented activities may intensify the dualism within the agricultural sector, as more mechanized and capital-intensive operations begin to crowd the smaller, usually more labor-intensive farms, contributing to labor displacement, underemployment, and increased urbanization; (4) since most of the marketing channels are controlled by multinational firms, the country may be vulnerable to an increased importance of agents whose operations are not effectively under national control; and (5) the additional exchange earned may be spent unproductively, as in luxury imports.

On the other hand, if a country's agricultural strategy aims at food self-sufficiency, other problems converge: (1) foreign exchange that otherwise could have been earned is foregone, as is some portion of new domestic and foreign investment that might have entered to finance a profitable export strategy; (2) given the maldistribution of income in Latin America, if the market is allowed freedom to set prices for basic foods, poorer groups often cannot meet their needs; but (3) if prices are artificially depressed (as through price controls), new investment is dampened and agricultural production depressed, sometimes stimulating "black" markets; and, (4) if government sets prices high enough to stimulate domestic staples production through substantial public subsidies, investment in other areas is hindered (and/or inflation fed). Also, self-sufficiency, taken far enough, implies cutting a country off from technological advances in agribusiness, which in some instances might imply risks (e.g., vulnerability to disease in the case of the improved seeds industry) (L. W. Goodman, 1983).

The imagery of dilemma helps to clarify the nub of the issue, but it must be qualified. First, it exaggerates the present state of the problem, except perhaps in Mexico, Chile, and Venezuela. Second, some countries (e.g., Haiti) must rely heavily on food imports because of population pressures and limited arable land. But the arable land/population ratio varies among countries, and in some cases the potential for increasing agricultural output is considerable by bringing more land under cultivation and/or intensifying production (Inter-American Development Bank, 1983:19–35).

A word about policy context might be in order. Agricultural policy in the region is typically a "trait taker" in the sense of responding to cues from other areas (as opposed, for example, to import-substituting industrialization [ISI], which acts more as a "trait maker") (Hirschman, 1967:131). Thus, in a structural sense, the changing composition of demand that accompanies industrialization shapes production patterns in agriculture; and economic growth rates in Europe and the United States tend to accelerate or brake the pace of production both through direct and indirect linkages. Also, agriculture is notoriously vulnerable to the weather, which amplifies the unpredictability of policymaking.

As a further caveat, our emphasis on trade-offs and choices understates the pull of market forces that operate where there is a commitment (usually tacit) by late developing, dependent countries to emulate advanced capitalist societies. Market forces will be heightened in the near future as the United States intensifies agricultural specialization due to domestic imperatives and engages in export competition with Canada and Argentina (and possibly the E.E.C.) in the Western Hemisphere and elsewhere.

We structure this chapter to sketch recent trends in the region, noting their implications for the domestic and international goals of agriculture. We then move to analyze interstate conflict and cooperation. We attempt in the conclusions to speculate about likely directions for the near term.

I. Overview of Trends and Implications

Table 7.1 sets out some basic information with which to begin a description of the setting for agricultural policy in the region. The table groups the Western Hemisphere countries in a way that facilitates analysis of the themes sketched above. The primary distinction is between net agricultural exporters and importers (by value) because we assume that exporters enjoy a greater margin in which to choose some balance between domestic and trade requirements. Exporters/importers are then classified according to per capita income, which provides some indication about resources potentially

Table 7.1

Situational Factors of Agricultural Policy in the Western Hemisphere

Percentage Population Urban	Malnutrition	Net Exports Per Capita Income – 1980			Net Imports Per Capita Income – 1980		
		High (>1,900)	Medium (1,000–1,900)	Low (250–1,000)	High (>1,900)	Medium (1,000–1,900)	Low (250–1,000)
High (75–90%)	Low 0–39%	United States Canada Uruguay Argentina 1				Chile	
	High > 40%		2	Columbia	Venezuela		
	Low	Cuba			Trinidad/Tobago 4		

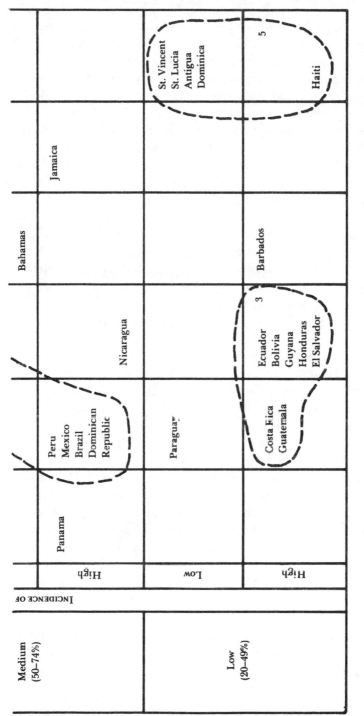

Panama

Peru
Mexico
Brazil
Dominican
Republic

Nicaragua

Paraguay

Costa Rica
Guatemala

Ecuador
Bolivia
Guyana
Honduras
El Salvador

3

Bahamas

Jamaica

Barbados

St. Vincent
St. Lucia
Antigua
Dominica

Haiti

5

High

Low

High

INCIDENCE OF

Medium
(50–74%)

Low
(20–49%)

Sources: Inter-American Development Bank (1981); *ibid.* (1979: 19); U.S. Department of Agriculture, Economics and Statistics Service (ESS) (1981); U.N. Food and Agriculture Organization (FAO), *Trade Yearbook*, 1980.

available to governments to finance policies. Grouping the countries by degree of urban population tells us something about the potential political pressures that consumers in a cash economy may generate as they pressure the government for cheap food policies. Finally, the 40 to 60 percent incidence of malnutrition in the countries indicates something about the seriousness of the nutrition problem.

Beginning with the net exporters, we stress first that the region as a whole is a net exporter of agricultural products (by value) as also are the majority of the countries in it. Second, the spread of wealth and urbanization in the region is fairly wide, although some clusters are identifiable. And third, malnutrition is prevalent in the Latin American subregion, using as a measure 0 to 39 percent of preschool children showing one or another degree of malnutrition as "low," and 40 to 82 percent as "high" (Inter-American Development Bank, 1979:19, 76).[1] This is the first of several indications that the general problem in the region is not the size of the aggregate agricultural product, but rather its composition and distribution.

Among net exporters, one cluster of countries is formed by the United States, Canada, Argentina, and Uruguay. An odd lot at first glance, these countries share a relatively high per capita income (at least U.S. $1,900 in 1980), have small rural populations (less than 30 percent), and exhibit a low incidence of malnutrition. Income distribution in this cluster tends to be relatively less unequal than in most of the rest of the Americas.

A second, and as we shall see especially interesting, country cluster consists of Colombia, Brazil, the Dominican Republic, Mexico and Peru. By adding an additional factor of population/arable land ratios, two distinct subgroups emerge from this cluster: Mexico and Peru, on the one hand, are really quite marginal net exporters with high population/arable land ratios; on the other hand and quite in contrast, Brazil, Colombia, and the Dominican Republic are strong exporters with relatively greater endowments of arable land per capita. These countries have reached an intermediate stage of economic development, with medium-to-high rates of urbanization and, with the exception of Colombia (U.S. $900 in 1980), medium levels of per capita income. Taken together, these countries account for 72 percent of the population and roughly 70 percent of the agricultural production in the Latin American subregion (Inter-American Development Bank, 1981:395, 404). These countries also have in common fairly high overall population growth rates (between 2.1 and 3.4 percent per year), large rural populations, and generally serious problems of malnutrition among young children. The governments in this cluster face in many respects the most vexing challenges: politicized urban groups demand cheap food; sustained industrialization requires export expansion; and income distribution is more unequal than in Group 1.

A third group among the net exporters includes the least developed, mostly Central American and Andean countries. These are small, largely agrarian economies, with low per capita incomes and large rural populations. All the Central American countries experience serious problems of malnutrition, which appears to a lesser extent in the Andean republics of Ecuador and Bolivia.

As one would expect, there is trade complementarity among the net exporters. The temperate zone countries of Group 1 export wheat, corn, sorghum, soybeans, edible beans, and meat products. Countries in Group 3 export sugar, bananas, cocoa, and coffee, for the most part. Except for Mexico and Peru, Group 2 countries export these commodities in appreciably greater volumes, and Brazil and Colombia also export soybeans and soybean products. Most of Group 2 and 3 countries are heavy wheat importers, and many import large volumes of corn, rice, beans, and feed grains. With these general observations, we can sketch a brief analysis of emerging trends in the context of policy choices.

Group 1: Wealthy Exporters

In agricultural terms, the United States, Canada, Argentina, and Uruguay are similar in many ways: each pursues similar policy goals of sustained growth with full employment; each vigorously pursues an agricultural export policy;[2] each is relatively highly urbanized; each has large urban labor and consumer groups that wield considerable political influence.

However, beyond these similarities it is useful to consider the countries in terms of matched pairs, with the United States and Canada forming one and Argentina and Uruguay the other. This is because the countries — as pairs — begin to diverge when we consider the degree of their agricultural mechanization and "technification," and sharply so when we consider the stability of the political and financial systems and the volumes of their production and sales.

Canada and the United States tend to share a basic vision of agricultural policy for the coming years. Both perceive agricultural exports to be of growing importance to their international trade and financial positions, and both have launched ambitious programs to promote export growth. Each sees a long-term trend toward tighter world grain markets, but nevertheless with export opportunities emerging especially in the Soviet Union and socialist bloc countries, and in the wealthier developing nations. Although analysts for both countries recognize that the 1980s will see considerable volatility in world grain markets and prices, it would appear that the United States agonizes more than Canada (at least publicly) about what sorts of policies to adopt to cope with the instability of the world food situation (O'Brien, 1981).

Canada's strategy for increasing grain production for export was unveiled by the Trudeau government in July 1981 in a policy paper titled "Challenge for Growth." The three main thrusts of the agrifood strategy are "market development, mission-oriented research and the upgrading and preservation of the basic land resources" (Whelan in *Agriculture Canada, 1981*:14). Canadian officials have been quite bullish about export prospects, setting a target of 36 million tons of grain by 1990 (compared with about 19 million tons in 1981) (Jarvis, 1981:4). These officials are confident that agricultural output can be increased by two-thirds by the end of the century if the technical and financial obstacles to production are removed. To assist in marketing, the Canadian agricultural export agency, CANAGREX, was established in June 1983.

Canadian grain production and exports have been at or near record levels during 1981–84, setting a pace even faster than planned. But strong world production of grains (except for the Soviet Union) and a slump in international wheat prices have hurt Canadian export earnings. Even so, the strength of the United States dollar (which gives the Canadians a market edge) and a less politicized commercial policy (including bilateral trade agreements) have acted to sustain Canadian exports, and farm earnings in 1982–83 have held up reasonably well.

As for the United States, its turn to increased production and export promotion marks a transition from a long period of inward-directed emphasis on policies to manage agricultural surpluses and support farm incomes. This period began with the mid-1930s New

Deal programs and continued with various efforts after World War II (D. Paarlberg, 1980:14–55). The transition began with the virtual doubling of world agricultural trade in the 1970s, which reinforced the overall national trend toward greater involvement in world trade and apparently changed United States farmers' attitudes and expectations. It was only logical for United States policymakers, regardless of ideological hue, to see exports as the ideal route to reduce domestic surpluses, increase farm and agribusiness incomes, and exploit an important comparative advantage. The Reagan Administration, with its zest for the magic of the marketplace, has brought a strong ideological commitment to free trade and the reduction of government involvement in farm programs.

The pro-export stance is seen in the words and deeds of the agriculture secretary, John R. Block. Summing up the Administration's two pillars of farm policy in his congressional statement of 1 April 1981, he stated: "One is to remove some of the risk from farming with the least possible cost to United States taxpayers. The second is to assure that the agricultural exports that have become so critical to this nation's economy will continue to be able to expand despite the difficult financial conditions many foreign countries are experiencing" (U.S. Senate, 1981:218).

Since then, however, the Agriculture Department has not devised a coherent export promotion policy. The secretary's main efforts in this regard have been to support modifications in the 1981 farm bill (discussed below), strengthen the Foreign Agriculture Service and gear more departmental activities toward exports, and travel extensively to potential market countries.

Congress's enthusiasm for exporting is clearly stated in the 1981 farm bill (PL 97–98), in which Title XII authorizes export credits, bilateral commodity supply agreements, discretionary export subsidies, embargo compensation, and continuation of PL 480. But somewhat in contrast to the executive's market orientation, the farm bill keeps alive an interest in international grain marketing agreements (providing that these benefit exporters). Also in contrast to the executive's market orientation, the farm bill keeps alive an interest in international grain marketing agreements (providing that these benefit exporters).

The years since 1979 have not been kind to United States farmers: record levels of production, depressed commodity prices (especially for wheat), and an agricultural depression in the midst of a gradual economic recovery. For the first time since the 1930s, land values and farm equity are on the decline. Among the several reasons, two stand out: production input costs, especially credit, are very high; and the export market has softened.

The Administration's response has been a dramatic retreat to surplus management together with a heightened, almost frantic search for export opportunities. In March 1983 the government announced its hastily conceived PIK (payment-in-kind) program, by which participating farmers take lands out of production in return for commodities from storage which they may use or sell. The rush to sign up was greater than expected, and PIK (along with crop losses due to drought) has provided some relief for the United States farm sector, while raising costs to the public (as consumers and taxpayers).

The longer-term implications of the export drive are both political and ecological. The export drive has reinforced the already pronounced trends toward land concentration and more sophisticated forms of agribusiness. This implies, as D. Paarlberg has noted (1980:5–12), that the family farm will continue to lose its symbolic sacredness as the public becomes increasingly aware of the reality of corporate agribusiness. Also, barring a sudden economic turnaround in the United States and elsewhere, income losses due to international trade may intensify pressure by farmers for government involvement in promoting trade (a topic reconsidered in the conclusion). Finally, a minority voice in the export debate maintains that the United States actually sacrifices by producing cheap grains, especially through soil deterioration and water depletion that result from intensive land cultivations (e.g., Soth, 1981).

Argentina and Uruguay also depend heavily on agricultural exports and are committed to increasing production for export. Argentina seeks to double its overall agricultural production by the year 2000. Argentina clearly has the resource capacity to reach this goal. The quality of its land and labor are among the best in the world. "Historically, less than 15 percent of Argentina's wheat acreage is fertilized, compared with 70 percent in the United States" (U.S. Department of Agriculture, Economic Research Service,* 1984c:7).

---

*All following references to U.S. Department of Agriculture, Economic Research Service will be listed U.S. Department of Agriculture/ERS.

The main impediment to Argentina's agricultural growth has been chronic and long-term economic mismanagement—reflected in frequent bouts of hyper-inflation, high interest rates (about 340 percent nominal per annum in 1983) and a frequently overvalued currency. On occasion (e.g., the Peronist interim of 1973–77), these problems have been complicated by pro-urban fiscal and commercial policies such as overvalued exchange rates with export tariffs on primary products that have in reality discouraged exports.

In contrast to the early Peronist fascination with import-substitution industrialization policies (1946–55) that directly penalized the traditional agricultural sector, a growing consensus has now been forged to promote exports, especially with a greater value added domestically through processing. The recent military governments (1976–83) sought to do this through market instruments; and one implication of the return to democratic rule is a shift toward more direct government intervention in the economy. But rather than a policy involving trade-offs between agriculture and industry, the choice concerns ways of promoting both sectors (and of better integrating them).

In sum, if financial impediments to promoting growth for export can be overcome, Argentina will raise its standing among major grain exporters. But the solution to financial constraints involves at base a solution to the half century of political crisis that is the root cause of the country's economic malaise.

Uruguay, a quite marginal agricultural exporter in comparison with Argentina, must also resolve its political disorganization in order to bring its economy under control and establish the basis for expanded production for export. In this respect, Uruguay enjoys perhaps brighter prospects than Argentina. Three factors figure here: (1) Uruguay's comparatively long experience with democratic rule has left society (including the army) committed to political democracy; (2) there is no movement comparable to Peronism; and (3) the Uruguayan army acted less brutally during 1973–83 and can thus disengage with less difficulty (González, 1983).

Agricultural self-sufficiency is virtually assured in the Group 1 countries, with the obvious exception of tropical products, such as coffee and cocoa. Certainly, food self-sufficiency is not a priority concern. Hunger is addressed by subsidy programs with direct payments to the poor (e.g., food stamps) or price controls on staples. Of

much greater concern is managing surpluses, maintaining farm incomes, and generating markets for exports.

The situation is dramatically different with the Group 2 nations.
Here market mechanisms produce serious distortions, affecting especially the lower income groups, who comprise a much greater portion
of the population than in Group 1. In Group 2 we find the choices
sketched in the introduction in starker form.

Group 2: Middle Income Exporters

A series of trends converge in these countries that lead to rapidly
increasing demands for agricultural products. Most of the trends are
well known and can be quickly summarized. Population growth has
been substantial in all the countries, and this per se has increased the
requirements for food; growing urbanization and rising urban incomes have also increased the total demand for food, and increased
consumption preferences for processed food products among lower
income groups is also apparent. This means that demographic and
economic growth translate geometrically into greater food demand.
Beyond this, industrial growth, intensely promoted since the 1950s,
has stimulated demand for agricultural products such as oilseeds,
cotton, wood, and sugarcane. Finally, agricultural products, long the
mainstay of most of these countries' export earnings, have regained
status with the turn away from import-substitution industrialization
and the increasingly outward-oriented growth of the late 1960s and
early 1970s (Keesing, 1981).

These trends promote a consolidation of agricultural lands and
an emphasis on production for middle and upper income groups
nationally and for exports generally. This is seen in such "new"
commodities as soybeans, fruits, and vegetables, which have joined
the traditional ones such as sugar, coffee, and cocoa; it is seen also in
sustained growth of the livestock industry, especially poultry. In
contrast, those commodities usually associated with lower class
diets—foods such as maize, beans, rice, and manioc—show a relatively "flat" performance, especially on a per capita basis. This,
taking into account skewed income distributions, suggests that the
nutritional situation of large portions of the population is probably
worsening.

Trends are even more dramatic with regard to imports. Here we see an impressive increase in sales, largely by the United States, of commodities such as dairy products, processed foods, and animal feeds, destined directly or indirectly for urban middle and upper income groups. In addition, United States exports of basic staples, such as wheat, rice, and edible oils, often are directed through government programs toward lower income groups, but nowhere on a scale commensurate with need.

Though there are variations on the theme in the various countries, at bottom the trends in production and trade reflect a setting of great income inequalities with pronounced dualism in the agricultural sector. In contrast to Group 1, these countries show a much lower and significantly less well distributed national income.[3] Thus there are significant differences in which the market functions to satisfy food needs. Middle sector groups and the better organized and paid industrial work force that live largely in the urban areas and comprise perhaps some 20–50 percent of the population participate well in the market as producers and consumers. For the small upper classes the market is a convenience, providing a range of goods and services comparable to the most advanced countries. But significant percentages of the populations simply cannot satisfy their dietary requirements through the marketplace. M. Selowsky (1979:8) has calculated that in the middle income countries (although his group includes Ecuador rather than the Dominican Republic) 25.4 percent of families are unable to finance an "efficient diet." This figure is lower than the observed incidence of persons experiencing calorie deficits, 36 percent in 1975.

Dualism, as used here, is taken to mean the coexistence of modern, well-managed production units (which may be of medium size, as in coffee or fruit; or quite large, as with soybeans, cotton, or sugar), alongside traditional, typically small-scale farming. The more modern units produce generally for middle and upper income groups, both domestic and foreign, and have access to credit as well as to public services designed to increase productivity. The more traditional producers typically lack these advantages, and produce more for subsistence, selling a variable surplus into the national markets. As Figueroa (1981) shows, the interactions of domestic urban growth and international trade do little to raise the incomes of the traditional farm sector. Beyond the small holders there is another stratum, often quite large, of landless laborers who live at the farthest margins of subsistence. To give some idea, Sloan (1980:49) cites a figure of 9 ½ million landless peasants in Brazil; the figure for Mexico is about 4 million.

The main factors that account for this pattern include a centuries-long history of extreme inequality, which has persisted largely unresolved (and probably worsened) into recent times. The surge of import-substitution industrialization (ISI) policies compounded the problem by diverting resources toward industry and neglecting (if not penalizing) agriculture. This implied slower relative growth for agriculture and a deepening of its dualistic nature. But politically, ISI allowed the double benefit of avoiding a confrontation with rural inequities and the power structure supporting them and of creating new bases of support for urban-oriented parties. There were, to be sure, efforts of varying intensity and effect to carry out land redistributions. By the mid-1970s, however, ISI and urbanization supported a shift in agrarian reform from distributionist policies (or rhetoric) to increasing production (Grindle, 1980).

Politically, then, the crux of the problem in the 1980s is how to manage systems with growing inequalities under generally worsening economic conditions (at least over the short run), as these countries, which developed inflation-prone and distorted economies in the ISI period, absorb the shocks of multiplied energy costs, heavy debt service, and global recession. One dimension of the problem is how to improve the production and thus the incomes of smallholders and their families, who still comprise large population percentages in group 2 countries. The problem is less a matter of government control or repression — although rural violence is frequent in most of these countries — than how nondisruptively to absorb these masses into an employment-scarce economy. The solution, whatever it might be, requires an enormous redistribution of resources and a reorientation of development strategies. In the absence of a solution, the rural poor migrate internally to the urban areas and internationally in search of employment.

The other dimension of the food problem concerns how to provide adequate nutrition for the urban poor. They are politically more visible and relevant to government stability than the rural poor. With open and disguised unemployment close to 25–40 percent of the work force in Group 2 countries, political stability is less assured, even under authoritarian governments. To date, urban outbreaks have taken the form of isolated protests, anomic eruptions (e.g., food riots in Brazil in July 1983), and large-scale social delinquency (e.g., crime, alcoholism) rather than of anti-system oppositions.

Brazil, Colombia, and the Dominican Republic are all fairly strong agricultural exporters, although on vastly different scales. They do have a margin for maneuver with regard to the putative trade-off between exports and self-sufficiency. Nevertheless, all rely heavily on agricultural products for essential foreign exchange to maintain economic growth; all have substantial urban populations and problems of income maldistribution; all suffer from dualism in their agricultural sectors; and all have large segments of their lower-income groups suffering nutritional deficiencies.

In the aftermath of Brazil's 1964 revolution, the new military government largely abandoned the anti-agrarian, cheap food policies of earlier populist regimes and emphasized an application of incentives for increased agricultural production, especially for export. With its enormous endowment of land, Brazilian policymakers could pursue both domestic and export goals by increasing production acreage and by intensifying the use of technology (Inter-American Development Bank, 1983:33). Export production benefited from preferential access to credit, relatively cheaper imports of fertilizers and machinery, and tax concessions. The result was a phenomenal growth of commercial agriculture, seen most dramatically in soybeans. In comparison, production of traditional food crops tended to lag behind (Barros and Graham, 1980) and the country was forced to use increasing amounts of foreign exchange to pay for imports of basic foods.

Brazil's growing reliance on wheat and other food imports began to create concern about balance of payments. Also, Brazilian authorities became more aware of the distributive implications of the pro-export policies, as agricultural smallholders fell into greater poverty. Thus, while agriculture remained a priority, the Figuereido government (1979–85) shifted emphases in 1979, largely to adjust agricultural policy to foreign exchange requirements: increased production of basic food crops and rapid development of alcohol from biomass (sugar cane) to reduce petroleum imports, and increased production of agricultural exports to earn foreign exchange.

After some progress in 1980–81 in promoting food production for domestic consumption, trends have acted to reinforce export promotion. These include credit restriction, currency devaluation, and anti-inflationary measures. Food production has stagnated while population growth has continued at about 2.5 percent per year. Nutrition programs have consistently ranked low among government priorities (Sanders, 1982b:17–18). Brazil has relied on United States wheat imports as a cheap staple, but in 1983 "since foreign exchange was severely limited, imports were not increaesd dramatically. The adjustment took place in demand — prices skyrocketed and per capita consumption fell" (U.S. Department of Agriculture/ERS, 1984c:5).

Using tax benefits as the main incentive, Colombia has been a leader in promoting and diversifying its agricultural exports. Disregarding illicit drugs as an example of successful innovation, Colombia has rapidly expanded its exports of soybeans, cut flowers, and cotton, benefiting largely the more commercialized producers (Grindle, 1980; Sanders, 1980). Land distribution, while important symbolically in the mid-1960s, virtually disappeared as an issue by the mid-1970s, and agrarian reform came to mean increased production by smallholders. The DRI (Integrated Rural Development) announced in 1976 and implemented after 1979 was directed toward farmers of 5 to 10 hectares. The principal thrust was to combine increased production inputs such as credit, fertilizer, improved seeds and irrigation, with additional requirements such as health care, education, and road building. Implemented in only 3 of Colombia's 18 departments by 1982, the government has maintained its commitment to DRI, but it is still too early to characterize the political and economic results.

With regard to provision of staples to the urban lower classes, Colombia's experiment with an administrative mechanism (IDEMA) in the later 1960s and early 1970s proved to be a financial disaster, although it did secure the political goal of undercutting support for the anti-government movement, ANAPO. Abandoning a public grain marketing agency, the government has relied on price supports for basic foods. These, however, have not provided sufficient incentives to small farmers, who find themselves in a severe cost squeeze due to high interest rates, land speculation (largely drug related), and increasing wages. Food prices have been allowed to rise with the market, and at rates generally higher than inflation. Organized consumers (e.g., union members, students) can find some protection in government-encouraged food-marketing co-ops, and public employees benefit from similar co-operatives administered by their agencies. It is not obvious how or whether the poorest and unorganized groups, which bear the full brunt of market forces, provide for their food requirements.

The Dominican Republic has long been a significant agricultural producer but has diversified exports perhaps less than Brazil or Colombia. However, like Brazil and Colombia, the Dominican Republic's recent policy trend toward smallholders emphasizes production, especially of staples; and government programs channel seeds, fertilizers, and credit as incentives. The Institute for Price Stabilization (INESPRE) was established in 1969 to regulate price supports and control imports. Thus far, the Dominican Republic has avoided the problem of heavy subsidies to producers and consumers. By granting INESPRE access to foreign exchange on favorable terms, the policy grants some degree of subsidy (about 10 percent currently) to urban consumers. The relatively greater reliance on imports by the Joaquín Balaguer government (1966–78) reflected a cheap food, urban bias. This was moderated by the shift toward staples production and increased attention to agriculture by the Guzmán Fernández (PRD) government (1978–82). Although the Dominican Republic, along with Jamaica and Trinidad, is a significant food importer, ". . . it would take very little acreage from export crops to make up the 20 percent food deficit" (Bolling, 1983a:8). This would imply, however, approximately a 15 percent reduction in exports and a cut in wheat products as well as in poultry and pork which are produced from imported feeds (*ibid.*).

Mexico and Peru, on the verge of becoming net importers, face perhaps a stiffer challenge. Peru, lagging decades behind most of the other Andean countries in political reform, experienced significant reforms under the Velasco Alvarado government (1968–75), which succeeded to some degree in redistributing resources (although limited somewhat to the relatively better-off workers and peasant groups) (Webb, 1975:121; and C. McClintock, Ch. 3, this volume). But the reforms, along with some adverse economic and climatic conditions, led to a serious economic recession during the latter 1970s. This was in turn complicated by bouts of bad weather during 1978–83. In all, per capita food and agricultural production dropped below the 1969–71 average. Despite the planning rhetoric of the Velasco period, one analyst (Kennedy, 1983) doubts that the government of the armed forces really followed a coherent food and agriculture policy. Regardless, reforms and the drops in agricultural production led to greater reliance on imports and an increase in subsidies on politically sensitive staples, rice and wheat.

More recently, the Belaúnde government (1980–   ) has shifted policy toward small farmers in ways that reflect concern over production (e.g., allowing cooperative members the option of private title to their holdings). Also, the anti-business rhetoric of the military reform government has been muted, and actions to promote agribusiness have been taken. The government has been attempting to dismantle the high levels of subsidies to consumers, a step that clearly has begged trouble for the fledgling democratic government.

As for Mexican agriculture, inadequate food production and deepening dualism have been evident since the mid-1960s. Mexico's close economic integration with the United States, seen for example in exports of winter vegetables, fruit, and feeder cattle and in wheat and sorghum imports, has created a more pronounced pattern of dualism than in most of the other countries of the region (Sanderson, 1981a, 1981b, and Ch. 5, this volume). By 1971, Mexico had begun to import food for the first time in several decades.

The oil bonanza, which got underway in 1977, was seen as the opportunity to attack the agricultural problem. Nearly half way through his term (1976–82) José López Portillo announced SAM (the Mexican Food System), certainly the most complex and ambitious of the integrated rural development schemes to date, designed to assist small-scale rainfed farming and to improve nutrition among the urban and rural poor. It was anticipated that much of its funding would come from the oil revenues.

The short-term goals were to achieve self-sufficiency in corn and beans by 1982 and in other products by 1985. Though SAM involved an array of policy instruments, the key was high support prices for food crops. In essence, Mexico's strategy was to increase financial subsidies to agriculture—from the improved seeds provided by PRONASE to the sale of products by CONASUPO—and to undertake a series of longer-term programs to increase production and reorient consumer behavior toward more nutritious diets. SAM, in conjunction with ideal growing conditions, produced dramatic production increases in 1981, and virtual self-sufficiency in corn and beans was indeed reached by 1982 (U.S. Department of Agriculture, Economic and Statistics Service, 1982).

However, the economic distortions created by the overheated, petrolized economy forced a 40 percent devaluation in February 1982, which in turn undercut the price supports. With subsequent devaluations, high inflation, and at least two years of fiscal austerity ahead, it is clear that the enormously expensive program of agricultural revitalization (about U.S. $13 billion in 1981) cannot be continued. But with widespread reliance on food subsidies to low-income consumers, neither is it clear how the program can be suspended. The recent increases in staples prices (corn tortillas and white bread rolls) demonstrate that the government of Miguel de la Madrid (1982–88) will move to stimulate production through the market (Bailey and Roberts, 1983).

Group 3: Least Developed Exporters

If conditions are serious in Group 2 countries, they are positively critical in Group 3. With regard to the Central American countries, all have experienced economic downturns, and several have endured severe economic contractions due to internal wars. These countries are largely exporters of traditional agricultural commodities: bananas, coffee, sugar, and cocoa. They have been, by and large, rather more market-oriented than Group 2 countries, with less direct government involvement in agriculture generally and less attention to the needs of traditional smallholders or the urban poor. Clearly, in Nicaragua (discussed in a separate section), El Salvador, and Guatemala, the internal wars stem in good part from agrarian grievances, and in some respects it seems accurate to think of the present violence in the region as the consequence of adjustments long postponed. The political-economic difficulties have retarded growth in overall agricultural production, which declined by about 1 percent in 1983, following a gain of less than 2 percent in 1982 (U.S. Department of Agriculture/ERS, 1984c:12). But El Salvador's agricultural output, due in large part to its protracted civil war, has declined nearly 28 percent during 1979–82 (U.S. Department of Agriculture, Economic and Statistics Service, 1982).

Among the most traditional and least developed of the South

American nations, Ecuador has made little progress in its agrarian reform efforts, taken to mean either land distribution or increased food production. Handleman (1980:11) found that "in sum, all agrarian reform efforts [from 1964] through 1979 have touched less than 20 percent of the peasant population and less than 15 percent of the agricultural land." Production of food crops generally kept pace with population growth until the latter 1970s when a decline set in (aggravated by drought).

Faced with stagnant production (and an increased capacity to import food, using petroleum revenues), Ecuador's food imports (primarily wheat) rose from $19.2 million in 1972 to nearly $100 million in 1978 (*ibid.*, 14).

Nor is there much political support for either increased land distribution or higher price supports for food crops, since the major parties are either urban-oriented or influenced by conservative landlords (*ibid.*, 17).

Bolivia, the poorest of the Andean countries, was the first in the region to experience relatively large-scale land redistribution. That 1952 reform is often cited to typify fall-off of agricultural production as land recipients improved their living standards and government failed to provide the needed support programs. During the Hugo Banzer dictatorship (1971–78), a period of relative political calm and economic growth, agricultural production increased (and the problems of illicit drug cultivation and processing, of considerable importance in agriculture and the economy, intensified, especially after 1976). Since then, the Bolivian economy has virtually stagnated, due in good part to political chaos, and agricultural production (with the exception of soybeans!) has dropped below the levels of 1969–71. When governments reach the stage of disorganization characterized by Bolivia, agricultural policy becomes fragmented and producer groups pursue defensive strategies to minimize risk. Regardless, malnutrition is a serious problem even during years of normal agricultural production. In times of drought, as in 1982–83, there are fears of famine, especially in areas as hard pressed as Potosí.

Worth noting in Group 3 is that Costa Rica in the mid-1970s attempted a limited policy of food self-sufficiency by raising support prices for grains. The costs proved so great, however, that as international grain prices fell in the latter 1970s, the policy was deemphasized.

Whatever the intensity of the trade-off between exports and self-sufficiency, and it is apparently considerable in the cases of Mexico, Peru, and Costa Rica, the countries of Groups 1–3 have some degree of maneuver in structuring their policies. This sort of "political space" diminishes as we shift our analysis to the net importers.

Group 4: "Petrolized" Importers

Both Venezuela and Trinidad/Tobago reflect the economic distortions of petroleum-led growth. The basic notion of petrolization is that a large portion of gross domestic product and of exports consists of petroleum. This is usually accompanied by an urban-oriented industrial and services bias, with agriculture relatively neglected. As part of progressive welfare policies, food subsidies for the urban population, particularly the lower income groups, are adopted. The consequence is to stimulate food imports, which are considered financially and politically "cheaper" in the short run than the modernization of agriculture to supply the local market. Once these processes get underway they become difficult to control and virtually impossible to reverse due to the accumulation of vested interests and popular expectations.

Venezuela is typical of this "petroleum syndrome." After the emphasis on agrarian reform under the Acción Democrática governments of 1945–48 and 1953–63, agriculture receded from importance. The demographic and economic factors that characterize the middle income countries were exaggerated by petroleum wealth. Through subsidies the government kept staple prices down, usually below world levels. In 1970, the Agricultural Marketing Agency was created to administer an increasingly complicated and expensive subsidy program. Liberalized food imports, decreed on an emergency basis in 1976, became in effect routine. By 1978, Venezuela was importing nearly 70 percent of its basic foodstuffs. The gradual attempt to shift the impact of agricultural policy away from income redistribution and toward increasing agricultural production has not succeeded, although some progress was reported for 1983–84. The key obstacle continues to be a cheap food policy that has discouraged production. The Christian Democratic (COPEI) government of Luís Herrera

Campíns (1978–83) attempted to reduce food subsidies and suffered politically for the effort (Martz, 1980:38–53). Venezuela continues to import more than 50 percent of its total food consumption, with nearly 60 percent originating in the United States (U.S. Department of Agriculture/ERS, 1984c:10).

While in Trinidad/Tobago petrolization is not so far advanced, the policy nevertheless has led to neglect of agriculture. Food production for domestic use increased by only 1.4 percent per year after 1960, barely matching population growth. Even so, the majority (65 percent) of the island's arable land is devoted to export crops. "In 1980, Trinidad produced only 35 percent of its own food needs but produced substantial quantities for export" (*ibid.*, 4).

Group 5: Least Developed Importers

These poorest countries of the Hemisphere — St. Vincent, St. Lucia, Antigua, Dominica, and Haiti — lack the basic infrastructure (skilled labor, energy) to attract foreign investment in meaningful quantities and thus participate more fully in the regional economy. The subregion is characterized by high unemployment and economic stagnation. Yet, with the exception of Haiti, which suffers high levels of malnutrition, the key problem of agriculture is not just population pressure on arable land but also realizing the production potential that exists. Output could be expanded greatly, and agribusiness might become the key to development if investment and effective management were available. But important attitudinal problems must be overcome. Outmigration is strong from the area, and a foreign-oriented mentality characterizes much of the population. As R. Palmer correctly notes (1981:5), "There is no greater obstacle to developing self-reliance at home than this, for it conditions the mind to think of abroad as where the good things are."

The countries described to this point have crafted policies in a more or less incremental fashion, attempting to reconcile competing goals by granting at least some attention to all, yet not succeeding completely in any. The final cluster of countries considered is characterized not by similar objective circumstances but rather by their nonincremental approaches to food and agriculture.

The Radical Exceptions: Chile, Cuba, Nicaragua

Chile: While several of the countries in the region have moved to reduce the role of government in the economy in order to increase efficiency of production, Chile stands alone in the radical nature of its liberalization policy. Certainly, intense hostility to the socialist program of Salvador Allende was a factor, but more important was the ability of a group of "true believers" in the market economy (the so-called "Chicago boys") to gain access to military leaders who were casting about for new policies (Sanders, 1983:2–3).

The Pinochet government (1973–   ) began with a wholesale commitment to dismantle his predecessor's administrative controls on the economy. But change in agriculture came about more slowly than in the other sectors. The early policy emphasis was to stimulate export crops, and the government offered research and extension services toward this end. After mixed results with several products, vegetables, fruits and viniculture proved successful. Production acreage was shifted in significant quantities into these areas. The decontrol of basic food prices came about more gradually, and the government did not decide to remove protection from foreign imports until late 1976. Even then, protection was granted to wheat growers. Gradually supports were removed; duties on wheat imports were reduced in 1977; bread prices were decontrolled in 1978; and the price support system was ended in early 1980. By this time, opposition was growing, not from the urban poor (firmly under control) but rather from producers, especially wheat growers. The contention was that Chilean farmers could compete effectively with foreign producers in very few areas. Yet even while economic policy seems to be unravelling in basic ways (e.g., high inflation, devaluation, foreign debt), the government has held firm on trade liberalization. Farmers must find satisfaction in government attempts to facilitate exports, ease tax treatment for certain types of landholding, and channel credit to agriculture; however, increased price support for wheat in 1983 may portend broader changes. With the economy reeling from a 15.4 percent plunge in GDP in 1982–83 (Inter-American Development Bank, 1984:252), pressures for change mount.

Cuba: Since 1959 the Cuban government has sought to raise rural living standards, increase agricultural production, and integrate the countryside into the Revolution. At times these goals have come into conflict. By way of gross generalization, one might characterize the period 1959–71 as one of abrupt swings in policy, followed by greater pragmatism and moderation during 1971–83.

Quickly on the heels of the 1959 land reform, the government attempted to deemphasize sugar production and to diversify agricultural production as part of a broader import-substituting industrialization scheme designed to reduce Cuba's dependency as a monocrop exporter in the world economy. This tack was abandoned in 1962, and the government returned to stressing sugar production for export. The export drive took on crusade-like zeal in the latter 1960s with the goal of achieving a 10-million-ton harvest for 1970. Though falling short of the goal, the country subsequently has retained a specialization-and-trade strategy, while at the same time working to increase domestic food production.

The radical shifts in agricultural policy created serious disruptions in the island's economy, and the policy style after 1971 was markedly more pragmatic and gradualist. Much effort went into raising living standards in rural areas, providing housing, education, and medical care on an impressive scale to workers on state farms.

The Castro government steadily pursued its goal of reducing private property, employing the tactic of persuasion (e.g., credit and other services to farmers who joined cooperatives). Smallholders had been organized into the National Association of Small Farmers (ANAP) in 1961, and the government used this association as a mechanism for regulation and consultation. Relations between the government and ANAP were strained during the latter 1960s and early 1970s as resources were devoted preferentially to the larger-scale sugar enterprises, and small farmers complained of inadequate prices offered through the government crop-purchasing system (*acopio*).

In the latter 1970s relations improved as Castro recognized the error of past discrimination against smallholders and promised to ease the pressure on them to transfer their plots to state farms. Subsequently the government increased tractor allocations to the private sector and raised *acopio* prices. A significant step was taken in May 1980 when the government established "farmers' free markets," allowing farmers to sell surpluses on the market after meeting their *acopio* quotas.

By the early 1980s, the Cuban government still faced two basic problems: First, the nation's record of food production had not been impressive (especially on a per capita basis), and the state farms had not done particularly well. Cuba still had to import substantial quantities of foodstuffs (especially wheat, beans, and meat). Second, the smallholders tended to be the more dynamic food producers; yet the government remained committed to the goal of socializing the rural sector (Forster, 1982).

On the consumption side, it is difficult to characterize trends in Cuba with much precision, due in good part to data problems. Yet, as Forster and Handleman (1982:6) point out:

virtually all analysts agree (and government statistics suggest) that per capita caloric consumption is probably a bit lower today than before the Revolution. *Average* consumption of basic foods such as rice, black beans, most vegetables and tubers, many fruits (excluding oranges), and of "luxury foods" such as meat and coffee is undoubtedly lower than in the years immediately preceding the revolution. Only in the consumption of eggs, fish, and some dairy products (yogurt) has per capita intake increased significantly.

On the other hand, experts agree that malnutrition among lower income groups, especially those in rural areas, has been virtually eradicated. The apparent discrepancy between fairly mediocre food production and average per capita consumption and the eradication of malnutrition "... lies in the effects of two government policies: first, dramatic income redistribution; and, second, mandatory equity—imposed through rationing—in the consumption of most basic foods" (*ibid.*, 7). Thus, urban middle income groups have suffered a decline in dietary standards since the Revolution, but more equitable distribution of income and food has improved the nutritional levels of lower income groups throughout the island (*ibid.*).

Though most are quick to deduce one or another lesson from the Cuban experience (usually to demonstrate the correctness of an ideological stance), it does seem to demonstrate two points: (1) political radicalism cannot define away the tensions between the trade and domestic goals of agriculture, and (2) the costs of attacking the centuries-old problem of maldistribution of wealth are impressively high.

Nicaragua: The FSLN came to power in Nicaragua in 1979, encountering food and agricultural problems typical of the subregion: serious malnutrition and highly skewed land tenure patterns, with most of the more capital-intensive units (many in the hands of the Somoza family) engaged in export activities while smallholders pursued subsistence agriculture or provided basic staples for the national market. The new government adopted the goals of raising rural living standards and providing affordable foodstuffs to urban groups. Some sacrifice of exports was acceptable in pursuit of the main goals. According to Colburn (1983), the agrarian reform sought to provide greater access to land at reduced costs for poorer peasants, the formation of cooperatives, and greater quantities of credit for rural producers. The reform ran into most of the typical difficulties: e.g., peasants resist joining cooperatives, preferring to work for and by themselves; credit without extensive inputs does little to increase production; peasants "misused" credit for immediate consumption and much of the money was not repaid. On the consumption side, measures were taken to set price controls on staples, subsidize the sales of imported foods, and channel retail marketing through a state agency (ENABAS), to provide cheap food, mainly for urban consumers. Even with price controls, the policy proved very expensive.

Considering that the total financial deficit of the government in 1980, according to the Plan of Reconstruction, was to be 900 million cordobas, the subsidy of ENABAS represented 17 percent of the deficit. This subsidy has increased every year. In the fourth year of the revolution, the subsidy to ENABAS was the largest government expenditure after defense (Colburn, 1983:14).

The real costs rise, of course, when one factors in the foreign exchange forgone by the displacement of exports.

Two additional findings are significant. First, the government's direct efforts to aid the rural poor with land and credit were overcome by general economic policies that tended to favor urban consumers (e.g., cheap food, overvalued exchange rates), resulting in a shift in the terms of trade against rural producers generally (including smallholders) and reducing incentives to expand production of staple crops. Second, the shift in power relations in the rural setting provided an opportunity to combine domestic and trade goals by emphasizing staple production on both large state farms and small holdings. Surpluses of maize and beans might have been exported to other countries in the subregion in part because Nicaraguan white corn is preferred to the United States yellow variety for preparation of corn meal (Colburn, 1983:24). But this opportunity has not been grasped.

If Dix (1983) is correct, both Cuba and Nicaragua are distinctive as modern revolutions in their relatively advanced stage of modernization (in comparison with Mexico or Russia) and the comparatively lesser importance of the peasantry in the seizure of power. The urban constituency and urban bias of the Sandinista leadership might account for aspects of the agricultural policy. The Castro government, however, moved quickly to radicalize the agrarian reform, debilitate the urban middle and upper classes, and establish a power base in the countryside. Perhaps clues to understanding lie in the broad-front nature of the Sandinista government and its collegial style of decision making, in contrast to Castro's ability to consolidate power quickly, eliminate his adversaries, and personalize decision making.

II. Interstate Cooperation and Conflict

Commerce, communications, and migrations have vastly intensified among the Western Hemisphere nations since the 1940s. For the most part, the dominant trend is an incomplete and frustrated pursuit of cooperation; and while conflict, except in isolated cases, is rather too strong a term to describe past relations in the region, its potential and probability are clearly increasing. Two broad areas affecting agricultural and food issues will be discussed here: subregional integration and bilateral relations. (Multilateral commodity agreements, while relevant to agriculture in the Hemisphere, go beyond the present scope.)

Since the disintegration of the Spanish and Portuguese empires, the Latin American countries have sought some form of reunion. These nations, along with the former French and English colonies, have turned to economic integration since the 1950s and 1960s. But significant results have not yet been achieved. The Inter-American Development Bank, a major proponent of integration, probably understates the situation. "Although political support for the integration process in general was expressed at the highest government levels, it was not translated into concrete activities and great wariness was to be noted in the adoption of community decisions" (Inter-American Development Bank, 1981:103).[4]

Economic integration of the Latin American region as a whole has not succeeded. In August 1980, the Latin American Integration Association (ALADI) was created to replace the Latin American Free Trade Area (LAFTA), and intra-zonal trade has increased somewhat in recent years, especially in fuels and food product. The Andean Common Market, suffering from internal strains and the withdrawal of Chile after 1973, appears to limit its activities in agriculture to plans and research. The Central American Common Market (CACM) is at a virtual standstill due to the violence and political conflict in the region. Not much constructive action can be expected over the short run, although the members will have to find some basis of cooperation to prevent the spread of coffee rust, which threatens the economies of all. The Caribbean Economic Community (CARICOM) is something of an exception with its emphasis on agriculture as the "cornerstone" of development. Several plans and studies to develop a food strategy for the subregion are underway, with the ambitious goal of shifting from traditional patterns of outward-oriented traditional crop export, ". . . to a course in which resources are specifically allocated to the joint development of food production" (Inter-American Development Bank, 1981:122). In all, the impression is one of plans and intentions. The major islands, especially the Dominican Republic—which would seem to be crucial to a food strategy—have shown interest but little concrete action. Nevertheless, the islands do cooperate where possible; there is increased consultation and interest in a food strategy; and there is a growing basis for limited forms of integration.

More tangible with regard to Caribbean economic cooperation is the extension of the Mexican-Venezuelan Oil Facility beyond Jamaica and Barbados to include the islands of the Eastern Caribbean. With the involvement of these regional powers, one might see a pattern of partial integration on a scale greater than CACM or CARICOM but less than ALADI.

De facto economic integration has long been underway in the northern parts of the Hemisphere, but formal association on a subregional basis remains at the idea stage and appears to have little prospect in the short term. The two most important concepts are the North American Accord and the Caribbean Basin Initiative.

The North American Accord enjoyed a brief flurry of interest in the opening stages of Ronald Reagan's 1980 presidential campaign. Involving Mexico, Canada, and the United States, the idea called in vague terms for closer forms of association. Neither the Mexicans nor the Canadians encouraged the proposal, and it quickly disappeared. Through 1984, the climate of cooperation between the United States and Canada worsened, and little progress in resolving outstanding issues was made between the United States and Mexico. The basic issues are economic: trade and investment. Both Canada and Mexico seek greater control over United States investment to assure its contribution to the national objectives; and both countries advocate local content requirements to increase national investment and employment and export requirements to assist balance of payments. In addition, Mexico seeks exceptions to United States trade restrictions due to its special status of an underdeveloped country sharing a border with the world's major economy, a situation unique in the world.

Industrial development, not agriculture, is the main concern in the North American idea, and it would seem that the basis for cooperation in agriculture, even where present, is not strong enough to overcome tensions on industrial development policy. Agriculture, in fact, might be taken hostage in the dealings on industry, since Canada can provide many of the same sorts of commodities as the United States. Thus, the Accord seems unlikely to prosper and is kept alive in the United States Senate by Max Baucus (D.-Montana), whose main interest is Canada and whose present tactic is to seek fairly specific and limited areas of agreement, such as automobile manufacturing.

Announced by President Reagan in February 1982, the Caribbean Basin Initiative shows his continued interest in subregional cooperation and represents an innovation in United States foreign policy:

This economic proposal is as unprecedented as today's crisis in the Caribbean. Never before has the United States offered a preferential trading arrangement to any region. This commitment makes unmistakably clear our determination to help our neighbors grow strong (*The Washington Post*, 25 February 1982:A12).

Although the Initiative proposes technical assistance, tax preferences (if Congress approves), and direct foreign aid, the main emphasis is one-way free trade with the United States. This would seem a bit puzzling, because as the U.S. Department of State (1982:10) notes:

Presently, the countries of the region are already afforded a liberal entry into the U.S. market. (In 1980, $6.4 billion out of total Caribbean basin exports to the U.S. of $10.5 billion were free of duty; a large part of dutiable trade was accounted for by petroleum — $2.7 billion — for which tariffs are not economically meaningful.) Nevertheless, some of the duties which remain in place are in sectors of special interest to the Basin countries. They also limit export expansion into many nontraditional products.

Agricultural modernization is a key feature of the Initiative, and the clear thrust is comparative advantage and market integration. "Caribbean basin countries need to better gear their agricultural production to the standards of the world market, to better serve their domestic and export needs both in terms of *quality and seasonal availability*" (*ibid.*, 20–21).

Whatever the intentions of the Initiative, it has encountered a skeptical reception in the subregion and within the United States. Mexicans have been cautious about the national defense overtones of the plan and have attached conditions to their cooperation; Venezuelans were more receptive until the United States supported Great Britain in the Falkland Islands war of May 1982, after which their support quickly diminished. In the United States, labor groups opposed the potential loss of jobs; liberals saw the initiative as a smoke-screen for greater United States military involvement in Central America; and conservatives opposed the foreign aid expenditures. Despite this, the Administration gained passage of the aid and trade portions of CBI in late 1982 and early 1983. The critical investment tax provision, however, was rejected by Congress.

With regard to bilateral dimensions of agricultural policy, the trend toward grain agreements has accelerated since 1974. The United States, Canada, and Argentina have entered into several such agreements, principally with nations outside the Western Hemisphere. (Mexico, which has supply agreements with both the United States and Argentina, is the main exception.) Suppliers seek grain agreements as a gesture of political good will and as a means to protect their shares of world markets. For the large or relatively dependent LDC importers, Huddleston (1982:6) suggests

the motivation is their desire to lock in future supplies in a world market they perceive as treating them unfairly and which they expect to be increasingly unreliable due to lower world stock levels and the unpredictability of Soviet demand.

There are sensible commercial reasons that bilateral grain agreements are unlikely to exert a major influence on world markets (*ibid.*, 5–7). Though bilateral pairings are conceivable, the main regional implication would seem to be that this sort of agreement might exercise a slight centrifugal pull outside the Hemisphere.

The so-called "food weapon," another item best treated under bilateral relations, exerts an interesting influence. The partial embargo on grain that President Carter placed against the Soviet Union in 1980 jolted many Latin American leaders into taking another look at their food circumstances. Even the conservative Inter-American Development Bank voiced concern about the level and rate of growth of food imports:

... the problem takes on special characteristics when expressed in terms of food security and dependency on unstable external markets, considerations that introduce elements that weaken the argument of comparative advantage in designing the agricultural policy of some countries (IDB, 1981:20).

The food weapon idea was given another boost by Secretary Block's remarkably inept statement prior to his confirmation hearings: "Food is a weapon but the way to use that is to tie countries to us. That way they'll be far more reluctant to upset us" (*The Washington Post*, December 24, 1980:A6). That thought, followed by the cancellation of PL 480 assistance to Nicaragua in March 1981, had the overall effect of creating support for political groups attempting to increase government attention toward agricultural production. The particular policies adopted depended on the traditions of the particular country, and the weight of the "food threat" varied. In Mexico, the food weapon was invoked frequently by President López Portillo to generate support for the highly statist SAM, and the intellectual author of the program stressed political pressure by the United States via food trade as a principal justification of the expensive program (Luiselli, 1980). Thus one might reach the perverse conclusion that United States threats rather than technical assistance are more effective incentives to increase food production in the region.

III. Speculations on the Near Term

Nowhere in the cases reviewed here have we seen a completely successful reconciliation of the export and domestic goals of agriculture. With such conflict the political aspects of policy choice become more significant. Although there is growing awareness of the nature of the tensions and tradeoffs, most countries have responded incrementally and incompletely. And efforts to meet goals through more radical approaches (e.g., Cuba, Nicaragua, Chile) also have fallen short. The case of Cuba reminds us of the enormity of addressing food sufficiency given the historical maldistribution of wealth.

If nation-states have not succeeded in reconciling export and domestic agricultural policies, the record of international organizations (e.g., ALADI, CACM) is even less encouraging. Part of the explanation for this is that the agriculture and nutrition problem is not of sufficient international concern to stimulate efforts. But there are also plausible structural factors that lead to skepticism about solutions via international organizations (R. L. Paarlberg, 1982).

Among these factors looms the international recession and financial crisis, a condition that obviously has exacerbated the food and agriculture problem. As of April 1984, the Latin American countries had amassed an external debt on the order of U.S. $340 billion (*The Washington Post*, 1 April 1984, F1). Brazil, Mexico, and Argentina lead the list of Third World debtors. With the exception of Venezuela, by mid-1984 all the major countries in the region were making use of various International Monetary Fund credit facilities or had begun negotiations with the Fund (*New York Times*, 11 March 1984).

The general implications of Fund agreements with debtor countries are fundamental in shaping food and agricultural policies. In very schematic terms, the logic of the agreements is to correct economic distortions such as inflation and balance-of-payments deficits in the short term and to induce more rational growth policies for the long term. This usually means cuts in public sector outlays and subsidies, contraction of credit, tax increases, layoffs of redundant personnel; in short, an induced recession. At the same time, devaluation is often prescribed to promote exports and reduce imports. Usually included among the cuts are public subsidies to food consumption and preferential credits to smallholders (recall the cases of Mexico, Brazil, and Peru). This typically results in higher food prices (through a combination of dampened production and reduced subsidies) and stormy political protests by the urban poor. Such outbreaks in Brazil and the Dominican Republic during 1984 have been labelled "IMF riots" by some. At the same time that subsidies and credit are restricted, the loan agreements encourage steps to promote exports as part of a general rationalization of the economy. This in turn reinforces the trend toward specialization and export, further reducing incentives for producing for the domestic food market.

The financial distress of the Latin American countries coincides

with a general decline in attitudes of cooperation among the countries and heightened United States and Canadian efforts to increase
exports. Throughout the region, nations are girding to compete in
agricultural exports, which—while less obvious than developments
in industrial export competition—is significant. Many countries use
tax policy to stimulate exports; many use a variety of production
subsidies to achieve this. Some are contemplating administrative
mechanisms to promote trade, with the Japanese-style trading company under close study (see McMillan, 1981). The United States is
maintaining its PL 480 program and has expanded credit guarantees
through the office of the General Sales Manager of the USDA. Credits
guaranteed to finance purchases by Latin American countries under
the GSM-102 program rose from U.S. $573 million in FY1982 to more
than 2.1 billion in 1983 and is expected to fall to about 1.5 billion in
1984.[5]

The net effect of the trend toward export promotion obviously is
increased competition among countries in areas of similar products;
but more importantly, it hastens the evolving patterns of increasing
specialization and complementarity. If such is the case, it would seem
that the sorts of distortions described by Figueroa (1981) and others
are likely to be intensified as the more advanced sectors of agriculture
respond to investment incentives while the more backward are either
ignored or displaced. One need not view such trends as automatic or
inevitable. It is conceivable to fashion policies to promote the involvement of traditional producers in the extension of an international
division of labor, and the more imaginative governments—those less
concerned about the transformation of the traditional sectors of their
societies—will attempt such a tack. But, as we have seen, the experience of Nicaragua in this respect is not encouraging.

If there is an intensification of international trade, the more likely
consequence in the less developed countries of the Western Hemisphere is a deepening of the dualistic nature of their economies as a
whole and of agriculture particularly. In its simplest terms, investment responds to effective demand, which is a function of income,
which remains highly skewed. Influence on policymaking requires
political capabilities (i.e., votes—where they count, organization,
leadership, strategic location in society) and skill. Peasants and landless groups score low on all counts. The more entrepreneurial of the
smallholders can participate if government policies are relatively

benign. The more fortunate of the landless can find better paying work and higher living standards in wage labor. But these will constitute the small minority of populations produced by decades of demographic and economic trends. The remainder will be further marginalized. Established elites will search for more comprehensive and sophisticated forms of manipulating these masses, using combinations of socialization, welfare concessions, and repression. Emigration will grow as a tacit policy response, and in one form or another, the consequences of present patterns of development will turn back on the developed countries.

On the face of it, Ray Goldberg's statement (1981:369) seems hyperbolic: "The greatest challenge in the world is the efficient and equitable development of the underdeveloped world food economies." As one thinks through the problem set, however, Goldberg seems not far from the mark.

Chapter 8

Food Aid and
Political Instability

LaMond Tullis

Various estimates indicate that about 10 percent of the world's population do not receive sufficient food (D. Paarlberg, 1980:274). For the
most part they are pregnant and nursing mothers, children, rural
landless laborers, the urban unemployed, the aged, the ill, and the
infirm. Every country has them, although most are in Asia and Africa,
and to some extent in Latin America.

One might suppose that a rich nation's giving massive quantities of
food to such people would provoke little commentary other than how
to do it more efficiently. Except during times of famine such as the
1966–67 failure of the monsoon in India and the 1984–85 catastrophic
effects of cumulative drought in Ethiopia (Nichols, 1984), this is not
so. Food aid is a controversial and emotional subject as much in the
literature on aid as on development.[1] Some writers accuse it of more
ills than it may be capable of producing;[2] others advance their own
highly diverse agenda in support of it.[3]

The controversy currently extends beyond traditional food-aid
debates over humanitarian principles, surplus food disposal, international political leverage, international market improvements,
appropriate beneficiaries, and even simple aspects of development.
Now the literature addresses the "integrated effects" that food aid may
have on its recipients.[4] People are increasingly concerned about
(1) the possible disincentive effects of food aid on local food production;[5] (2) income distribution consequences;[6] (3) the effect on development and development policies, particularly as they relate to
domestic policy reforms;[7] (4) price stabilization problems;[8] and (5)
dependency.[9]

Even as levels of per capita global food aid to lesser developed countries declined in the late 1970s and early 1980s (see Figure 8.1), the debate as to the appropriateness of such income transfers seemed to get more lively.[10] Interested observers—professional, practical, and academic—both in donor and recipient countries, increasingly voiced strong opinions.[11]

What seems certain is that the integrated effects of food aid on recipient countries are to a great extent time and circumstance specific, therefore making generalizations on the basis of a few variables extremely difficult and probably wrong. This matter is further complicated by data availability and measurement problems, by the normative and ideological tensions associated with the subject, and because food aid, in terms of its domestic effects, cannot be separated easily from other forms of aid, trade, or diverse international financial flows. Yet a consideration of integrated effects obviously has been important, for otherwise it would be hard to account for so much discussion of effects in the literature, or the continuing expenditure of so many billions of dollars in a global food-aid enterprise. On balance, there seems little question that food aid has in fact met the expectations, some of the time, both of its supporters and detractors.

Infrequently appearing in the discussion of effects is the relationship of food aid to a recipient country's "political stability."[12] This infrequency may derive from the general, almost unquestioned assumption that food aid of necessity contributes directly to a recipient country's social and therefore political stability. For the principal donors this clearly is one of the intended effects: "Stability is desirable; instability threatens U.S. interests" (Bloomfield, 1972–73:45).

But does food aid actually enhance political stability in a recipient country? As with other controversial dimensions of food aid, the answer is probably yes and no depending on existing conditions. What are the principal differentiating conditions? This chapter attempts to offer insights for an answer.

Were it possible to identify all the relevant variables (which I think unlikely) and then control them statistically (assuming discriminating measurements on the variables were possible which, given the present state of data collection, I thoroughly doubt), one could approach an answer to the question head on. Given the absence of that possibility, could we not tease out some insights through the "back door," namely by inquiring into the likely condition under which

Figure 8.1

Shipments of Food Aid in Cereals Compared to Growth
in Population Bases to which Aid Is Sent
Showing Declining Levels of Per-Capita Food Aid

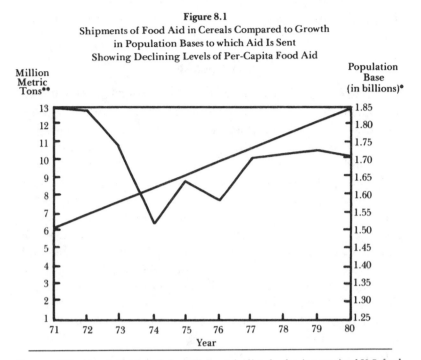

Sources: *The population base is from 72 countries listed as having received U.S. food aid shipments in 1979 [U.S. Department of Agriculture, *Global Food Assessments, 1980a*, Economics, Statistics and Cooperative Foreign Agricultural Economic Report #159, pp. 15, 22, 31, 41, 54, 64, 76 and 87]. Population figures are calculated from a base estimate of 1979 for the countries listed and projected by a weighted average growth rate of 2.3% [U.S. Department of Commerce, Bureau of the Census, *World Population 1979: Recent Demographic Estimates for Countries and Regions of the World* (Washington, D.C., U.S. Superintendent of Documents, 1980)]

**Food and Agriculture Organization (1980:1–27).

food aid may enhance the prospects for political *instability* in a re-cipient country, or at least the conditions in which such an outcome would seem to be likely? If under certain conditions food aid likely contributes to political instability, then donors may desire to enquire into those conditions in making their food aid decisions.

To explore such "negative" conditions and examine how they may relate to food aid is not advanced here as a general argument against food aid, only a call to examine empirically each case to determine the conditions in which the integrated effects may contribute to political instability.

Before examining probable relationships between food aid

and political instability it is useful to review briefly food aid as an institution.

Background

The giving away of massive quantities of food began principally as a consequence of the need of the United States to dispose of huge surpluses amassed during the latter 1940s, 1950s and early 1960s (see Table 8.1). Some of the world's people were hungry. Economically they could not enter an international grain market.[13] In the United States, storage costs were becoming difficult to manage politically if not economically. It was a time when Washington could use its national treasury on behalf of its domestic farmers in a humanitarian gesture. Then other countries joined. But even as late as 1963 the United States was contributing over 95% of all international food aid — $3.249 billion in 1982 dollars (see Table 8.2). Producers' surplus, their domestic political clout, worldwide food deficits, humanitarian instincts, the desire to develop new markets, and perhaps other factors combined to initiate what in modern times has become institutionalized simply as "food aid." A large portion of the more than $74 billion (1982 dollars; see Table 8.2) has constituted a net economic transfer. Since the close of the Marshall Plan era, the transfers have been principally from North Atlantic countries and Japan to underdeveloped countries in Asia, Africa and Latin America.

In recent years the per capita amount of global food aid has declined (Figure 8.1), and its composition and the political and other considerations attached to it have changed.[14] Yet the generally unsettled nature of the world food situation[15] coupled with prospects of a renewal of food disposal problems in the United States[16] and the continuing desire to exercise international political leverage through food have given rise to the newly evolving impact issues mentioned above.

While food aid to Third World countries of Asia, Africa, and Latin America was made practically possible by continuing surpluses, the rationalizing model for international political and strategic concerns, especially from the vantage of the United States, went something like this:

— Hunger and poverty in the Third World lead to domestic strife and political instability.

Table 8.1

U.S. Wheat Production, Utilization and End-of-year Carryover

Crop year (July-June)	Production (in million bushels)	Utilization (in million bushels)		Stocks: end of year carryover (in million bushels)	
		Total (a)	Export	Total (b)	Government owned
1948	1,294.9	1,185.0	503.6	307.3	227.2
1949	1,098.4	983.2	302.9	424.7	327.7
1950	1,019.3	1,055.7	365.9	399.9	196.4
1951	998.2	1,163.6	475.0	256.0	143.3
1952	1,306.4	978.5	317.5	605.5	470.0
1953	1,173.1	850.6	216.7	933.5	774.6
1954	983.9	885.4	274.0	1,036.2	975.9
1955	937.1	949.7	346.0	1,033.5	950.7
1956	1,005.4	1,137.8	549.1	908.8	823.9
1957	955.7	993.9	402.3	881.4	834.9
1958	1,457.4	1,051.4	442.8	1,295.1	1,146.6
1959	1,117.7	1,106.7	509.8	1,313.4	1,195.4
1960	1,354.7	1,264.9	661.5	1,411.3	1,242.5
1961	1,232.4	1,327.4	719.4	1,322.0	1,096.6
1962	1,092.0	1,224.2	643.8	1,195.2	1,082.5
1963	1,146.8	1,444.5	856.1	901.4	828.9
1964	1,283.4	1,368.6	725.0	817.3	828.9
1965	1,315.6	1,598.6	867.4	535.2	340.0
1966	1,311.7	1,423.6	744.3	425.0	124.0
1967	1,522.4	1,408.9	761.1	539.4	102.0
1968	1,570.4	1,298.1	544.2	818.6	162.7
1969	1,460.2	1,378.0	606.1	884.7	301.2
1970	1,378.5	1,506.0	738.0	730.2	369.9
1971	1,639.5	1,487.0	632.0	865.3	366.5
1972	1,544.8	1,970.9	1,186.3	438.4	209.2
1973	1,705.2	1,900.0	1,148.7	247.4	18.9

(a) including exports

(b) including government owned and under loan to the government

Source: M. Wallerstein (1980:12–13).

— Domestic political instability invites Communist intervention.

— Communist intervention is threatening to world peace, and therefore to the national security interests of the United States.

— World peace is best preserved by turning back Communist aggression and influence.

— Communist aggression and influence are best turned back by a

Table 8.2
Value of Farm Products Shipped as P.L. 480 Food Aid
(Millions of Dollars)
(Does not include administrative overhead or freight)

| | United States Food Aid | | | | Other OECD Countries | | Estimated 1982 Dollar Value |
| | | | | | U.S. % of | | |
	Title I*	Title II*	Title III	Total PL480[1]	Global Total	Global Total	Adjusted to 1982 Price[3]
1955	73	187	125	385	99e[2]	389	1019
1956	439	247	298	984	99e[2]	994	2545
1957	908	206	401	1525	99e[2]	1540	3850
1958	657	224	100	981	99e[2]	991	2418
1959	724	161	132	1017	99e[2]	1027	2440
1960	824	143	149	1116	99e[2]	1127	2615
1961	951	221	144	1316	99e[2]	1329	3004
1962	1049	248	198	1495	98[11]	1526	3357
1963	1145	263	48	1457	96[7]	1518	3249
1964	1104	270	43	1418	95[2]	1492	3103
1965	1300	238	32	1570	94[11]	1670	3373
1966	1047	267	32	1346	91[7]	1479	2899
1967	981	267	23	1271	85[2]	1495	2840
1968	1023	250	6	1280	80[2]	1600	2944
1969	773	265	1	1039	77[11]	1349	2401
1970	815	241	—	1056	70[11]	1509	2595
1971	743	280	—	1023	80[2]	1279	2123
1972	678	380	—	1058	77[7]	1374	2198
1973	667	287	—	954	55[11]	1735	2672
1974	584	292	—	867	48[11]	1806	2673
1975	762	339	—	1101	59[11]	1866	2650

1976	650	257	—	907	699	1511	2055
1977[4]	1076	411	—	1487	657	2288	2974
1978	739	335	—	1074	588[8]	1851	2295
1979	748	389	—	1137	571[0]	1995	2354
1980	—	—		1307[5]	50[5]	2614	2927
1981	—	—		1339[12]	55e	2434e	2580e
1982	—	—		1163[6]	55e	2115e	2115e
Estimated Global Totals					$ 43,903		74,268

Title I includes sales for local currency and long-term dollar and convertible local currency credit sales.

Title II includes government to government donations, donations to the World Food Program, and donations through relief agencies.

Title III includes bartered material for supplemental stockpile.

1. Sources for P.L. 480 contributions include: USDA, *Food for Peace, 1979* (USDA: January 1981), Appendix, Table 1; and USDA, *Global Food Assessment, 1980*, Economics, Statistics and Cooperative Foreign Agricultural Economic Report #159, p. 98.

2. Christopher Stevens, *Food Aid and the Developing World* (London: Croom Helm, 1979), p. 25; and, USDA, *Global Food Assessment, 1980*, Economics, Statistics and Cooperative Foreign Agricultural Economics Report #159, p. 98.

3. Assumes long-term average annual depreciation of the dollar at 6%.

4. Includes an extra three months in the accounting period.

5. From OECD, *Development Co-operation Review*, 1981, p. 183. OECD and USDA do not use the same accounting system. Thus some discrepancies appear (e.g., OECD gives 1979 data as 1,302 rather than 1,137).

6. Budgetary proposals of the Reagan administration. OECD, "Food Aid," *Development Co-operation Review*, 1981, p. 146.

7. Mitchell B. Wallerstein, *Food for War — Food for Peace: United States Food Aid in a Global Context* (Cambridge, Mass.: The MIT Press, 1980), p. 68.

8. OECD, *Development Co-operation Review*, 1979, pp. 212–213.

9. OECD, *Development Co-operation Review*, 1978, pp. 200–201.

10. OECD, *Development Co-operation Review*, 1981, pp. 180–181.

11. OECD, *Development Co-operation Review*, 1976, p. 148.

12. USDA, *Food for Peace*, 1981 Annual Report on Public Law 480, p. 1 of printer's draft.

strong military posture in the Free World and the reduction of hunger and poverty abroad.

— The reduction of hunger and poverty abroad is best achieved by politically stable regimes that are development oriented.

— Economic development will in turn enhance political development and therefore the prospects for long-term political stability.

— Economic development and therefore political development can be accelerated through international transfers of capital, technology, and commodities, of which *food aid* can play an important part.

A number of political development models acquired currency in the 1960s[17] and helped to sustain and to legitimize the thinking on the relationship of food aid and stability. In their minimal considerations one might call them an "economic theory of political stability," or, in more expansive ones, an "economic theory of democracy."[18] They made possible an intellectually justified and practically inspired link between domestic grain producers, the United States government, and the security of the "Free World."

Even after the politically destabilizing effects of modernization and rapid economic changes in lesser developed countries became well-known[19] the models did not lose their appeal. Note the following widely circulated statement from a 1969 pro-aid report:

More rapid growth and rising incomes will not necessarily win friends and allies or ensure peace and stability in the less developed countries. On the contrary, real progress involves a break with the past and may induce highly destabilizing political and social change. But profound changes are already under way in the less developed world regardless of what the United States does or does not do. The long-term political rationale for aid, therefore, rests on the calculated risk that accelerating the modernization process, and reducing the sacrifice to achieve it, will enhance the odds of an earlier evolution of responsible and independent states in the low-income regions of the world. By the same token, the risk of involvement by the great powers in crises and power vacuums abroad will thereby be reduced.[20]

"Development," as viewed in the West and as applied to lesser developed countries, was understood to be best achieved with a strategic emphasis on capital investment in areas that would lend themselves to import-substitution industrialization.[21] The ensuing investments, quite naturally, went to the larger cities where infrastructure and manpower were more readily available. The words "trickle down" became part of the lexicon in those days, for it was thought that enhanced economic activity would reach down in the social pyramid to produce a stable middle class and, eventually, even relieve the poor and impoverished of some of their suffering.[22] Clearly, this was seen as being in the national security interests of the United States. It was an argument sufficiently persuasive to invoke billions of dollars in foreign assistance. For some countries the food-aid component of that assistance was rather significant.

Once institutionalized, food aid has continued even though surpluses have declined[23] and terms of transfer have become "harder."[24] Thus, quite aside from continuing food transfers in recent years for humanitarian and other concerns (e.g. disaster and war relief in Nigeria, the Sahel region of Africa, Cambodia, and also Poland in 1982), three basic types of food aid have evolved and continue in force: food-for-cash, food-for-nutrition, and food-for-wages.[25] All probably constitute, for the most part, "additional" net economic transfers over other forms of aid. This is because of the "surplus push" for decision-making in some countries, a politically attractive feature not associated with hard cash.[26]

The principal donors in the West participating in one or more of the above food-aid activities are the United States, Canada, the European Economic Community and its individual members, and the World Food Program.[27] The United States still contributes the vast bulk of all global food aid (see Table 8.2, column 6).

Stability, Coercion and Consensus

To examine the relationship of food aid to political instability or stability requires first a description of what is meant by political stability and an analysis of conditions that contribute to it. Thereafter we may examine food aid's likely effect on those conditions.

"Political stability," valued by those who advocate food aid for a donor country's national security, may be understood as describing a regime that has shown resistance to sudden change, dislodgment, or overthrow. From a Western food donor's perspective, it may also be characterized as a regime demonstrating an absence of radical political solutions to any outstanding problems of distribution and equity among its subjects or electorate. It may be understood, therefore, as a

224 Food, the State, and International Political Economy

regime able to evoke sufficient political order for international trade, business, financial, educational, and other transactions to occur with regularity, predictability, and security.

What is the basis of such stability? Two extreme sources traditionally have been noted: "consensus" and "coercion" (C. Johnson, 1982:15–39). By "consensus" we mean a people's general agreement or accord with the way they are governed. This accord might not—probably does not—extend to the way all social and economic assets are distributed or policies decided and implemented. However, any potentially destabilizing discontent is usually diffused by a generally held belief in a "change function" in the political system. Usually this is an electoral process that allows people to consider their constitution inviolate while at the same time permitting them to change policies and political procedures of present leaders, and the leaders themselves, through political campaigns and votes. "Consensus" does not necessarily say anything about the real world an outside observer might view, only of the belief system that insiders have about that world. Take *inequality*, often cited as a cause of political instability and a justification, therefore, for the giving of food to help redress its political consequences. In objective terms a highly skewed or uneven distribution of social and economic goods and political power might prevail in a country and yet people generally agree that it is appropriate. They might see the political marketplace balancing inequities of wealth arising from the economic marketplace, and the private economic marketplace providing alternatives to public power in the political marketplace. Private wealth may be seen as balancing public power, and public power having the ability to reallocate private wealth according to preferences of consumers and producers, citizens and politicians (Apter, 1977:310). Inequality as a "cause" of political instability may be nothing of the sort unless it is seen as being unjust and unchangeable under present political arrangements. A group must perceive itself as being disadvantaged, judge the situation to be relevant to their own conditions, appraise it as being illegitimate, feel anger, frustration and resentment over it, and then make demands for greater equality that they are prepared to prosecute with sufficient organizational, leadership and other capabilities either to shift the government's position or to evoke the alternative condition for stability—coercion.

By political coercion we mean the forcing of a people to act in a prescribed manner by pressure or threat, which may involve the country's judicial apparatus as well as its security forces. In the absence of consensus or regime alteration toward a new political arrangement, coercion is a likely outcome of any destabilizing tension, a condition that pits the government against vast segments of its people. In the early 1980s Poland, El Salvador, and Nicaragua were dramatic cases within this category. A decay in a government's willingness or capability to exercise force under these conditions is often noted as a prelude to revolution (Tullis, 1973:278–86).

The social fabric may be torn along ethnic, social and economic class, racial, or religious grounds as well as political-ideological ones. Coercion may prevent the appearance of manifest forms of political instability even under conditions of extreme internal tension. The society is held together not from any notion of loyalty to a ruling group or national political institutions but rather by force. In multi-ethnic nations where extreme ethnic competition over scarce resources has been noted the social glue may be little more than the police and army. The same may be true in highly class-structured societies governed by either a traditional elite or their new-rich counterparts of the industrialization era. In all conditions of this general type, national security forces frequently become the last stabilizing element short of outside intervention or revolution and a new political code. Invariably, at least in the short run, the result is to integrate the society on the basis of coercion rather than consensus. This phenomenon has become so prevalent that a whole new genre of literature has been advanced to try to explain it.[28]

All regimes that produce political stability through coercion are noted for the absence of the rule of law, for the denial of civil rights, and some even for official terrorist or torture tactics to invoke compliance with regime norms (e.g., Guatemala). Indeed, Latin America has long been noted for regimes of coercion over regimes of consensus, at least as seen by increasing numbers of its own citizens as well as outside observers. The same applies to Eastern Europe since World War II, for which the case of Poland should now be instructive to everyone too young to remember Hungary and Czechoslovakia.

"Consensus" and "Coercion" may be thought of as polar ends of a continuum, somewhat ideal-type in nature, but still sufficiently close to the real world to be instructive as regards political practices in such opposites as New Zealand and Guatemala. Most of the nations of the world lie in varying places along the continuum, some exhibiting a little more consensus than coercion (e.g., the United States) and others a little more coercion than consensus (e.g., Brazil) in their political practices and procedures. Most "developing" countries are classified as being more coercive than consensual in their political arrangements, governed, as most of them are, either by military or civilian authoritarian regimes. Those that appear to be situated less toward the coercive side of the continuum also seem to be the most economically prosperous and, for the moment at least, more politically stable.

It takes considerably less institutional energy to maintain political stability in a country when consensus prevails than when the society must be held together by guns, where security forces function as the principal mechanism of internal order and where, in order to do so, they consume large portions of the country's GNP.[29]

Stability by consensus is hard to undermine in the short run, particularly if the economy of a country is delivering well and if distributional and equity issues have not consumed the political thinking of large numbers of citizens. If economic satisfactions or an ideology evoking positive institutional support are strong at home, missionaries of an alien faith have trouble making much headway.

Stability by coercion, on the other hand, is ephemeral, awaiting only the perception of change in the balance of power for profound transformations to occur. Among ancient societies not often noted in the literature, the fall of the Aztecs and Incas is a case in point, not to mention the often cited and far-flung empires of the Romans and the Ottomans.

Advocates of food aid, given that they come mostly from North Atlantic democracies, clearly prefer stability over disorder, and stability based on consensus rather than coercion. However, if they have to make a choice between political disorder, which they fear may open the ground for ideological competitors, and stability based on coercion, they will take the latter. Thus, while they have known that much of the food aid they have sponsored, at least since the early 1960s, has gone to countries in which coercion prevailed over consensus,[30] they have nevertheless thought that humanitarian principles and the development effort for which food aid was seen to play a part would ultimately prevail, and that one of the principal beneficial outcomes would be the gradual integration of the society on the basis of consensus.[31]

Stability and Development

But is the logic sound? It is thought that food aid enhances stability through its effects on economic development, for the political instability so characteristic of lesser developed countries allegedly derives from a lack of development, not as a consequence of it.

Consider that assumption. Countries for which food aid targeted for development purposes is considered appropriate are, on the whole, being subjected to rapid social and economic changes that operate independently of cyclical aggravations directly affecting internal food-production capabilities. (e.g., the droughts occurring with regularity in Brazil's northeast and Africa's Sahel). Decolonization was a consequence of some of the changes, followed by increasing levels of industrialization, urbanization, increased literacy, communications and political awareness. All of these tended to be accompanied by value changes producing what Karl Deutsch once termed "social mobilization" (Deutsch, 1961:494). They were, and are, changes in which "major clusters of old social, economic and psychological commitments are eroded or broken and people become available for new patterns of socialization and behavior" (Deutsch, 1961:494).

The capacities, wants, and expectations of those involved expand at an alarming pace. A natural consequence is that people so mobilized desire participation in their country's politics, economics, and society in ways that may not be governed or sanctioned by existing norms or procedures. Peasants want to vote and acquire economic benefits and personal freedoms; students want to make public policy; the economic middle class wants to do—and enjoy—everything; the old aristocracy wants to hang on to its privileges and unshared power.

Usually the wants and expectations of newly mobilized people rise considerably faster than the existing capacity or willingness of a developing nation's elite and existing institutions to respond satisfactorily to them. The resulting gap between, on the one hand, the expectations and availability of socially mobilized people for new commitments and, on the other, their opportunities to realize those expectations and engage in the new commitments helps to produce political instability; it may also set the stage for serious civil disorders.

Enhanced social mobilization deriving from almost any form of development effort is just *part* of the problem of political instability. Contemporary literature in the field of international political economy shows how the very development models selected frequently contribute to the problem. Consider the empirical definition advanced by Cardoso and Faletto (1979:23–24) that describes the real development world they have observed:

... we do not mean by the notion of "development" the achievement of a more just society. These are not consequences expected from capitalist development, especially in peripheral economies. ... Development, in this context, means the progress in productive forces, mainly through the import of technology, capital accumulation, penetration of local economies by foreign enterprises, increasing numbers of wage-earning groups, and intensification of social division of labor.

If the above observation correctly portrays an empirical model of development frequently experienced by lesser developed countries in the contemporary era, one rather clearly sees why regimes of coercion rather than regimes of consensus tend to accompany the development effort. If a "trickle down" effect is not readily apparent (which usually it is not) people in wholesale lots begin to protest the absence of quality-of-life improvements they had grown to expect.

The matter is further complicated because lesser developed countries generally have a low institutional capacity to bridge the rapidly rising expectations-opportunity gaps, regardless of the development models they may have selected or the nature of their integration in the international political economy. Thus, quite aside from problems deriving from a development model or the nature of a country's international economic integration, which of themselves may pose serious problems, the countries may have too few (or unknown) resources to exploit, an insufficient income to distribute, or less than a realistic vision of how to make investments and reap profits. They may be plagued with corrupt businessmen and conniving politicians, ruled by old leaders unwilling to make a commitment to change, or may be overwhelmed with clerics who perceive all environmental and value change as a threat to the holy sanctity of their world. They may be controlled by an oligarchy that fosters economic development but, being fearful of the social and political consequences, clamps down hard to maintain the status quo in areas of power, privilege, and prestige. Old authority patterns suffer. They no longer ask the right questions or provide the answers. People begin to look elsewhere for solutions to newly perceived problems.

In the wake of these dissatisfactions, the old political arrangements tend to lose their legitimacy among the socially mobilized but less satisfied groups in the society. Yet new patterns of authority embodying complex bureaucratic and legal norms in institutions that have both the capacity and the will to react adequately to new situations are slow to emerge. In the resulting wasteland operate military coups, frightened authoritarian despots, revolutionary and charismatic leaders, external intervenors, and social chaos.

Rapid economic and social change does not impinge on all groups in a country at the same time. It tends to begin in the large cities. Even there, in the early stages, change drastically affects only selected groups. However, as more individuals become involved, the expectations-opportunity gaps loom ever more pervasive, frustrating, and even frightening. The political effect of rapid economic change is not unlike a fire under a teakettle. Unless the flames are dampened or the teakettle cooled with additional water, the molecules, as people, eventually begin to jump.

If a country's political authorities do not (whether out of lack of desire or ability) respond in such a way as to relieve the social tearing, the forces for change, given sufficient time, tend to overwhelm the old elite, weaken their means of resistance and coercion, and eventually remove them from power either through coups, revolutions, or assassinations.

Such violent acts do not resolve gap problems. Sometimes they make them worse. Accordingly, there frequently emerges from the tensions yet another characteristic of rapid environmental and value change. We shall call it "amoral groupism," a condition in which victorious politicians end up fighting among themselves just as previously, together, they may have fought against an entrenched elite. One of the consequences may be the "bureaucratic authoritarianism" about which Guillermo O'Donnell and his associates have long spoken[32] and the international "dependency" that tends to accompany it.[33] Thus more often than not developing countries today tend to exhibit political systems integrated more on coercion than consensus. They may be "stable." That stability may also be highly transitory.

If out of the "natural" processes of "development" a new economy and a new society tend to arise, the same certainly cannot necessarily be said of a stable polity. No easy solutions are offered for replacement of political institutions when values and environment rapidly change. Thus political instability and coercive political regimes associated with rapid development frequently extend well beyond the days after rises in GNP become a booming reality. The gap between wants and their fulfillment, expectations and their achievement, and capabilities and the opportunity to exercise them continues. The failure of the old order to respond effectively to the dilemma has undermined its legitimacy. Yet, throughout, little purposeful groundwork is laid for an institutional replacement capable of amelioration and resolution. The gaps remain, frequently becoming worse. Instability, or coercive efforts to contain it, therefore continues. It is this threatening instability that charismatic leaders appropriate to their advantage, and that military officers and bureaucratic authoritarian dictators attempt to control for theirs. It is also this same threatening instability that policy makers and politicians in many food-donor countries perceive as being against their own national interests and for which they hope food donations and other aid will make a stabilizing difference.

In spite of food and other developmental aid, political instability frequently continues. Thus the donors supplement food and other economic grants with military hardware, logistics and training of counter-insurgency specialists. It follows that the societies continue to be integrated principally on the basis of coercion rather than consensus. People may "eat," food aid and all, but the political stability of the country is transitory when integrated by coercion, with the food-aid donor usually being more disliked than appreciated for the "generosity."

In the countries where the above analysis holds, it follows that long-term political stability based more on consensus than coercion — if it occurs at all — will be associated with structural realignments in the society, economy and polity, and that these will not necessarily be associated with any "trickle down" effect of economic development. In the society they entail an increase in the permeability of class, regional, or vertical-ethnic boundaries (Horowitz, 1971; Enloe, 1973:28–29). In the economy they imply not only a global increase in national wealth but also distributional realignments (Christensen, 1978a), first to accommodate some of the expectations of newly mobilized groups, and secondly to appeal to their sense of fairness. In the polity the structural realignments imply an opening of a competitive political process such that new groups may be co-opted by a system as opposed to developing a counter elite that seeks to overthrow it. Nothing is more damaging to a revolutionary cause than the infertility of the domestic soil.

"Political Stability" may be achieved on the basis of consensus or coercion. Most lesser developed countries—insofar as they have achieved political stability at all—have done so largely by coercion. Such an experience might be classified as a kind of "unstable stability." Development, given the economic models selected, the social forces unleashed and the nature of the international political economy that interacts with a domestic developing economy, tends to create, in the short run, at least, conditions that seem to evoke more, not less political coercion. Thus development seems to be inherently destabilizing, at least when attempted under conditions of the present era. But might food aid *contribute* to that instability?

Having now set the stage, let us examine that specific question.

Food Aid and Political Stability

Given the tensions associated with contemporary rapid social and economic changes, many political leaders who value both their positions and the welfare of their countries obviously have attempted to resolve the dilemmas. Reports are laden with descriptions of their efforts. Many have backfired. Consider the interrelated although most likely unintended effects of the following two of many *illustrative* popular policies that help to assure that a country will be a candidate for food aid and will, as a consequence, not likely improve its position on any index of consensual political stability:

(1) Price Controls on Basic Foodstuffs

The logic for the policy is clear enough. Food costs have a clear relationship to wages—especially for blue-collar industrial workers who have a penchant for joining unions and engaging in strikes. Food costs frequently account for up to 60% of a worker's income. If food prices are kept low, pressures for wage increases may also be kept low. Lower wages, made possible in part by relatively low costs of basic foodstuffs, are therefore related to other important economic questions, such as the ability of a firm to compete in international markets. Low wages improve the investment climate—all other things being equal—for finance and venture capital; they help make exports more competitive; and, they help to reduce political unrest in the cities.

The widely practiced policy of price controls on food constitutes a net economic transfer from rural to urban areas. A portion of the income that under relatively unfettered market conditions would flow to the rural producers is retained in the urban economic centers, mostly among upper income groups. The economic argument for this, in relation to savings and investment, is well known.[34]

Capital and other economic transfers from rural to urban areas are quite unremarkable because they are expected and frequently planned. Equally unremarkable are income transfers that concentrate rather than redistribute wealth, because that occurs all the time in lesser-developed countries (Beitz, 1981:321–46). But under certain conditions such transfers and concentration of wealth create production disincentives that reduce domestically grown foodstuffs, thereby requiring the country to import to cover its food deficits.[35] As food shortages satisfied by imports tend to drive up unsubsidized prices, the effect is to contribute to political unrest. To maintain a subsidized price promotes budgetary deficits and inflation.

Enter food aid. It saves a country's foreign exchange, for it replaces food imports that otherwise may have to be purchased. It helps to balance a government's current accounts, and it may reduce short-term political tension. But it may, in specific cases, also further aggravate the production incentive problem, contributing to further food shortages; mass migration of people to the cities in search of work; frightfully high levels of unemployment among the migrants and underemployment in the countryside;[36] and glaring income disparities that, while usually not affecting politically the first generation migrants, certainly do their children.[37] There follows a need for coercive measures to control a tense and frustrated population. Food aid sometimes helps to legitimize coercion if it relieves a government of the responsibility to deal with the structural disincentives associated with its food-deficits and the issues of "unfairness" they promote (Beitz, 1981). In so doing it contributes to long-term political instability.

(2) Export Substitution Agriculture

In an effort to enhance their foreign exchange position and continue to develop their countries economically, Third World political and economic elite look for every available means. During the 1960s "import substitution" was tried in order to industrialize and to diversify economically. That fell far short of expectations, in part because internal markets were easily saturated by high-priced products produced under the "infant industry" import-protection doctrines.[38] Then, during the 1970s countries tried to develop new export markets with value-added goods (Gereffi and Evans, 1981:31–64), thereby lessening their vulnerability to fluctuating prices on primary commodities (O'Donnell, 1973; Collier, 1979a). Sometimes falling short there, in part because of intense international competition from the already industrialized nations, some policy makers in lesser developed countries reverted back to enhancing exports of traditional commodities and attempting to bargain for a "new international economic order" with Japan and the North Atlantic countries.[39]

Nevertheless, some countries have been partially successful in finding a commercial or industrial process at which they have acquired an international comparative advantage and have begun to provide new goods for an international market—hence "export-substitution industrialization." And some countries have begun to succeed at what the United States has done so well—"export agriculture," principally through stunning production transformations characterized by Green Revolution technology and capital-intensive mechanization.

But consider what happens in countries such as Brazil, Mexico and several in Black Africa when certain kinds of export-substitution agriculture are pursued—capital intensive procedures introduced in a labor-surplus environment more in order to reduce a foreign exchange crisis, facilitate imports and external debt servicing (Wionczek, 1981; Aronson, 1979, 1985) and satisfy external markets than respond to food needs at home. Malnutrition and hunger increase among some population sectors as traditional food crops are displaced,[40] and structures that enhance the probability of political tensions are reinforced—high horizontal but low vertical mobility; high unemployment; low effective market demand at a production-incentive price.

The lack of sufficient internal markets exists, in part, because of the failure of structural realignments that would integrate more people, especially in the rural areas, into a growing industrial economy. Export-substitution agriculture, under these conditions, assures their further marginalization. (Unemployed people do not, as a matter of course, greatly improve internal market demand). This further marginalization enhances conditions that may lead to political instability, for it enhances "gap" conditions that turn people's attention to extreme politics in search of solutions.

Food aid is thought of as one way to help resolve the problem because it can provide food to people who are displaced and marginalized and thereby assist in stabilizing the "development process." If it were only a short-run requirement, and if the "trickle down" development models actually worked,[41] the argument could be impressive. But the countries's enhanced commercial agricultural position is not meant to meet domestic food needs, for it is the absence of effective domestic demand at an affordable domestic price that turns maize lands into soya lands and that enhances export earnings at the apparent expense of production for domestic consumption. That countries where this has happened have been scenes of intense political conflict, where the societies have had to be held together principally on the basis of coercion, is not an unrelated accident.[42]

Now that even Mexico's food position is deteriorating after years of surplus following the Green Revolution (Bailey, Ch. 7, and Sanderson, Ch. 5, this volume) it will be interesting to see if it can salvage itself from the problem. Income from energy exports might buy some time just as it has done in Venezuela and Saudi Arabia (but failed to do in Iran). But, in the long run, that will not be an effective substitute. Income from energy exports to buy food is, in some sense, just like food aid. It is, first, a "bonus" to the economy. Second, it is "terminable" (depletable). If the funds derived from it are employed with little emphasis on structural realignment they will help to create the very political conditions they were meant to resolve (Todaro, 1981:63–64), especially if, as in the case of aid, they are suddenly cut off or, as in the case of oil, the international market deteriorates. Indeed, Mexico is faced with a frightful dilemma as it has not been able to find international buyers for its oil at a level high enough to fuel its growth at the expected levels (Bizzarro, 1981). No amount of food aid, therefore, will assure good long-term political stability prospects. Indeed, it may just make political-stability matters worse.

In each case illustrated above — price controls and export substitution — a chief consequence under the conditions that normally obtain in lesser developed countries has been conditions that may lead to political instability. Both policies have contributed to domestic food scarcities that have had to be satisfied either by commercial food imports or by food aid, or both. Both policies have allowed for the maintenance of rural-urban disparities that aggravate distribution problems, displace large populations, and marginalize more and more people. Food aid, along with other forms of aid, may fill the void for a time, but hardly solve the problem of stability, for they interface with instability in such a way as to help to assure that it will continue not to be resolved, at least in a manner approximating consensual politioo.

If one of the purposes of food aid is to enhance the prospects for consensual political stability in a recipient country, it follows that such aid ought not to be given to countries fostering policies that subvert domestic food-production capabilities, that legitimize the wholesale displacement of much of their population, and that help to sustain distributional patterns that more and more people increasingly view as being unjust, and which require, therefore, coercive policies as a substitute for government by reasonable consent. If aid subverts the markets on which adherents of the capitalist system believe an important production advantage exists, and if it helps to marginalize people whom it pretends to serve, it may help to prolong regimes for whom stability is synonymous with coercive institutions. But it thereby enhances conditions that either encourage political instability in the long run (by helping to maintain regime short-term coercive capabilities while at the same time creating disincentives for structural reforms) or at least does nothing to ameliorate contributing conditions in the short run. Under these conditions food aid may be a bad long-term investment.

Final

Food aid for humanitarian purposes, which should be supported on its own merits, and food aid for development purposes thought to enhance the national interests of the donor country, certainly do one thing — they get rid of surplus food, and sometimes they create new export markets. Food aid thus appeases an important political group at home through domestic income redistribution. All that may be in the donor country's national interest—to assure that food-production capability at home remains high and that there be a domestic food self-sufficiency with adequate margins to handle weather or other cyclical crises.

Food aid can make important contributions to recipient countries. In making that contribution it need not have disincentive effects on local food production, need not contribute to worsened income distribution that marginalizes and displaces people, can have a positive effect on development programs, can help to stabilize consumer food prices so that the poor eat less poorly, and does not necessarily lead to dependency. Food aid need not necessarily contribute to political instability. The conditions where all these benefits and few liabilities obtain are not general but rather country specific and to a certain extent manipulable. Where they do not obtain, and where conditions are not propitiously manipulable, it seems highly counter productive to give food aid except on a short-term basis for strictly humanitarian reasons.

This is not a call for less food aid. Let there be more aid. Let it be given under conditions wherein the long-term prospects for consensual political stability are enhanced rather than made less likely.

PART III

Technology
and Food

Chapter 9

Technology Transfer and Food Security: Pluses, Minuses, and Desirable Policy Changes

David W. McClintock

Technology transfer is a constantly discussed but frequently misunderstood factor in the global food equation. Some people have the misguided notion that if somehow the extraordinary technology-based know-how of the United States and a few other agriculturally advanced nations could be spread throughout the populous developing world, impending food crises could be averted and development could move forward in quantum leaps. Others perceive the benefits of technology transfer as being unidirectional — i.e., occurring essentially as a form of aid from the First World *to* the Third. In the context of the North-South dialogue, these people see the developed world paying all the costs and the lesser-developed countries reaping all the benefits — hence a variant of the zero-sum game.

On a more reasoned basis, attitudes among concerned individuals in developed nations range from enthusiasm for a likely solution to the politically and economically destabilizing world hunger problem to interest in enhancing export earnings through technology sales. On the negative side, there is concern in the developed nations about the possible loss of agricultural competitiveness, about the costs of transferring technology through foreign aid programs, and the apparent futility of outracing Third World population gains. In Third World eyes, technology transfer is seen variously as compensation for past injustices, as an essential stepping stone to industrial development, or at times as an inappropriate and unassimilable Western import.

While opinions differ according to vantage point and the specific agricultural problem being discussed, there is generally broad agreement that technology and its proper dissemination are essential to global agricultural progress in the late 20th century. As noted by Hopkins et al. (1982:6), technology—along with food supplies and population patterns—has constituted one of three key factors in a cyclical pattern of social and economic relationships ever since the time of Malthus. The carrying capacity of the entire human system is determined by the interaction of these factors, each of which represents a limit. If any one of the three changes, either positively or negatively, the others must change as well.

With world population almost certain to exceed six billion by the year 2000 and with the prospect of food shortfalls (albeit partially from maldistribution), it would be difficult to regard agricultural technology transfer as anything less than a critical global policy issue in the mid-1980s. It is of equal concern to neo-Malthusians worried about predicted food crises, to distributionists disturbed by income disparities and social injustices, and to productionists who believe that various shortcomings in the world food system can be overcome on the supply side.[1]

Viewed holistically, agricultural technology transfer may be seen as a highly complex set of responses to the world food problem, offering various positive and negative features to both transferers and transferees. This chapter presents the broad economic and political implications for the developed and developing nations, and then focuses on Third World impacts, donor nation interests, the needs of the global community, and finally on the policy and planning challenges that confront both worlds. This discussion is based on the premises that technology interchange is in fact two-way rather than unilateral, and that the process is neither a long-term panacea nor a "quick fix" for meeting global food requirements. Rather, it is a modicum for complex interactions among political and social groups that could have either positive or negative impacts. Its political implications are as important as its economic or agronomic impacts.

In their brief but incisive study "Food in the Global Arena," Hopkins et al. (1982:25–26) define technology as consisting not only of physical artifacts (machinery, chemicals, etc.) and theoretical techniques, but also of social tools and policies. It is a sum of all the products and procedures that humanity has devised to deal with its physical and social environment. Furthermore, technology is "amoral" in that it has no intrinsic positive or negative value

unto itself. How society applies technology and interprets the consequences of that application assigns something of good or bad value to
the process. The idea that any problem can be solved through expertise, capital and technology is not necessarily valid, although it is
admittedly appealing to the "have" nations which are reluctant to
invest (or give up) anything more. However, technological fixes can
be inappropriate solutions to social problems if wealthy countries
develop them for poor nations where overwhelming constraints on
capital, expertise and resources exist.

This definition applies especially well to agricultural technology
transfer and underscores the problem of assessing the politico-
economic impacts of such diverse matters as foreign agricultural
training programs, the introduction of hybrid seeds and Green Revolution agronomic techniques, cooperative agricultural research,
plant germplasm collection and specimen exchange, global climate
and crop forecasting, nutritional interventions, "downstream" food
processing techniques, and modern marketing methods.

It is apparent that these and many other components of the transfer
process are of concern to different constituencies in both the transferring and transferee nations. For example, political policy makers in
transferring countries may perceive agricultural technology transfer
positively both as a foreign aid device and as a modestly priced
response to Third World demands for know-how. Trade officials who
realize that "service" exports (i.e., technology) can be as profitable as
commodity exports may also share this positive view. But others may
view transfer negatively in terms of the possible impact of enhanced
foreign agricultural productivity on domestic farm exports. (The
granting of U.S. technical aid to promote overseas palm oil production some years ago at the expense of domestic oil producers is a case
in point.) Nevertheless, underwriting a second phase of the Green
Revolution and applying domestic expertise to overseas rural development may be perceived as good insurance against political upheavals that could also be economically injurious. Politically stable
trading partners are likely to become more prosperous economically
and hence better future customers for manufactured and agricultural
exports. The scientific community is not directly concerned with
these political and economic factors but has considerable interest in
the technological challenges. A humanitarian constituency, represented by many organizations dedicated to solving the world hunger

problem, perceives knowledge-sharing from yet another angle, and so on.

Viewpoints and attitudes in the cooperating lesser-developed countries (LDCs) can be similarly diverse. For example, a political elite may be preoccupied with the problems of its urban poor and disinclined to devote resources to rural development, or — alternatively—highly interested in foreign agricultural technology as a cure for politico-economic ills. Third World farmers may be anxious to try "miracle seeds" or conversely reluctant to abandon their traditional production techniques. LDC planners may view agricultural technology suspiciously as an invidious means of locking their countries into single-crop plantation agriculture, or too costly in terms of resource inputs, too difficult to implement in terms of local skills and infrastructure, or a combination of the above.

Thus it is not possible to assess the technology transfer process in simple terms of profit or loss, advantage or disadvantage. Clearly each incremental transfer constitutes a special case that must be evaluated on its own merits. The political and economic benefits for the donors and the impact on the political economy of the recipients cannot be conveniently merged but must remain heterogeneous. Broadly considered, this does not represent a zero-sum game between North and South, but instead one means of dealing with a precarious world food situation with which the global food community is only marginally able to cope.

The tendency to overlook the diversity of agricultural technology transfer issues carries over into governmental policy-making. In the United States particular misperceptions result from the notion that a monopoly exists over a discreet body of transferable information and that it is possible to control its transfer at the governmental level. In reality, many of the "artifacts" and theoretical techniques defined above are uniquely suited to First World agricultural settings and hence are not even amenable to transfer. Control over artifacts and techniques in fact is divided among government at various levels, corporate patent holders, public and private research institutions, land grant colleges, local extension services and conservation districts, and among farmers themselves. Technology is so diversified that coordinating bodies at the Federal level such as the Agency for International Development and the Foreign Agricultural Service would be hard pressed to assemble truly comprehensive information for intergovernmental transfer even if required to do so. Secondly, information transfer occurs constantly outside official channels. Examples include commercial sales of hybrid seeds, pesticides, herbicides, advanced-technology agricultural machinery, and private consulting contracts. Individual scientists are constantly corresponding, exchanging specimens, and attending symposia. Massive quantities of technical literature are available to foreign readers through simple purchase.

When considering the role of donor nation governments in technology transfer the issue thus is not control but rather facilitation and adaptability and the ability to fund the collection of needed information and to package and deliver it to foreign users. Even in this latter area there are numerous private, non-profit foundations operating in parallel with government.

The foregoing raises several policy questions. If donor governments cannot or do not wish to monopolize the technology transfer process, how is it possible to coordinate among foreign nations regarding priority needs? Is it not possible that the objectives of non-profit foundations and humanitarian organizations will differ from those of governmental policymakers, or even among similar entities? For example, the Rockefeller Foundation has long focused on technical issue areas in international agriculture whereas the Ford Foundation has tended to concentrate on social aspects of rural development. Factoring in the commercial side of the transfer process, it is also possible that private trade efforts may conflict with the policy objectives both of governments and foundations. Examples in this latter instance would be pesticide and hybrid seed sales to nations where government and foundation efforts were being focused on the rural environment and the avoidance of monocropping to avoid blights. The idea that agricultural technology is a neatly swept arena for governmental policies and action thus does not square with global realities.

Consideration also must be given to the role of the Second World vis-à-vis the First and Third Worlds. Agricultural technology transfer occurs not only between Western industrial nations and LDCs, but also involves the centrally planned economies as providers of artifacts, theoretical techniques and foreign aid programs, and as collaborators in international research. To complicate this picture, several important Second World nations — e.g., the USSR, China and

Poland — are agricultural customers of the United States and Canada and in this sense are clients of North American agricultural technology. The information flow therefore is trilateral rather than bilateral. A case could also be made that these transfers are multi-directional, since scientific research usually involves a two-way information exchange between any two parties.

Effects on the Developing Nations

Having described the complicated setting in which agricultural technology transfer occurs, we may now move to the key issue of the impact of such transfers on the political economies of the developing nations. While these nations do not share any universal set of characteristics, most observers agree that lagging rural development is a common problem in the Third World and that this in turn frequently results from problems of geography, demography, and political and economic deficiencies. The following discussion therefore focuses on these commonalities while recognizing that each LDC faces its own unique challenges.

Lagging rural development tends to result from the multiple causes of intentional neglect by urban-oriented political elites, from conflicts in development priorities, or from complex shortages of human and physical resources. Bleak rural lifestyles have impelled many inhabitants to move to the cities where even slum conditions seem preferable to the desolation of the village. This new and expanding class of urban poor creates difficulties for the ruling elites, who must reorient economic planning or face the political consequences. One of the salient features — and accompanying problems — of the typical LDC political economy is thus subsidized foodstuffs for the urban poor. The riots that erupted in Cairo when Sadat's regime attempted to raise food prices exemplify this problem, as also the January 1984 riots in Tunisia when bread prices were decontrolled.

Subsidizing urban consumers (usually through price controls) in turn provides disincentives for local farmers to increase food production, since it is usually unprofitable to do so. Productionists who perceive the world food problem only in terms of lagging farm technology or the incapacity of LDC farmers to meet their nations' food needs tend to overlook or at least downplay this social factor. Experience has shown that in most instances farmers will grow enough for their own subsistence needs if it is unprofitable to grow more, but can be surprisingly efficient producers—even with traditional methods—if profits are to be made. This raises the question as to whether imported technology is in fact central or peripheral to rural development in the typical LDC. As Lester Brown (1978:3) notes, whether the exciting advances that agricultural technology offers ever materialize and become commercially applicable remains to be seen. In any event, considerable unrealized food production potential in the Third World can be tapped using existing agricultural technologies.

An additional problem relates to the physical size and characteristics of the traditional LDC farmstead. As discussed by Harwood (1979:3) in his thoughtful work *Small Farm Development*, the factors that limit food-producing capacity on small LDC farms in the tropics and subtropics are virtually unlimited—small plots (under 5 hectares on the average), low soil fertility and poor soil structure, poor seeds, water shortages, extreme temperatures, and a lack of access to inputs and markets. Unfortunately, agricultural development programs tend to concentrate on those few factors that seem most crucial to crop production and are easiest to improve. This does not necessarily lead to more food production or an increase in the well being of peoples who have been largely untouched by the new technologies. A question thus arises as to the efficacy of transferring existing technologies when special ones relevant to LDCs may have to be invented.

To the extent that developed-nation agricultural technology is transferable, an additional question pertains to LDC absorptive capacity as determined by local research capacity and institutional infrastructure. As Crosson (1975:17) observes, three conditions must be observed if farmers are to utilize modern technology: i) the new technology already must be invented; ii) farmers must know how to use it; and iii) they must have incentives to use it efficiently. The extent to which these three conditions can be satisfied depends on the institutional structure within which the farmer lives and works. In this sense some of the major obstacles to technological advance are institutional; all institutions in principle may be limiting. Thus a fruitful point of departure in assessing the ability of the LDCs to accelerate food production is to identify the set of institutions most likely to limit adoption of new technologies. In particular one should pay attention to agricultural extension programs, government meteorological services, farm credit agencies, and college-level agricultural training programs.

While institutions can raise barriers to progress, their absence — in the instance of scientific research — can also be a barrier. It has been estimated for the developing countries as a whole that two to three times as much growth can be obtained per dollar spent on research than from any other form of investment. The presence of a "local" (i.e., national) research capability naturally increases the benefits of such investment in agricultural research (Evenson and Kislev, 1975:507–21).

Comparing the traditionally small scale of LDC agriculture geared for local food consumption with the roles of research and local institutions, it should be noted that foreign technology on the one hand can be intrusive and a vehicle for undesirable change, or on the other it can be adapted and rendered appropriate. What the impact is essentially depends on policy and planning choices. Hybrid seeds again offer an illustration. While widespread use of these seeds is a natural outcome of the Green Revolution and hence desirable within the Revolution's objectives, uncritical acceptance and use of hybrids as marketed on a massive global scale has driven LDC agriculture toward dependence on imported seeds, pesticides, herbicides, and other technology necessary to support this non-traditional farming method. Too often the individual farmer's willingness to shift to hybrid varieties is based on admiration for the plant specimen rather than an appreciation of what inputs the new technology requires. Other examples of uncritical acceptance can be found in the purchase of oversize farm machinery ill adapted to small plots and thin soil, the utilization of pesticides and herbicides without appreciation of the potential health and environmental hazards, and the decision to plant new crops or raise animals for markets which have not yet been established.

The non-meshing of imported technology with local conditions would not be an especially serious matter if introduced on a trial-and-error, localized basis. Negative effects can be much more serious if introduced on a large scale and forced into implementation by government decree. If the result is an undesirable change in scale or agricultural practice, the negative effects not only can be economic but also political and even societal. Misapplied technology in the extreme case could disestablish a small farm economy simply because its members could not bear the costs. The successor farm economy could depend on larger landholdings, in some instances owned by absentee landlords using the tenant or sharecropper labor of former yeoman farmers. Regardless of the economic validity of such change, the political and social results could be disastrous. As Harwood (1979:27ff) observes, it is difficult to measure the well-being of small farmers by traditional commercial measures such as crop yield. New indices heavily infused with social indicators must be developed before we can be certain that economies of scale dictated by "modern" methods are the right ones.

The relationship between technological and social change in the LDCs can be seen as especially sensitive if the domestic experience of the technology-exporting United States, which is presumably better able to adapt to such changes, is taken into account. As Leo Mayer (1981:48) noted in a General Accounting Office report:

The bottom line is that research and innovation is destabilizing to a society. This became clear in the United States in the 1950s and 1960s when improved farm productivity brought with it one of the most massive migrations in history . . . Our cities today still reflect much of what generally was an influx of untrained and poorly educated workers . . . Other nations, the European Community is one example, have chosen not to allow the full effects of farm mechanization and other improved production methods to impact on their agricultures.

While the so-called "hamburger revolution" can hardly be described as transferring technology to the Third World, it does represent a kind of technological innovation in the First World that may have adverse social impacts in the LDCs, and further illustrates the negative effects of abrupt changes in land use patterns. As pointed out by a State Department contract study, the production of beef cattle in Central America for the North American market has prompted landowners to carve new pasturage out of tropical forest land; small tenant farmers have been forced to relocate on mountain slopes where cultivation promotes erosion. The negative ecological effects are reversible but the social ones possibly are not (Shane, 1980).

Notwithstanding Mayer's concerns about the social effects of technological innovation on a farm population as advantaged as the American one, the United States has made a successful transition from labor intensive to capital intensive agriculture within a brief span of years. High investment in research (especially through the century-old land grant colleges), elaborate extension efforts to turn theory into practice, sophisticated machinery, and energy intensive techniques have enabled fewer farmers to produce more food while the national economy absorbed surplus farm labor. However, while the economic rationale for such a transition may be valid in the United States, Canada and a few other major grain exporting nations, the resultant agricultural system inevitably becomes technology oriented and capital dependent. Indeed, the U.S. farm depression of the past few years suggests that there are limits to capital substitution even in the most advanced farm economies. While it is now evident that technology at this level cannot be injected into an LDC economy without serious risks, many foreign aid programs in the first two decades after World War II frequently committed this error.

Capital and labor policies in the LDCs are not driven solely by external forces. As noted in a report by the Development Coordinating Committee to President Carter in 1978, the policies pursued by many LDCs in an effort to hasten their development occasionally favor the adoption of inappropriate technology by underpricing capital and overpricing labor. These policies, sometimes inadvertent and sometimes adopted to meet the demands of dominant political or social groups, foster the use of more capital-intensive techniques to the detriment of two of the major pronounced economic and social goals of most LDCs — more equity in income distribution and more employment in the modern sector (Shane, 1978:95).

Large capital investments in the LDCs involving difficult-to-assimilate technology still occur, but not always as a result of planning errors or a lack of sophistication. There is an increasingly common, controversial trend to use large LDC land areas to produce tropical and subtropical export crops. High capital investment and specialized technologies together produce economies of scale. Some of the most massive efforts have been undertaken on Brazilian forest land, although results have been disappointing due to problems with soil structure and resultant leaching and erosion. On the other hand, North Carolina State University efforts in the Amazon watershed of Peru suggest that it may be possible to overcome problems of tropical soil infertility; benefits presumably could accrue either for high technology plantation agriculture or traditional farming at the family level. The large scale fruit growing operations in Central and South America, the Philippines and elsewhere in the tropics in many instances have been in place so many years that they can be described as originally capital-intensive and only recently technology-intensive.

Whether described as neo-plantation agriculture or multinational corporate farming, the political, economic and social impacts of the above practices are a subject of continuing policy debates. On the positive side, it may be argued that such investment and technology transfer creates jobs, builds export markets where none existed before, provides downstream benefits to workers in the processing and handling sectors, and permits access to capital for other development needs. Critics, among whom the most articulate is Frances Moore Lappé (1978:277ff), argue that the practice is in fact neo-colonialistic, that wages and working conditions are undesirable for native laborers, that LDCs are held hostage to single crop economies, and that excessive corporate profits and comparatively low product prices perpetuate income disparities between developed and developing nations. Value judgements admittedly are required to assess these arguments. However, evidence provided elsewhere in this paper would tend to support the critics. Capital and technology transfers on such a scale cannot help but be disruptive of traditional agricultural patterns and hence socially contentious. There is ample evidence that economic benefits accrue to numerically small LDC elites and fail to "trickle down" to laborers who have no employment alternatives. At the national level, dependence on a single export cash crop creates a dependency on market prices which frequently fail to keep pace with world inflation and hence the prices of imported manufactures from the First World. To the extent that capital intensive technology reduces labor requirements, the subject LDC faces additional job creation challenges, most likely in the already over-crowded urban sector.

Some development specialists have suggested that LDCs which promote rural development and reach an economic take-off stage in the middle-to-long-run become better customers for value-added U.S. food and technology exports which they can more readily afford and which are more profitable to the United States as exports than unprocessed grain. Lappé points out, however, that under conditions of LDC income inequality, excessive imports of value-added foodstuffs by the middle and upper classes can distort the development process (1978:277ff). The latter argument also extends to the issue

of whether the transfer of some food-processing technology is super-
fluous to the legitimate needs of developing nations. On the one hand
carbonated beverages may be a harmless semi-luxury for the LDC
poor; on the other, technically concocted infant formulas may be as
potentially dangerous with contaminated water added as they are
expensive and defeating of the post-pregnancy nonfertility cycle. A
more enthusiastic case could be made for the transfer of poultry
production technology — ironically part of the United States fast-food
revolution but quite applicable to the protein needs of the LDCs.

Considerable debate on the appropriateness of agricultural technology transfer relates to the energy intensiveness of many Western
agricultural methods. This is especially true of food processing,
packaging, transport and handling "downstream" from the farmstead. As noted by Pimentel et al. (1975:125–56), food production in
the United States requires the B.T.U. equivalent of 112 gallons of
gasoline per capita per year, or 336 gallons if processing, distribution
and preparation are added. If petroleum were the only energy source
and we used *all* petroleum reserves solely to feed the world population using U.S. agricultural methods, total known world oil reserves
would last only 12 years, or 53 years utilizing all potential reserves.
Contrary to popular belief, U.S. food production costs are high by
world standards; the percentage of income spent on foodstuffs is low
only because per capita income is high. Significantly, Green Revolution agriculture—which is a focal point for technology transfer—is
also dependent on high energy inputs.

It is useful to consider the implications of these energy costs for the
LDCs in the context of petroleum price history following the precip-
itous 1973 rise rather than in the probably misleading context of
a present presumably temporary decline in prices due to dissension
within OPEC. While the 1973 and subsequent price increases im-
pacted Western economies severely, the most devastating blows were
struck at the developing nations, a majority of which are not oil
exporters. Inflation and ultimately stagflation have reduced First
World demand for LDC raw materials and products while prices of
Western manufactured goods have risen; foreign investment lags
while debt service burdens increase. The drop in petroleum prices
may ease the situation somewhat, but a global economic recovery
could be expected to drive prices up again.

Since rural development projects inevitably involve long term commitments, new technology imports can scarcely be energy intensive if they are to be workable. This leads us back to the conclusion that the most appropriate technology is that which does the least to disrupt existing agriculture patterns. While it may be overstating the case, the more successful traditional LDC systems are based on energy use patterns that might well inspire a reverse technology transfer in the event of a future energy crisis. As observed by the Steinharts (1975:39), "primitive" cultures can obtain 5 to 50 food calories for each calorie of energy invested; industrialized food systems require 5 to 10 calories of fuel to obtain 1 food calorie. If some of the energy subsidy for food production could be supplied by on-site, renewable resources such as sun and wind, we might be able to sustain more energy intensive food systems. Otherwise, the choices appear to be either less energy intensive food production or famine for many areas of the world.

The foregoing discussion should not lead to the conclusion that transfers of technology from the agriculturally advanced nations to the LDCs are consistently inappropriate or doomed to failure. On the contrary, information transfer is inherently preferable to food aid in the form of commodity shipments. It must be admitted that the latter aid has been motivated by the need to support supplier country prices and to draw down stored surpluses as well as by humanitarian intentions, although the latter should not be discounted. While there has been (and presumably always will be) a place for free food in genuine famine relief situations, the temptation to regularize such shipments is reinforced by the combined concerns of donors with surplus stocks and recipient elites with urban feeding problems. Both the First and Third Worlds have learned by doing. Ironically, this improved understanding of foreign aid realities has come at a time in 20th century history when donor nations are less able to afford the transfer costs and when economic protectionism is resurgent.

Third World demands for a New International Economic Order (NIEO) at times have been shrill, and Western reactions have been defensive or, alternatively, non-responsive. In Finding #6 of its 1980 report, the U.S. President's Commission on World Hunger (1980:17) stated that "during the past decade there has been a significant decline in the Agency for International Development's capacity to deliver high quality technical assistance to help recipient nations sustain self-reliant national agricultural systems. Moreover, in many countries AID's activities fail to achieve their maximum potential impact upon food consumption by the poor because that objective is seldom explicitly incorporated as a program goal." Hence there is an issue of program quality as well as program objectives. The Commission continued by pointing out that many of the most experienced aid specialists have resigned or retired, and experts in other U.S. Government agencies are difficult to lure away from their career development ladders. Furthermore, U.S. universities are training fewer agricultural specialists with an international career orientation. AID's so-called New Directions legislation has shifted development efforts to the most needy countries—a commendable reform given past problems with the misappropriation of AID funds by LDC elites—but this legislation may be hampering needed efforts to strengthen LDC institutional infrastructures where immediate payoffs for the ultra-poor cannot be demonstrated (ibid:118).

Recognizing that it is no easy task to formulate, fund and deliver appropriate agricultural technology or for a recipient nation to make efficient use of it, we might ask what are the best areas for program focus. It would appear that the efforts most likely to succeed are those in which there are mutual benefits to be obtained by both donor and recipient. Happily, cooperative research and information exchange are productive areas involving such mutual payoffs. The possibilities are especially appealing in the field of remote sensing, which necessitates the launching of sophisticated satellites by the United States and European Space Agency nations but also elicits valuable information from other nations that in turn facilitates weather prediction, crop forecasting, and the identification of water and other resources. The promise for this new technology is exceptionally great because of the massive quantities of useful data that can now be yielded. Agro-climatic modelling techniques such as developed by an Aspen Institute pilot program in Venezuela, when combined with vastly expanded weather data from satellites and more efficient extension programs in the LDCs, should enable Third World farmers to overcome many uncertainties in the planting and harvesting cycles. (In the tropics considerable guesswork is involved in estimating the onset of rainy seasons; the potential for crop failure is great.) In arid regions satellites can help in locating new water resources for irrigation and monitor desertification processes. Also, remote sensing has valuable applications in crop forecasting, which in turn can help to anticipate famines and in normal times reduce speculation and fluctuation in world grain prices (Abel and Meer, 1979).

There is also need in the Third World for an international grain agreement whereby reserves, ongoing deliveries, and storage requirements could be more rationally calculated. First World suppliers would benefit as well, although international competition to date has made it difficult to find a time when one supplier or another would not be disadvantaged and thus unwilling to support a broad-based compact. Crop-estimation [grain-sizing] techniques are technology-based, and this is yet another area where knowledge transfer can produce mutual benefits.[2]

Certain breakthroughs in agricultural technology should offer secondary payoffs in terms of energy saving and thus should receive priority attention. For example, biological pest control methods and wider applications of integrated pest management techniques in the LDCs should reduce global requirements for petroleum-based pesticides. Innovative weed control techniques similarly should reduce the need for petroleum-based herbicides. Most significantly, a breakthrough in nitrogen fixation would offer enormous savings in fertilizer inputs. Some Asian nations already have developed advanced, small-scale technology to produce methane gas from animal wastes that could be more widely applied in the First and Third Worlds. Improved crop rotation, no-till agriculture (to the extent herbicide use does not rise disproportionately), and selective plant breeding are additional areas where payoffs in the LDCs could be significant without undue cost to donors, who in turn would be enjoying benefits within their own agricultural systems.

Plant germplasm conservation provides yet another example of an area where scientific and technological cooperation can provide simultaneous benefits for aid recipients and donors as well. However, various misunderstandings and policy differences appear to be impeding an effort that is vital to the whole global community. The LDCs frequently are the best sources for plant specimens whose germplasm must be preserved as a basis for future breeding and as a hedge against loss through man's alteration of the landscape and through over-reliance on mono-cropping. By contrast, the scientifically advanced nations undertake most of the collection efforts and provide storage facilities. The latter service is essential because only the developed nations can incur the expense and because storage facilities such as Fort Collins, Colorado are more secure from physical threats or potential neglect. On the other hand, LDC critics of this system complain that First World repository nations control priceless germplasm and utilize it to their own advantage, selling new seed varieties back to a "captive" LDC market. Their plea is for a global system of local repositories. But the United States and other key holding nations fear these could be vulnerable to political instability, underfunding or various natural disasters. Meanwhile, specimens continue to be collected and stored on a haphazard basis while countless species are lost through lack of a more coherent system. Since most of the endangered plant species—many of which have not even been catalogued or evaluated for future use—are located in the tropics, this is a unique area for technology transfer arrangements in which specimens can flow in one direction while compensatory information moves in the other.[3]

Impacts on the Developed Nations

The preceding discussion has focused primarily on the impact of technology transfers on the developing world. It is now appropriate to turn to the special circumstances affecting the possessors of technology—in most instances the developed nations. Foreign aid is an accepted feature of contemporary international relations and perhaps even a "moral imperative"; however, what about the evolving situation in which information transfer implies potential economic losses as well as the payment of political and humanitarian "dues"? S. Rajaratnam (1981:144ff) suggests: "In the economic field, the postwar zeal for promoting development in the Third World has evaporated. ... The major powers' need to recruit Cold War allies from the Third World is ... not as pressing as it once was. The other and more important reason is the fear of competition from economically successful Third World countries [which] ... have demonstrated a capacity to compete successfully with advanced countries. ... These fears about an economically dynamic Third World are both groundless and self-defeating. But in light of the fact that the advanced countries have already entered a recessionary phase, this minor challenge from the Third World has stimulated further protectionist tendencies."

The American farm crisis of the 1980s has prompted government support for a major push in agricultural exports, so another question arises as to which competitors might nullify this effort. The protectionist European Community is seen as an agricultural adversary as are Canada, Argentina and other grain-exporting nations; however, what about the populous LDCs which have turned into good agricultural customers with their modest gains in spendable income? Might not the transfer of agricultural know-how undercut the export push on which the United States may become dependent? As noted previously, the palm oil chapter in United States aid history provided unwelcome evidence of such a possibility. Theoretically at least, LDC progress toward producing basic foodstuffs is raising income levels to a point where these nations are becoming better customers for *higher* priced (i.e., processed) foodstuffs in which the United States still has a producer advantage. However, theory does not guarantee Congressional support for program funds to share technology so long as such a risk exists. It is therefore timely to reexamine potential benefits to the United States and other technology producers.

It should be noted that technology itself can be a money-earning export. We are used to thinking of commodities and manufactured goods as staples of the export trade, but are reminded that the late 20th century is the "information age"; software, technical knowledge and services are the staples of the post-industrial economy. In the agricultural sector, references already have been made to such diverse subjects as sophisticated space hardware supportive of data services, to hybrid seeds, advanced farm machinery, and innovative farm management methods. Whether the subject is hardware or software, patents and copyrights link knowledge to proprietary rights. Intellectual property is presently very salable and likely to become more so in the future. For example, recent advances in biotechnology have built hopes for revolutionary advances in crop production, animal breeding and human and animal health. One prominent official in this fledgling industry estimates that 13 key products, including animal growth hormones, human and animal food-feed additives, and sweetener raw materials, presently have an annual global market value of about $600 million; with a biotechnology-based industrial strategy this could grow to $1.7 billion as early as 1990 (Glick, 1982:290–91). Exports that will help to meet this market demand will include research data and processed information as well as tangible products. Thus, technology transfer is once again demonstrated to be an inseparable part of the agricultural export trade.

The U.S. Supreme Court's Chakrabarty decision upholding the patentability of life forms has expanded proprietary rights.[4] But U.S. and European patent laws are mutually conflicting. For both domestic and international business reasons, industrial secrecy thus may take precedence over knowledge sharing. Had not laboratory safety standards been markedly relaxed through growing confidence in the safety of biotechnology processes, the possibility existed that this type of technology might have been transferred prematurely to the Third World — not in the form of development aid but rather through manufacturers' offshore flight from regulations.

The commercial bonanza that is expected to result from exports of genetically engineered agricultural processes and products may involve a paradox. Driven by the need for venture capital, this industry has sought (or acquiesced in) foreign financial intervention through research contracts, mergers, and outright corporate acquisitions. The result of such interventions usually involves a short-term financial gain for the U.S. firm, but technology inevitably is transferred to the foreign investors. In this case the transfer is *within* the First World rather than between the First and Third Worlds. Once transferred, the technology can be used by the foreign beneficiary to sell products and processes that may compete directly with those originally offered by the U.S. firm. The implications for the agriculture sector are especially great in view of the growing world market for genetically engineered animal vaccines, animal feed additives, and substitutes for petroleum-based pesticides and fertilizers.

It may be argued also that multinational corporations transfer technology — agricultural and other — for their individual profit, irrespective of the impact on their parent-developed nations or the developing areas where they may operate. The adverse effect on parent nations thus far seems to be in the area of tax losses, but in the future an information drain may pose additional problems. This is especially true with regard to processes that support domestic employment. A different case, probably beneficial to the United States and a few other "headquarters" nations, involves a limited number of giant land development corporations. Their methods involve the reclamation of large tracts of unproductive land with earth-breaking devices, the development of elaborate irrigation works, highly mechanized production techniques, and plantation-style harvesting and marketing of products. This technology repatriates profits which obviously do not take into account negative social impacts at the operational sites and hence negative political reactions to indirect parent-nation involvement.

There appears to be a consensus that exports of value-added — i.e., processed — agricultural products from the United States are more profitable than those of raw foodstuffs. It could be argued, therefore, that technology transfers that enable (or encourage) developing nations to undertake this type of processing on a post-importation basis will undercut profitability for exporters. In the silvaculture area, the United States already finds itself in the predicament of exporting raw lumber to Japan where it is processed (with great technical efficiency) into plywood for re-export back to the United States. The implications of forfeiting technological advantages in the more sophisticated areas of food processing are thus sobering. Profits presumably can be made with the initial transfer of know-how in the service sector but subsequently lost in the manufacturing sector. (Transnational corporations, as distinguished from national enterprises engaged in international trade, may be partially immune from this danger by virtue of their offshore capabilities.)

The implications of agricultural technology transfer for originating nations such as the United States must also be assessed in terms of what they gain from reverse flows of knowledge and data. Germplasm conservation already has been cited as an area in which specimens collected from the Third World are stored in First World repositories to the obvious benefit of plant breeders and seed companies. Indeed, the future of U.S. agriculture is vitally dependent on continued access to those irreplaceable materials. Offshore data likewise is an essential component in the functioning of information and monitoring projects which depend on Western engineering, sophisticated hardware and software, and distribution facilities. It may be argued also that the primarily tropical Third World constitutes a giant laboratory where — because of climate, soil and other conditions — much of the research on future agricultural technologies must be carried out.

Overseas research possibilities are so numerous that the only practical approach appears to be a cooperative one. Research and technical assistance networks are already in place to facilitate such scientific interchange. While there are perennial problems of funding and coordination, the existing infrastructure at least reflects decades of institution building and trial-and-error approaches to complex missions. As described by Wortman and Cummings (1978:129ff), one of the most valuable research networks exists under the aegis of the Consultative Group for International Agricultural Research (CGIAR), an outgrowth of the International Rice Research Institute. The nine component institutions are unique in that they are governed by autonomous boards of trustees, enjoy talented international staffs, are mission-oriented, can develop programs quickly, tailor programs and training to specific requests and needs, institutionalize the knowledge gained, and maintain continuity in their work. When United Nations special agencies, national aid and research entities and private organizations are considered in tandem with CGIAR, it may be seen that adequate conduits for information flow between the developed and developing worlds are already in place.

The World Food and Nutrition Study undertaken by the National Research Council (1977) summarized the key benefits that accrue to the United States and the developing nations from collaborative research:

— Reduced production costs that increase the profitability of farming; stimulate food output, development and reciprocal trade; permit more stable food prices; and help to control inflationary pressures.
— Reduced year-to-year fluctuations in world supplies of grains and other major foods, which are accompanied by sharp price fluctuations that cause economic difficulties for U.S. and developing country farmers and consumers.
— Reduced environmental pollution and consumption of energy and scarce minerals.
— Increased knowledge about the complex interrelationships among diet, health, life style, and factors in the physical and socioeconomic environments.

Specific examples of research benefits already obtained by the United States include the adoption of virus-resistant South American Pangola grass to restructure beef pastures in the Southeast; $50 million in annual savings from utilization of a wheat strain from Turkey; and the use of Israeli oat varieties to resist crown rust infestation.

Technology Transfer in the Global Context

Having briefly examined the special implications of agricultural technology transfer for the First and Third Worlds and the special benefits of two-way information flow, it is now appropriate to consider this interchange in the context of global community interests. The concepts of "Spaceship Earth" and global interdependence perhaps have been overused. Nonetheless, present-day political and economic realities make it virtually impossible for any nation to remain immune from global problems. Food is one of these.

The neo-Malthusians, distributionists and productionists view global food problems from different vantage points and propose different solutions; each approach is partially correct and multiple solutions are indeed required. Agricultural technology transfer is especially relevant to the efforts of the productionists, whose challenge was succinctly stated in a recent workshop sponsored by the National Research Council: "World food production must double in the next 40–80 years, depending on the rate of population growth. In 1975, when the world population was 4 billion, 3.3 billion tons of food were produced. If population grows at an annual rate of 2 percent, the 8 billion people in the year 2015 will require 6.5 billion tons of food. Two-thirds to three-fourths of this increase must come from intensified production on existing land and the rest from bringing new, marginal lands into production. Both tasks will require new and appropriate technology" (Lewis, 1982:147).

Political leaders in both the developed and developing worlds have a common interest in seeing that this fundamental human need is satisfied, since inadequate food supplies surely can lead to uncontrollable political upheavals. There is therefore a political imperative for expanding and improving the flow of information that will enhance world food supplies. However, in the real world, attention tends to be given to clearly defined, short-range problems for which decision makers may be held accountable. A challenge exists for economists, political scientists, planners, and aid specialists to translate long-term needs into such near-term requirements. One task is to determine how agricultural technology transfer can serve the needs of the global community while being supportable by donor nations, assimilable by recipients and injurious to none. As Hopkins and

Puchala (1980:183–86) observe, very little effort has been made to undertake new types of research that could lead to changed government priorities, or to cultural and social changes. They add that American policy should continue to uphold the principle that agricultural science and technology are collective goods developed for the benefit of mankind. The U.S. government should similarly adhere to, and emphasize, the conviction that information about agricultural conditions within any nation must be available to all nations, since the orderly evolution of markets and development plans depends critically on such information.

It should be reiterated that information transfer will occur on a fairly broad international scale *outside* governmental channels and irrespective of governmental desires, filling limited needs and objectives. It is not in governmental interests to alter this process by attempting to monopolize knowledge transfer, but rather to focus on vital areas where only public action will bridge the gaps, and to provide needed coordination. Some costs of technology transfer can only be borne by public funds. Obvious examples include: support for international research networks and consortia; contributions to specialized international agencies such as the FAO; the dedication of a portion of costly space programs to agricultural remote sensing; large-scale research on agricultural energy problems; nutritional interventions; and germplasm conservation. Such cooperative efforts should strengthen the existing infrastructure for technological exchange as well as lead to a better sense of priorities among all nations.

The benefits of agricultural technology transfer must be recognized as simultaneously economic, political, social and scientific, even if only one or two of these several objectives are pursued. As a senior official of the World Bank noted, there is not one but many food problems, and a surprisingly large number of them are the result of human and governmental decisions rather than immutable forces (Walters, 1975:26). Unfortunately, decision making on the part of most governments and nongovernmental institutions occurs on an incremental basis and tends to be addressed to near-term problems perceived as economically or politically "urgent." The multiple problems of world feeding, of which agricultural technology transfer is an important component, are inherently long-term and their urgency is not always understood or appreciated. Therefore, better international agricultural transfer policies can only result from more coherent, long-range thinking about the world food problem as a whole.

Chapter 10

Unbalanced Technological Change and Income Disparity in a Semi-Open Economy: The Case of Brazil*

FERNANDO HOMEM DE MELO

Since the 1950s many economists have emphasized the importance of technological change for economic growth and, in particular, for increases in agricultural productivity (e.g., Solow, 1957; Griliches, 1963, 1964). Several studies have even estimated the rate of return of public investments in new technology research, mainly for specific crops (Griliches, 1957, 1958; Ayer and Schuh, 1971).

More recently, the literature has given attention to the distributive effects of technological change, that is, how such change affects patterns of income distribution and therefore individual well-being in the countries involved. Bieri, de Janvry, and Schmitz (1972) were already calling attention to the lack of theoretical and empirical efforts in this area at a time when large public-sector investments were being made in agricultural research. Other studies followed. Akyno and Hayami (1975), for example, focused attention on aspects of rice research in the economic development of Japan. Scobie and Posada (1978) investigated the impact of technological change in the rice sector of Colombia, and Hayami and Herdt (1977) discussed the effects of such change among subsistence farmers.

We seek in this chapter to add to this more recent line of emphasis by focusing attention on the distributive implications of technologi-

*Earlier versions of this paper were presented at the 18th Conference of the International Association of Agricultural Economists, Jakarta, Indonesia, August 1982 and the 12th World Congress of the International Political Science Association, Rio de Janeiro, Brazil, August 1982.

cal innovations on low-income food consumers in less-developed countries. In the words of Singer and Ansari (1978:47), "even the ultimate objective of development is a great deal more than a mere increase in per capita income; questions relating to the use and distribution of this income are as important dimensions of development policies as its increase."

Our starting point to open this discussion is an economy characterized as "semi-open," in the context of Myint's conception, in which ". . . a large part of the domestic economy must remain insulated from the impact of foreign trade and comparative costs. . . ." (1975:32). In such cases, which are likely to correspond to the actual situation found in many less-developed countries, we intend to show that a pattern of technological change concentrated on agricultural exports can impair the growth of domestic crops, alter relative prices (domestic-exportables) and bring negative effects (in terms of real income) for low-income consumers. As an illustrative case, we make specific reference to technological changes and their distribution effects in the 1967–1979 massive expansion of soybeans in Brazil.

Technological Change, Resource Use, and Price Effects

In this section we show how major technological innovations can affect resource use among the subsectors of Myint's "semi-open" economy. Let us take a hypothetical case of an important agricultural innovation that has two fundamental characteristics: First, it is significant with respect to individual crops and regions benefited; second, it is spread over a relatively short period of time. Such an innovation would provide the necessary conditions for changing farmers' expected returns from available options and could therefore encourage them to alter the composition of their output (e.g., maize, rice, or beans to soya). As the new technology became diffused and available, farmers could thus be encouraged to transfer resources away from their current farming arrangements to the activities that the new technology favored. Not only that, if they could expand their total acreage by bringing new lands under cultivation they would do so, and the expansion would quite likely be oriented predominantly towards those crops that the new innovations favored.

Whether resource transfers would be made and new lands, if available, brought under cultivation would depend on the type of technological innovation, market conditions, and the possibility of factor substitution. As for type of technological innovation, in this chapter we shall examine the so-called "bio-chemicals,"[1] crop varieties arising through the work of selection and varietal improvement, including a greater response to fertilizer application (although greater dependence on chemicals for pest and disease management). They result in greater yields, cause practically no change in the quality of the final product, and reduce production costs (Kuznets, 1972). They have been widely applied not only on lands traditionally used for older and sometimes entirely different crops, but new lands as well.

Concerning market conditions as being important for determining the degree to which resources will be transferred and therefore affect crop mixes in favor of the new technology, we refer here to price elasticity of demand.[2] The higher the value of price elasticity of demand the more likely will new innovations be adopted and production expanded and therefore resources transferred.

This general conclusion can also be obtained indirectly from Castro's (1974) analysis of demand for new agricultural lands on which to apply new technology.[3] His is a two-stage (two sub-functions) production function with four factors: land and land-saving capital (bio-chemicals) on the one hand, and labor and labor-saving capital (machinery) on the other. The substitution possibilities are high within each subfunction but low between them. Assuming constant prices for all four factors mentioned above, Castro has shown that the demand for land would increase if $S_T\eta + S_L\lambda > \lambda_T$, where S corresponds to factor shares of the aggregate factors (land plus bio-chemicals; labor plus machinery), η to the price-elasticity of demand, λ to the elasticity of substitution among the two subfunctions, and λ_T to the same parameter in the land subfunction (land and bio-chemicals).[4]

As a reference, it should be mentioned that the elasticity of substitution measures the extent to which the land-bio-chemicals ratio changes in response to changes in the ratio of the price of land to the price of bio-chemicals. With a pattern of land-saving technical change (bio-chemicals innovations) and a high elasticity of substitution for land-bio-chemicals (λ_T) a key parameter determining whether the demand for land would increase is the price elasticity of demand for the crop (η). The higher this value, the more likely is the increase in the demand for land to be cultivated with the crop experiencing technical change.

Suppose now that an attractive technology, encouraging market conditions and proper factor substitutability are all in order, to the extent that demand for land is increased. Suppose further that we place all these matters into the Myint-type "semi-open" economy that we described earlier, that is, a subsector closed and another open to international transactions. Under these conditions what the resource transfer effect is becomes clearer as we look at who the beneficiaries of that transfer are. It has been surprising, perhaps, for the outcome under some circumstances to be increased poverty and malnutrition. This is because if farmers transfer resources away from domestically consumed crops to exportables, basic food prices tend to rise (or if price controls are in effect, food just gets more scarce) and any poor who must buy that food find it increasingly difficult to feed their families.

The situation just described, where a part of agriculture is closed to international transactions and another is open (imports or exports) is recognized more and more in the literature. For instance, Abbott (1979) mentions the case in which food self-sufficiency is a national policy and the government allows consumption to increase or to decline with the level of domestic production. If resources are transferred out of domestic production in favor of exportables, domestic prices can rise and the poor eat less well. In addition, Castro and Schuh (1977) show that because of the different responses of quantity demanded to given price changes — greater for exportables and lower for domestic crops — the choice of products to receive public investments is important for determining who the beneficiaries of agricultural research will be.

To pursue these matters further, in the following analysis we assume the agricultural sector to consist of two subsectors: exportables and domestic products. The distinction is based on the functioning of domestic markets, that is, if they are open or closed to international transactions (imports, exports).

In an open market economy, domestic prices are determined by the functions of supply and demand of exports, while in a closed market economy prices are determined by the relevant internal functions. A closed economy is usually a consequence of a country's commercial policy enacted through instruments such as tariffs, import licensing and, in the extreme, import prohibitions which, along with internal cost conditions, determine prices. Now, if we assume a "small country" case in international trade, the domestic price of an exported crop will be determined by the international price, the exchange rate, and marketing costs. In such cases, prices and profitability of exported crops influence prices of domestic crops (although domestic crop prices do not influence the price of exportables). As a result, if supply is low or the country in question through import restrictions has adopted a closed market, it is possible for internal domestic crop prices, due to inadequate internal production and import restrictions, to stay above their price in the world market.

With such a situation in mind we can analyze the distributive implications for consumer families of technological change biased, in a certain time period, towards one or more exportable crops. If we consider the case of land-saving bio-chemicals, the individual marginal cost curves and the market supply curve would shift to the right. This results from the fact that technical change will bring about a decrease in production costs of farmers when comparison is made between the old and the new technique at their optimal combination of factors and with their prices constant. With a perfectly elastic export demand, the cultivated average of the export crop would increase,[5] with all these effects occurring with a constant product price. In this specific case domestic producers appropriate all direct benefits from technological change,[6] including increase in land prices.

When total acreage is fixed, the change in the expected rate of return of the exportable crop (or crops) benefited by innovations would lead to the attraction of resources previously employed in the domestic subsector (possibly, also, from exportables not benefited) and, consequently, the real prices of domestic crops would increase. This would continue until a new equilibrium relative price is attained, always assuming no change in the commercial policy which brought the domestic subsector into existence. In other words, the composition of output would be affected in favor of the exportables benefited by technological change.

A second possibility is when total cultivated acreage can increase. In such a case, the process of acreage growth would tend to be directed towards the favored crops, in addition to the effect in regions already under cultivation. In those cases where the innovations are specific to a certain agricultural region of the country, the unfavored ones could show an increase in the production of domestic crops (because of

higher real prices) — by assumption, crops not benefited by technological innovations — partly compensating the production fall in the
former region. The important point to emphasize is that, as a result of
such pattern of innovations, prices of domestic crops internally may
stay above the international ones.

Furthermore, if the so-called domestic crops include important
foods, in terms of budget shares of low income families, the real price
increases following the change in growth rates would be like a tax with
regressive incidence. As a result, the unbalanced nature of the process of technological change among crops with different market characteristics could bring a worsening of income distribution (from the
expenditure side). For that scenario, it is necessary that we maintain
the assumption of no changes in commercial policy or, alternatively,
that the international market, at least for certain commodities, is not a
supplier able to complement domestic production. In addition, an
intermediate case should be mentioned; internal prices of domestic
crops stay above the export prices but below the import ones.[7]

With these ideas in mind we can now clarify recent trends in Brazil
with respect to the soybean industry.

Evidences from the Brazilian Case

For some time Brazilian agriculture has been characterized by the
existence of two subsectors, exportables and domestic crops, the first
being open and the second closed to international transactions.[8] Over
time the first group has included soybeans, oranges, sugar, tobacco,
cocoa, coffee, peanuts and cotton, while the second, with some variations over time, has consisted mostly of rice, edible beans, manioc,
corn, potatoes and onions — important foods for low-income families.
It should be noted that at least some of the domestic crops are potential
exportables since there exists either well-developed international
markets (corn, rice) or a developing one (manioc). However, in varying degrees, over time, internal costs have prevented a favorable
competitive position internationally and, as a result, such crops have
not been exported regularly or on a significant basis.[9]

In this section we will show that one of the main reasons for the
tremendous growth in soybean production (see Table 10.2 below) for
the early sixties were technological innovations occurring in Southern Brazil. In addition, we will show this growth resulted in signifi-

cant changes in the composition of output against domestic-food crops, resulting in an inadequate rate of output growth. Finally, we will attempt to show the effects of such changes in the index of food prices for families at different income levels.

We hasten to note that our focus on technological innovations is not meant to imply that Brazil has not benefited from its new soybean technology. Surely the country's stronger export performance has been of great importance in helping to control the magnitude of its external debt crisis.[10] Our objective, however, is to focus attention on the distributive implications of an unbalanced pattern of crop growth induced by technological change.

We also note that technological innovation in soybeans was only one of three main factors favoring exportables in Brazil from the mid sixties. The other two were: a) the introduction, in 1968, of exchange minidevaluations, and b) a favorable period of international prices, mainly during the first half of the seventies. Consequently, the evidences of price effects, presented below, must not be understood as deriving exclusively from technological change in soybeans production. Nevertheless, we will show that "technology" is of great importance in explaining the change in crop mix that began in the second part of the sixties and which resulted in the expansion. Hopefully, in the future a more complete evaluation will be possible focusing on the relative importance of each factor.[11]

In Brazil, soybeans represent the most recent example of a large expansion in acreage during a short time interval and in a limited geographic extension. In 1960, total soybeans acreage was 177 thousand hectares, with 159 thousand in the state of Rio Grande do Sul. By 1980, the respective figures were 8,965 thousand and 3,988 thousand.[12] The increase in international prices started in 1971–72 and reached maximum levels in 1973 and 1974. In 1972, total soybean acreage already was at 2,292 thousand hectares. Certainly, the favorable period of international prices during the early seventies made a positive contribution in the growth of acreage. However, this was not the principal factor behind the commencement of soybeans expansion in Brazil, since during the sixties prices remained practically constant in nominal terms. In addition, it should be noted that several commodities had price increases during certain years in the seventies, but none of them experienced an expansion even comparable to that of soybeans.

Table 10.1

Time of Introduction and Adoption of New Soybean Varieties
in Brazil and Effects in Yields

Period	Average Yield Brazil (Kg/Ha)	New Varieties
1960	—	Amarela comum, Abura, Pelicano e Mogiana.
1960–68	1,060	Hill, Hood, Majos, Bienville e Hampton.
1969–74	1,394	Bragg, Davis, Hardee, Santa Rosa, Delta, Campos Gerais, IAC-2, Viçoja e Mineira.
1975–80	1,541	IAS–4, IAS–5, Planalto, Prata, Perola, BR–1, Paraná, Bossier, Santana, São Luiz, IAC–4 e UFV–1.
1980	1,740	BR–2, BR–3, BR–4, Ivaí, Vila Rica, União, Cobb, Lancer, CO-136, IAC–5, IAC–6, IAC–7, UFV–2, UFV–3, Cristalina e Dokko.

Source: M. Kaster and E. R. Bonato, "Contribuição das Ciências Agrárias para o Desenvolvimento: A Pesquisa em Soja," *Revista de Economia Rural* 84 (1980:405–34).

Table 10.1 shows a summary of the agronomic research for soybeans in Brazil, in terms of new varieties, the time of introduction and the impact in actual yields. Two of these varieties—Santa Rosa and Hardee—were very important for the expansion of soybeans during the late sixties and early seventies. The first one originated at Campinas Agronomic Institute, São Paulo, beginning with the introduction of American varieties and, later on, the development of lineage L-326 in 1958. In the mid sixties it became commercially available in Rio Grande do Sul under the name of Santa Rosa. The variety Hardee, also of American origin, was studied and adapted at Campinas after 1965. Such facts also reveal the importance of international knowledge transfer for the process of technological change in Brazilian soybeans, mainly by obviating the need to repeat research completed elsewhere and so leading, as in the case discussed by Guttman (1978), to a decline in research costs. Also of note is that from the 48 varieties recommended for planting in 1980, 26 had originated in national programs and 22 came from the United States, half of which were in the form of lineages.[13]

Over the years the research centers emphasized several other agronomic aspects of the crop (Kaster & Bonato, 1980): selection of Rhizobium's lineages; direct planting; control of weeds, diseases and pests; density; and planting time. By the late seventies soybeans research was one of the most developed in the country, and recently the centers have helped develop production systems for regions other than Southern Brazil (East and Center-West). In addition, "the research is aiming to develop technology specific for soybeans production in regions with latitudes below 15°S. The prospects for obtaining varieties specifically adapted to lower latitudes, as well as for knowledge about crop management are excellent, and new in the world" (Kaster & Bonato, 1980:432). During 1970–75, the average annual rate of growth of soybeans yields per hectare in Brazil was 7.5 percent (12.3 percent in the state of Paraná), a rate well above those observed for other crops, either exportables or domestics.

Table 10.2 shows the domestic production growth rates during

Table 10.2
Annual Rates of Growth of Domestic Production, Brazil,
14 Commodities, 1960/69, 1967/75 and 1970/79 (in %)

Commodities	1960/69	1967/76	1970/79
1. *Domestic*:			
Rice	3.20	2.47	1.46
Edible Beans	5.37	−1.93	−1.90
Manioc	6.05	−1.86	−2.09
Corn	4.74	3.55[a]	1.75[a]
Potatoes	4.34	1.34	3.73
Onions	3.87	4.77	9.27
2. *Exportables*:			
Soybeans	16.31	35.03	22.47
Oranges	6.01	12.73	12.57
Sugarcane	3.63	5.10	6.30
Tobacco	5.30	−	6.16
Cocoa	2.55	−	3.73
Coffee	−7.10	−6.34[a]	−1.54[a]
Peanuts	5.89	−6.80[a]	−12.06
Cotton	1.51[a]	−1.99	−4.41

[a] This letter indicates the coefficient as not significantly different from zero at the 5 percent level.

Source: Production data from FIBGE-Fundação Instituto Brasileiro de Geografia e Estatística.

1960–69, 1967–76 and 1970–79 for fourteen exportable and domestic crops. The data show that from the sixties to the seventies Brazilian agriculture experienced a number of important changes: after a relatively uniform performance among crops during the sixties, in the seventies the country had a substantial deterioration in domestic crop performance and a greater expansion of certain exported ones — a process clearly led by soybeans. The worst cases were manioc and edible beans — each showing large declines — while rice and corn production stagnated. These are Brazil's basic foodstuffs, declining at the same time the country's population was growing at the annual rate of 2.47 percent.

If the first five domestic-food commodities of Table 10.2 are aggregated in terms of "per capita" caloric/protein availability,[14] the data show an annual rate of decline (1967–79) of 1.44 percent and 1.42 percent respectively. The availability in Brazil of rice, corn and edible beans was only very slightly increased by imports. These five domestic-food crops, in addition to cotton and pasture land, were the agricultural activities most affected by the substantial expansion of soybeans in Southern Brazil.[15] Furthermore, as mentioned in the previous section, the substitution effect of technological change was not limited to domestic crops. As can be seen, cotton, an exported crop, was also negatively affected.

Even when we consider other food products such as sugar, wheat, meats (beef, pork and poultry), eggs and milk, total per capita caloric/protein availability declined during 1967–75 (annual rates of 0.58 percent and 0.60 percent respectively), with a small recovery during 1976–79. The importance of wheat and sugar also increased over the period, the former being a traditionally imported food which had a policy of price subsidies for consumers beginning in 1972 (Carvalho, 1982:32–42). During 1970–79, the growth rate of wheat availability was greater than that for domestic production, indicating a greater role of imports. Without the policy of consumption subsidies and larger wheat imports, the fall in caloric/protein availability would have been larger than that observed.

As a consequence of this unbalanced performance of domestic production and food-product availability, it is relevant to investigate how different family income classes were affected. To do this, the information from the 1974–75 family budget survey (ENDEF-FIBGE)[16] carried out in the states of São Paulo, Rio de Janeiro, as well as South and Northeast regions can be used. Such data show important differences in consumption among expenditure classes[17] and regions. For instance, in the four regions the share of rice and edible beans in total food expenditure varied between 21.1–27.9 percent in the lowest income (expenditure class) and between 3.3–7.2 percent in the highest one.[18] Similar behavior was observed for the shares of corn and its products, wheat and its products (except in the Northeast), tubercle and roots (manioc, potatoes) and sugar. The contrary, however, was seen to occur in the case of meats and eggs/milk/cheese, that is, increasing shares as incomes rise. Also, a few important differences could be observed in the Northeast: manioc was much more important in lower income classes, while wheat was more important for higher income classes.

These strong differences in consumption structures over income (expenditure) classes, as well as the distinct behavior of physical availabilities, are good reasons for expecting an uneven impact in terms of prices and real incomes for Brazilian families. This would occur through changes in market prices and consequent income effects via each product's share in total food expenditure. After examining the price behavior of thirteen food items in São Paulo during 1967–79, those with largest increases were manioc, edible beans, beef, pork and corn, three of them being domestic foods[19] originating in the crop sector and of greater importance to lower-income families.

In an attempt to verify the distributive effects of this situation, we estimated the increase of the food-price index by income classes (based on ENDEF-FIBGE, 1974–75) for the states of São Paulo, Rio de Janeiro, and the South and Northeast regions. We computed the indices from the shares (weights) of each product in total food expenditures for the two states and two regions of Brazil and the observed prices in São Paulo (cost of living index). Excepting São Paulo it should be clear that we are only approximating the situation that families over different income classes face. One can expect, however, that the various prices will vary mostly because of spatial distribution of production and consumption, without significantly affecting the rates of growth over time.

Table 10.3 shows the estimated food-price index for the Northeast region only. The direction of the change, however, was the same in the two states and the other region analyzed. Larger price increases showed up for the lower-income families. Lower-income families

Table 10.3

Indices of Nominal Food Prices, Expenditure Classes, Northeast Region, 1967/79

(1967 = 100)

Years	<1.0	1.0–1.5	1.5–2.0	2.0–3.5	3.5–5.0	5.0–7.0	>7.0
1967	100	100	100	100	100	100	100
1968	126	124	123	122	122	121	120
1969	160	155	152	150	148	148	147
1970	198	191	188	185	183	181	181
1971	253	243	237	231	229	225	223
1972	319	302	291	280	275	270	268
1973	430	407	389	374	365	359	356
1974	557	533	514	498	490	483	479
1975	766	721	688	658	640	624	606
1976	1,133	1,033	970	912	876	848	817
1977	1,546	1,401	1,317	1,242	1,195	1,156	1,124
1978	2,087	1,947	1,856	1,768	1,720	1,671	1,631
1979	3,311	3,081	2,917	2,770	2,686	2,609	2,542
Annual Rate	28.6	28.0	27.5	27.0	26.7	26.5	26.2

Source: Primary data, ENDEF-FIBGE (Weights) and FIPE-Fundação Instituto de Pesquisas Econômicas (Prices in São Paulo).

were therefore those mostly affected by the transformations which occurred in the composition of agricultural output in response to technological innovations in soybeans and to changes in external variables (prices and exchange rate). The situation in the Northeast was the most serious and for that reason in Table 10.3 we have reproduced all the data. When we compare the lowest and highest income classes in terms of annual rates of growth of nominal food prices we see that during 1967/79 they were 28.6 percent and 26.2 percent respectively. Alternatively, the cumulated increase over the 1967–79 period, for the lowest income class was 32.9 percent more than for the highest income class. Given that the lowest income class in the Northeast spent more than 60 percent of its total income on food as compared to 17 percent for the highest income class, we can see that the poorest groups suffered the most in terms of losses in real income. For São Paulo, Rio de Janeiro and Southern region these greater cumulated increases were 10.0 percent, 12.7 percent and 8.7 percent more for the lowest income class as compared with the highest one.

In discussing the different results among states and regions, two main reasons should be mentioned: a) the greater importance of manioc and edible beans for lower-income families in the Northeast as compared to other regions (26.7 percent against 2.4 percent among the income extremes in that region, versus 14.2 percent against 1.4 percent in the South). These two commodities were the ones with greater increases in retail prices during 1967–79. b) the relatively small importance of wheat in the consumption habits of lower-income families in the Northeast (4.2 percent against 10.0 percent among the extremes in the Northeast, and 8.9 percent against 7.1 percent in the South). It should be recalled that, beginning in 1972, the Brazilian government subsidized wheat prices to all consumers, which, in the Northeast, had a regressive incidence, since it was consumed relatively more by higher income classes. Results such as those described, particularly for the Northeast, can aggravate those obtained for nominal income distribution in Brazil with the census data of 1970 and 1980, in the sense of greater concentration of the real income distribution,[20] since food prices, a key component in the cost of living of lower income families, increased much more for them, which had a larger negative impact on their purchasing power.

Conclusion

We have sought to investigate possible distributive implications of an unbalanced pattern of technological innovations in a "semi-open" economy composed of two subsectors in agriculture — production for export and production for domestic consumption. The case of most interest is where innovations are concentrated in export crops during a relatively short time period. In such circumstance our conclusion is that the composition of total agricultural output might change in favor of exportables. Without changes in commercial policy, prices of domestic crops will rise. If these are important foods for lower-income families, real income distribution will be adversely affected.

We have also given attention to the Brazilian case where a semi-open agricultural economy has long existed. In the domestic subsector important foods can be found, mainly in terms of budget shares for lower-income families. We examined the technological innovations in the soybeans industry, its extraordinary expansion and the subsequent transformations in the composition of total agricultural output. We concluded that lower-income Brazilian families have suffered the most from food price increases during 1967–79 induced, in part, by these technological innovations.[21] To the extent that real income distribution is taken into account when deciding on public investment in agricultural research, our results indicate the need to increase such investments for domestic food crops. In the beginning, the benefits will appear as lower food prices for consumers. Later on, society as a whole should also gain, since as a result of declines in costs and prices some of the crops would become exportables and provide foreign exchange earnings (rice, corn, manioc, etc.). For crops without a well-developed international market (edible beans) most of the benefits would go to domestic consumers. It is also highly likely that indices of malnutrition among the poor could be reduced, perhaps significantly.

Notes

Notes to the Introduction

1. The most frequently cited case is Mexican emigration to the United States.

2. By International Political Economy (IPE) we mean the *complexe* of social, political, and economic relationships, institutions, and practices, both domestic and international, that shape, and are shaped by, international economic transactions (e.g., trade, foreign investment, international business transactions and organizational patterns, international banking and monetary dealings, and foreign aid). Students of international political economy assume an interdisciplinary perspective, calling upon the research insights of political science, economics, sociology and other disciplines in the social sciences.

3. All the authors in this volume broach this subject.

4. In part because they have mostly ceased buying land, preferring to give financial and marketing incentives to producers on a "contract-out" basis.

5. Susanna Davies, "Markets, States, and TNCs: Power and the World Grain Trading System," unpublished manuscript.

6. Christopher D. Scott, "The Determinants of Investment and Divestment by Transnational Corporations in the Latin American Food Industries," unpublished manuscript.

7. Ibid.

8. Moore (Ch. 4) notes that even in the relatively successful South Korean case income distribution patterns are now turning against the small farmer.

Notes to Chapter 1

1. Food security as a basic need shaping the organization of social life is explored by Mair (1962). Its basic importance is also well stated in A. Berg (1973).

2. For elaborations of this see Mair (1962), I. Wallerstein (1974), Tilly, ed. (1975), especially chapter 5.

3. In 1973–75, when production dipped for the first time in twenty years, millions of people's attention shifted to food problems. Newspaper headlines mentioning food increased several fold, and major efforts to improve national and international food security were undertaken. *New York Times* front page headlines with food references, for instance, increased from an average of six to eight a week to over twenty a week during this period; this evidence was uncovered in a study by Brunner (1975).

4. A good example of the overly heavy focus on malnutrition as the major impact of food shortages is the Report of the Presidential Commission on World Hunger, *Overcoming World Hunger: The Challenge Ahead* (Washington: G.P.O., March 1980) which focuses on the physical aspects of food and blames hunger on poverty. The latter point, while true, is about as helpful as blaming death on the character of the human organism. Debates on the size of the hunger problem are reviewed in Poleman (1983).

5. See the World Food Council, *Report of the 5th World Food Council Meeting* (Ottawa, September 1979).

6. See for example Tilly, ed. (1975); I. Wallerstein, *The Modern World System* (1974), and Wolff (1974).

7. On this point see Bates, *Markets and States in Tropical Africa* (1981), and also Lipton (1977).

8. Alamgir (1980); and see Srinivasan's (1983b) review of A. K. Sen's latest book *Poverty and Famines: An Essay on Entitlement and Deprivation*.

9. For the statistics for this judgment see D. Johnson (1983):1–34; and also D. Johnson (1975).

10. This is not to suggest also that the management of famine is not reliably addressed by such organizations as the United Nations Disaster Relief Organization, or the International League of the Red Cross, or that no improvement is desirable in the early detection, quick delivery and more effective administration of food relief. A number of steps proposed by various experts would improve the situation. See for example Jean Mayer (1974 and 1977).

11. See Reutlinger and Selowsky (1976), and also Polemen (1983) and Srinivasan (1983a).

12. For an insightful discussion of peasant predicaments see J. Scott (1976): 13–55.

13. On peasant behavior see Goran Hyden (1981).

14. Central America occasionally has heavy storms that damage crops, but its weather-related production variability is modest, especially compared to the Soviet Union.

15. Indeed, they are probably more important than international agreements on wheat. See Daniel T. Morrow (1980).

16. For a discussion of this growing world condition see Lindbloom (1977), and I. Wallerstein (1974).

17. See, for example, Wortman and Cummings, Jr. (1978), and the numerous reports of the World Food Council and FAO on Food Security, e.g., *Report of the Ninth Session of the Committee on World Food Security* (Rome: FAO, CL86/10, May 1984), especially paragraph 33.

18. See Lappe and Collins (1978), Tony Jackson (1982), and George (1977).

19. Generally, this is the strategy preferred by economists such as C. Peter Timmer, Walter P. Falcon, and Scott R. Pearson (1982).

20. This is the general conclusion of work reported in Alberto Valdes, ed. (1981).

21. See Cochrane (1979) and Mancur Olson Jr. (1965) who describe the collective good aspect of the county agent system.

22. See Hyden (1983) who makes an excellent case for the over-ambition of state efforts. The classic critique of Africa is Berg (1981).

23. The European commitment has grown in 1972 when the United Kingdom and Ireland joined and again in 1981 when the FAC increased from 4.5 to 7.6 million tons and the EEC went from roughly a 1.3 to a 1.67 million ton pledge.

24. See Alex McCalla (1967) who puts forward the now common explanation for international stability in 1950-1970 as due to the larger role played by U.S. and Canadian surpluses of grain held off the market to support domestic farm programs

25. See Valdes and Castillo (1984). Peter Svedberg (1984) seems to offer a more optimistic view of the ability of developing countries to keep up with import needs. He shows evidence that when import costs rise so do the export prices of the agricultural commodities of LDCs, and thus ease the balance-of-payments crunch. However, he does not address agricultural exports' real value relative to other needed imports of industrial goods from developed countries, as this chart does. While prices rise together, this does not help the already large portion of an LDC import bill that is spent on food imports rather than other needed goods, or help the overall terms of trade experienced in the international market.

26. Such a view is advocated by John W. Mellor and Bruce Johnston (1984).

27. This is the classic example of the "prisoner's dilemma."

28. These and other examples of the weakness of food power as a diplo-

matic mode versus food policy based on domestic politics may be found in Robert Paarlberg (1983).

29. For a major look at the expanded responsibility of the state see the entire volume of *Daedalus* on The State (Fall 1979).

30. This and other cases of the importance of food and politics are cited in Hopkins (1980).

Notes to Chapter 2

1. In 1983–84, the United Nations Food and Agriculture Organization (FAO) identified twenty-four countries with serious food emergencies. These countries include some affected by the current drought, such as Benin, Botswana, Cape Verde, Chad, Ethiopia, Gambia, Ghana, Ivory Coast, Lesotho, Mauritania, Mozambique, Rwanda, South Africa, Senegal, Swaziland, Togo, Zambia, and Zimbabwe, as well as countries with more chronic food problems, such as Angola, Somalia and Tanzania. In 1984–85, the food emergency countries were: Burkina Faso, Cape Verde, Chad, Mali, Mauritania, Niger, Senegal, Burundi, Ethiopia, Kenya, Rwanda, Somalia, Sudan, Tanzania, Angola, Botswana, Lesotho, Mozambique, Zambia, and Zimbabwe. Import requirements are generally defined as imports necessary to maintain per capita consumption at previous levels (generally already below FAO's minimum nutritional standards) and are not projections of what countries will actually import. Actual imports will depend on purchasing power and food aid allocations. For a more detailed description of import and food aid calculations, see United States Department of Agriculture/ERS, *Food Aid Needs and Availabilities, 1983* (Washington, D.C.: 1983).

2. The regional descriptions draw heavily on the previous and ongoing work of country experts in the Africa Middle-East Branch of USDA/ERS. We thank Susan Buchanan for information on the Horn of Africa, Peter Riley for information on Mozambique, Angola, Zambia and Zimbabwe, Margaret Missiaen for analysis of West Africa, and Mary Burfisher and Nadine Horenstein and Mary Bohman for work on the Sahel. For evaluation of country-specific situations, see U.S. Department of Agriculture/ERS (July 1984b).

3. For a good summary of recent economic changes and their impact, see Carol Lancaster (1983:149–166).

4. FAO estimated that the twenty-four countries with serious food emergencies would require 3.6 million tons of assistance in 1983–84. ERS, using slightly different approaches, arrived at nearly three million tons for 19 countries. As of May 1984, the bulk of these needs had been covered. ERS estimates that 34 Subsaharan African countries would require 4.8 million tons of food aid in 1984–85 to keep consumption levels at the status quo level. See U.S. Department of Agriculture/ERS (July 1984a).

5. See, for example, Agricultural Development Council (ADC) (1982).

6. For a discussion of macroeconomic and international linkages affecting U.S. agriculture, see Edward Schuh, "Economic and International Relations: A Conceptual Framework," *American Journal of Agricultural Economics* 63 (December 1981):767–78.

7. See, for example, Sara Berry, "Agrarian Crisis in Africa? A Review and Interpretation," African Studies Association (Boston, MA: December 1983).

8. "Cash crops" and "export crops" have frequently been synonymous in the African context, primarily because colonial structures incorporated African food producers into the market via exports, under the (then correct) assumption that traditional food production and trading patterns could be adequate to feed the local population. In some cases (e.g., rice in Senegal) imported food was used as a wage good for the then relatively small urban population.

9. For an excellent overview of African production systems, see Bede N. Okigbo, "Agriculture and Food Production in Tropical Africa," in Agricultural Development Council (1982).

10. U.S. Department of Agriculture/ERS (1981), *Food Problems and Prospects in Subsaharan Africa*, provides an overview of technological problems and constraints.

11. For projections of food import requirements, see U.S. Department of Agriculture/ERS, *Food Problems*, and Huddleston (1984).

12. For an extensive discussion of the role of non-production factors in hunger, see Christensen (1978a:745–74).

Some studies have in response down played the importance of increased production—often because it is associated with changes which increase income and affect inequality. See, for example, Lappe and Collins (1978); George (1977). For an analysis of the need for increased production under African conditions, and the importance of regional differences, see Christensen (1978b:181–220).

13. See the World Bank, *Accelerated Development in Subsaharan Africa*, (Washington, DC, 1981) (commonly known as the Berg Report).

14. For the classic statement of the "urban bias" thesis, see Lipton (1977). For a good discussion of the politics in Africa (domestic) setting, see R. Bates (1981).

15. For strong critiques of these institutions, see Bates (1981), and World Bank (1981a). U.S. Department of Agriculture/ERS (1981) provides detailed listing of parastatals and government practices.

16. For a somewhat technical discussion of the conditions under which devaluation may not stimulate economic activity by triggering such a shift, see James Hanson, "Contractionary Devaluation, Substitution for Production and Consumption and the Role of the Labor Market," *Journal of International Economics* 14 (1983):179–89.

17. The term state generally refers to a government organized within established territorial bounds and able to exercise authority over the people within its frontiers. A nation, on the other hand, is a community of people who feel that they belong together because they share elements of a common heritage and have a common future destiny. While the normative ideal of a nation-state includes both state and nation within common frontiers, this is not achieved in many developing countries. Cf. Crawford Young (1976), especially pages 66–97.

18. See Lindbloom (1977:24–25).

19. Some of the reasons for lack of organization flow from the classic public choice literature. Cf. Norman Frolich and Joseph Oppenheimer (1978). For an expert application to Africa, see Bates (1981).

20. For an extensive discussion of the differences see Browne and Cummings (1984).

21. This section draws heavily on the discussion by Timmer, Falcon, and Pearson (1983:215–34).

22. World Bank (1981a) provides a classic development perspective. For the IMF view, see J. de Larosiere (1982); S. Kanesa-Thasan (1981); and S. M. Nsouli (1982).

23. For greater detail on price changes, see Christensen and Witucki (1982).

24. Unofficial exchange rates are taken from *Pick's Currency Yearbook*.

Notes to Chapter 3

1. There is some controversy about the exact levels of current calorie consumption. The World Bank (1981:35) estimated that daily calorie intakes in the rural highlands were 1,971 calories per capita in 1980, but the Bank itself suggested that these figures were optimistic. The estimate on malnutrition is from the World Bank (1981b:35). The 420 calories per day figure is reported by *Quehacer* (October 1982:43).

2. The points in this paragraph are described and documented in detail in McClintock (1981:60–63) and McClintock (1982:138–140).

3. I am indebted to my colleague Catherine Allen, an anthropologist who studied in a rural area of Cuzco in the mid-1970s, for this point.

4. In 1974, about 80 percent of respondents in two coastal cooperatives and two highlands peasant communities belonging to a larger cooperative reported that the cooperative "helps some" or "helps a lot." For details on this survey item, see McClintock (1981:289). In 1981, when the cooperative system was under attack, peasants in two communities belonging to the same large highlands cooperatives were even more enthusiastic about their enterprise. The 20-odd respondents in a non-random survey stated unanimously that the

new cooperative was better and more socially just than the haciendas.

5. See McClintock (1980:11–13) for details. Workers' wages in the three cooperatives I studied increased from approximately 50–60 soles a day in 1973–74 to between 470 and 676 soles a day in 1980. The inflation rate for the period 1973 through the first quarter of 1980 was officially 275 percent; the U.S. dollar was worth about six times as much in March 1980 as in the 1969–1975 period.

6. See McClintock (1980:34–35); McClintock (1981:226, footnote 11); Matos Mar and Mejía (1980b:265–270); and Martínez and Tealdo (1982); and Billone, Carbonetto, and Martínez (1982) for details.

7. Almost 100 percent of sugar, 68 percent of cotton, and 26 percent of rice are produced on cooperatives. See Caballero and Alvarez (1980:80–81).

8. While the recent analyses of Peru's reform provide little specific data on production, they never indicate production declines. See Matos Mar and Mejía (1980b:88–93) and Eguren (1982:116–122).

9. There are few discussions of the types of products in the cooperatives. Data are not broken down by type of enterprise. However, data for agricultural exports and production in recent decades indicate very little change in product type (Caballero, 1980:27; Eguren, 1982:102–109; OAS, 1981:54). Also, the products receiving official credit have barely changed at all during the 1970s; about 80 percent is destined to cotton, rice, corn, and potatoes (Matos Mar and Mejía, 1980b:287). The only significant exception to this pattern on continuity is for poultry and eggs; production approximately doubled during the 1970s for these goods.

10. On production patterns in SAIS Cahuide, see the Annual Reports mimeographed by the enterprise.

11. Peru's agricultural exports declined at a rate of 5 percent annually during the decade 1970–1980; "traditional" exports (cotton, coffee, sugar, and wool) accounted for about 95 percent of all exports (Martínez and Tealdo, 1982:139–141). While nontraditional agricultural exports (cacao, spices, nuts, tobacco, insects, asparagus, etc.) increased at a 4.6 percent annual rate, they still did not account for more than 5 percent of agricultural exports and are not on lists of Peru's "major exports" (Martínez and Tealdo, 1982:142–143; OAS, 1981:71).

12. Such recommendations were made to me in interviews with Norval E. Francis, Jr., Agricultural Attache, U.S. Embassy, Lima, on July 7, 1983 and with David Flood, Chief for Agriculture, U.S. AID/Peru, in Lima on July 14, 1983.

13. Estrella's manager said that he would emphasize livestock production if the enterprise had been his own. As mentioned in footnote 9, poultry production increased considerably in Peru in the 1970s, almost entirely on private holdings.

14. See C. Scott (1981:303) and Maletta (1982:424). Many of these jobs were in the upper jungle area (Amazonic uplands), but employment on the coast, where the major cooperatives are, also probably rose. Scott emphasizes various other reasons than do I for the rise.

15. See especially Matos Mar and Mejía (1980b:270–271).

16. Data courtesy of ENCI. Price increases were roughly double inflation in 1978, 1979, and 1982.

17. Interview with Ing. Manual Villatana of ENCI, in Lima, July 12, 1983.

18. Calculation from ENCI data.

19. See Martínez and Tealdo (1982:104). The major source is the official Agrarian Bank.

20. The coast has about 15 percent of the farm population, and during the last decade received roughly 65 percent of the credit; the highlands, with approximately 70 percent of the farm population, has received merely around 15 percent. For farm population figures, see Larson and Bergman (1969:303); for loan data, see Martínez and Tealdo (1982:102) and Maletta and Foronda (1980:118).

21. Belaúnde government officials were quite open on this score in interviews with me in early 1983. See also the government's new laws, especially the *Informativo Legal Agrario*, No. 10, which includes the entire text and commentary of the new *Ley de Promoción y Desarrollo Agrario*.

22. No data on subdivisions have been compiled. This estimate is based on discussions in both the countryside and Ministry of Agriculture offices, February and July 1983.

23. Figures for the 1968–69 and 1977–78 bienniums from Portacarrero (1982:439) and for 1981 from Peru National Planning Institute (1982:4). Figures are for funds spent, not programmed. 1981 *soles* were estimated to be worth 10 percent of 1970 *soles*.

24. Figures for 1960–67 from Fitzgerald (1976:88); for 1968–69 and the for the 1970s from Portocarrero (1982:440); for 1981, from the Peru National Planning Institute (1982:5); and for 1982, from the Peru Presidency of the Republic (1983:216–228 and 292).

25. See Peru Presidency of the Republic (1983:215–228) for 1982 data. Population figures from Peru, Presidency of the Republic (1983:front matter).

26. Discussions and documents from the World Bank, the United States Department of Agriculture, and the Peruvian Ministry of Agriculture.

27. See World Bank studies and also Caballero (1981 and 1984).

28. See the Centro de Investigación de la Universidad del Pacífico (1980: 70 and 85).

29. See "Proyecto Majes," a collection of data on the project from the Peruvian Central Reserve Bank.

Notes to Chapter 4

1. Between 1960 and 1979 the economy grew at an average rate of about 10 percent per year (Kim and Joo, 1982:13).

2. Between 1960 and 1979 agricultural production grew at an average rate of about 4 percent per year (Ibid.:13).

3. Ban, et al. (1980:414–415) and Korea, Ministry of Agriculture and Fisheries, *Yearbook of Agriculture and Forestry Statistics* (1982:Table 127).

4. Additional agricultural incomes have accrued disproportionately to producers of these specialist crops located near or within easy access of the two main urban conglomerations, Seoul and Pusan (Keidel, 1981).

5. "In 1982 alone, about 100 people from 15 foreign countries received Saemaul education . . ." (*Saemaul in New Age*, 1982:189).

6. By 1982, 16,000 foreigners had been to Korea "to study or observe the Saemaul Undong" (Ibid.:189).

7. Major Speeches by President Park Chung Hee (n.d.:171 and 175).

8. Most of what is said here about South Korea applies equally to North Korea.

9. In contrast to the mass of the population, the contemporary South Korean elite is marked by a degree of cultural heterogeneity arising from varying experiences of foreign education (Dore, 1977:199).

10. Korea, Ministry of Agriculture and Fisheries, *Yearbook of Agriculture and Forestry Statistics* (1975:Table 12).

11. Ibid.:Tables 10 and 11.

12. Ibid.:Table 89.

13. Ban, et al. (1980:307). The question of whether there are changes in agrarian structure is discussed in E. Lee. One major problem in interpretation of trends lies in doubts about the validity of data series on tenancy. While tenancy is in principle almost completely illegal, no attempts have been made to enforce the law on tenancy and land transfer. Farmers are in large degree willing to report tenancy. However the data on tenancy in the main official data series, reported in the annual *Yearbook of Agriculture and Forestry Statistics*, clearly understates tenancy by a large margin. See E. Lee (1979:54) and Land Economics Research Centre (1966).

14. On the politics of this period see Hahn (1975).

15. On the history of the agricultural research and extension services see Ban, et al. (1980:Ch. 6 and 269–270).

16. For Taiwan see Yu (1978:175–176).

17. For detailed figures see *Basic Agricultural Statistics, Republic of China* (1983:Table 24) and Korea, Ministry of Agriculture and Fisheries, *Yearbook of Agriculture and Forestry Statistics* (annual). For the broad comparison see Ho (1982:978).

18. For details of these policy changes see Kim and Joo (1982:Ch. 4); Ban, et al. (1980:Ch. 8 and *passim*); and Korea Development Institute (1982:Chs. 1–3).

19. For a description of the Office for Rural Development see Ban, et al. (1980:Ch. 9).

20. See, for example, the annual *Saemaul in New Age*, and *Major Speeches by President Park Chung Hee*.

21. For less critical examples see Kim and Lee (1978) and Whang (1981). A more analytical and insightful account is given by Choe (1978).

22. For example Wade (1982 and 1983) and Aqua (1976).

23. On the KMT in Taiwan see Winckler (1981a and 1981b); and Clough (1978:Ch 2).

24. Figures supplied to the author by the Ministry of Agriculture in Seoul.

25. Korea, Ministry of Agriculture and Fisheries, *Food and Agriculture in Korea*, 1983:62–63.

26. Kim and Joo (1982:39); Korea Development Institute (1982:7 and 47); and Korea, Economic Planning Board, *Korea Statistical Yearbook* (1981:497).

27. The government eliminated its fertilizer deficit in 1976 and incurred only a small loss in 1977, but the 1978 increase in oil prices led to an increase in the subsidy both in terms of the ratio of government purchase to sales price and in absolute cash terms.

28. National Livestock Cooperation Federation, *Quarterly Review* 3:2 (1983:109–111).

29. This observation comes from the author's field research in Taiwan.

30. Korea, Economic Planning Board, *Korea Statistical Yearbook* (1967: Table 87); and Korea, Ministry of Agriculture and Fisheries, *Yearbook of Agriculture and Forestry Statistics* (1982:Table 76).

31. Average farm size has been increasing slowly, rising from 0.92 hecatres in 1971 to 1.08 hectares in 1981 (Korea, Ministry of Agriculture and Fisheries, *Yearbook of Agriculture and Forestry Statistics*, 1982:Table 8). But the absolute number and proportion of farms covering more than three hectares is continually declining (Ibid.:Table 12).

32. The promotion of rural industrialization and of non-farm income is now a major component of rural policy. "The Off-Farm Income development Planning Group, which is chaired by the Vice Minister of the Economic Planning Board, has been established since 1981 as a national level planning and coordination organization for the rural industrialization program" (Korea, Ministry of Agriculture and Fisheries, *Food and Agriculture in Korea*, 1983:63).

Notes to Chapter 5

1. See, for example, Winrock International, 1981; Mexico, (SINE-SAM), 1980–81; Rojko and Schwartz, 1976; Regier, 1978.

2. Mexico, Secretaría de Programación y Presupuesto, *La Población de México, Su Ocupación, y Sus Niveles de Bienestar* (Mexico: SPP, 1979).

3. This association is confounded statistically by the great differences in scale among herds, exports and consumption. Further analysis requires the standardization of the relationship about a common mean.

4. Coefficients of pasturage are determined by the Secretariat of Agriculture to determine how much land per head of cattle is permitted in various regions under the agrarian reform law.

5. Note that some of that soya production is for export to the European Economic Community where it is ground and processed for oil and cattle feed.

6. U.N., Center on Transnational Corporations, *Transnational Corporations in Food and Beverage Processing* (New York: United Nations, 1981), p. 23.

7. Much of the more specific information in this paper comes from case studies of Mexico. While Mexico in no way represents a "modal" type for Latin America, it is suggestive of some of the larger relationships indicated by aggregate data presented for all of Latin America. Obviously, case studies on all of the major cattle countries would be required to validate this thesis completely. For more information on the Mexican case, see S. Sanderson (1985).

8. Unión Nacional de Empacadoras, T.I.F., (1970).

9. S. Sanderson, 1982; Dyer and O'Mary, 1977; Ebeling, 1980; and "Beef Extra: The Changing Face of Cattle Feeding," *Farm Journal* 106 (No. 1, January 1982).

10. Simpson (1978; 1979a); U.S. Department of Agriculture (1978a); Choi (1977); McCoy (1979).

11. Aside from the methodological issues arising from great differences in herd scale, complicating factors in this assessment include the aggregation of production for domestic consumption with production for export, and the permeability of the U.S.-Mexican border. Nevertheless, when cattle numbers are standardized and correlated, Mexico's cattle cycle correlates with the U.S. ($r = .799$), as does Argentina (.732), Brazil (.853), Canada (.949), and Australia (.910).

12. The reader is reminded to note that raw data have been standardized in the figure about a mean of 0.

13. U.N., Center on Transnational Corporations (1981).

Notes to Chapter 6

1. Companion papers discuss the historical relationship between Britain and Third World sugar producers, and the history of international sugar agreements. See Mahler (1981) and Mahler (1984).

2. As put by John Adams, "I do not know why we should blush to confess that molasses was an essential ingredient in American independence. Many great events have proceeded from much smaller causes" (cited in Sheridan 1973:339). For discussions of the sugar trade in the seventeenth and eighteenth centuries see Dunn (1972); Sheridan (1973); and I. Wallerstein (1980: 160–175).

3. Indeed, the sugar boom of the seventeenth and eighteenth centuries resembled in many ways the oil boom of the present. Just as the Persian Gulf has become an area of supreme strategic importance during the 1970s and 1980s, so the Caribbean was one of the key arenas of global politics in the eighteenth century, with the Spanish, Dutch, French, Portuguese and English all vying for territory and influence. The Caribbean became "a cockpit of great naval campaigns" which were concluded by omnibus treaties in which various islands were swapped among the Great Powers "in the Olympian way in which eighteenth-century statesmen decided the fate of the outer world" (Bowle, 1974:115).

4. Carman (1930:199). Colonial ships returning from French ports typically tied up briefly in Jamaica, where they received a false statement that their cargo had been obtained there. Deerr (1950:414) quotes a contemporary commentator:

This trade is now grown barefaced. . . . There are now at the North Side three ships from London under pretence of loading there, which is in truth not able to load one ship. But we are assured that they go loaded with French sugar and indigo. . . . For God's sake, put a stop to it . . . and we are such mercenary wretches as to give them all the assistance we can for our own undoing, by furnishing them with all materials for Sugar Works.

5. In 1739 Parliament in part compensated West Indian merchants for its leniency by passing a Sugar (Direct Trade) Act allowing them to sell their sugar directly in European markets without passing through British ports — a privilege the French allowed their own West Indian colonies. During the mid-1700s sugar prices were relatively high, alleviating pressure on British West Indian producers and helping to mute somewhat their opposition to North American smuggling.

6. The first two quotations are from Rothbard (1976:48–49); the third is from Morison et al. (1969:144). A useful discussion of the transformation from particular grievances to general principles is offered in Bailyn (1967). A number of pamphlets protesting the Sugar Act are reprinted in Bailyn (1965).

7. The United States prohibited participation in the slave trade by *American* shippers in 1792.

8. In practice, some smuggling of slaves continued until the abolition of slavery in all British colonies in 1834.

9. The refining industry in the United States grew very rapidly in the 1850s, particularly in major port cities which were accessible to imported sugar. As described by one contemporary observer, referring to New York City, "the sugar refining interest of New York has increased, within a few years, to a business of great magnitude, till the city is nearly encircled by enormous refining establishments, easily recognized by their lofty walls and chimneys." Between 1850 and 1856 alone American sugar refining experienced an extraordinary fourfold increase (Eichner, 1969:39).

10. A classic description of sugar in Louisiana is offered in Sitterson (1973, reprint of 1953 book).

11. A detailed description of the emergence of beet sugar is offered in Deerr (1950). The later development of beet cultivation in the United States is described in Eichner (1969:229–263).

12. For a number of years Hawaii had been granted special treatment in the American market over other foreign producers. The McKinley Tariff of 1890 eliminated this preference and, indeed, offered bounties to sugar planters in the United States. The desire of influential Hawaiian planters to regain preferred access to the American market was a central motivation for the power play that resulted in the deposition of Queen Liliuokalani in 1893 and the annexation of Hawaii by the United States in 1898. For a detailed discussion of this fascinating episode in American history see Tate (1965).

13. A Democratic Congress briefly eliminated bounties for domestic sugar in 1895, but they were soon restored when high-tariff Republicans regained a majority. Among other incentives the government offered potential beet sugar growers seeds imported from Europe. See Thomas (1971:458).

14. Article III, cited in Huberman and Sweezy (1960:15). For a detailed discussion of the adoption of the Platt Amendment see Thomas (1971:450–458). For other useful historical discussions of Cuban-American relations see Farber (1976); O'Connor (1972); and Goldenberg (1965). Finally, for a classic critique of American-Cuban relations see Jenks (1928).

15. A detailed chronology of the Sugar Program is offered in Gerber (1976).

16. Most of the belligerents during World War II entered into bulk purchasing arrangements for the supply of primary commodities in an effort to ensure supply and avoid major price increases. The British, for example, enacted bulk purchasing agreements with Commonwealth sugar producers; see Moynagh (1977) for a discussion.

17. An interesting discussion of Cuban sugar policy since the break with the United States is offered in Roca (1976).

18. The Kennedy Administration at one point had Cooley's telephone tapped, but criminal charges were never filed. Aside from possible criminal misconduct, it was evident that sugar quotas were often granted on a blatantly political basis. In 1965, for example, the House Agriculture Committee, as a favor to house Speaker John McCormick of Massachusetts, awarded a sugar quota to Ireland, which normally exported no sugar at all. With the offer of a guaranteed market in the United States Ireland began to export some of its domestic sugar to the United States at 6 cents per pound while importing sugar for its own needs from Poland at 2 cents per pound (Livernash, 1979:832).

19. The largest quota recipient, the Philippines, was allocated about a quarter of the foreign sugar quota for 1974. Other quota recipients for 1974 included (in order of the size of the quota) the Dominican Republic, Brazil, Mexico, Peru, Australia, Ecuador, Argentina, Taiwan, Indian, Costa Rica, Colombia, Nicaragua, Panama, Guatemala, Venezuela, West Indies, South Africa, El Salvador, Fiji, Belize, Haiti, Mauritius, Swaziland, Thailand, Malawi, Honduras, Bolivia, Paraguay, and Ireland. Cuba and Rhodesia retained formal quotas that had been suspended by executive order (Andrews, 1975:1297, note 95; and *Congressional Quarterly Almanac*, 1975:227).

20. Sugar price fluctuations are influenced by the unusual nature of sugar as an agricultural commodity. Unlike any other major cash crop sugar derives from two entirely different sources, cane and beet, which are affected by very different climatic forces. Cane sugar prices tend to fluctuate in cycles of some 8 to 10 years. Cane plants typically (there are exceptions) have a life span of about eight years, with peak production occurring in the second or third year and then gradually falling off. Since heavy plantings occur in times of high prices, when planters have both the desire and the resources to invest in replanting, large numbers of plants tend to mature at essentially the same time, driving down prices. Prices usually rise again as the yields of mature plants diminish and fields have to be replanted, forcing planters to wait for a year or more until large yields begin again. During each cycle planters tend to be locked into cane since replanting requires a major investment that must be recouped over a number of years.

Beet sugar is subject to no such cycle, and sugar beets are usually planted as part of a crop rotation. The unstable prices one would expect to result from the natural forces affecting cane sugar are thus somewhat mitigated by beet production. But since the majority of sugar traded internationally has traditionally been cane, this is less true than might be expected.

For an excellent discussion of the more technical aspects of sugar as a commodity see Hagelberg (1975). For basic series of statistics on non-U.S. sugar production see U.S. Department of Agriculture, Foreign Agricultural

Service (periodic); for U.S. domestic production figures see U.S. Department of Agriculture, Crop Reporting Board (periodic).

21. Sugar Act payment provisions were extraordinarily complex — intentionally so, some argued, in order that only cognoscenti would be fully aware of how they operated. See *Congressional Quarterly Almanac* (1974:227) for a summary of the main provisions.

22. A 7-million ton import quota for foreign sugar remained in effect, but this was considered meaningless since imports at this time were only about 5 million tons.

23. In the 1977–78 marketing year, for example, sugar producers in the European Community were guaranteed more than twice the world price; see Commission of the European Communities (1979).

24. This discussion of American ratification of the ISA follows closely the discussion in Mahler (1984). Actually, quotas were imposed when the market price of sugar reached 14 cents per pound and lifted at 15 cents. Buffer stocks, financed by a levy of 0.28 cents per pound on free market trade, were authorized up to 2.5 million metric tons and were to be released in three equal stages at 19, 20 and 21 cents per pound.

Note that, alone among major sugar producers and consumers, the European Community did not ratify the International Sugar Agreement.

25. There was a permanent minimum duty on sugar of 0.625 cents per pound that applied even if world prices were high enough that no action was necessary to defend U.S. domestic producers. Current U.S. sugar policy is described in Womach (1983).

26. This open-ended authorization is similar to the variable levy of the European Community about which American policy makers so often complain.

27. Honduras received 52 percent of the reallocated quota, Costa Rica 30 percent and El Salvador 18 percent.

28. Sugar producers find some refuge in the fact that under current technology corn sweeteners are not easily granulated, and are thus not adaptable to many of sugar's traditional uses.

29. See Mahler (1980) for a detailed discussion of these issues.

30. These efforts live on in the sugar policies of the European Community; the Common Agricultural Policy for beet sugar is as generous as American support programs and has stimulated production to the extent that Third World sugar producers must now in most years compete in export markets with a substantial Community sugar surplus. For discussions of the place of the Community in the world sugar economy see Mahler (1981:489–92) and Mahler (1984).

Notes to Chapter 7

1. Malnutrition appears in different degrees of seriousness and may be caused by improper diets as well as by lack of nutrients *per se*. A study on malnutrition in Latin America by the Inter-American Development Bank (1979:3) reports that

Malnutrition and undernutrition apparently significantly affected at least 71 million people, or one-fourth of the population. At least 57 million suffered from *undernutrition* (i.e., "hunger" level intakes of food so inadequate in quantity as not to permit healthy and active life); *primary malnutrition* (i.e., inadequate food intakes in quality of diet directly leading to physical and mental impairment such as anemia due to lack of iron, sight impairment due to vitamin A shortages; loss of weight or slow growth due to improper balance of calories and proteins); and *secondary malnutrition* due to malabsorption of nutrients caused by genetic or environmental factors and leading to intestinal disorders and infectious diseases.

2. During 1977–79 agricultural exports, as a percentage of a country's total merchandise export earnings, ranged between a low of 10 percent (Canada) to a high of 94 percent (Argentina); U.N., Food and Agriculture Organization (1981).

3. See the discussion of ranking countries by degree of income maldistribution by Amartya Sen (1980:55–58); and *World Bank Development Report 1983*, Table 27, pp. 200–201.

4. For an extended recent discussion of regional integration, see Inter-American Development Bank, *Economic and Social Progress in Latin America, 1984 Report*.

5. Interview material, December 1984.

Notes to Chapter 8

1. Perhaps for this reason the literature on food aid has become disproportionately large, "characterized by its singular failure to reach any kind of agreement on the fundamental issues. These include whether there should be food aid at all, the most appropriate commodities to be used, the types of use to which food aid should be put and the criteria for deciding who should receive it, on what scale and under what conditions" (Maxwell, 1983:21).

2. See Dalibor (1984) on the economic crisis in Nepal, and Riding (1977) on Guatemala. In general, food-aid critics argue that it depresses agricultural production either directly or indirectly, imposes alien food tastes on recipients, marginalizes the rural population, and justifies a recipient government's dysfunctional agricultural policies. See D. Gale Johnson (1978), Nicholson and Esseks (1978), and U.S. Department of Agriculture, *Global Food Assessment, 1980a*:692.

3. Discussions frequently argue that food aid should be used to:

a. succor the poor and starving people of the world;
b. assist farmers in advanced market economies to dispose of surpluses, thereby supporting their incomes through a higher priced food market;
c. develop new trading patterns that may enhance the donor's export markets;
d. contribute to the overall development of recipient countries by helping them to grow economically and to improve the quality of life for their people;
e. alleviate poverty and thereby make less attractive communist solutions to hunger, such as revolution;
f. support diplomatic initiatives.

In specific cases food-aid supporters have given an almost endless list of its achievements—"improvement of animal husbandry, crop diversification, settlement of new lands, rehabilitation, regeneration of natural pastures, reduction of unemployment and underemployment, community development, vaccination, improvement of health, alertness and proficiency of school children, control of cholera and typhoid, educational reform including improvement of urban/rural balance, slum clearance, promoting fairer income distribution, increasing labor productivity, and even training in carpet making!" (The quote is from Stevens, 1979:25, but does not necessarily reflect his position as he was simply illustrating arguments).

4. Illustrative in this trend towards integrated understanding are Maxwell (1983) and Clay and Singer (1982). Singer and Maxwell (1983) note four arguments for food aid and four arguments against it. In favor: that it helps to stabilize prices; and that it is additional aid. Against: that it has a disincentive effect on production; that it is inefficient; that it creates dependency; and that it is allocated using mainly political criteria.

5. Theodore W. Schultz (1960), first raised the question in the academic community, followed seven years later by Jitendar S. Mann (1967). The points raised in these articles have been repeated in most of the literature critical of aspects of food aid. See, for example, Kern (1968), Isenman and Singer (1977), Dudley and Sandilands (1975), U.S. General Accounting Office (1975), Bethke (1980), Hayes (1981).

The theoretical counterthrust was begun by Franklin M. Fisher (1963), who argued that Schultz and others overstated the negative price effects of food aid by implicitly assuming that the elasticity of domestic supply is zero and that there is a single market for imported and domestic commodities so that distribution of concessional imports substituted directly for domestic demand. The theory, that price disincentives on internal markets can be reduced if food aid is distributed outside domestic market channels in such a way that it creates effective new demand, was tested positively in India by

Srivastava, Heady, Rogers, and Mayer (1975). Christopher Steven's work (1979) in four African countries showed no negative consequences. John W. Mellor (1981) sees food aid as having the potential to contribute to economic development and therefore to an enhanced food market demand. But *The Economist* (London: December 26, 1981):79–81 sees the relationship as being mostly negative, and others make an impressive case for alterations in the program if it is to have a desirable economic impact. See Austin and Wallerstein (1979), and Puchala and Hopkins (1978). The whole controversy has been sufficiently stinging to advocates of food aid that some now advance the following recommendations for allocation and distribution so as to insure that food aid does not have adverse effects on food production in recipient countries:

i) the flows of food aid must not replace domestic production;
ii) food aid must not lead to a reduced effort by the government in question to maintain and develop domestic production;
iii) food aid should not turn consumers away from food products which are or can be produced domestically.

Aside from all that, "donors should also try to establish linkages between deliveries of food aid and action to promote agricultural development." Concrete suggestions are given. OECD (1981):147.

A bibliography covering the mid-1960 to mid-1970 period listing twenty-two Indian case studies and seven from Colombia (the next most popular case) has been prepared by H. Schneider (1975).

6. See, for example, Sinclair (1981), Christensen (1978a), AID, *Policy on Agricultural Assets Distribution: Land Reform*, PD-72 (Washington: AID, January 16, 1979) in which recent AID director John Gilligan is quoted as saying that if studies show that aid exacerbates the plight of the poor then the Agency would be prepared to consider withholding it; and, Lappe, Collins, and Kinley (1980:79).

7. See, for example, Srivastava, et al. (1975), Puchala and Hopkins (1978), Stevens (1979), Rogers (1971), Nicholson and Esseks (1978), Griffin (1974), and even a popular but central organ for the aid community, Agenda, which published Edward W. Coy's "Latin America: A Search for Solutions Amid Turmoil," (May 1981):7–11.

8. With specific reference to Botswana, Lesotho, Upper Volta and Tunisia, see Stevens (1979: 68, 73–75, 166, 172–79, and 187). Tarrant (1980:256) argues that food aid, under specific circumstances associated with domestic price elasticity of supply related to risk and stability, can contribute to long-term price stability to the benefit of food producers and consumers.

9. The "dependency" literature is huge and may even be unmanageable. One of the best brief classifications is by Ronald H. Chilcote (1981:296–312). A short but extraordinary review is by James A. Caporaso (1980). Discussions of

food aid and "dependency" generally do not enjoy a profound explicit sensitivity to dependency literature, although they do address analogous themes. See, for example, Nicholson and Esseks (1978:679–719) and Lofchie and Commins (1984). It is of interest that of the several political problems that appear to surround food issues as increasing population puts pressure on existing supplies and as poverty exacerbates hunger in lesser developed countries, the USDA picked "international dependency" as one to emphasize. See U.S. Department of Agriculture (1980a:712–719). Tarrant (1980:259), speaks of food aid, dependency and problems of a "beggar mentality." A growing concern is the degree to which commercialization of agriculture in developing countries to garner new export markets reduces their domestic food production, a process made possible, in part, by food aid imports which cover a portion of the food deficit. See P. Bye (1980), and all the chapters in this volume. Sometimes the resulting deficits simply mean higher levels of "marginalization" and malnutrition among low income groups as Fernando Homem de Melo argues in this volume. All these issues are at the forefront of discussions on food aid even among its most faithful supporters. See OECD (1980: 51–69, but especially 57–61).

10. As illustrations, see George (1976), Lappé, et al. (1980), Wortman and Cummings, Jr. (1978:95–97), and Bergesen (1980:285–302).

11. Aside from the uncompromising statements emanating from the Institute For Food and Development Policy in San Francisco (e.g., *World Hunger: Ten Myths*; *Food First: Beyond the Myth of Scarcity*; *Aid to Bangladesh: For Better or Worse?*; *Aid as the Obstacle*), the Agency for International Development itself has tried more and more to put its best foot forward. See Sommer (1981:2–5), and Schuh (1979).

12. Of the half dozen entries indexed under "food aid and politics" that appear in a 1981, fairly comprehensive, annotated bibliography on food aid and development, most deal with the politics of food aid in donor countries (competition among producers to get on the government's subsidy export list), politics among distribution agencies (competing for the food so they can distribute it) and the politics of governments (as recipients bargain on conditions under which they would be willing to accept food aid). None deals with the relationship of food aid to political stability in a recipient country. See Cadet (1981; index). The issue of suppliers' participation has been of sufficient political importance to trigger legislative hearings. See U.S., General Accounting Office (1980b).

13. The most poignant example of problems that low-income populations have in the international cereals markets emerged during the world drought of 1972–74 when world stocks were severely depleted, much of the grain being bid up in price to service feedlot beef. Because of income disparities, those bidding for cereals for direct consumption were frequently outbid by those

wanting to consume it indirectly via red meat. For arguments that relate hunger to income, not production or distribution, see, as an example, Tarrant (1980:7ff).

14. Good background information on P.L. 480 may be found in Saylor (1977:199–211), and Srivastava, et al. (1975:4–13). In 1966 significant shifts were made from local currency sales to long-term dollar sales, from a 96.7/3.3 ratio in 1962 to a 52/48 ratio in 1968, and grants, as a percentage of total food aid commitment have declined (Srivastava, et al., 1975:66). In 1974 Congress approved an amendment to P.L. 480 requiring that 70 percent of all food aid go to countries hardest hit by food and oil price increases, following in 1975 with a new foreign aid assistance bill requiring that 75 percent of P.L. 480 loans go to countries where annual per capita gross national product was less than $300 (the 1980 limit was $625) and also denying food aid to any government that "consistently violates recognized human rights" of its citizens. Then, in 1977, the "Food-for-development" clause was added to the food aid law, which requires that any recipient government use the proceeds from its sale of the food to undertake development programs in agriculture, nutrition, health services and population planning. See the *Annual Reports* on Public Law 480 published by the United States Department of Agriculture, e.g., 1975:3 and 13; 1977:11–12; 1979:7–8. See, also, Lappé, et al. (1980:103).

15. World food production fell nearly 2.5 percent in 1979, the first decline in seven years. Although output increased in South and Central America, it declined in most African countries and South Asia. Greatest food needs exist in the sub-Saharan African regions and South Asia, but certain Central American, Caribbean and South American countries also showed signs of being in trouble. See U.S. Department of Agriculture (1980a:2–8). The mid-1980s disaster in the Sahel region of Africa was widely noted (see Christensen and Witucki, Ch. 2, this volume). In 1985 Russia stepped up its purchases after yet another grain shortfall due, in part, to uncooperative weather.

16. American agriculture is in an economic crisis unparalleled since 1932. Demand relative to production is so low that in 1982–84 farmers had their lowest "parity" since 1932. There is immense political pressure in Washington to do something for the farmers. The table below indicates the gravity of the matter.

U.S. Farmers
Ratio of Index of Prices Received to Index of Prices Paid
1910–14 = 100

1929 – 92	1948 – 110	1967 – 73
1930 – 83	1949 – 100	1968 – 73
1931 – 67	1950 – 101	1969 – 73
1932 – 58	1951 – 107	1970 – 72

1933 – 64	1952 – 100	1971 – 70
1934 – 75	1953 – 92	1972 – 74
1935 – 88	1954 – 89	1973 – 91
1936 – 92	1955 – 84	1974 – 86
1937 – 93	1956 – 83	1975 – 76
1938 – 78	1957 – 82	1976 – 71
1939 – 77	1958 – 85	1977 – 66
1940 – 81	1959 – 81	1978 – 70
1941 – 93	1960 – 80	1979 – 71
1942 – 105	1961 – 79	1980 – 65
1943 – 113	1962 – 80	1981 – 61
1944 – 108	1963 – 78	1982 – 57
1945 – 109	1964 – 76	
1946 – 113	1965 – 76	
1947 – 115	1966 – 79	

Source: U.S. Department of Agriculture Statistical Reporting Service, Courtesy Don Mellom, Crop Reporting Board, Economics and Statistics Service, June 8, 1982, and January 24, 1984, Washington, D.C.

17. A competent survey of some of the literature is to be found in Apter (1977:Ch. 15) and Chilcote (1981:Ch. 7). The assumption of unilinearity in political development as in economic development, implicit or explicit, generally predates the publication of Samuel P. Huntington's *Political Order in Changing Societies* (1968) which emphasized that political decay was as much a likelihood as political development. Unilinearity is illustrated by Organski's *The Stages of Political Development* (1965), which was influenced by Walt W. Rostow's *The Stages of Economic Growth: A Non-Communist Manifesto* (1960). The ensuing struggles with "political development" as a concept is illustrated by Kesselman's "Order or Movement? The Literature of Political Development as Ideology" (1973) and the acknowledgement of heated replies published in a subsequent issue of *World Politics* 27, 4 (July 1974):622. "Nonunilinearity" has now become, in the face of the facts, the current academic vogue. See Merkl (1981). The best discussion of what "Political Development" is, or is not, is Huntington and Dominguez (1975).

18. An early persuasive statement that set the tone for much later writing is Seymour Martin Lipset (1960), preceded by Lipset's (1959) major synthesis of criteria relating to democracy and development. Lipset's own impressive transformation is best stated in his "The Limits of Social Science" (1981). Within the large literature dealing with different aspects of the relationship of economic development to democracy, and aside from the citations to Lipset above, two other important initial studies are Coleman (1960), and Cutright (1963). The whole approach is well critiqued by Packenham (1973).

19. The matter was argued especially by Huntington (1965), and Eisenstadt (1966). Claude Ake's attempts (1974) to downgrade the destabilizing effects did not gain wide notice.

20. Research and Policy Committee, *Assisting Development in Low-income Countries* (New York: Committee for Economic Development, 1969), p. 2.

21. The best example of early arguments for import-substitution industrialization were developed by the Argentine Raúl Prébisch (1963) and his group with the United Nations Economic Commission for Latin America. On this, as on other like issues, one should always read the insights of Albert O. Hirschman (1968).

22. The models presumed that distributive inequalities were required for maximizing the rate of growth. Economic development was seen primarily as a process of capital formation. Capital formation derived from savings, the availability of which in turn was a function of the rate of savings. As the rich save a larger share of their income than do the poor, income returns from economic development highly skewed to the better off would, in effect, make more savings available for investment, therefore for capital formation, therefore for enhanced economic growth. By the same token, the investment of the savings was best done in cities where the marginal rate of return on investment was seen as being highest. Thus economic growth could be maximized. The resulting increased inequalities between countryside and city and among social classes were not only inevitable, but desirable. Through the increased economic activity everyone would be better off than they were before ("trickle down"). That this orientation has come under increasing fire suggests that its applicability to currently underdeveloped countries—as opposed to "previously underdeveloped countries that are now developed"—is highly suspect. See, for example, Mellor (1976), and Beitz (1981).

23. Ending stocks of wheat in excess of minimum working stocks have fluctuated significantly among the world's four major grain exporters—the United States, Canada, Australia, and Argentina. From a high of 32 million metric tons in 1960/61, stocks in the United States declined to 6.67 in 1966/67, rose to 18.74 in 1969/70, fell to 0.12 in 1973/74, rose to 22 in 1977/78, but then declined again in 1978/79 to 14.49 million metric tons. The pattern for Canada was the same. Australia and Argentina cycled differently, but their stocks are relatively small. Morrow (1981:227 and Table 1).

24. See Srivastava, et al. (1975:64–86), and also the references in note 14, this chapter.

25. The three types of food aid are distinguished on the basis of their major goals. Food-for-cash includes a variety of applications, including sales in the recipient country's open market to raise money for its governmental budgets, matching funds in specific development projects in which the donor country has an interest, special feeding projects at schools in order to promote a

national educational development plan, dairy industry development, or even market stabilization to keep rising food prices from getting politically too high. In all these illustrated cases the primary goal is to turn the food into its money equivalent for use in the recipient country. Who the beneficiaries are depends a great deal on how the recipient government then spends the money or authorizes it to be spent. With food-for-nutrition, the object is to tie feeding programs to a specific development-related project or idea. Generally, supplemental nutrition is given to category-specific people judged to be particularly vulnerable to malnutrition and whose debilitated condition would reflect quite negatively on strategic human resource development in the recipient country. These categories include expectant mothers, school children, and workers on specific development projects who could not earn enough to feed themselves or their families in the absence of a supplemental nutrition program. Food-for-nutrition generally excludes old people. Food-for-work, the last of the food-aid categories, is project tied. The donor government's agent and the recipient country's counterpart agree upon a development-related project that meets minimum political as well as economic criteria and use the food either as full or partial payment for labor on the project. Usually such aid is for road construction or other infrastructure to facilitate farm-to-market transit or improve the productivity of agriculture and the economic well-being of the rural poor. See Stevens (1979:67–131; 197–199).

26. Still, there is now heightened awareness among legislators to be concerned about the impact of food aid on recipient countries. See U.S. House, Committee on Agriculture (1981:1).

27. The best discussion of donor country programs and amounts is Mitchell B. Wallerstein (1980). A comparative table on donations from 17 countries appears on p. 71 of his book.

28. The most important early example is Huntington (1968), followed by Philippe C. Schmitter's edited volume on Military Rule (1973). Some of the best of the current literature is to be found in Collier, ed. (1979b), which includes a treatment of recent discussions deriving from Guillermo O'Donnell's influential work (1973). As for the military itself, a useful review is Perlmutter (1980).

29. Comparative data are summarized by Sivard (1981) and prior years under the same title but different years.

30. See the interesting discussion by Lars Schoultz (1981:183–84) on indirect support of oppression in Latin America.

31. See Jeffrey M. Puryear (1983) on the problems that developmental-assistance agencies face in countries characterized by widespread political repressions.

32. O'Donnell (1973). See also Collier (1979a:19–32).

33. Sunkel (1981:93–111), and Caporaso (1980:605–28) address the matter in a contemporary state of the world and "dependency" literature.

34. The best citations of this extensive literature are found in Beitz (1981: 324, note 11).

35. See *Latin American Regional Reports: Brazil 7* (London), 7 August 1981, for an illustrative discussion on Brazil.

36. An important work on the relationship of population, employment and income distribution is Rodgers, Hopkins, and Wery (1978). See also Beitz (1981). Insofar as "trickle down" is to have a significant positive impact on unemployment and underemployment in the short run, the development model proposed by John Mellor (1976) may need to be taken seriously. By reversing the patterns of investment from urban to rural and smaller-town areas, its success could enhance structural changes in relations between the countryside and the city.

37. See Tullis (1973:270–271), Germani (1969–70:171–172), Hirschman (1970:43, 76, 106, and 111), and Huntington (1968:281–283).

38. The theoretical discussion is raised by Todaro (1981:374–380).

39. A perspective that focuses upon the new challenges to international law created by such a posture is Bedjaoui (1979). A summary of historical developmental types leading to the present dialogue, along with a discussion of the values that permeate contemporary approaches, is Henriot (1979). See also Jordan (1982).

40. Nicholson, Esseks, and Khan (1979); and, *Latin American Regional Reports-Brazil* (London), 7 August 1981, pp. 6–7 reporting on the work of Fernando Homem de Melo at Brazil's Fundacão Instituto Paulista de Economia (FIPE). See also Homem de Melo, Ch. 10, this volume.

41. See, for example, the discussions, now reaching semi-popular dissemination, of K. K. S. Dadzie (1980).

42. Examples are several regions in Brazil as a representative of integration into the "semi-periphery" of the capitalist world and Cuba as one integrated into the periphery of the Communist world. However, on the whole, at least in 1982-85, Brazil seemed to be less coercive than, say, in 1976.

Notes to Chapter 9

1. A more extensive discussion of the neo-Malthusian, distributionist and productionist approaches may be found in John G. Merriam's "The Politics of Hunger," a paper delivered at the 24th annual convention of the International Studies Association at Mexico City, April 7, 1983.

2. For a complete discussion of grain sizing, see David J. Eaton, et al., *Grain Reserve Sizing: A Multi-Objective and Probabilistic Analysis* (Austin: University of Texas, Lyndon B. Johnson School of Public Affairs, n. d.).

3. A comprehensive discussion of the germplasm conservation issue may be found in *Proceedings of the U.S. Strategy Conference on Biological Diversity* (Washington, D.C.: Department of State Publication No. 9262, April 1982).

4. For a discussion of the Chakrabarty case, see *Impacts of Applied Genetics: Micro-Organisms, Plants and Animals* (Washington, D.C., Congress of the United States, Office of Technology Assessment, April 1981), pp. 240–42.

Notes to Chapter 10

1. For a discussion of innovation types, see Hayami and Ruttan (1971).

2. The responsiveness of the quantity of a good demanded to changes in its price, expressed as the percentage change in quantity demanded divided by the percentage change in price.

3. The principal thrust of Castro's model is an analysis of distributive questions.

4. See also de Janvry (1977).

5. This would be similar to the possibility mentioned by Myint (1975: 336): "in peasant economies, not excepting densely populated countries like India, peasant producers have been generally observed to respond to relative price changes by flexibly reallocating resources between subsistence production and cash crops, including export crops."

6. Schuh (1976:795–801).

7. See the discussion about import and export prices in Hinshaw (1975: 475–78).

8. See Fernando Homem de Melo (1983a:57–58) for details of this segmentation. Evidence is also presented that internal prices have been above international ones for domestic crops.

9. Among the domestic crops during 1967–79, corn was the only one showing some, although quite irregular, exports: in four of the 13 years exports were less than 1.2 percent; in two, 3.4 percent and 5.1 percent, and in seven, between 6.8 percent and 10.3 percent of domestic production.

10. The positive employment effects of increased soybeans production has not been as important as the benefit to foreign exchange because labor requirements per cultivated acreage are significantly the lowest among the eleven most important Southern Brazilian crops. See Homem de Melo and Fonseca (1981:87).

11. We also recognize that the change in labor legislation in the first half of the sixties that lead to a reduction in payments in kind may have reduced domestic crop production (subsistence plots). However, the unavailability of relevant evidence for Brazil forces us to leave the issue for future analysis.

12. In 1980 soybeans exports were US$ 2.5 billion, about 12 percent of total Brazilian exports. During the sixties the annual growth rate of soybeans

acreage was 16.3 percent; in the seventies, 20.7 percent.

13. See Kaster and Bonato (1980:422). These evidences suggest that the emphasis on soybeans research may have resulted from the expectation that, given the international transfer of knowledge, it would be "easier" to obtain significant breakthroughs.

14. That is, domestic production minus exports plus imports. We did not consider use as seeds, losses and change in stocks, because of lack of annual data. For a more detailed discussion see Homem de Melo (1983b).

15. For other details, see Zockun (1980).

16. For other details see Homem de Melo (1983b).

17. Defined in terms of consumption expenditures plus taxes as well as labor and retirement/health contributions.

18. The lowest and highest expenditure classes were not always coincident among regions.

19. For a detailed discussion see Homem de Melo (1983b). Even beef and pork meat are closer to the subsector of domestic products than of exportables. Some exports/imports were made during the seventies but in relatively small amounts when compared to domestic production.

20. For an analysis about wage goods and distributive inequality in the United States, see Williamson (1977:29–41).

21. We mentioned in the text the interplay of two additional variables. With the increase of certain international prices during the early seventies and modifications in Brazil's exchange rate policy, the results we report should not be imputed entirely to the unbalanced pattern of technological innovations, but to all factors together. We recognize that to the extent we were unable to quantify each factor's contribution to the observed behavior of Brazilian agriculture we leave a part of the initial question still open. We hope to make progress on that in the near future.

Bibliography of Works Cited

Abbott, P. C. (1979) "Modelling International Grain Trade with Government Controlled Markets." *American Journal of Agricultural Economics* 61(1): 22–31.

Abel, Martin E. and S. Ahmed Meer (1979) "Impact of Improved Information on the Structure of World Grain Trade." A paper delivered at the International Conference on Cybernetics and Society, Boulder, Colorado.

Agricultural Development Council (ADC) (1982) *The Developmental Effectiveness of Food Aid.* New York: ADC.

Agriculture Canada (1981) *Proceedings of the Canadian Agricultural Outlook Conference.* Ottawa: Agriculture Canada.

Aharoni, Y. (1966) *The Foreign Investment Decision Process.* Cambridge, Mass.: Harvard University Press.

Ake, Claude (1974) "Modernization and Political Stability: A Theoretical Exploration." *World Politics* 26(4) (July):576–91.

Akyno, M., and Yujiro Hayami (1975) "Efficiency and Equity in Public Research: Rice Breeding in Japan's Economic Development." *American Journal of Agricultural Economics* 57(1):1–10.

Alamgir, Mohiuddin (1980) *Famine in South Asia.* Cambridge: Oelgeschlager, Gunn, and Hain.

Almeida, Silvio, et al. (1975) *World Hunger: Cases and Remedies.* Washington, D.C.: Transnational Institute.

Alvarez, Elena (1983) *Política Ecónomica y Agricultura en el Perú,* 1969–1979. Lima: Instituto de Estudios Peruanos.

Amat y León, Carlos (1981) *La Desigualdad Interior en el Peru.* Lima: Centro de Investigación de la Universidad del Pacífico.

Amin, Samir (1974) *Accumulation on a World Scale.* New York: Monthly Review Press.

Andrews, E. Sherrill (1975) "The Expiration of the Sugar Act: Bittersweet Prospects for Nonregulation." *Law and Policy in International Business* 7 (Fall):1287–1304.

Apter, David (1977) *Political Analysis*. Cambridge: Winthrope.

Aqua, R. (1974) *Local Institutions and Rural Development in South Korea*. Ithaca: Cornell University Rural Development Committee.

Aronson, Jonathan David, ed. (1979) *Debt and the Less Developed Countries*. Boulder, Colo.: Westview Press.

————. (1985) "Muddling Through the Debt Decade," in *An International Political Economy*, W. Ladd Hollist and F. LaMond Tullis, eds., pp. 127–51. Boulder, Colo.: Westview Press.

Austin, James E. (1978) "Institutional Dimensions of the Malnutrition Problem," in *The Global Political Economy of Food*, Raymond F. Hopkins and Donald J. Puchala, eds., pp. 171–201, Madison: University of Wisconsin Press.

Austin, James E., and Mitchell B. Wallerstein (1979) "Reformulating U.S. Food Aid Policy for Development." *World Development* 7(6):635–46.

Ayer, H. W., and G. E. Schuh (1971) "Social Rate of Return and Other Aspects of Agricultural Research: The Case of Cotton Research in Sao Paulo, Brazil." *American Journal of Agricultural Economics* 54(4):557–69.

Bach, C. L. (1978) "U.S. International Transactions, First Quarter, 1978." *Survey of Current Business*, part II (June):1–17.

Bailey, John J. (1980) "Presidency, Bureaucracy, and Administrative Reform in Mexico: The Secretariat of Programming and Budget." *Inter-American Economic Affairs* 34(1) (Summer):27–59.

————. (1981) "Agrarian Reform in Mexico." *Current History* (November): 357–60, 391–92.

Bailey, John J., and D. H. Roberts (1983) "Mexican Agricultural Policy." *Current History* 82(488) (December):420–24, 436.

Bailyn, Bernard, ed. (1965) *Pamphlets of the American Revolution 1750-1776*. Cambridge, Mass.: Belknap Press of Harvard University Press.

————. (1967) *The Ideological Origins of the American Revolution*. Cambridge, Mass.: Belknap Press of Harvard University Press.

Balassa, Bela (1971) *The Structure of Protection in Developing Countries*. Baltimore: Johns Hopkins University Press.

————. (1983a) "The Adjustment Experience of Developing Countries after 1973," in *IMF Conditionality*, John Williamson, ed., pp. 145–74, Washington, D.C.: Institute for International Economics.

————. (1983b) "Policy Responses to External Shocks in Subsaharan Africa." *Journal of Policy Modelling* 5(1):75–105.

Bale, Malcolm D., and Ronald C. Duncan (1983) "Food Prospects in the Developing Countries: A Qualified Optimistic View." *American Economic Review*. 73(2):244–248. Reprinted as World Bank Paper #275.

Ban, S. H., et al. (1980) *Rural Development: Studies in the Modernization of the Republic of Korea, 1945-1975*. Cambridge, Mass.: Harvard University Press.

Banco Agrario del Perú (1982) *Estadística de Préstamos* (Ejercicio 1981) Lima: Banco Agrario del Peru.

Barkin, David (1978) *Desarrollo regional y reorganización campesina.* Mexico: Editorial Nueva Imagen.

Barkin, David, and Blanca Suárez (1982) *El fin de la autosuficiencia alimentaria.* Mexico, D.F.: Centro de Ecodesarrollo/Editorial Nueva Imagen.

Barker, Ronald, Eric C. Gabler, and Donald Winkleman (1981) "Long Term Consequences of Technological Change on Crop Yield Stability: The Case for Cereal Grain," in *Food Security for Developing Countries*, Alberto Valdes, ed., pp. 53–78. Boulder, Colo.: Westview Press.

Barraclough, Solon. (1977) "Agricultural Production Prospects in Latin America." *World Development* 5(May-July):459–476.

Barros, J. R. M. de, and D. Graham (1980) "Brazilian Agricultural Development and the Problems of Constrained Modernization." Paper presented to the Center for Brazilian Studies, SAI – The Johns Hopkins University, 25 September.

Basic Agricultural Statistics, Republic of China (Annual) Taipei: Council for Agricultural Planning and Development.

Bates, Robert (1981) *Markets and States in Tropical Africa: The Political Basis of Agricultural Policies.* Berkeley: University of California Press.

Bedjaoui, Mohammed (1979) *Towards a New International Economic Order.* London: Holmes and Meier.

Beitz, Charles R. (1981) "Economic Rights and Distributive Justice in Developing Societies." *World Politics* 33(3) (April):321–346.

Berg, Alan (1973) *The Nutrition Factor.* Washington: The Brookings Institution.

Berg, Elliot (1981) *Accelerated Development in Sub-Saharan Africa.* Washington, D.C.: The World Bank.

Bergesen, Helge Ole (1980) "A New Food Regime: Necessary but Impossible." *International Organization* 34(2) (Spring):285–302.

Bergsten, C. F., T. Horst, and T. H. Moran (1978) *American Multinationals and American Interests.* Washington, D.C.: The Brookings Institution.

Berry, Sara (1983) "Agrarian Crisis in Africa? A Review and Interpretation." African Studies Association, Boston, Mass., December.

Bethke, Siegfried (1980) "Food Aid – A Negative Factor?" *Aussenpolitik* 31: 180–195.

Bieri, J., Alain de Janvry, and A. Schmitz (1972) "Agricultural Technology and the Distribution of Welfare Gains." *American Journal of Agricultural Economics* 54:801–08.

Billone, Jorge, Daniel Carbonetto, and Daniel Martínez (1982) *Términos de Intercambio Ciudad-Campo 1970–1980.* Lima: CEDEP.

Bizzarro, Salvatore (1981) "Mexico's Oil Boom." *Current History* 80(463) (February):49–52.

Bloomfield, Lincoln (1972–73) "Foreign Policy for Disillusioned Liberals." *Foreign Policy* 9 (Winter):55–68.

Bolling, H. C. (1983a) "Dominican Republic: Factors Affecting Its Capacity to Import Food." Washington, D.C.: United States Department of Agriculture/ERS Economic Report #183.

———. (1983b) "Trinidad and Tobago: Factors Affecting Its Capacity to Import Food." Washington, D.C.: United States Department of Agriculture/ERS Economic Report #178.

Bornschier, Volker and Thahn-huyen Ballmer-Cao (1979) "Income Inequality: A Cross-national Study of the Relationships Between MNC-penetration, Dimensions of Power Structure and Income Distribution." *American Sociological Review* 44 (June):487–506.

Bowle, John (1974) *The Imperial Achievement.* London: Secker Warburg.

Brandt, V. S. R. (1971) *Korean Village Between Farm and Sea.* Cambridge, Mass.: Harvard University Press.

Brandt, Willy (1980) *North-South: A Program for Survival.* Cambridge, Mass.: MIT Press.

Broehl, Wayne (1968) *The International Basic Economy Corporation.* New York: National Planning Association.

Brown, Lester R. (1970) *Seeds of Change.* New York: Praeger.

———. (1974) *By Bread Alone.* New York: Praeger.

———. (1978) *The Twenty Ninth Day.* New York: Norton.

Browne, Robert S. and Robert J. Cummings (1984) *The Lagos Plan of Action vs. The Berg Report.* Lawrenceville, Va.: Brunswick Publishing Co. (for Harvard University, 1984).

Brunner, Ronald D. (1975) *Politics, Communications and Social Tension.* Ann Arbor: University of Michigan.

Buckley, P. J., and R. D. Pearce (1977) "Overseas Production and Exporting by the World's Largest Enterprises: A Study in Sourcing Policy." University of Reading (Great Britain) Discussion papers in International Investment and Business Studies, No. 37, September.

Buckley, P. J., and M. Casson (1976) *The Future of the Multinational Enterprise.* New York: Holmes and Meier.

Burbach, Roger, and Patricia Flynn (1980) *Agribusiness in the Americas.* New York: Monthly Review Press.

Burgess, E. W. and F. H. Harbison (1954) *Casa Grace in Peru.* Washington, D.C.: U.S. National Planning Association.

Bye, P. (1980) "L'Agro-Industrie dans les Pays en Voie de Development: Autonomie ou Dependance?" *Economie et Humanisme* 256 (1980):33–37.

Caballero, José María (1980) *Agricultura, Reforma Agraria, y Pobreza Campesina.* Lima: Instituto de Estudios Peruanos.

———. (1981) *Economía Agraria de la Sierra Peruana.* Lima: Instituto de Estudios Peruanos.

———. (1984) "Agriculture and the Peasantry Under Industrialization Pressures: Lessons from the Peruvian Experience," *Latin American Research Review* 19(2):3–41.

Caballero, José María, and Elena Alvarez (1980) *Aspectos Cuantitativos de la Reforma Agraria.* Lima: Instituto de Estudios Peruanos.

Cabieses, Hugo, and Carlos Otero (1977) *Economía Peruana: Un Ensayo de Interpretación.* Lima: DESCO.

Cadet, Melissa Lawson (1981) *Food Aid and Policy for Economic Development: An Annotated Bibliography and Directory.* Sacramento, Calif.: Trans Tech Management Press.

Cahn, Linda A. (1980) "National Power and International Regimes: United States Commodity Prices, 1930–1980." Unpublished Ph.D. dissertation, Stanford University.

Caldwell, Malcolm (1977) *The Wealth of Some Nations.* London: Zed Press.

Caporaso, James A. (1980) "Dependency Theory: Continuities and Discontinuities in Development Studies." *International Organization* 34(4) (Autumn): 605–628.

Cardoso, Fernando Henrique (1973) "Associated-dependent Development: Theoretical and Practical Implications," in *Authoritarian Brazil: Origin, Policies, Futures,* Alfred Stephan, ed., pp. 142–176. New Haven: Yale University Press.

Cardoso, Fernando Henrique, and Enzo Faletto (1979) *Dependency and Development in Latin America,* translated by Marjory Mattingly Urquidi. Berkeley: University of California Press.

Carman, Harry J. (1930) *Social and Economic History of the United States,* vol. 1, "From Handicraft to Factory, 1500–1820." Boston: D.C. Heath.

Carvalho, L. E. (1982) "O Caráter Social da Política de Subsidio ao Trigo." *Alimentos e Nutrição*:32–42.

Casson, M. (1979) *Alternatives to the Multinational Enterprise.* New York: Holmes and Meier.

Castillo-Vera, Gustavo del (1982) "Las relaciones entre el ejecutivo y el poder legislativo vistas dentro del contexto del Sistema Generalizado de Preferencias Norteamericano." *Cuaderno Semestral* 10 (Mexico City: Centro de Investigación y Docencia Economicas [CIDE]).

Castro, J. P. R. (1974) "An Economic Model for Establishing Priorities for Agricultural Research and a Test for the Brazilian Economy." Ph.D. Dissertation, Purdue University.

Castro, J. P. R., and G. E. Schuh (1977) "An Empirical Test of an Economic Model for Establishing Research Priorities: A Brazil Case Study," in *Resource Allocation and Productivity*, T.M. Arndt, Dana G. Dalrymple and Vernon W. Ruttan, eds., Minneapolis: University of Minnesota Press.

Cater, Douglass (1964) *Power in Washington*. New York: Random House.

Caves, R. E. (1982) *Multinational Enterprise and Economic Analysis*. Cambridge, U.K.: Cambridge University Press.

Centro de Investigación de la Universidad del Pacífico (1980) *Perú 1980: Elecciones y Planes de Gobierno*. Lima: Universidad del Pacífico.

Chilcote, Ronald H. (1980) *Theories of Comparative Politics: The Search for a Paradigm*. Boulder, Colo.: Westview Press.

Cho, S. C. (1975) "The Bureaucracy," in *Korean Politics in Transition*, E. R. Wright, ed., pp. 71–84. Seattle: University of Washington Press.

Choe, Y. B. (1978) *The Korean World of Rural Saemaul Undong: Its Structure, Strategy and Performance*, Working Paper 4. Seoul: Korean Rural Economics Institute.

Choi, Wonyoung (1977) "The Cattle Cycle." *European Review of Agricultural Economics* 4(2):119–136.

Choo, H. K. (1982) *Widening Urban-Rural Income Differentials in Korea: A Re-Examination*. Working Paper Series 82–05. Seoul: Korean Development Institute.

Christensen, Cheryl (1978a) "World Hunger: A Structural Approach," in *The Global Political Economy of Food*, Raymond F. Hopkins and Donald J. Puchala, eds., pp. 171–201. Madison: University of Wisconsin Press.

———. (1978b) "The Right to Food: How to Guarantee." *Alternatives* 4(2) (October):181–220.

Christensen, Cheryl, and Lawrence Witucki (1982) "Food Problems and Emerging Policy Responses in Subsaharan Africa." *American Journal of Agricultural Economics* 64(5) (December):879–96.

Clairmonte, Fredrick F. (1980) "U.S. Food Complexes and Multinational Corporations: Reflections on Economic Predation." *Economic and Political Weekly* 15:1815–30.

Clay, Edward J., and Hans W. Singer (1982) "Food Aid and Development: The Impact and Effectiveness of Bilateral PL480 Title I-type Assistance." *AID Program Evaluation Discussion Paper No. 15*. Washington, D.C.: USAID.

Cleaver, Harry M. (1972) "The Contradictions of the Green Revolution." *American Economic Review* 72 (May):177–88.

Cleaves, Peter S. and Martin J. Scurrah (1980) *Agriculture, Bureaucracy and Military Government in Peru*. Ithaca: Cornell University Press.

Clough, R. (1978) *Island China*. Cambridge, Mass.: Harvard University Press.

Cochrane, Willard W. (1979) *The Development of American Agriculture: A Historical Analysis*. Minneapolis: University of Minnesota Press.

Colburn, F. D. (1983) "Nicaragua's Agrarian Reform." Paper prepared for delivery at the Latin American Studies Association Meetings, Mexico City, September. (Mimeographed.)

Coleman, James S. (1960) "Conclusion: The Political Systems of the Developing Areas," in *The Politics of the Developing Areas*, Gabriel A. Almond and James S. Coleman, eds., Princeton: Princeton University Press.

Collier, David (1979a) "Overview of the Bureaucratic-Authoritarian Model," in *The New Authoritarianism in Latin America*, David Collier, ed., pp. 19–32. Princeton: Princeton University Press.

―――. (1979b) *The New Authoritarianism in Latin America*. Princeton: Princeton University Press.

Commission of the European Communities (1979) *Annual Report on the Development Cooperation Policies of the Community and its Member States*. Brussels: by the Commission.

Connor, J. M. (1977) *The Market Power of Multinationals: A Quantitative Analysis of U.S. Corporations in Brazil and Mexico*. New York: Praeger.

Cook, J. (1980) "Handsome is as Handsome Does." *Forbes*, March 3:43–48.

Corden, W. M. (1971) *The Theory of Protection*. Oxford: Clarendon Press.

Corporate Data Exchange, Inc. (1979) *CDE Stock Ownership Directory No. 2: Agribusiness*. New York: Corporate Data Exchange.

―――. (1980) *Directory and Fact Book 1979–80*. Englewood Cliffs: CPC International, Inc.

Coy, Edward W. (1981) "Latin America: A Search for Solutions Amid Turmoil." *Agenda* (May):7–11.

CPC International, Inc. (1979–80) *CPC Directory and Fact Book*. Englewood Cliffs: CPC International, Inc.

Crosson, Pierre R. (1975) "Institutional Obstacles to Expansion of World Food Production," in *Food: Politics, Economics, Nutrition and Research*, a Special SCIENCE Compendium, Philip H. Abelson, ed., pp. 17–22. Washington, D.C.: American Association for the Advancement of Science.

Cutright, Phillips (1963) "National Political Development: Measurement and Analysis." *American Sociological Review* 27 (April):253–264.

Dadzie, K. K. S. (1980) "Economic Development." *Scientific American* 243(3) (September):58–65.

Dalibor, Gudrun (1984) "When Aid is Little Help." *The Guardian* (Manchester and London), 2(March):21.

Davies, Susanna (1984) "Markets, States, and the TNCs: Power and the World Grain Trading Systems." Unpublished manuscript.

Deerr, Noel (1949; 1950) *The History of Sugar*, 2 vols. London: Chapman and Hall.

de Janvry, Alain (1977) "Inducement of Technological and Institutional Innovations: An Interpretative Framework," in *Resource Allocation and*

Productivity, T. M. Arndt, Dana G. Dalrymple and Vernon W. Ruttan, eds. Minneapolis: University of Minnesota Press.

————. (1981) *The Agrarian Question and Reformism in Latin America*. Baltimore: The Johns Hopkins University Press.

de Larosiere, J. (1982) "The International Monetary System and the Developing Countries." *IMF Survey* 11(29) (November):377–380.

Deutsch, Karl (1961) "Social Mobilization and Political Development." *American Political Science Review* 55(3) (September):493–514.

Dietz, Henry A. (1982) "National Recovery vs. Individual Stagnation: Peru's Urban Poor Since 1978." Paper presented at the 44th International Congress of Americanists, University of Manchester, Manchester, England (September).

Dix, R. H. (1983) "The Varieties of Revolution." *Comparative Politics* 13(1) (April):281–294.

Dore, R. (1977) "South Korean Development in Wider Perspective." *Pacific Affairs* 50(2):189–207.

dos Santos, Theotonio (1970) "The Structure of Dependence." *American Economic Review* 60 (May):231–36.

————. (1971) "The Structure of Dependence," in *Readings in U.S. Imperialism*, K. T. Fann and Donald Hodges, eds., pp. 225–236. Boston: Porter-Sargent.

Drouin, M. J., and H. Malgren (1981) "Canada, the United States, and the World Economy." *Foreign Affairs* 60 (Winter):393–413.

Dudley, L., and R. J. Sandilands (1975) "The Case of P. L. 480 Wheat in Colombia." *Economic Development and Cultural Change* 23(1) (January): 325–336.

Dunn, Richard S. (1972) *Sugar and Slaves: The Rise of the Planter Class in the English West Indies, 1626-1713*. Chapel Hill: University of North Carolina Press for Institute of Early American History and Culture, Williamsburg.

Dunning, J. H. (1977) "Trade, Location of Economic Activity, and the MNE: A Search for an Eclectic Approach," in *The International Allocation of Economic Activity*, Bertil Ohlin, Per-Ove Hesselborn, and Per-Magnus Wijkman, eds., pp. 395–418. London: Macmillan.

Durán-Juárez, Juan Manuel (1982) "Aspectos de la migración en el noroeste de Michoacán. Transformación agrícola y migración en la Ciénaga de Chapala." Paper presented at the Fourth Anthropology and Regional Studies Conference, Zamora, Michoacán, 30 July.

Dyer, I. A., and C. C. O'Mary, eds. (1977) *The Feedlot*, second edition. Philadelphia: Lea and Feiberger.

Eaton, David J., et al. (n.d.) *Grain Reserve Sizing: A Multi-Objective and Probabilistic Analysis*. Austin: University of Texas Lyndon B. Johnson School of Public Affairs.

Ebeling, Walter (1980) *The Fruited Plain: The Story of American Agriculture.* Berkeley and Los Angeles: University of California Press.

Edirisinghe, Neville (1984) *The Implications of the Change from Ration Shops to Food Stamps in Sri Lanka for Fiscal Costs, Income Distribution, and Nutrition.* Washington, D.C.: International Food Policy Research Institute (IFPRI).

Eguren, Fernando (1980) "Política Agraria vs. Producción de Alimentos?" *Quehacer* (3) (March):34–41.

———. (1982) *Situación Actual y Perspectivas del Problema Agrario en el Peru.* Lima: DESCO.

Eichner, Alfred S. (1969) *The Emergence of Oligopoly.* Baltimore: Johns Hopkins University Press.

Eisenstadt, S. N. (1966) *Modernization: Protest and Change.* Englewood Cliffs: Prentice-Hall.

Ellis, Frank (1982) "Agricultural Price Policy in Tanzania." *World Development* 10:263–83.

Emery, Walter C. ed. (1982) *Commodity Yearbook, 1982.* New York: Commodity Research Bureau.

Emmanuel, Arghiri (1972) *Unequal Exchange.* New York: Monthly Review Press.

ENCI [Empresa Nacional de Comercialización de Insumos] (1977) *Memoria Anual.* Lima: ENCI.

Enloe, Cynthia H. (1973) *Ethnic Conflict and Political Development.* Boston: Little, Brown.

Evenson, Robert E. and Yoav Kislev (1975) "Investment in Agricultural Research and Extension: A Survey of International Data." *Economic Development and Cultural Change* 23(3) (April):507–521.

Farber, Samuel (1976) *Revolution and Reaction in Cuba, 1933–1960: A Political Sociology from Machado to Castro.* Middletown, Conn.: Wesleyan University Press.

Feder, E. (1978) *Strawberry Imperialism: An Enquiry into the Mechanisms of Dependency in Mexican Agriculture.* Mexico City: Editorial Campesina.

———. (n.d.) "Ganadería y estructura agraria en Chiapas." Mexico: unpublished manuscript.

Fernández Ortíz, Luís Ma., and María Tarrio G. de Fernández (n.d.) "Cattle Raising, Farmers, and Basic Grain Products: A Study in Chiapas." Mexico: unpublished ms.

Fernández-Baca, Jorge (1982) "La Producción de Alimentos en el Perú: Un Problema Indigesto." *Quehacer* 17 (June):86–94.

Fernández-Baca, Jorge, Carlos Parodi-Zevallos, and Fabian Tume-Torres (1983) *Agroindustria y Transnacionales en el Perú.* Lima: DESCO.

Figueroa, A. (1981) "Effects of Changes in Consumption and Trade Patterns on Agricultural Development in Latin America." *Quarterly Review of Economics and Business* 21(2) (Summer):83–97.

Fisher, Franklin M. (1963) "A Theoretical Analysis of the Impact of Food Surplus Disposal on Agricultural Production in Recipient Countries." *Journal of Farm Economics* 45 (November):863–875.

Fitzgerald, E. V. K. (1976) *The State and Economic Development: Peru Since 1968.* London: Cambridge University Press.

———. (1979) *The Political Economy of Peru 1956–78: Economic Development and the Restructuring of Capital.* New York: Cambridge University Press.

Forster, N. (1982) *The Revolutionary Transformation of the Cuban Countryside.* American Universities Field Staff Reports, North America, #26.

Forster, N. and H. Handleman (1982) *Government Policy and Nutrition in Revolutionary Cuba: Rationing and Redistribution.* American Universities Field Staff Reports, South America, #19.

Foweraker, Joe (1981) *The Struggle for Land: A Political Economy of the Pioneer Frontier in Brazil from 1930 to the Present Day.* Cambridge, U.K.: Cambridge University Press.

Frank, Andre Gunder (1967) *Capitalism and Underdevelopment in Latin America.* New York: Monthly Review Press.

———. (1969) *Latin America: Underdevelopment or Revolution.* New York: Monthly Review Press.

Frankel, Francine R. (1971) *India's Green Revolution: Economic Gains and Political Costs.* Princeton: Princeton University Press.

Frolich, Norman, and Joseph Oppenheimer (1978) *Modern Political Economy.* Englewood Cliffs, N.J.: Prentice-Hall.

Frundt, H. J. (1975) "American Agribusiness and U.S. Foreign Agricultural Policy." Ph.D. Dissertation, Department of Political Science, Rutgers University.

———. (1979) *Gulf and Western in the Dominican Republic: An Evaluation.* New York: Interfaith Center on Corporate Responsibility.

George, Susan (1977) *How the Other Half Dies: The Real Reasons for World Hunger.* New York: Penguin Books.

Gerber, David J. (1976) "The United States Sugar Quota Program: A Study in the Direct Congressional Control of Imports." *The Journal of Law and Economics* 19 (April):103–147.

Gereffi, Gary, and Peter Evans (1981) "Transnational Corporations, Dependent Development, and State Policy in the Semiperiphery: A Comparison of Brazil and Mexico." *Latin American Research Review* 16(3):31–64.

Germani, Gino (1969–70) "Stages of Modernization in Latin America." *Studies in Comparative International Development* 5(8):171–72.

Glick, J. Leslie (1982) "The Industrial Impact of the Biological Revolution." *Technology in Society* 4(4):283–93.

Goldberg, R. and R. C. McGinity (1979) *Agribusiness Management for Developing Countries: Southeast Asian Corn System*. Cambridge, Mass.: Ballinger.

Goldberg, Ray (1981) "The Role of the Multinational Corporation." *American Journal of Agricultural Economics* 6(2) (May):367–374.

Goldenberg, Boris (1965) *The Cuban Revolution and Latin America*. New York: Praeger.

Gonzalez, L. E. (1983) "Uruguay, 1980–1981: An Unexpected Opening." *Latin American Research Review* 18(3):63–76.

Goodman, David and Michael Redclift (1981) *From Peasant to Proletarian*. New York: St. Martin's Press.

Goodman, L. W. (1983) "Food, Transnational Corporations, and Developing Countries." Paper prepared for delivery at the Latin American Studies Association Meetings, Mexico City.

Graham, E. M. (1974) "Oligopolistic Imitation and European Direct Investment in the U.S." Ph.D. Dissertation, Harvard Business School.

Green, Rosario (1981) *Estado y banca transnacional en México*. México, D.F.: Nueva Imagen, Co-ediciones con el CEESTEM.

Griffin, Keith (1974) *The Political Economy of Agrarian Change: An Essay on the Green Revolution*. Cambridge, Mass.: Harvard University Press.

Griliches, Zvi (1957) "Hybrid Corn: An Exploration in the Economics of Technological Change." *Econometrica* 25:501–22.

———. (1958) "Research Costs and Social Returns: Hybrid Corn and Related Innovations." *Journal of Political Economy* 66(1):419–431.

———. (1963) "The Sources of Measured Productivity Growth: United States Agriculture, 1940–60." *Journal of Political Economy* 71(1):331–46.

———. (1964) "Research Expenditures, Education and the Aggregate Agricultural Production Function." *American Economic Review* 54(6):961–74.

Grindle, M. (1980) *Whatever Happened to Agrarian Reform? The Latin American Experience*. Austin: Institute of Latin American Studies, University of Texas, Technical Papers Series #23.

Guttman, J. M. (1978) "Interest Groups and the Demand for Agricultural Research." *Journal of Political Economy* 86(3):467–84.

Hagelberg, G. B. (1975) "Sugar," in *Commodity Trade of the Third World*, Cheryl Payer, ed., pp. 104–128. New York: Wiley.

Hahn, K. S. (1975) "Underlying Factors in Political Party Organisations and Elections," in *Korean Politics in Transition*, E. R. Wright, ed., pp. 85–104, Seattle: University of Washington Press.

Handleman, H. (1980) *Ecuadorian Agrarian Reform: The Politics of Limited Change*. American Universities Field Staff Reports, South America, #49.

Hanrahan, Charles, and Cheryl Christensen (1981) "Food Policy in Subsaharan Africa." Paper presented at the African Studies Association Meetings, Indiana University, Bloomington, Indiana, October 21–24.

Hanson, James (1983) "Contractionary Devaluation, Substitution for Production and Consumption and the Role of the Labor Market." *Journal of International Economics* 14(1/2):179–89.

Hardy, R. W. F. (1977) *A Treatise on Di-nitrogen Fixation: Section IV, Ecology and Agronomy.* New York: Wiley.

Harwood, Richard R. (1979) *Small Farm Development: Understanding Land Improving Farming Systems in the Humid Tropics.* Boulder, Colo.: Westview Press.

Harris, J., and M. Moore, eds. (1984) *Development and the Rural-Urban Divide.* London: Frank Cass.

Hayami, Yujiro, and R. W. Herdt (1977) "Market Price Effects of Technological Change on Income Distribution in Semisubsistence Agriculture." *American Journal of Agricultural Economics* 59(1):245–56.

Hayami, Yujiro, and Vernon W. Ruttan (1971) *Agricultural Development: An International Perspective.* Baltimore: Johns Hopkins University Press.

Hayes, Harold (1981) "A Conversation with Garrett Hardin." *Atlantic Monthly* 247 (May):60–68.

Henriot, Peter J. (1979) "Development Alternatives: Problems, Strategies, Values," in *The Political Economy of Development and Underdevelopment,* 2nd edition, Charles K. Wilber, ed., pp. 5–22, New York: Random House.

Hinshaw, Randall (1975) "Non-traded Goods and the Balance of Payments: Further Reflections." *Journal of Economic Literature* 13:475–78.

Hirschman, Albert O. (1967) *Development Projects Observed.* Washington, D.C.: The Brookings Institution.

———. (1968) "The Political Economy of Import-substituting Industrialization in Latin America." *Quarterly Journal of Economics* 82(1) (February): 2–32.

———. (1970) *Exit, Voice, and Loyalty: Responses to Decline in Firms, Organizations, and States.* Cambridge, Mass.: Harvard University Press.

Ho, S. P. S. (1978) *Economic Development of Taiwan, 1860–1970.* New Haven and London: Yale University Press.

———. (1982) "Economic Development and Rural Industry in South Korea and Taiwan." *World Development* 10(11):973–990.

Hofhienz, R., and K. E. Calder (1982) *The East Asian Edge.* New York: Basic Books.

Hollist, W. Ladd (1979) "Brazil's Debt-burdened Recession: Consequences of Short-term Difficulties or of Structures of Production and Consumption," in *Debt and the Less Developed Countries,* J. D. Aronson, ed., pp. 171–187. Boulder, Colo.: Westview Press.

———. (1981) "Brazilian Dependence: An Evolutionary, World-System Perspective," in *World System Structure: Continuity and Change,* W. Ladd Hollist and James N. Rosenau, eds., pp. 202–220. Beverly Hills: Sage.

————. (1983) "Dependency Transformed: Brazilian Agriculture in Historical Perspective," in *North/South Relations: Studies in Dependency Reversal,* Charles F. Doran, George Modelski, and Cal Clark, eds., pp. 157–186. New York: Praeger.

Hollist, W. Ladd, and F. LaMond Tullis, eds. (1985) *An International Political Economy.* Boulder, Colo.: Westview Press.

Hollist, W. Ladd, and James A. Caporaso (1985) "International Political Economy Research: What is It and Where Do We Turn for Concepts and Theories," in *An International Political Economy,* W. Ladd Hollist and F. LaMond Tullis, eds., pp. 27–49. Boulder, Colo.: Westview Press.

Homem de Melo, Fernando (1983a) "Commercial Policy, Technology and Food Prices in Brazil." *Quarterly Review of Economics and Business* 23(1): 58–78.

————. (1983b) *O Problema Alimentar no Brasil: A Importancia dos Desequilibrios Tecnologicos.* São Paulo: Editora Paz e Terra.

Homem de Melo, Fernando, and Eduardo Fonseca (1981) *Proalcool, Energia e Transportes.* São Paulo: Pioneira.

Hood, N., and S. Young (1979) *The Economics of Multinational Enterprise.* London: Longman.

Hopkins, Raymond F. (1965) "Game Theory and Generalization in Ethics." *Review of Politics* 27 (October):491–500.

————. (1980) *Food, Politics and Agricultural Development.* Boulder, Colo.: Westview Press.

Hopkins, Raymond F., and Donald J. Puchala (1978) "Perspectives on the International Relations of Food," in *The Global Political Economy of Food,* Hopkins and Puchala, eds. Madison: University of Wisconsin Press.

————. (1980) *Global Food Interdependence: Challenge to American Foreign Policy.* New York: Columbia University Press.

Hopkins, Raymond F., Robert L. Paarlberg and Mitchel B. Wallerstein (1982) *Food in the Global Arena,* Global Issues Series, James E. Harf and B. Thomas Trout, eds. New York: Holt, Rinehart and Winston.

Horowitz, Donald L. (1971) "Three Dimensions of Ethnic Politics." *World Politics* 23(2) (January):232–244.

Horst, T. (1974) *At Home Abroad.* Cambridge: Ballinger.

Horton, Douglas E. (1974) *Land Reform and Reform Enterprises in Peru.* A report submitted to the Land Tenure Center and the World Bank, June.

Huberman, Leo and Paul M. Sweezy (1960) *Cuba: Anatomy of a Revolution.* New York: Monthly Review Press.

Huddleston, Barbara (1982) "World Food Security and Alternatives to a New International Wheat Agreement." *New International Realities* 6(2) (March).

————. (1984) *Closing the Cereals Gap with Trade and Food Aid.* Washington, D.C.: International Food Policy Research Institute (IFPRI)

Huntington, Samuel P. (1965) "Political Development and Political Decay." *World Politics* 17(3) (April):386–430.

———. (1968) *Political Order in Changing Societies.* New Haven: Yale University Press.

Huntington, Samuel P., and Jorge Dominguez (1975) "Political Development," in *Handbook of Political Science: Macro Political Theory*, Fred I. Greenstein and Nelson W. Polsby, eds., pp. 1–119, vol. 3. Reading, Mass.: Addison-Wesley.

Hyden, Goran (1981) *Beyond Ujamaa.* Berkeley: University of California Press.

———. (1983) *No Short Cuts to Progress.* Berkeley: University of California Press.

Ibingira, Grace (1980) *African Upheavals Since Independence.* Boulder, Colo.: Westview Press.

Iffland C., and A. Galland (1978) *Les Investissements Industriels Suisses au Mexique.* Lausanne: Centre de Recherches Europeennes.

Independent Commission on International Development Issues (Brandt Commission) (1980) *North-South: A Program for Survival.* Cambridge, Mass.: MIT Press.

Inter-American Development Bank (IDB) (1979) *Nutrition and Socio-Economic Development of Latin America.* Washington, D.C.: by the Bank.

———. (1981) *Economic and Social Progress in Latin America: 1980–81 Report.* Washington, D.C.: by the Bank.

———. (1983) *Economic and Social Progress in Latin America: Natural Resources.* Washington, D.C.: by the Bank.

———. (1984) *Economic and Social Progress in Latin America, 1984 Report.* Washington, D.C.: by the Bank.

International Food Policy Research Institute (IFPRI) (1976) "Meeting Food Needs in the Developing World: The Location and Magnitude of the Task in the Next Decade," Research Report No. 1 (February).

Isenman, Paul J., and H. W. Singer (1977) "Food Aid: Disincentive Effects and Their Policy Implications." *Economic Development and Cultural Change* 25 (January):205–239.

Jackson, Rosemary P. (1979) "United States-Mexican Relations, Issue Definition in the U.S. Role in a Changing World Political Economy: Major Issues for the 96th Congress." Compendium of papers submitted to the Joint Economic Committee, Congress of the United States, June 25.

Jackson, Tony (1982) *Against the Grain.* London: Oxfam.

Jain, Thail (1975) *Size Distribution of Income.* Washington, D.C.: World Bank.

Jansen, Doris (1981) "Agricultural Pricing Policy in Subsaharan Africa." Mimeo. Washington, D.C.: The World Bank.

Jarvis, W. E. (1981) "Market Demand and Production Requirements for

Prairie Grain." Paper presented to the Prairie Production Symposium, October 28–31, Saskatoon, Saskatchewan, Canada.

Jenkins, R. O. (1977) *Dependent Industrialization in Latin America — the Automotive Industry in Argentina, Chile, and Mexico.* New York: Praeger.

Jenks, Leland Hamilton (1928) *Our Cuban Colony: A Study in Sugar.* New York: Vanguard Press.

Johnson, Bruce (1980) "Agricultural Production Potentials and Small Farmer Strategies in Subsaharan Africa," in *Agricultural Development in Africa: Issues of Public Policy,* Robert Bates and Michael Lofchie, eds., pp. 67–97. New York: Praeger.

Johnson, Chalmers (1982) *Revolutionary Change,* 2nd ed. Boston: Little Brown.

Johnson, D. Gale (1974) *The Sugar Program: Large Costs and Small Benefits.* Washington, D.C.: American Enterprise Institute for Public Policy Research.

———. (1975) *World Food Problems and Prospects.* Washington, D.C.: American Enterprise Institute.

———. (1978) "World Food Institutions: A 'Liberal' View." *International Organization* 32(3) (Summer):837–854.

———. (1983) "The World Food Situation: Recent and Prospective Developments," in *The Role of Markets in the World Food Economy,* D. Gale Johnson and G. Edward Schuh, eds. Boulder, Colo.: Westview Press.

Johnson, D. Gale and G. Edward Schuh, eds. (1983) *The Role of Markets in the World Food Economy.* Boulder, Colo.: Westview Press.

Jordan, Robert S. (1982) "Why a NIEO? The View from the Third World." In *The Emerging International Economic Order: Dynamic Processes, Constraints and Opportunities,* H. Jacobson and D. Sidjanski, eds., 59–83. Beverly Hills: Sage Publications.

Kanesa-Thasan, S. (1981) "The Fund and Adjustment Policies in Africa." *Finance and Development* 18(3) (September):20–24.

Kaster M., and E. R. Bonato (1980) "Contribuicão das Cîencias Agrarias Para o Desenvolvimento: A Pesquisa em Soja." *Revista de Economia Rural* (Brazil) 84:405–34.

Katz, J. (1976) *Importación de tecnología, aprendizaje local e industrialización dependiente.* México: Fondo de Cultura Económica.

Keesing, D. (1981) "Exports and Policy for Latin American Countries: Prospects for the World Economy and for Latin American Exports, 1980–1990." *Quarterly Review of Economics and Business* 21(2) (Summer):18–47.

Keidel, A. (1981) *Korean Regional Farm Product and Income: 1910–1975.* Seoul: Korean Development Institute.

Kennedy, P. (1983) *Food and Agricultural Policy in Peru, 1960–1977.* Austin: Institute of Latin American Studies, University of Texas, Technical Papers Series #39.

Kern, Clifford R. (1968) "Looking a Gift Horse in the Mouth: The Economics of Food Aid Programs." *Political Science Quarterly* (March):59–75.

Kesselman, Mark (1973) "Order or Movement? The Literature of Political Development as Ideology." *World Politics* 27(1) (October):139–154.

Keys, A., J. Brozek, A. Henschel, O. Mickelsen, and H. Taylor (1950) *The Biology of Human Starvation.* Minneapolis: University of Minnesota Press.

Kim, Dong-Hi, and Yong-Jae Joo (1982) *The Food Situation and Policies in the Republic of Korea.* Paris: OECD.

Kim, K. D., and O. J. Lee (1978) "Korea's Saemaul Undong: Social Structure and the Role of Government in Integrated Rural Development," in *Korea: A Nation in Transition,* S. J. Kim and C. W. Kang, eds., pp. 21–43. Seoul: Research Center for Peace and Unification.

Kinley, David (1980) *Aid as Obstacle: Twenty Questions About Our Foreign Aid and the Hungry.* San Francisco: Institute for Food and Development Policy.

Klaren, P. (1973) *Modernization, Dislocation and Aprismo.* Austin: University of Texas Press.

Knickerbocker, F. T. (1974) *Oligopolistic Reaction and Multinational Enterprise.* Cambridge, Mass.: Harvard University Press.

———. (1976) *Market Structure and Market Power Consequences of Foreign Direct Investment by Multinational Corporations.* Occasional Paper No. 8. Washington, D.C.: Center for Multinational Studies.

Kojima, Kiyoshi (1978) *Direct Foreign Investment: A Japanese Model of Multinational Business Operations.* London: Croom Helm.

Korea Development Institute (1982) *Programs for Increasing Rural Household Income.* Seoul: by the Institute.

Korea, Economic Planning Board (annual) *Korea Statistical Yearbook.* Seoul: by the Board.

Korea, Economic Planning Board (monthly) *Monthly Statistics of Korea.* Seoul: by the Board.

Korea, Ministry of Agriculture and Fisheries (annual) *Yearbook of Agriculture and Forestry Statistics.* Seoul: by the Ministry.

Korea, Ministry of Agriculture and Fisheries (annual) *Food and Agriculture in Korea.* Seoul: by the Ministry.

Korea, National Livestock Cooperation Federation (1983) *Quarterly Review* 3(2).

Krishna, Raj (1967) "Agricultural Policy and Economic Development," in *Agricultural Growth and Economic Development,* H. M. Southworth and B. F. Johnston, eds., pp. 497–540. Ithaca, N.Y.: Cornell University Press.

Kuznets, Simon (1972) "Innovations and Adjustments in Economic Growth." *The Swedish Journal of Economics* 74:431–51.

Lall, S. and Paul Streeten (1977) *Foreign Investment, Transnationals and Developing Countries.* London: Macmillan.

Lancaster, Carol (1983) "Africa's Economic Crisis." *Foreign Policy* 52 (Fall): 149–66.

Land Economics Research Centre (1976) *A Study of Land Tenure System in Korea.* Seoul: by the Centre.

Lappé, *Frances Moore and Joseph Collins (1978) Food First: Beyond the Myth of Scarcity,* revised edition. New York: Ballentine Books.

Lappé, Frances Moore, Joseph Collins, and David Kinley (1980) *Aid as Obstacle: Twenty Questions About Our Foreign Aid and the Hungry.* San Francisco: Institute for Food and Development Policy.

Larson, Magli S., and Arlene G. Bergman (1969) *Social Stratification in Peru.* Berkeley: Institute of International Studies, University of California.

Ledogar, Robert J. (1975) *Hungry For Profits: U.S. Food and Multinationals in Latin America.* New York: IDOC.

Lee, E. (1979) "Egalitarian Peasant Farming and Rural Development: The Case of South Korea," in *Agrarian Systems and Rural Development,* D. Ghai et al., eds., pp. 24-73. London: Macmillan.

Lee, J. H. (1981) *A Study on the Adjustment of Agricultural Land Systems for Increased Productivity in Korea, Third Interim Report.* Seoul: Economic Planning Board.

Lee, T. H. (1971) *Intersectoral Capital Flows in the Economic Development of Taiwan 1895-1960.* London and Ithaca, N.Y.: Cornell University Press.

Lele, Uma (1975) *Design for Rural Development.* Baltimore: Johns Hopkins University Press (for the World Bank).

Levinson, James F. (1974) *Morinda: An Economic Analysis of Malnutrition Among Children in Rural India.* Cambridge: International Nutrition Policy Series.

Lewis, Lowell (1982) "Agriculture Overview," in *Priorities in Biotechnology Research for International Development: Proceedings of a Workshop,* pp. 147-58. Washington, D.C.: National Academy Press.

Lindbloom, Charles E. (1977) *Politics and Markets.* New York: Basic Books.

Lipset, Seymour Martin (1959) "Some Social Requisites of Democracy: Economic Development and Political Legitimacy." *American Political Science Review* 53 (March):69–105.

———. (1960) *Political Man: The Social Bases of Politics.* New York: Doubleday.

———. (1981) "The Limits of Social Science." *Public Opinion* 4 (October/November):2–9.

Lipton, Michael (1977) *Why the Poor Stay Poor: A Study of Urban Bias in World Development.* London: Temple Smith.

Little, I. M. D., T. Scitovsky, and M. Scott (1970) *Industry and Trade in Some Developing Countries: A Comparative Study.* London: Oxford University Press.

Livernash, Bob (1979) "Power of Sugar Lobby Wanes, But It Still Helps Write the Bill." *Congressional Quarterly Weekly Report* (May 5):831–35.

Lofchie, Michael F., and Stephen K. Commins (1984) *Food Deficits and Agricultural Policies in Sub-Saharan Africa*. The Hunger Project Papers, No. 2, Beverly Tangri, ed. San Francisco: The Hunger Project, September.

Lowenthal, Abraham F. ed. (1975a) *The Peruvian Experiment*. Princeton: Princeton University Press.

———. (1975b) "Peru's Ambiguous Revolution," in *The Peruvian Experiment*, Abraham F. Lowenthal, ed., pp. 3–43. Princeton: Princeton University Press.

Lowi, Theodore J. (1969) *The End of Liberalism: Ideology, Policy and the Crisis of Public Authority*. New York: W.W. Norton.

Luiselli, F. C. (1980) "Por que el SAM? Objetivos y programa del Sistema Alimentario Mexicano." *Nexos* 25.

Mahler, Vincent A. (1980) *Dependency Approaches to International Political Economy: A Cross-National Study*. New York: Columbia University Press.

———. (1981) "Britain, the European Community and the Developing Commonwealth: Dependence, Interdependence and the Political Economy of Sugar." *International Organization* 35 (Summer):467–492.

———. (1984) "The Political Economy of North-South Commodity Bargaining: The Case of the International Sugar Agreement." *International Organization* 38 (Autumn):709–731.

Mair, Lucy (1962) *Primitive Government*. London and Baltimore: Penguin.

Major Speeches by President Park Chung Hee (n.d.) Seoul: Samhwa Publishing Co.

Maletta, Hector (1982) "El Empleo Rural en el Perú: Situación y Perspectivas," in *Situación Actual y Perspectivas del Problema Agrario en el Perú*, Fernando Eguren, ed., pp. 397–468, Lima: DESCO.

Maletta, Héctor and Jesús Foronda (1980) *La Acumulación de Capital en la Agricultura Peruana*. Lima: Centro de Investigación de la Universidad del Pacífico.

Mann, Jitendar S. (1967) "The Impact of Public Law 480 on Prices and Domestic Supply of Cereals in India." *Journal of Farm Economics* 49(1) (February):131–146.

Mares, David (1982) "Agriculture and Dependent Development: Politics in an Evolving Enclave Economy." Ph.D. dissertation, Department of Government, Harvard University, 1982.

Martínez, Daniel and Armando Tealdo (1982) *El Agro Peruano 1970–1980: Análisis y Perspectivas*. Lima: CEDEP.

Martínez-Saldaña, Tomás (1980) *El costo social de un éxito político*. Chapingo, México: Colegio de Postgraduados.

Martz, J. (1980) "Approaches to Agricultural Policy in Venezuela." *Inter-American Economic Affairs* 34(3) (Winter):25–53.

Matos Mar, José, and José Manuel Mejía (1980a) *Reforma Agraria: Logros y Contradicciones 1969-1979.* Lima: Instituto de Estudios Peruanos.

——. (1980b) *La Reforma Agraria en el Perú.* Lima: Instituto de Estudios Peruanos.

Maxwell, Simon J. (1983) "From Understudy to Leading Star: The Future Role of Impact Assessment in Food Aid Programmes," in *Bulletin* 14:2, Institute of Development Studies, University of Sussex, England, April.

Maxwell, Simon J., and Hans W. Singer (1981) "Food Aid to Developing Countries: A Survey," in *Recent Issues in World Development: A Collection of Survey Articles*, Paul P. Streeten and Richard Jolley, eds., pp. 219-240. Oxford and New York: Pergamon.

Mayer, Jean (1974) "Coping With Famine." *Foreign Affairs* 53(1) (October): 98-120.

——. (1977) *Acts of Nature, Acts of Man: The Global Response to Natural Disasters.* New York: United Nations Association.

Mayer, Leo V. (1981) "Farm Productivity—Balancing Technological Land Social Goals," in *Food in the Future: Proceedings of a Planning Symposium*, pp. 36-48. Washington, D.C.: U.S. General Accounting Office.

McCalla, Alex (1967) "Duopoly Model of World Wheat Pricing." *Journal of Farm Economics* 48(1):711-17.

McCalla, Alex, and A. Schmitz (1979) "Grain Marketing Systems: The Case of the United States Versus Canada." *American Journal of Agricultural Economics* 61(2) (May):199-212.

McClintock, Cynthia (1980) "After Peru's Agrarian Reform: Are the Peasants More Conservative, or More Radical?" Paper presented at the Latin American Studies Association Meeting in Bloomington, Indiana (October).

——. (1981) *Peasant Cooperatives and Political Change in Peru.* Princeton: Princeton University Press.

——. (1982) "Post-Revolutionary Agrarian Policies in Peru," in *Post-Revolutionary Peru: The Policies of Transformation*, Stephen M. Gorman, ed., pp. 135-156. Boulder, Colo.: Westview Press.

McClintock, Cynthia, and Abraham F. Lowenthal, eds. (1982) *The Peruvian Experiment Reconsidered.* Princeton: Princeton University Press.

McCoy, J. (1979) *Livestock and Meat Marketing.* Westport, Conn.: AVI Publishers.

McMillan, C. J. (1981) "The Pros and Cons of a National Export Trading House." *Canadian Public Policy* 7(4) (Autumn):569-583.

Meissner, F. (1980) "Agribusiness Development of Latin America: The Role of the Inter-American Development Bank." Mimeo prepared for Seminar on International Agriculture, Cornell University, 16 April.

Mellor, John W. (1976) *The New Economics of Growth, A Strategy for India and the Developing World*. Ithaca: Cornell University Press.

———. (1981) "Commentary on Josling," in *Food and Agriculture Policy for the 1980s*, D. Gale Johnson, ed., pp. 147–49. Washington: American Enterprise Institute.

Mellor, John W., and Bruce Johnston (1984) "The World Food Equation: Interrelations Among Development, Employment, and Food Consumption." *Journal of Economic Literature* 22 (June):531–74.

Merkl, Peter H. (1981) "Democratic Development, Breakdowns, and Fascism." *World Politics* 34(1) (October):114–135.

Merriam, John G. (1983) "The Politics of Hunger." A paper delivered at the 24th annual convention of the International Studies Association, Mexico City, April 7.

México, Secretaría de Programación y Presupuesto (1979) *La población de México, su ocupación, y sus niveles de bienestar*. México: by the Agency.

México, Sistema Nacional de Evaluación, Sistema Alimentario Mexicano (SINE-SAM) (1980–81) *Sistema integral de carne bovina*, five volumes. Mexico, D.F.: SINE-SAM.

Mohr, A. Fuentes (1977) "The Latin American Multinational Enterprise of Agricultural Cooperation: A Practical Expression Among Developing Countries." *Nueva Sociedad*; special issue.

Montavon, R. (1979) *L'implantation de deux entreprises multinationales au Mexique*. Paris: Presses Universitaires de France.

Moody's Industrial Manual (1979) New York: Moody Publishing Co.

Moon, Chun-In (1984) *The Political Economy of Bilateral Economic Relations: The Case of Korea and Saudi Arabia*. Baltimore: University of Maryland. (Mimeographed.)

Moore, M., and G. Wickremesinghe (1980) *Agriculture and Society in the Low Country* (Sri Lanka). Colombo: Agrarian Research and Training Institute.

Morison, Samuel Eliot, Henry Steele Commager and William Leuchtenberg (1969) *The Growth of the American Republic*. New York: Oxford University Press.

Morrow, Daniel T. (1980) *The Economics of the International Stockholding of Wheat*. Washington, D.C.: International Food Policy Research Institute (IFPRI), report #18, September.

———. (1981) "The International Wheat Agreement and LDC Food Security," in *Food Security for Developing Countries*, Alberto Valdes, ed., pp. 213–39. Boulder, Colo.: Westview Press.

Moynagh, Michael (1977) "The Negotiation of the Commonwealth Sugar Agreement, 1949–51." *Journal of Commonwealth and Comparative Political Studies* 15 (July):63–76.

Myint, Hla (1975) "Agriculture and Economic Development in the Open Economy," in *Agriculture in Development Theory*, L.G. Reynolds, ed., pp. 327–54. New Haven: Yale University Press.

National Academy of Sciences (Committee on World Food) (1975) *Population and Food: Critical Issues*. Washington, D.C.: National Academy of Sciences.

National Research Council (1977) *World Food and Nutrition Study: The Potential Contributions of Research*. Washington, D.C.: National Academy of Sciences.

Nichols, Peter (1984) "24 African Nations Need Urgent Food Aid, Says UN." *The Times* (London), January 20:4.

Nicholson, Norman K., and John D. Esseks (1978) "The Politics of Food Scarcities in Developing Countries." *International Organization* 32(3) (Summer):679–719.

Nicholson, Norman K., John D. Esseks, and Ali Akhtar Khan (1979) "The Politics of Food Scarcities in Developing Countries." in *Food, Politics and Case Studies in the Public Policy of Rural Modernization*, Raymond F. Hopkins, Donald J. Puchala, and Ross B. Talbot, eds. Boulder, Colo.: Westview Press.

Nsouli, S.M. (1982) "The Role of the Fund in Financing and Adjustment with Particular Reference to the Sahel Countries." *IMF Survey* 11 (February 22):50–55.

Nuccio, Richard A. (1981) "The Redefinition of U.S.-Mexican Relations, 1977–1980." Williamstown, Mass.: Williams College Department of Political Science.

O'Brien, P. (1981) "Global Prospects for Agriculture," in *Agriculture-Food Policy Review: Perspectives for the 1980s*, pp. 2–27. Washington, D.C.: USDA.

O'Connor, James (1972) "Cuba: Its Political Economy," in *Cuba in Revolution*, Rolando Bonachea and Nelson P. Valdes, eds., pp. 52–81, Garden City, N.Y.: Anchor Books.

O'Donnell, Guillermo (1973) *Modernization and Bureaucratic-Authoritarianism: Studies in South American Politics*. Institute of International Studies, University of California, Berkeley, Politics of Modernization Series No. 9.

OECD (1979) *Impact of Multinational Enterprises on National Scientific and Technical Capacities: Food Industry*. Directorate for Science, Technology and Industry. Paris: OECD. (Mimeographed.)

OECD (1980) "The Important but Elusive Issues of Aid Effectiveness." *Development Cooperation Review*. 51–69.

OECD (1981) "Food Aid." *Development Cooperation Review*. Paris: OECD.

OECD (annual) *Development Cooperation Review*. Paris: OECD.

Okigbo, Bede N. (1982) "Agriculture and Food Production in Tropical Africa," in *The Developmental Effectiveness of Food Aid*, Agriculture Development Council, pp. 11–68. New York: by the Council.

Olson, Mancur, Jr. (1965) *The Logic of Collective Action.* Cambridge, Mass.: Harvard University Press.

Organization of American States (OAS) (1981) *Short-Term Economic Reports: Vol VII 1981 Peru.* Washington, D.C.: OAS.

Organski, A. F. K. (1965) *The Stages of Political Development.* New York: Alfred A. Knopf.

Paarlberg, Donald (1980) *Farm and Food Policy: Issues of the 1980s.* Lincoln: University of Nebraska Press.

Paarlberg, R. L. (1982) "Managing Global Food Problems: The Unique Institutional Assets of the State." Paper prepared for delivery at the XII World Congress of the International Political Science Association, Rio de Janeiro, August.

Paarlberg, Robert (1978) "Shifting and Sharing Adjustment Burdens: The Role of the Industrial Food Importing Nations," in *The Global Political Economy of Food*, Raymond F. Hopkins and Donald J. Puchala, eds. Madison: University of Wisconsin Press.

———. (1980) "Lessons of the Grain Embargo." *Foreign Affairs*, 59(1) (Fall): 144–62.

———. (1983) "Food Power: Myth or Reality." Manuscript, Wellesley College.

Packenham, Robert A. (1973) *Liberal America and the Third World.* Princeton: Princeton University Press.

Painter, Michael (1983a) "Agricultural Policy, Food Production, and Multinational Corporations in Peru." *Latin American Research Review*, 18(2): 201–18.

———. (1983b) "The Political Economy of Food Production in Peru," *Studies in Comparative International Development*, 28(4):34–52.

Palerm, Ángel (1976) *Modos de producción y formaciones socioeconómicas.* México, D.F.: Editorial EDICOL.

Palloix, Christian (1977) *Las firmas multinacionales y el proceso de internacionalización.* Mexico: Siglo XXI.

Palmer, R. (1981) "The Eastern Caribbean: Problems of Peripheral Development." Paper presented at a conference on the Eastern Caribbean sponsored by the U.S. Department of State. Washington, D.C., November.

Pearson, S. R., J. D. Stryker, C. P. Humphries, et al. (1981) *Rice in West Africa: Policy and Economics.* Stanford: Stanford University Press.

Pease García, Henry (1981) *Un Perfil del Proceso Político Peruano: A Un Año del Segundo Belaundismo.* Lima: DESCO.

Pellicer de Brody, Olga (1981a) Comments presented at the Binational Consultation on U.S.-Mexican Agricultural Relations. San Diego, California, February.

————. (1981b) "U.S. Concerns Regarding Mexico's Oil and Gas: Evolution of the Debate, 1977–1980." Research Report No. 10, Center for U.S.-Mexican Studies, University of California, San Diego, LaJolla, California.

Penn, J. B. (1981) "Economic Developments in U.S. Agriculture During the 1970s," in *Food and Agricultural Policy for the 1980s*, D. Johnson, ed., pp. 3–47. Washington, D.C.: American Enterprise Institute for Public Policy Research.

Perelman, Michael (1977) *Farming for Profit in a Hungry World*. Montclair, N.J.: Allanheld, Osmun.

Perkins, P. (1979) "Multinationals in Brazilian Agricultural Production." Unpublished manuscript.

Perlmutter, Amos (1980) "The Comparative Analysis of Military Regimes." *World Politics* 33(1) (October):96–120.

Peru, Ministry of Agriculture (1982) *Producción, Superficie Cosechada y Rendimiento de los Principales Cultivos por Región Agraria 1977–1981*. Lima: Ministry of Agriculture.

Peru, National Planning Institute (1982) "Informe Socioeconómico: Evaluación del Programa de Inversiones," Vol. II. Lima: INP (Mimeo)

Peru, Presidency of the Republic (1982–83) *Peru 1981*. Lima: Presidency of the Republic.

————. (1983) *Peru 1982*. Lima: Presidency of the Republic.

————. (1984) *Peru 1984*. Lima: Presidency of the Republic.

Phelps, D. M. (1969) *Migration of Industry to South America*; reprinted 1st ed. Westport, Conn.: Greenwood Press.

Pick's Currency Yearbook (annual) New York: Pick Publishing Corporation.

Pimental, David, et al. (1975) "Food Production and the Energy Crisis," in *Food: Politics, Economics, Nutrition and Research*, a Special SCIENCE Compendium, Philip H. Abelson, ed., pp. 121–27. Washington, D.C.: American Association for the Advancement of Science.

Poleman, Thomas (1983) "World Hunger: Extent, Causes, and Cures," in *The Role of Markets in the World Food Economy*, D. Gale Johnson and G. Edward Schuh, eds. Boulder, Colo.: Westview Press.

Portocarrero, Felipe M. (1982) "The Peruvian Public Investment Programme, 1968–1978." *Journal of Latin American Studies*, 14(2):433–54.

Prebisch, Raúl (1946) "Panorama general de los problemas de regulación monetaria y crediticia en el continente americano: América Latina," in Banco de México, Memoria: Primera reunión de técnicos sobre problema de banco central del continente americano, pp. 25–28, México: Banco de México.

————. (1959) "International Trade and Payments in an Era of Coexistence." *American Economic Review: Papers and Proceedings* 49(2):251–73.

————. (1963) *Towards a Dynamic Development Policy for Latin America*. New York: United Nations.

Puchala, Donald J. and Raymond F. Hopkins (1978) "Toward Innovation in the Global Food Regime." *International Organization* 32(3) (Summer): 855–68.

Puryear, Jeffrey M. (1983) "Higher Education, Development Assistance and Repressive Regimes." Paper reprinted by the Ford Foundation and adapted from this article appearing in *Studies in Cooperative International Development*, 17, No. 2 (1982).

Rajaratnam, S. (1981) "The Crisis of the Third World," in *At Issue: Politics in the World Arena*, pp. 139–48. New York: St. Martin's Press.

Rama, R., and R. Vigorito (1979) *Transnacionales en América Latina: El complejo de frutas y legumbres en México*. México City: Instituto Latinoamericano de Estudios Transnacionales, Editorial Nueva Imagen.

Rawls, John (1972) *A Theory of Justice*. Cambridge, Mass.: Harvard University Press.

Regier, Donald W. (1978) "Feed Demand in the World GOL Model." *Agricultural Economics Research* 30(2) (April):16–24.

Republic of China, Council for Agricultural Planning and Development (annual) *Basic Agricultural Statistics, Republic of China*. Taipei: by the Council.

Research and Policy Committee (1969) *Assisting Development in Low-Income Countries*. New York: Committee for Economic Development.

Reutlinger, Shlomo, and Marcelo Selowsky (1976) *Malnutrition and Poverty: Magnitude and Policy Options*. Baltimore: Johns Hopkins Press.

Rico, Carlos (1980) "Method and Madness: Looking for a Typology of Issue Areas in U.S. Foreign Policy-Making." Mexico, D.F.: Centro de Investigación y Docencia Económicas, Instituto de Estudios Estados Unidos. (Mimeographed.)

Riding, Alan (1977) "U.S. Food Seen Hurting Guatemala." In *New York Times*, November 6.

Rifkin, Jeremy (1981) *Entropy*. Toronto: Bantam Books.

Ripley, Randall B., and Grace A. Franklin (1980) *Congress, the Bureaucracy and Public Policy*. Homewood, Ill.: Dorsey Press.

Robinson, Joan (1962) *Economic Philosophy*. Chicago: Aldine.

Roca, Sergio (1976) *Cuban Economic Policy and Ideology: The Ten Million Ton Sugar Harvest*. Beverly Hills: Sage Professional Papers in International Studies.

Rodgers, Gerry, Mike Hopkins, and Rene Wery (1978) *Population, Employment, and Inequality: The BACHUE Model Applied to the Philippines*. New York: Praeger.

Rogers, Keith D. (1971) "Theory and Application of Food Aid in Economic Development." Ph.D. Thesis, Iowa State University, Ames.

Rojko, Anthony S., and Martin W. Schwartz (1976) "Modeling the World Grain-Oilseeds-Livestock Economy to Assess World Food Prospects." *Agricultural Economics Research* 28(3) (July):89–98.

Rostow, Walt W. (1960) *The Stages of Economic Growth: A Non-Communist Manifesto.* Cambridge, U.K.: Cambridge University Press.

Rothbard, Murry N. (1976) *Conceived in Liberty,* vol. 3 of "Advance to Revolution, 1760–1775." New Rochelle, New York: Arlington House.

Saemaul in New Age (annual) Seoul: Republic of Korea.

Sanders, Thomas (1980) *Food Policy Decision-Making in Colombia.* American Universities Field Staff Reports, South America, #50.

———. (1982a) *Argentina Before and After the War.* American Universities Field Staff Reports, South America, #33.

———. (1982b) *The Problems of Nutrition in Brazil.* American Universities Field Staff Reports, #16.

———. (1983) *Chile's Economic Crisis and Its Implications for Political Change.* American Universities Field Staff Reports, South America, #4.

Sanderson, Fred (1978) *Japan: Food Prospects and Policies.* Washington, D.C.: Brookings Institution.

Sanderson, Steven E. (1981a) "Florida Tomatoes, U.S.-Mexican Relations and the International Division of Labor." *Inter-American Economic Affairs* 35(3) (Winter):23–52.

———. (1981b) *The Receding Frontier: Aspects of the Internationalization of U.S.-Mexican Agriculture and Their Implications for Bilateral Relations in the 1980s.* University of California-San Diego, Program in U.S.-Mexican Studies, Working Papers #15.

———. (1982) *Trade Aspects of the Internationalization of U.S.-Mexican Agriculture and their Implications for Bilateral Relations in the 1980s.* La Jolla: University of California-San Diego Monographs in U.S.-Mexican Studies.

———. (1985) *The Transformation of Mexican Agriculture: International Structure and the Politics of Rural Change.* Princeton University Press.

Saylor, Thomas Reese (1977) "A New Legislative Mandate for American Food Aid," in *Food Policy: The Responsibility of the United States in the Life and Death Choices,* Peter G. Brown and Henry Shue, eds., pp. 199–211. New York: The Free Press.

Scheibal, Ken (1982) "Plan to Feed World Hungry is Proposed." *Washington Times,* June 1:3A.

Schmitter, Philippe C., ed. (1973) *Latin America: Function, Consequences and Perspectives.* Beverly Hills: Sage Publications.

Schneider, H. (1975) *The Effects of Food Aid on Agricultural Production in*

Recipient Countries: An Annotated Selective Bibliography. Paris: OECD.

Schoultz, Lars (1981) *Human Rights and United States Policy Toward Latin America*. Princeton: Princeton University Press.

Schuh, G. Edward (1976) "The New Macroeconomics of Agriculture." *American Journal of Agricultural Economics* 58(5):801–11.

———. (1979) "Food Aid: Does It Help the Poor?" Agenda (June):10–16.

———. (1981) "Economics and International Relations: A Conceptual Framework." *American Journal of Agricultural Economics* 63 (December):767–78.

Schultz, Theodore W. (1960) "Impact and Implications of Foreign Surplus Disposal on Underdeveloped Economies." *Journal of Farm Economics* 42(4) (November):1019–30.

Scobie, Grant M., and R. Posada (1978) "The Impact of Technical Change on Income Distribution: The Case of Rice in Colombia." *American Journal of Agricultural Economics* 60(1):85–92.

Scott, Christopher D. (1978) *Technology, Employment and Income Distribution in the Sugar Industry of the Dominican Republic*. Report to the International Labour Office (PREALC), Regional Employment Programme for Latin America and the Caribbean, March.

———. (1980) "Transnational Corporations and the Food Industry in Latin America: A Preliminary Analysis of the Determinants of Investment and Divestment." Paper presented at the Woodrow Wilson Center for International Scholars, Washington, D.C.

———. (1981) "Agrarian Reform and Seasonal Employment in Coastal Peruvian Agriculture." *Journal of Development Studies* 17(4) (July):282–306.

———. (1984) "Transnational Corporations and Asymmetries in the Latin American Food System." *Bulletin of Latin American Research* 3(1).

———. (1984) "The Determinants of Investment and Divestment by Transnational Corporations in the Latin American Food Industries." Unpublished manuscript.

———. (forthcoming) "Transnational Corporations, Comparative Advantage and Food Security in Latin America," in *Economic Imperialism and Latin America*, C. Abel and C. Lewis, eds. London: Athlone Press.

Scott, James C. (1976) *The Moral Economy of the Peasant*. New Haven, Conn.: Yale University Press.

Seligson, M. A. (1977) "Agrarian Policies in Dependent Societies: Costa Rica." *Journal of Inter-American Studies and World Affairs* 19(2):201–32.

Selowsky, M. (1979) *Balancing Trickle Down and Basic Needs Strategies: Income Distribution Issues in Large Middle-Income Countries, with Special Reference to Latin America*. Washington, D.C.: World Bank Staff Working Paper #335.

Sen, Amartya (1980) *Levels of Poverty: Policy and Change*. Washington, D.C.: World Bank Staff Working Paper #401.

Shane, Douglas R. (1978) "Development Issues: U.S. Actions Affecting the

Development of Low Income Countries." The Third Annual Report of the President Transmitted to the Congress. Washington D.C.: Agency for International Development, publication #78/852 (April)

————. (1980) "Hoofprints on the Forest: An Inquiry into the Beef Cattle Industry in the Tropical Forest Areas of Latin America." A study prepared for the U.S. Department of State. Washington, D.C.: U.S. State Dept., contract #1751–900416 (March).

Shepherd, Jack (1975) *Politics of Starvation*. New York: Carnegie Endowment.

Sheridan, Ricahrd B. (1973) *Sugar and Slaves: An Economic History of the British West Indies 1623–1775*. Baltimore: Johns Hopkins University Press.

Silva Herzog, James (1982) *Los Angeles Times*, 19 May.

Simpson, James R. (1978) "Cattle Cycles: A Guide for Cattlemen." Food and Resource Economics Department Staff Paper, Institute for Food and Agricultural Sciences, University of Florida, Gainesville.

————. (1979a) "World Cattle Cycles and the Latin American Beef Industry." Food and Resource Economics Department Staff Paper, Institute for Food and Agricultural Sciences, University of Florida, Gainesville.

————. (1979b) "An Assessment of the United States' Meat Import Act of 1979." Unpublished manuscript.

Sinclair, Ward (1981) "Food Exports: Worries in Land of Plenty." *Washington Post* (August 17):1.

Singer, Hans W. (1950) "The Distribution of Gains Between Investing and Borrowing Countries." *American Economic Review: Papers and Proceedings* 40(2) (May):473–85.

Singer, Hans, and Javed Ansari (1978) *Rich and Poor Countries*. London: George Allen and Unwin.

Singer, Hans W., and Simon J. Maxwell (1983) "Development Through Food: Twenty Years' Experience." Paper submitted for discussion at the World Food Program/Government of the Netherlands Seminar on Food Aid marking the twentieth anniversary of the World Food Program, 3–5 October, The Hague.

Sitterson, J. Carlyle (1973 reprint of 1953 book) *Sugar Country: The Cane Sugar Industry in the South, 1753–1950*. Westport, Conn.: Greenwood Press.

Sivard, Ruth Leger (1981) *World Military and Social Expenditures 1981*. Leesburg, Va.: World Priorities.

————. (1982) *World Military and Social Expenditures 1982*. Leesburg, Va.: World Priorities.

Sloan, J. (1980) "Comparative Public Policy in Cuba and Brazil." Paper presented at the American Political Science Association Convention, Washington, D.C.: August.

Smith, Ian (1975) "Sugar Markets in Disarray." *Journal of World Trade Law* 9 (February):41–62.

Solow, R.M. (1957) "Technical Change and the Aggregate Production Function." *Review of Economics and Statistics* 39(1):312–20.

Sommer, John G. (1981) "Does Foreign Aid Really Help the Poor?" *Agenda* (April):2–5.

Soth, Leonard (1981) "The Grain Export Boom: Should It Be Tamed?" *Foreign Affairs* 59(4) (Spring):895–912.

———. (1982) "The U.S. Farm Export Booms." *Foreign Affairs* Fall, 1982.

Srinivasan, T. N. (1983a) "Hunger: Defining It, Estimating Its Global Incidence, and Alleviating It," in *The Role of Markets in the World Food Economy*, D. Gale Johnson and G. Edward Schuh, eds. Boulder, Colo.: Westview Press.

———. (1983b) "Review of A. K. Sen's Poverty and Famines: An Essay on Entitlement and Deprivation." *American Journal of Agricultural Economics* 65(1) (February):200.

Srivastava, Uma K., Earl O. Heady, Keith Rogers, and Leo V. Mayer (1975) *Food Aid and International Economic Growth*. Ames: The Iowa State University Press.

Stavrianos, L.S. (1981) *Global Rift*. New York: William Morrow.

Stein, Leslie (1978) "The Green Revolution and Asian Development Strategy." *Studies in Comparative International Development* 12(13):58–69.

Steinhart, J. S. and C. E. Steinhart (1975) "Energy Use in the U.S. Food System," in *Food: Politics, Economics, Nutrition and Research*, a Special SCIENCE Compendium, Philip H. Abelson, ed., pp. 33–42. Washington, D.C.: American Association for the Advancement of Science.

Stevens, Christopher (1979) *Food Aid and the Developing World: Four African Case Studies*. London: Croom Helm.

Stevens, William K. (1982) "Punjab Farmers: A Shining Example." *New York Times*, October 7:4.

Stohl, Michael S., and Harry Targ, eds. (1982) *The Global Political Economy in the 1980s*. Cambridge: Schenkman.

Sunkel, Osvaldo (1981) "Development Styles and the Environment: An Interpretation of the Latin American Case," in *From Dependency to Development*, Heraldo Munoz, ed., pp. 73–114. Boulder, Colo.: Westview Press.

Svedberg, Peter (1984) Food Insecurity in Developing Countries: Causes, Trends and Policy Options. UNCTAD/CD/301. June, Geneva. (Mimeographed.)

Swanberg, K. G. (1981) "Implications of the Drought Syndrome for Agricultural Planning in East Africa: Tanzania." Washington, D.C.: USAID/USDA PL480 Mission to Tanzania. (Mimeographed.)

Targ, Harry (1982) *International Relations in a World of Imperialism and Class Struggle: An Essay on the History of Ideas*. Cambridge: Schenkman.

Tarrant, John R. (1980) *Food Policies*. New York: Wiley.

Tate, Merze (1965) *The United States and the Hawaiian Kingdom: A Political History*. New Haven: Yale University Press.

Thomas, Hugh (1971) *Cuba: The Pursuit of Freedom*. New York: Harper and Row.

———. (1979) *A History of the World*. New York: Harper and Row.

Thorp, Rosemary, and Geoffrey Bertram (1978) *Peru 1890–1977: Growth and Policy in an Open Economy*. London: Macmillan.

Tilly, Charles, ed. (1975) *The Formation of National States in Western Europe*. Princeton: Princeton University Press.

Timmer, C. Peter, Walter P. Falcon, and Scott Pearson (1983) *Food Policy Analysis*. Baltimore: Johns Hopkins University Press.

Todaro, Michael P. (1981) *Economic Development in the Third World*, 2nd ed. New York: Longman.

Tucker, Robert W. and David C. Hendrickson (1982) *The Fall of the First British Empire: Origins of the War of American Independence*. Baltimore: Johns Hopkins University Press.

Tullis, LaMond (1970) *Lord and Peasant in Peru*. Cambridge, Mass.: Harvard University Press.

———. (1973) *Politics and Social Change in Third World Countries*. New York: John Wiley and Sons.

———. (1984) "The Current View on Rural Development: Fad or Breakthrough in Latin America?" in *An International Political Economy*, W. Ladd Hollist and F. LaMond Tullis, eds., pp. 223–54. Boulder, Colo.: Westview Press.

U.N. *Preliminary Assessment of the World Food Situation*. Rome: United Nations.

———. (1978) *Transnational Corporations in World Development: A Re-examination*. United Nations.

U.N., Center on Transnational Corporations (1981) *Transnational Corporations in Food and Beverage Processing*. New York: United Nations.

U.N., CEPAL (1975) *La industria de la carne de ganado bovino en México*. Mexico: Fondo de Cultura Económica.

U.N., Food and Agriculture Organization (FAO) (1980; 1981) *Trade Yearbook*, 34:316–30.

———. (1980) *The State of Food and Agriculture, 1979*. Rome: FAO.

———. (Annual) *FAO Production Yearbook*. Rome: FAO.

———. (1984) *Report of the Ninth Session of the Committee on World Food Security*. Rome: FAO, CL86/10, May.

U.S. Agency for International Development (1979) *Policy on Agricultural Assets Distribution: Land Reform*. Washington, D.C.: by the Agency.

U.S., Congress, Office of Technology Assessment (1981) *Impacts of Applied Genetics: Micro-Organisms, Plants and Animals*. Washington, D.C.: by the Office. April.

U.S., Department of Agriculture (1978a) *Livestock and Meat Situation* (September).

————. (1978b) "Meat Boom Sparking Latin American Demand for U.S. Soy Products." *Foreign Agriculture* 16 (July):2–5.

————. (1980a) *Global Food Assessment, 1980*, report #159. Washington, D.C.: Economics, Statistics, and Cooperatives Service of USDA.

————. (1980b) "Mexican Government Concerned over Lag in Meat Production." *Foreign Agriculture* 18 (April):10.

————. (1983) *Attache Report* (from Lima) Report No. PE–3010.

————. (annual) *Food for Peace: Annual Reports on Public Law 480*. Washington, D.C.: USDA.

U.S., Department of Agriculture, Economic Research Service (ERS) (1981) *Food Problems and Prospects in Subsaharan Africa*. Foreign Agricultural Economic Report (FAER) #166. Washington, D.C.: USDA.

————. (1983) *World Food Aid Needs and Availabilities, 1983*. Washington, D.C.: USDA.

————. (July 1984a) *World Food Aid Needs and Availabilities, 1984*. Washington, D.C.: USDA.

————. (July 1984b) *Subsaharan Africa: Outlook and Situation Report*. Washington, D.C.: USDA.

————. (1984c) *Latin America Outlook and Situation Report* (RS-84–9, July 1984).

————. (1984d) *Sugar and Sweetener Outlook and Situation Report* (Washington, D.C.: Government Printing Office).

U.S., Department of Agriculture Economic and Statistics Service (ESS) (1981) *Agricultural Situation: Western Hemisphere, Review of 1980 and Outlook for 1981*. Washington, D.C.: USDA.

————. (1982) *Agricultural Situation: Western Hemisphere — Preliminary Working Draft*. Washington, D.C.: USDA.

U.S., Department of Agriculture, Foreign Agricultural Service (1981a) "Brazil: Agricultural Situation, 1980." January. (Mimeographed.)

————. (1981b) "Colombia: Annual Agricultural Situation Report." January. (Mimeographed.)

————. (1981c) "Peru: Agricultural Situation Report." January. (Mimeographed.)

————. (periodic) *Foreign Agriculture Circular: Sugar*. Washington, D.C.: USDA.

U.S., Department of Agriculture, Crop Reporting Board (periodic) *Sugar Market Statistics*. Washington, D.C.: USDA.

U.S., Department of Commerce (1976) *U.S. Direct Investment Abroad, 1966 Final Data*. Washington, D.C.: Government Printing Office.

U.S., Department of State (1982) "Fact Sheet: Caribbean Basin Policy." Washington, D.C.: by the Department. (Mimeographed.)

U.S., General Accounting Office (1975) *Disincentives to Agricultural Production in Developing Countries, Report to the Congress.* Washington, D.C.: General Accounting Office, November 26.

———. (1980a) *Promoting Agricultural Exports to Latin America.* Washington, D.C.: General Accounting Office, December.

———. (1980b) "Competition Among Suppliers in the P.L. 480 Concessional Sales Programs." report to the chairman, Subcommittee on Limitations of Contracted and Delegated Authority, Senate Committee on the Judiciary, by the Comptroller General of the United States. Washington, D.C.: by the Office.

U.S., House of Representatives, Committee on International Relations (1977) *Use of U.S. Food Resources for Diplomatic Purposes—An Examination of the Issues.* Washington, D.C.: U.S. Government Printing Office.

U.S., House, Committee on Agriculture, 97th Congress (1981), 1st Session, Hearings, July 21–23. *World Hunger Situation.* Washington, D.C.: U.S. Government Printing Office.

U.S., Presidential Commission on World Hunger (1980) *Overcoming World Hunger: The Challenge Ahead.* Report of the Presidential Commission on World Hunger. Washington, D.C.: U.S. Government Printing Office.

U.S., Senate (1981) *Agriculture and Food Act of 1981: Report of the Committee on Agriculture, Nutrition, and Forestry.* Washington, D.C.: U.S. Government Printing Office.

Unión Nacional de Empacadoras, T.I.F. (1970) *Industrialización del Ganado en México.* México: by the Unión.

United Nations Association (1977) *Acts of Nature, Acts of Man: The Global Response to Natural Disasters.* New York: UNA-USA.

Valdés, Alberto, ed. (1981) *Food Security for Developing Countries.* Boulder, Colo.: Westview Press.

Valdés, Alberto (1982) "Agricultural Protectionism: The Impact on LDCs." *Ceres* 15 (November-December):13–16.

Valdés, Alberto, and Anna Castillo (1984) *The Role of Food Trade in the Food Security of Developing Countries.* UNCTAD/CD/300, May, Geneva. (Mimeographed.)

Vernon, Raymond (1966) "International Investment and International Trade in the Product Cycle." *Quarterly Journal of Economics* 80(2):190 207.

———. (1971) *Sovereignty at Bay: The Multinational Spread of U.S. Enterprises.* New York: Basic Books.

———. (1977) *Storm Over the Multinationals: The Real Issue.* London: Macmillan.

Von Braun, Joachim, Harold Alderman, and Saki Ahmed Sakr (1982) *Egypt's Food Subsidy and Rationing System: A Description.* Washington, D.C.: International Food Policy Research Institute (IFPRI), report #34.

Wade, R. (1982) *Irrigation and Agricultural Politics in South Korea.* Boulder, Colo.: Westview Press.

————. (1983) "South Korea's Agricultural Development: The Myth of the Passive State." *Pacific Viewpoint* 24(1):11–28.

Wall, D. (1979) *Industrial Processing of Natural Resources.* World Bank Commodity Working Paper No. 4. Washington, D.C.: World Bank.

Wallerstein, Immanuel (1974) *The Modern World System: Capitalist Agriculture and the Origins of the European World Economy in the Sixteenth Century.* New York: Academic Press.

————. (1976) "Semi-peripheral Countries and the Contemporary World Crisis." *Theory and Society* (Winter):461–83.

————. (1980) *The Modern World System II: Merchantilism and the Consolidation of the European World Economy 1600–1750.* New York: Academic Press.

Wallerstein, Mitchell B. (1980) *Food for War — Food for Peace: United States Food Aid in a Global Context.* Cambridge, Mass.: MIT Press.

Walters, Harry (1975) "Difficult Issues Underlying Food Problems," in *Food: Politics, Economics, Nutrition and Research,* a Special SCIENCE Compendium, Philip H. Abelson, ed., pp. 122–28. Washington, D.C.: American Association for the Advancement of Science.

Warman, Arturo (1976) *Y venimos a contradecir. Los campesinos de Morelos y el estado nacional.* México, D.F.: Ediciones de la Casa Chata, Centro de Investigaciones y Estudios Superiores del INAH.

Webb, Richard (1975) "Government Policy and the Distribution of Income in Peru, 1963–1973," in *The Peruvian Experiment,* Abraham F. Lowenthal, ed., pp. 79–127. Princeton: Princeton University Press.

————. (1977) *Government Policy and the Distribution of Income in Peru, 1963–1973.* Cambridge, Mass.: Harvard University Press.

Whang, I. J. (1981) *Management of Rural Change in Korea: The Saemaul Undong.* Seoul: Seoul National University Press.

Wilkins, M. (1974) *The Maturing of Multinational Enterprise: American Business Abroad, 1914–70.* Cambridge, Mass.: Harvard University Press.

Williamson, Jeffrey G. (1977) "Strategic Wage Goods, Prices, and Inequality." *American Economic Review* 67(29):41.

Winckler, E. A. (1981a) "National, Regional and Local Politics." in *The Anthropology of Taiwanese Society,* E. M. Ahern and H. Gates, eds., pp. 13–37. Stanford: Stanford University Press.

————. (1981b) "Roles Linking State and Society," in *The Anthropology of Taiwanese Society,* E. M. Ahern and H. Gates, eds., pp. 50–86. Stanford: Stanford University Press.

Winrock International (1981) *Technical Report: The World Livestock Product, Feedstuff, and Food Grain System.* Morrilton, Ark.: Winrock International.

Wionczek, Miguel S. (1981) "External Indebtedness of Less Developed Countries," in *The Yearbook of World Affairs, 1981*, George W. Keeton and Georg Schwartzenberger, eds., pp. 114–20. Boulder, Colo.: Westview Press.

Wolff, Richard D. (1974) *The Economics of Colonialism*. New Haven: Yale University Press.

Womach, Jasper (1983) *Agriculture: The U.S. Sugar Program* (Washington, D.C.: Library of Congress, Congressional Research Service, mini brief no. MB82239).

Wood, Charles (1982) "The Political Economy of Infant Mortality in São Paulo, Brazil." *International Journal of Health Services* 12(2):215.

World Bank (1979) *World Development Indicators*. Washington, D.C.: by the Bank.

———. (1980) *World Tables*, 2nd ed. Washington, D.C.: by the Bank.

———. (1981a) *Accelerated Development in Subsaharan Africa* (The "Berg Report") Washington, D.C.: by the Bank.

———. (1981b) *Peru: Major Development Policy Issues and Recommendations*. Washington, D.C.: the Bank.

———. (1982) *World Development Report 1982*. New York: Oxford University Press.

———. (1983) *World Bank Development Report 1983*. New York: Oxford University Press.

World Food Council (1979) *Report of the 5th World Council Meeting*. Ottawa, September.

———. (1984) *The World Food and Hunger Problem: Changing Perspectives and Possibilities, 1974-84*. Addis Ababa, Tenth Session: World Food Council, WFC/1984/6.

Wortman, Sterling and Ralph E. Cummings, Jr. (1978) *To Feed This World: The Challenge and the Strategy*. Baltimore: Johns Hopkins University Press.

Wright, E. R., ed. (1975) *Korean Politics in Transition*. Seattle: University of Washington Press.

Young, Crawford (1976) *The Politics of Cultural Pluralism*. Madison: University of Wisconsin Press.

Yu, T. Y. H. (1978) "Farm Family Income Distribution by Region in Taiwan," in *Agricultural Economic Research Papers*, Economic Digest Series No. 23, pp. 171–186. Taipei: Joint Commission on Rural Construction.

Zockun, M. H. G. (1980) "A Expansão de Soja no Brasil: Alguns Aspectos de Produção." *Ensaios Econômicos No. 4*. São Paulo: Instituto de Pesquisas Econômicas, Universidade de São Paulo.

Subject Index

Index of Authors Cited